Origins of Inequality in Human Societies

Since the beginning of social life human societies have faced the problem of how to distribute the results of collaborative activities among the participants. The solutions they found ranged from egalitarian to unequal but caused more dissension and conflict than just about any other social structure in human history. Social inequality also dominated the agenda of the new field of sociology in the nineteenth century. The theories developed during that time still inform academic and public debates, and inequality continues to be the subject of much current controversy.

Origins of Inequality in Human Societies begins with a critical assessment of classical explanations of inequality in the social sciences and the political and economic environment in which they arose. The book then offers a new theory of the evolution of distributive structures in human societies. It examines the interaction of chance, intent and unforeseen consequences in the emergence of social inequality, traces its irregular historical path in different societies, and analyses processes of social control which consolidated inequality even when it was costly or harmful for most participants. Because the evolution of distributive structures is an open process, the book also explores issues of distributive justice and options for greater equality in modern societies. Along with its focus on social inequality the book covers topics in cultural evolution, social and economic history and social theory.

This book will appeal to scholars and advanced students of sociology, economics and anthropology – in particular sociological theory and social inequality.

Bernd Baldus is Professor Emeritus of Sociology at the University of Toronto, Canada.

Routledge Advances in Sociology

158 **Aging in Contexts of Migration**
Edited by Ute Karl and Sandra Torres

159 **Twentieth Century Population Thinking**
A Critical Reader of Primary Sources
Edited by Population Knowledge Network

160 **The Synchronization of National Policies**
Ethnography of the Global Tribe of Moderns
Pertti Alasuutari

161 **Retail and the Artifice of Social Change**
Steven Miles

162 **Theorizing Social Memories**
Concepts and Contexts
Edited by Gerd Sebald and Jatin Wagle

163 **Addiction, Modernity, and the City**
A Users' Guide to Urban Space
Christopher B.R. Smith

164 **Medicine, Risk, Discourse and Power**
Edited by John Martyn Chamberlain

165 **Pragmatic Humanism**
On the Nature and Value of Sociological Knowledge
Marcus Morgan

166 **The Social After Gabriel Tarde**
Debates and Assessments, 2nd edition
Edited by Matei Candea

167 **Dynamics of National Identity**
Media and Societal Factors of What We Are
Edited by Peter Schmidt, Josef Seethaler, Leonie Huddy and Jürgen Grimm

168 **Beyond Capital**
Values, Commons, Computing, and the Search for a Viable Future
David Hakken, Maurizio Teli and Barbara Andrews

169 **Values, Economic Crisis and Democracy**
Edited by Malina Voicu, Ingvill C. Mochmann, Hermann Dülmer

170 **Understanding Southern Social Movements**
Edited by Simin Fadaee

171 **Sharing Lives**
Adult Children and Parents
Marc Szydlik

172 **The Reflexive Initiative**
On the Grounds and Prospects
of Analytic Theorizing
*Edited by Stanley Raffel and
Barry Sandywell*

173 **Social Movements in Violently
Divided Societies**
Constructing Conflict and
Peacebuilding
John Nagle

174 **Challenging Identities**
European Horizons
Edited by Peter Madsen

175 **Cool Nations**
Media and the Social Imaginary
of the Branded Country
Katja Valaskivi

176 **Thanatourism and Cinematic
Representations of Risk**
Screening the End of Tourism
Rodanthi Tzanelli

177 **The Decent Society**
Planning for Social Quality
*Pamela Abbott, Claire Wallace
and Roger Sapsford*

178 **The Politics and Practice of
Religious Diversity**
National Contexts, Global Issues
Edited by Andrew Dawson

179 **São Paulo in the Twenty-First
Century**
Spaces, Heterogeneities,
Inequalities
*Edited by
Eduardo Cesar Leão Marques*

180 **State Looteries**
Historical Continuity,
Rearticulations of Racism, and
American Taxation
*Kasey Henricks and
David G. Embrick*

181 **Lesbian, Gay, Bisexual and
Trans* Individuals Living with
Dementia**
Concepts, Practice and Rights
*Edited by Sue Westwood and
Elizabeth Price*

182 **Family, Culture, and Self in the
Development of Eating
Disorders**
Susan Haworth-Hoeppner

183 **Origins of Inequality in Human
Societies**
Bernd Baldus

184 **Confronting the Challenges of
Urbanization in China**
Insights from Social Science
Perspectives
*Edited by Zai Liang,
Steven F. Messner, Youqin Huang
and Cheng Chen*

185 **Social Policy and Planning for
the 21st Century**
In Search of the Next Great
Social Transformation
Donald G. Reid

186 **Popular Music and Retro
Culture in the Digital Era**
Jean Hogarty

187 **Muslim Americans**
Debating the Notions of
American and Un-American
Nahid Kabir

Pieter Bruegel the Elder (c.1525–1569). *The Battle of the Moneybags and the Strong Boxes.* Image credit: Yale University Art Gallery.

Notes
Two recurrent themes in Bruegel's art were paintings and drawings of ordinary people and satirical portrayals of greed and acquisitiveness in the bustling and sometimes violent merchant culture of Antwerp where he spent part of his life. The Flemish inscription, freely translated, reads "Go to it, you piggy-banks, barrels and chests. It's all about money and goods, this fighting and twisting. Although they will tell you otherwise, don't believe it. That's why we fly the grappling hook banner which has never failed us. They try to find ways to subdue us, but they will not succeed until there is nothing left to rob."

Origins of Inequality in Human Societies

Bernd Baldus

NEW YORK AND LONDON

First published 2017
by Routledge
711 Third Avenue, New York, NY 10017

and by Routledge
2 Park Square, Milton Park, Abingdon, Oxon OX14 4RN

Routledge is an imprint of the Taylor & Francis Group, an informa business

© 2017 Taylor & Francis

The right of Bernd Baldus to be identified as author of this work has been asserted by him in accordance with sections 77 and 78 of the Copyright, Designs and Patents Act 1988.

All rights reserved. No part of this book may be reprinted or reproduced or utilized in any form or by any electronic, mechanical, or other means, now known or hereafter invented, including photocopying and recording, or in any information storage or retrieval system, without permission in writing from the publishers.

Trademark notice: Product or corporate names may be trademarks or registered trademarks, and are used only for identification and explanation without intent to infringe.

Library of Congress Cataloging in Publication Data
Names: Baldus, Bernd, 1941– author.
Title: Origins of inequality in human societies / Bernd Baldus.
Description: New York : Routledge, 2016. | Series: Routledge advances in sociology
Identifiers: LCCN 2016008457| ISBN 9781138671829 (hardback) | ISBN 9781315616773 (e-book)
Subjects: LCSH: Equality. | Distributive justice.
Classification: LCC HM821 .B35 2016 | DDC 305–dc23
LC record available at http://lccn.loc.gov/2016008457

ISBN: 978-1-138-67182-9 (hbk)
ISBN: 978-1-315-61677-3 (ebk)

Typeset in Times New Roman
by Wearset Ltd, Boldon, Tyne and Wear

Contents

1	Dimensions of Inequality	1
2	Contested Terrain: The Rise of Modern Theories of Social Inequality	26
3	Theories of Social Inequality: Classical Paradigms	49
4	Inequality's Inner Secrets: The Cultural Evolution of Social Inequality	98
5	Variation: Pathways to Inequality	142
6	Selection: Self-Reinforcement and Social Control	173
7	Possible Worlds: Pathways to Equality	197
8	Epilogue	234
	Index	240

1 Dimensions of Inequality

Three themes recur in the accounts of the first European explorers who reached the coasts of Africa, South America, the Pacific Islands and Asia. One is the dream of wealth and conquest. Apart from the press gangs only the hope for riches could motivate men, most of them poor, to succumb to the hardship of life and death at sea. The second are rumors of sexual license among the natives. Stories, embellished in the telling, that their marriages "are not with one woman but with as many as they like, and without much ceremony, and we have known someone who had ten women" must have been much on the minds of men who lived out their teens and early twenties onboard ship deprived of female company. The third theme, commented on with a mixture of disbelief and fascination, is the social structure of the societies they met. Vespucci, surveying the land he saw on his voyage to Brazil in 1502, fancied himself "near the terrestrial paradise." The climate was warm, the air was fragrant with the scent of blossoms and food was abundant, but what impressed him most was the apparent equality of the natives.

> I tried very hard to understand their life and customs because for twenty-seven days I ate and slept with them. They have no laws or faith, and live according to nature. They do not recognize the immortality of the soul, they have among them no private property, because everything is in common; they have no boundaries of kingdoms and provinces, and no king! They obey nobody, each is lord unto himself; no justice, no gratitude, which to them is unnecessary because it is not part of their code.
> (Cited in Bergreen 2003: 98, 99)

In 1521, Antonio Pigafetta, official chronicler for Magellan's voyage around the globe, felt on more familiar ground when he visited the Raja of Brunei, guarded by 300 bodyguards with drawn rapiers. Pigafetta's delegation could address the king only through a hierarchy of messengers, the highest of whom would whisper through a speaking tube in a wall. On the other side, unseen, one last servant would convey the message to the king. When they finally were allowed into his presence they had to make elaborate obeisance before addressing him.

Inequality preoccupied human beings long before these events. Distributive structures, from egalitarian to unequal, are among the earliest documented features of social life. Reactions varied just as much, from Aristotle's assertion that "It is ... just and clear that there are by nature free men and slaves" to Rousseau's complaint that "man was born free, and he is everywhere in chains." Short of sex and salvation, nothing has roused human passions more than the question who should get what.

Inequality continues to divide today's societies. In the US the share of total income going to the top 10 percent of the population reached a high of 49 percent in 1928, then fell sharply during the Second World War, remained stable just below 35 percent until 1978, and then rose rapidly to 49.7 percent in 2007 (Piketty and Saez 2010). Between 1979 and 2007, after-tax incomes rose by 18 percent for the lowest fifth of American households, and by 275 percent for the top 1 percent. During this period, overall shares in income declined for all but the top fifth of the population (United States Congressional Budget Office, 2011). Inequality also varied significantly between countries. Whereas top incomes increased substantially over the past 30 years in English-speaking countries and in India and China, the increase was much lower in continental Europe and Japan (OECD 2008; Atkinson et al. 2009). Poverty rates show similar changes over time and between countries (Brady 2009). On the international scale the number of countries in the poorest category increased from 25 in 1960 to 43 in 1976, and to 71 in 2000 (Milanovic 2005). A recent decline in global inequality was mainly due to growing incomes in India and China and the stalled economies of Western countries (Milanovic 2013). Last but not least, income and wealth disparities were also major causes of social conflict. The duration and casualties of post-1960s civil conflicts around the world were positively associated with levels of social inequality (Milanovic 2013). Such long-term variations offer a first glimpse of the volatility of inequality and its social consequences.

When sociology emerged as an academic discipline in the nineteenth century, the search for the causes of social inequality was the primary concern of Saint-Simon, Comte, Spencer, Sumner, Marx and Durkheim. If they were the founding fathers of the new field of sociology, inequality was its founding problem. They created the archetypical explanations of social inequality as a result of domination and power, as a reflection of inherited differences or biological advantages, or as a functional response to societal needs. These views laid the groundwork for later, more specialized debates: whether inequality was a product of social conflict or impersonal imperatives, whether it was a functional structure of empty spaces waiting for competent applicants or a segmented labor market shaped by economic and political power, whether it was based on material differences or on identity and status, or whether in modern societies class divisions were replaced by a fluid post-modern diversity.

An Outline of the Book

This book offers a comprehensive new theoretical analysis of the nature of social inequality in human societies. There are two reasons for such a project. First, theories matter because they guide our research. They tell us what evidence to collect and what questions to ask of it. They can lead us to important features of the social world but can also obstruct our view. If we think that social processes are governed by laws, we are unlikely to see the causal role of chance in human affairs. If we presume that human actions are shaped by external determinants or rational constraints, we will not have much interest in creative or non-rational behavior. If we assume that the long-term effects of inequality are beneficial or inevitable, we will see harmful outcomes as transient and unimportant and dismiss the search for more egalitarian social structures as pointless. Such assumptions are reflected in research. Scientific journals overwhelmingly publish articles reporting strong relationships between variables, whereas only a small portion of those that find null (chance) results are written up and submitted, and few of these are accepted (Mervis 2014). It is rare to find studies which argue that failing rather than efficient markets, and irrational rather than rational choices, contributed to inequality in current societies (Hacker and Pierson 2010; Stiglitz 2012), or that its history is turbulent and unpredictable rather than a steady progress towards ever greater prosperity (Piketty 2014).

The second reason is that over the past decades sociological interest has shifted from the roots of inequality to its symptoms. In one of the more curious recent twists, research on material inequality declined at the same time as discrepancies in wealth and income increased in many societies, (Coelho et al. 2005; Dollery et al. 2008). Sociologists turned instead to racial, ethnic or gender differences (Myles 2003; Baldus 2004). Such sectoral studies revealed important empirical characteristics, but they also moved away from asking basic theoretical questions. Talcott Parsons' work in the 1950s was one of the last attempts to develop a general theory of the causes and functions of inequality in social systems.

A re-examination of this topic is thus long overdue. The central problem I explore in this book is how the results of collaborative efforts can be distributed among the participants. More specifically I want to understand how and why distributive structures emerge, stabilize and change in complex, contingent environments which offer multiple options for human action.

Chapter 1 outlines the book's content and defines the social resources involved in distributive decisions. It then examines how these resources were divided in three exemplary inequality structures: European feudalism, the Indian caste system and an African slave-holding society. In each case the growth of inequality began with small precipitating causes whose consequences were not anticipated. Its subsequent consolidation was due to separate dynamics of social control which reinforced these inequality structures even though they were detrimental to the welfare of most of the people involved. These case studies also illustrate the capricious historical course of inequality. Feudalism came to a relatively sudden and spectacular end, whereas caste and slavery endure in varying forms to this day.

Chapter 2 puts early sociological theories of inequality into the context of pre-industrial religious ideas, of seventeenth and eighteenth century philosophical and economic debates and of the political and social turbulence surrounding the industrial revolution. Nineteenth century sociologists, in particular, faced a world of rapid and far-reaching change, of spectacular new wealth and appalling poverty, of political unrest and social tensions. These conditions profoundly affected their views of inequality.

Chapter 3 offers a critical examination of five classical explanations of social inequality which still inform sociological and public debates. They saw the causes of inequality in biological processes of competition and selection, in class struggle, in institutional and organizational dynamics, in hierarchy as a necessary prerequisite for the pursuit of social goals and in subjective needs for domination and conspicuous social status. Subsequent writing has elaborated and criticized these theories, but I have considered it only where it substantively added to classical ideas.

The goal of this chapter is threefold. First, I want to give a concise critique of each explanation of social inequality which avoids their authors' often lengthy excursions into unrelated or period-bound areas. My second objective is to show that most of these theories were based on common premises: inequality was derived from universal causes, emerged largely independent of people's will, endured because its advantages outweighed its costs and developed along predictable historical lines. They therefore paid little attention to the subjective motives and responses of the participants, to the dynamics that maintained inequality even where it was dysfunctional or harmful, and to options for alternative distributions of wealth.

Third, I want to highlight a number of rarely noted references in the work of Marx, Spencer, Sumner and Durkheim to the role of chance and contingency in the growth of inequality, to the power of persuasion and force to shape subjective responses to inequality and to its irregular historical growth. These insights were for the most part incidental by-products of their authors' historical research and did not change their convictions. Worried or, in the case of Marx, encouraged by an unsettled time, and with an envious eye on the rapid progress of the natural sciences, classical theorists preferred the retrodictive fallacy of taking the frequency and longevity of inequality in human history as signs of the providential working of social laws or universal needs.

Such deterministic and rational-functional logics exacted a price: crucial aspects of the rise of social inequality in human societies disappeared from view. Chance as a causative factor became "a very unwelcome guest, ubiquitous but studiously concealed, ignored and even denied the right to exist by virtually everyone" (Boudon 1986: 173). As for harmful consequences, sociologists sided with Durkheim that no human institution based on error and lies could last, and that "irrational hierarchy maintenance along with potentially self-interested, malicious conduct will dissolve and be replaced by the relatively neutral goals of organizational efficiency and productivity" (Roscigno 2011: 358). The same held for biological explanations of inequality. Theories of cultural evolution, from Herbert Spencer to modern Neo-Darwinism which transformed Darwin's theory early in the twentieth century, had a strong bias toward the positive and adaptive. Harmful consequences of social inequality were seen as the natural purging from society of the weak or unfit, or were altogether ignored.

Sociological and biological determinism also reduced or eliminated the role of individuals in the genesis of social inequality. Sociologists talked much about agency but focused mostly on its effects. Even Marx, who stressed the need for class action, felt he had to enlist historical necessity as a midwife to give birth to his favorite child, an egalitarian communist society. In spite of repeated calls to bring people back into sociology, "recognizably human actors seem to escape our grip: the stage is set, the script is written, and the roles are handed out, but the actors strangely never reach the scene" (Giddens 1979: 253). Neo-Darwinist theories of cultural evolution were just as averse to studying individual agency. For them evolution was driven by the external forces of mutation and selecting environments. Individuals therefore had no autonomous selection-influencing role. What appeared to be intent or free will was in fact guided by inherited predispositions toward adaptive, "viable" or "competent" behaviors. Redundant, irrational or harmful cultural traits were negligible by-products of a fundamentally beneficial selection.

Deterministic or rationalist bias also influenced the long-term view of inequality. Social theories produced a plethora of developmental schemes where history followed predetermined paths, and hoped that statistical snapshots of arbitrarily chosen historical event sequences would reveal general social mechanisms which worked independent of time and context. The twists and turns of real history were dismissed as "mere noise, a nuisance in the process, a form of instability or unreliability, a lack of robustness, not meaningful change that requires explanation" (Isaac and Lipold 2012: 7).

Not all analyses suffered from these limitations. One of the best recent studies of the evolution of social inequality argues that

> Inequality results from people's efforts to be thought of and treated as superior. Whatever the supporting role of factors such as population growth, intensive agriculture, and a beneficent environment ... inequality does not occur without active manipulation of social logic by human agents.
>
> (Flannery and Marcus 2012: 191)

I share this premise, but only as a first step. Anyone who explores the origins of a major cultural institution such as social inequality eventually needs to look into the origin of culture itself. Social scientists, although they sometimes used evolutionary language, believed that the uniqueness of human culture was an existential fact so obvious that it required no explanation. By contrast, Darwin and most evolutionists after him emphasized the evolutionary continuity between animal and human behavior. As a result, relations between the two disciplines became strained and sometimes hostile, especially after Wilson's *Sociobiology* (1975) signaled the growing interest of biologists in the evolution of human culture. Sociologists suspected that evolutionists wanted to force their complex cultural world into a genetic straightjacket. Evolutionists feared that their sociological colleagues were trying to destroy their beautiful theory with nasty little facts. Social inequality frequently became the flashpoint of these disputes.

Chapter 4 follows Darwin in treating culture, including the growth of inequality in human societies, as a natural evolutionary product. I know of no other defensible explanation. At the same time I want to avoid the constraints

6   *Dimensions of Inequality*

imposed by recent Neo-Darwinist approaches which interpreted culture as an analog or extension of genetic variation and selection and had to explain specific cultural traits and institutions in terms of their adaptive, heritable effects. Chapter 4, therefore, moves to a sphere of evolution which has rarely been examined: how people actually experience and participate in evolution during their lifetime. Lived, cultural evolution is only partially shaped by genetic selection. What makes it natural is that it follows a fundamental principle underlying all evolution: it produces spontaneous variety in response to uncertain environments. In cultural evolution this principle produces distinct characteristics. Culture evolves over the short term, variation and selection are mostly internal and cognitive, and the results are highly variable. Applied to the evolution of social inequality, this framework makes it possible to explore the complex beginnings of inequality structures, to separate the causes which precipitate such structures from those which maintain them over time, and to examine the role of social agents without assuming from the start that their actions serve functional or adaptive ends. Inequality appears as a fluid historical product of social choices made in a dynamic and often unpredictable world. It is a temporary, although often long-lasting, result of ordering and destabilizing social forces, of precipitating accidents and self-reinforcing consequences, of trust and cooperation and of deception and defection. These dynamics can produce workable solutions but can also institutionalize error and harm.

Chapter 5 examines historical pathways to inequality. It traces initial and often accidental changes in the material and social environments of early egalitarian societies which led to unplanned but long-lasting distributive change. It identifies regions of opportunity where such pathways are particularly likely to start and shows that the long-term evolution of inequality moves irregularly between growing disparities and egalitarian reversals rather than following a predetermined trajectory.

Chapter 6 examines why the causes with which inequality begins cannot explain how it becomes entrenched in a society. Additional social control processes are required to make it endure: strategies of persuasion and coercion, but also behavior by deprived groups which helps them cope with their situation while unintentionally reinforcing their dependence. Such processes can make inequality, once established, self-sustaining and resistant to change. Chapter 6 concludes with an examination of historical changes in social control from pre-industrial to modern inequality structures.

If, as this book suggests, social inequality is not a product of necessity but of an open-ended cultural evolution, we can also look for alternative ways of distributing collectively achieved gains. Chapter 7 explores possible criteria for a fair or just distribution. It first examines four major theories of social justice: neo-liberal views which base justice on rights created by individual acquisition and possession, John Rawls' argument that a just distribution must take account of the contribution of chance and uncertainty to collective achievements, utilitarian efforts to link justice and personal satisfaction, and Habermas' search for forms of public debate which can lead to a consensus about social justice. The chapter then develops a theoretical argument for greater equality and examines practical efforts to achieve more equality in the organization of work and distribution in contemporary societies.

An Epilogue (Chapter 8) summarizes the main arguments of the book.

What is Inequality?

Proceeds from collaborative efforts can be distributed in a variety of ways – from complete equality where each party receives the same share to complete inequality where all gains go to one participant. Inequality exists where people are engaged in a collaborative project, and where the resulting gains in wealth, power or social standing flowing to some are not shared by others, or are obtained at their expense by increasing their deprivation, powerlessness or social exclusion. This requires, first, that winners and losers are involved in a joint project. Differences in wealth, power or wellbeing between unconnected individuals or groups do not constitute inequality. People in one part of the world may be better off than in others, but unless we can show that such differences derive from their participation in cross-national or global economic or political networks there is no point in speaking of inequality between them. Occupational success, life expectancy or health may vary substantially from person to person, but they suggest inequality only if they are due to differential access to social positions, living conditions or health care in a shared social system. Similarly, historical comparisons of different societies can tell us much about varying forms and recurrent characteristics of inequality, but they do not reveal processes which "call forth stratification ... with universal necessity" (Davis and Moore 1966: 47). We can learn from history, but history itself, like all evolution, does not repeat itself.

Second, although there are no limits to the ways people can value things or actions and turn them into objects of exchange and distribution, social inequality typically involves strategic resources. Resources are strategic if their possession increases opportunities for further accumulation. Four categories of resources are particularly likely to have such compounding effects: the ownership of material wealth, the control of knowledge, the use of influence, authority and power over other people, and the ability to include or exclude others from social relations. Gaining control of each of these resources creates typical benefits and restrictions for winners and losers. Ownership of strategic wealth such as land or water can be used to extract profit and services from those who have no access to this resource. Strategic technical or ritual knowledge can become a monopoly of expertise and social capital. Power over others, whether achieved by conquest, religion or charisma can create lasting relations of obedience, subservience and command. The social exclusion of others can establish status boundaries, discrimination and closure of access to valued social positions. Inequality structures often combine several of these effects.

Control of strategic resources merely creates opportunities for increasing inequality. It does not dictate choices or actions. Whether and how opportunities are used remains a matter of chance, personal discovery and cultural values. Material wealth can be privately or communally owned. Authority can be cooperative or hierarchical, and power accountable or arbitrary. Knowledge may be freely shared or monopolized by castes, guilds or professions. Licensing and educational credentials may enhance the quality of service or turn into barriers that reduce competition and inflate earnings. Social relations can be participatory and democratic or exclusive and discriminatory.

Third, all stages of the distribution of jointly achieved results, especially where they lead to inequality, involve subjective evaluation and choice. Economists and sociologists have often portrayed individuals as rational maximizers of given needs in known environments. The nuances of emotions and feelings, the rationalization of mistakes and errors, and the imperfect knowledge of current and future events were not considered (Goldthorpe 2001). In the real world, what people perceive as scarce, rewarding or discriminatory involves complex and malleable judgements. Just about any material or intangible good can be transformed into an object of desire, indifference or loathing. Wealth and power may be flaunted through a conspicuous lifestyle or enjoyed behind tightly closed doors. Poverty can appear as injustice or as a punishment for one's sins, and wealth as exploitation or as a sign of God's calling. Possessions can be generously shared and avariciously defended. How people react to inequality may veer far from what might be considered their objective interests, and their social identities may diverge widely from their structural position. Pascal pointed out that people never do evil so completely and cheerfully as when they do it from religious conviction. Social inequality can evoke similar reactions. People can be persuaded or forced into accepting their exploitation, but just as frequently in human history they have demanded more equality.

Inequality is therefore first and foremost a cultural product, a system of socially constructed limitations which prevent some individuals or groups from having access to strategic resources which are available to others. Later chapters of this book examine details of this process, but how its components interact is best seen by looking at inequality structures in their entirety. Each of the three following historical examples involves the control of a strategic resource. In European feudal societies a monopoly of agricultural land created the basis for a highly unequal society. The Indian caste system rested primarily on norms of social discrimination and closure. In the third example, an indigenous African slave-holding society, the command over labor was the key strategic resource. In each case particular attention is given to the way control over these resources was first obtained, how it was used to divide benefits and costs between winners and losers, and how strategies and beliefs on both sides maintained these inequality structures over time.

European Feudal Societies

Origins

Feudal inequality prevailed in most European societies from about the tenth century AD to the French Revolution and survived in Russia for another century. European powers exported feudal structures to other parts of the world, such as seventeenth and eighteenth century New France in Canada. Similar forms of inequality arose independently in India, China, Japan and Africa.

Feudalism established itself in Europe with remarkable speed. In the turbulent period between the ninth and eleventh century, local gangs of marauders and cut-throats transformed themselves into a powerful and often immensely wealthy aristocracy which controlled virtually all arable land. They proclaimed their exclusive status through heraldic symbols, conspicuous life style and a "noble" ancestry although few of them were able to trace their descent back beyond AD 800 (Bloch 1961: 284, 285). Elaborate rules came to govern the control of land, the key source of wealth, and led to perpetual land hunger, recurrent internal conflict and the expansion of feudal rule into eastern and southern Europe, the Near East, and eventually overseas territories (Bartlett 1993: 46). On the other side, free peasants who in the eighth century still owned small pieces of land and made up the majority of the population, had two centuries later become a largely landless class.

The immediate event that precipitated these changes was the collapse of the empire of Charlemagne (AD 742–814) which covered much of today's France, Germany and northern Italy and was held together by frequent military campaigns, terror, political skill and a measure of luck. Carolingian society was not yet feudal, but it began to degrade older Germanic traditions which treated land as collective property assigned to individual families for temporary use and where assemblies of warriors made major decisions and elected leaders. The army was a popular army, called up when needed, and disbanded after each campaign.

Charlemagne's military campaigns relied still largely on this levy of free peasants, but its earlier egalitarian features eroded under his rule. He surrounded himself with an elite corps of armed vassals who enjoyed legal immunity and were freed from agricultural work. Permanent service strengthened the bonds of loyalty and obligation between retainer and lord. It became shameful to leave the battlefield alive if the lord died. In return, followers shared in the prestige and the magnanimity of a lord. This expectation of mutual support between lord and vassal was to become a cornerstone of aristocratic power.

Standing corps of vassals weakened the position of peasants. Peasants were still called up for military service and had to bring enough food for three months and enough weapons and clothing for six, but the greater frequency of campaigns interfered with agricultural production and caused the ruin of many smallholdings. Charlemagne was not insensitive to this problem and raised the minimum acreage at which peasants had to serve. But many state and church officials used their power to deprive peasants of their land, forcing them to choose between becoming beggars and vagrants or entering the service of wealthier landowners. An inquiry by Charlemagne revealed that such abuses were widespread.

> The peasants complain that they were robbed of their property; and this complaint they raise against bishops and abbots and their administrators, as well as against the counts and their officials. They say also that, whenever someone refused to hand over his property to bishop, abbot, count, judge or

official, these would search for reasons to be able to sentence him, or to demand repeated military service until he was impoverished and was then by necessity forced to entrust himself and his property to their protection, or to sell his holding to them.

(Cited in Kalckhoff 1987: 16)[1]

Such takeovers were made more attractive by new ways of exploiting the now landless labor. Peasants assumed the risks of farming while guaranteeing the new owners of land a steady flow of returns. They were granted a subsistence plot on the lord's land in exchange for having to work on the lord's own fields and provide customary gifts, rents and services. Profits grew in direct proportion to the amount of land the lord controlled. In a relatively short time, the feudal principle of *nulle terre sans maître* concentrated virtually all arable land in the hands of the feudal nobility.

After Charlemagne's death, central authority disintegrated. By AD 1000, power had shifted to anyone able to collect a band of armed followers to compete for territory. Predatory behavior was their main route to prominence. Theft and pillage became indistinguishable from "legitimate" warfare. Hordes of warriors, claiming to protect an area against "wicked men," namely themselves, forced peasants to submit to plunder while seizing control of their land.[2] They were aided by two innovations in military technology. One, arriving from Asia in the early eighth century, was the stirrup. The other was the motte and bailey castle, an inexpensive adaptation of the defensive hill forts which had been used in Europe since the Stone Age. The stirrup changed the conduct of war. Armies had employed cavalry for a long time, but mounted soldiers threw mostly javelins, shot arrows or used their superior mobility to get behind an enemy and then dismount and fight on foot. Their precarious position on the back of the horse made it difficult to use heavier weapons. The stirrup provided much greater support and allowed riders to wield battle-axes, lances and swords. Its use spread quickly and caused further innovations: the breeding of heavy horses, armor for horse and rider, and heraldic symbols on shield, helmet and pennant to distinguish fully armored friends from foes. This new military technology decisively changed the military and political balance. The core of feudal armies was now a shock force of mounted knights, each of them estimated to be the equivalent of 100 foot soldiers.

The cost of armor, horses and luxurious lifestyle could be met either by acquiring more land or by extracting more surplus from peasants. That simple equation defined the economics of feudal rule. The motte and bailey castle was a perfect tool for seizing new territory. In about 20 days, some 100 people rounded up in nearby villages could dig a circular ditch, build an earthen wall and a central mount, and top them with wooden palisades (Fichtenau 1992: 467). During the tenth and eleventh century, such castles spread throughout central Europe, reaching densities of one for every 10 square miles (Bartlett 1993: 67). The aim was to advance one's claims for land and resist subsequent sieges by competitors, a game that was "guaranteed to endure at least until treason opened the gates or the seigneur himself was captured" (Bur 1983: 134).

Cheap to build and easy to defend, castles gave their occupiers a clear military edge. Together with the stirrup they facilitated the rapid social transformation of the armored knights into an aristocratic class. Infantry formations, from the hoplite phalanx of ancient Greece to the Germanic military levy and the Swiss square, democratized their society because hand-to-hand combat required cooperation and mutual assistance. By contrast, the armored knight on horseback was a quintessentially individual combatant. The immediate social effect was to generate a culture which celebrated individual deeds of bravery and aloofness from the "common" society. By the twelfth century, the aristocracy had become a socially closed hereditary elite. This did not prevent internal division. Intensely competitive and constantly in search of more land, feudal lords were never certain of the loyalty of their followers. Treachery and changes of alliance among liege men were common; trustworthiness "stood in inverse proportion to the length of one's sword" (Fichtenau 1992: 534). Although feudal structures began to stabilize with the ascendance of monarchies from the twelfth century onward, petty aristocratic rivalries frequently escalated, and while they often thinned the ranks of the competitors, their brunt was born by the peasants who were stuck in their muddy villages in glutinous immobility.

The Distribution of Costs and Benefits

By the twelfth century, feudal society had become a rigidly hierarchical system. At the top stood an aristocracy with clear internal rank differences, from dukes and magnates who controlled vast stretches of countryside to lesser knights who eked out a modest existence on land granted to them as fief, although they jealously maintained their contempt for anyone of lower rank. Internally, this privileged class was held together by marital alliances, political and military ideology, and an overbearing arrogance toward those they considered social inferiors.

The peasantry whose work was the main source of this wealth also became more homogeneous. Pre-feudal distinctions between serfs, leaseholders and free disappeared; all became villains (Heer 1962: 44). The lever for this transformation was the aristocracy's monopoly over arable land. At the lowest level of society it created a protection racket where services and payments were extorted from peasants by promising to shield them from ills of which the aristocracy itself was the primary cause. The extent of the services and payments villains owed for the "privilege" of using the lord's land was shaped by the arbitrary demands of the aristocracy on one side, and the peasants' sullen resistance on the other. Even where these duties became a more permanent custom of the manor they were always subject to the whims of local lords and their ever-present need for more income to finance dowries, wars and luxurious lifestyles.

Peasant obligations fell into three broad categories: labor, payments for monopoly services and rents. Work was mainly done on land reserved for the lord's own use, the *demesne*. Here, villains had to plough, sow and harvest, tend the lord's cattle and spread manure. They also had a myriad of less regular tasks such as fencing, construction and repair of houses and roads, lodging the lord's messengers or beating the moat with branches to silence the frogs which disturbed the lord's sleep. Such work was to be done "for the love of the lord." It was often not known in the evening what service had to be rendered in the morning (Bennett 1971: 103). Entire families and villages were sometimes expected to turn out. The lord customarily offered food or drink. The time required varied from as little as two to as much as six days per week through much of the year. The impact on the peasant could vary a great deal depending on age, health or family size.

The second form of feudal obligations were fees required for using the lord's monopoly of mills or bake-ovens, for fishing in rivers and ponds, and for gathering fuel in the lord's forest. Payments were also due when the head of the family died, when rights to holdings were transferred to other peasants, or when animals were sold. Without the lord's permission villains were not able to leave the manor or to marry. Transgressions were fined, with the lord acting as judge in all but serious crime. The villain could do few things

> without his lord's permission "prayed and obtained." The lord's power was about him on all sides: not only did he fear the occasional visit of the steward – armed with powers of life and death as it seemed – or the more frequent visits of the itinerant bailiff, whose authoritative commands everyone learned to respect, but he also came under the supervision of the local village officials.... All these were constantly influencing his actions, and to some extent infringing on his freedom.
>
> (Bennett 1971: 129)

Peasants customarily delivered a tenth of their own harvest to the tithe barn of their lord, and another tenth to the church. Actual payments varied widely. By the thirteenth century the growth of markets made cash payments more common. Villains could now buy out their labor obligations or hire poorer villagers for such work. For the lord, cash facilitated the purchase of luxury goods or the payment of dowries. The right of local rulers to mint their own coin also opened the door for a lucrative devaluation of money by reducing its silver content. Unbeknownst to lord, peasant or merchant, this growing money economy would eventually spell the end of feudal rule.

Maintenance and Social Control

In the medieval literature

> peasants were often depicted as filthy, subhuman, and comical, the reverse of the civilized and the courtly ... the *villain* was everything that the knight was not: lowly, servile, grossly materialistic, cowardly, malformed, and unfit for the service of love.... Peasants appeared in art and iconography as coarse and ill-favored. Likened to domestic animals or even (by means of filth and excrement) to the land he tilled, the peasant was rendered as large, grotesque, and rather sluggish. He craved food, yawned, scratched himself, was partial to drink, and enjoyed sleeping.
>
> (Freedman 1999: 157)

Such images were not likely to reconcile peasants to their fate. A sounder basis was needed to secure their work. Just as pre-existing social arrangements and technologies facilitated the rise of feudal power, aristocratic groups used established religious concepts to sanctify feudal inequality and transform it into an eternal reality that stifled peasant resistance. One was the idea of a divine order that gave all things their natural purpose and place. The Old Testament described different ranks of angels, suggesting that hierarchy was a fundamental ordering principle in heaven. Augustine (AD 354–430) argued that each occupation, even prostitutes and executioners, had its God-given role. Medieval justice tried swords because they had fallen from their place on the wall, and pigs and rats for actions considered outside their proper sphere. Such ideas could be readily used to prove the providential nature of feudal inequality. Feudal ideologues such as the eleventh century Bishop Adalbéron of Laon depicted inequality as a mutually beneficial relationship between three orders. The church prayed for everyone to assure their spiritual salvation. In return, it was exempt from taxation. Aristocrats risked their lives in the defense and protection of others. They therefore had the right to levy taxes. The natural duty of peasants was to work and support the other two classes. John of Salisbury (AD 1115–1180) drew a parallel between the organs of the body and the structure of feudal society, anticipating nineteenth century organic models of inequality in sociology by some 700 years. The church was the soul which gave the body its life. The ruler was the head, the crown council the heart, and judges and lower administration represented the eyes, ears and tongue of the feudal lords. The court which surrounded them was the chest, and officials and armies were the civil and military arm of the body politic. The financial administration performed the digestive functions of the intestines. Craftsmen, merchants and peasants were the legs and feet that carried the body.

The biblical tale of Adam and Eve's surrender to temptation which enslaved humanity to lower passions was also employed to justify feudal rule. In the sixth century, Pope Gregory had already argued that God created all people equal, but that peasants were more prone to sin and therefore in need of chastisement (Duby 1980: 35). They bore the brunt of God's curse that Adam would have to earn his bread by the sweat of his brow.

> God, in his great grace, has forced servitude upon those for whom he has realized freedom is not suitable. And although baptism has removed the Original Sin from all believers through the grace of God, the just God has divided the life of men in such a way that he made some into servants and others into lords, so that the possibility of sinning by the servants should be curtailed by the power of the lords.
> (Burkhardt of Worms cited in Brackert 1975: 27)

This message was reinforced by others, such as the Old Testament story of the three sons of Noah who, when returning home, found their father drunk and partially naked. When one of them ridiculed him, Noah cursed the offender and all his descendants. This passage fueled the feudal image of the unequal children of

Eve: the cursed brother fathered the peasants who were permanently subordinated to the descendants of his more respectful siblings.

Such beliefs justified the existing social order and deferred hopes for greater equality and justice to a time after death. Peasants could enter heaven provided they accepted their God-willed role in this life and redeemed their sins through their work (Duby 1980: 160, 161). Such ideas were backed by terror, the second of the two great pillars of *amor et timor*, love and fear, which propped up the feudal system. As early as the seventh century, Bishop Leodgar justified aristocratic violence in a way that still echoed through Luther's defense of the repression of the German peasant rebellion some 900 years later.

> Man on this earth can, if he receives from God the power to do so, persecute, seize, rob, burn and kill: we can in no way escape that. Even if we are temporarily delivered to punishment, this must not cause us to despair, but to anticipate with joy forgiveness in the future.
>
> (Cited in Kalckhoff 1987: 190)

Violence was sinful but also necessary to contain the boundless wickedness of human nature. Blinding, torture and execution were staged as public spectacles of intimidation. The contorted features of Christ on the cross, the detailed accounts of the agony of Christian martyrs, and the vivid portrayal of the fearsome fate awaiting sinners in hell all told the peasant that suffering was part of the pilgrimage through this world, and that only its acceptance could bring redemption in the next.

Not all of these justifications were imposed from above. Peasants invented their own ways of making their life bearable. They took a dogged pride in securing their family's survival and even a modest prosperity. They appealed to saints for help with specific problems, sought physical and spiritual succor from folk remedies and from the ubiquitous relics – a splinter from Christ's cross, a bone from a martyr's finger. They helped each other, drowned their frustrations in drink, or vented them in senseless violence (Bloch 1961: 412). These adaptations, too, became an enduring part of the web of feudal social control.

How widely accepted such beliefs were is difficult to assess. The poor and illiterate leave few historical records. Feudal social control was not a seamless web. Aristocrats did not hesitate to express their contempt for the "stinking peasant," but many of them probably also believed that lord and peasant were bound to the higher authority of God and, when the occasion warranted, they could romanticize the peasants' simple wisdom and praise their role in feeding "God's people by means of their sweat" (Mundy 1973: 228, 223). The wealth and privilege of the church was challenged by monastic movements which advocated a life of penitence, poverty and work. Many of these, like the Cistercians or Franciscans, eventually returned to more comfortable ways of existence. If they became a threat to the established order they were brutally repressed; the first heretics were burnt at the stake in Orleans in France in 1022 (Heer 1962: 201). Peasants, too, shifted between faith, loyalty, private resentment and collective resistance. Rebellions were endemic in feudal societies, from peasant uprisings in Normandy at the end of the tenth century to the peasant rebellions in England and Germany in the fourteenth and sixteenth century. They, too, often began with biblical allusions. The corrosive power of the question "When Adam delved and Eve span, who was then the gentleman?" slowly but fatally weakened feudal power until it could no longer prevent the vast disadvantaged majority from breaking its bonds.

Caste

Origins

If feudal power rested on the control of land, caste inequality was based on identity and exclusion. Bétaille (1969: 274) defines caste as

> a small and named group of persons characterized by endogamy, hereditary membership and a specific style of life which sometimes includes the pursuit by tradition of a particular occupation and is usually associated with a more or less distinct ritual status in a hierarchical system, based on the concepts of purity and pollution.

Although most extensive in India, the avoidance or exclusion of groups deemed to be polluting or stigmatized is common to many human cultures, from the treatment of the *eta* or *burukamin* in feudal Japan to the ghettoes and gated communities of modern cities.

The first descriptions of caste traditions are found as early as 1200 BC in texts derived from oral sources. Castes had acquired their basic forms by about 300 BC. Beside the four major castes *(Varna)* there existed a fifth group, the untouchables who were considered to have been born ritually unclean. India's current constitution prohibits discrimination against untouchables and guarantees them access to administrative positions, schools and universities. But caste inequality continues, especially in rural India. About 15 percent of the Indian population are classified as *Harijan* or scheduled castes. They refer to themselves as *Dalit*, "poor and downtrodden."

A long history of migration and of social transformations of the Indus and Ganges regions make it difficult to establish the early origins of caste. Genetic evidence (Moorjani et al. 2013) suggests that an ethnic mixture between Indo-European and South Indian groups was followed by a relatively rapid emergence of endogamous caste distinctions. Theories of caste have also disagreed whether caste inequality is primarily relational or distributive, with Dumont (1970) arguing that caste was an all-encompassing code of conduct while others claimed that it merely obscured an underlying exploitative class structure (Meillassoux 1973: 98). Whatever its origins, the caste system created a complex web of notions of purity, social distance and social closure which established an inequality structure of uncommon longevity and stability.

The Distribution of Costs and Benefits

Caste distinctions were not the only ordering principle in Indian society. As in so many agricultural societies, major economic and political inequalities divided society into kings and local rulers, court and religious retainers, armies and officer classes, and the vast mass of peasants whose taxes maintained courts and military. It was at the local level of villages and towns that caste affected the lives of ordinary people most directly, and where it survived when states collapsed or new ruling groups took over. Here the four *Varna* ran broadly parallel to occupational distinctions. The three highest castes were: *Brahmin*, traditionally priests and keepers and interpreters of sacred texts; *Kshatriya*, traditionally warriors; and *Vaishya*, traders and merchants. Below them ranked the *Shudra* (meaning low or insignificant) whose ritual impurity relegated them to the role of servants and providers of material support for higher castes. The fifth, lowest rank, *Pariah* or untouchables, performed tasks which other castes considered defiling. These general ranks were overlaid by 3000 or more local sub-castes (Dutt 1968: 5) which developed their own religious and cultural practices and made caste boundaries more ambiguous. *Shudra*, for instance, could reach social positions of prominence and wealth, and many major land-owners in agricultural sub-castes were *Shudra* (O'Hanlon 1985: 5).

Whereas social relations within castes tended to be shaped by norms of solidarity and equality, relations between castes were hierarchical and were governed by norms of social distance. Contact with lower castes, whether by touching, eating and drinking, or sex, was seen as polluting and required ritual purification. Severe pollution such as eating food prepared by an untouchable or sexual relations between higher caste women and lower caste men could mean expulsion from one's caste.

Social exclusion often requires symbolic markers which identify and enforce social boundaries. Different castes lived in different parts of villages and towns and used different wells. Spacial segregation was most severe for untouchables. They were not allowed to enter the houses or shops of upper castes and were barred from entering temples. Food cooked by lower castes could not be accepted by higher castes. Sharing food indicated caste equality; giving food generally denoted the lower standing of the recipient. "The kind of food, the question whether it is cooked in butter or water, the caste of the person cooking it, and the place (whether temple or home) where the food is cooked, all go to determine its acceptability" (Srinivas 1969: 268). The pursuit of learning, the familiarity with Sanskrit and with the complex caste rituals concentrated strategic knowledge in the hands of Brahmins and served as a symbol of high social status. The avoidance of manual labor also set Brahmins apart; ritual rules prohibited their use of the plow. Manual work was reserved for lower castes, although in rural areas agriculture was practiced by all castes. Raising, tending and butchering animals or selling animal products or liquor symbolized servile work and low caste food and was traditionally performed by *Shudra*. The most despised work, such as working on funeral pyres, removing garbage and animal carcasses, or working with animal skins (tanning or shoe-making) was restricted to untouchables. Such distinctions persist to the present. As a high caste member put it,

> They are at a lower level, they are low. Because they are lowest – the shoemakers ... the sweepers. As a matter of fact, as far as it counts for me, you have blood, I have blood, we are people, aren't we? I think this (caste system) is nothing. But what to do? This tradition was established a long time ago, and people have feelings about it. They feel uneasy. Although on the outside we say this (that people are same), in our minds, we feel troubled. For example now, consider the untouchables, the Shoemakers, the Sweepers. They are dirty.... Their work matches their kind.
> (Cited in Parish 1996: 59)

Caste differences could run parallel to economic differences, but class and caste did not necessarily coincide. Brahmins might live off alms and have few permanent possessions, whereas lower caste wealth occasionally overcame caste barriers. The same was true for physical differences. Brahmins tended to be fair-skinned and were thought to have more refined bodily features. Light skin color was generally valued; a dark-skinned Brahmin girl could become a burden to her family because they could not find a husband for her. "Dark *Brahmin* and light *Pariah* are not proper" (cited in Bétaille 1969: 276). The stigma created by such distinctions is still keenly felt:

> villagers never forgot, nor did they let us forget, that we were untouchables. High – caste children sat inside the school; the Bauri children, about twenty of us, sat outside on the veranda and listened. The two teachers, a Brahman outsider and a temple servant, refused to touch us, even with a stick. To beat us, they threw bamboo canes. The higher-caste children threw mud at us. Fearing severe beatings, we dared not fight back.
> (Cited in Freeman 1979: 67)

Maintenance and Social Control

In the early Vedic literature the four basic castes are described as being created from the mouth, the arms, the thighs and the feet of the Creator, an image similar to the feudal analogy between inequality and the organs of the body.

> This caste system is like our body. If our body did not have eyes, we could not see. If we did not have hands, we could not work. Without ears, we could not hear. In the same way, we need people of all castes in society. If we are to eat meat, the Butchers are necessary. We need the Sweepers to clean. We need the Brahmans to recite religious lessons.
> (Cited in Parish 1996: 142)

Specific caste obligations are defined by *Dharma*, a code of conduct which outlines behavior appropriate for each caste. Serious violations are thought to destroy the social order. As a legal code of social control, *Dharma* is deemed to protect essential elements of society: property, family, and caste.

The acceptance and observance of *Dharma*, combined with Hindu and Buddhist beliefs in reincarnation, in turn determines a person's *Karma*. *Karma* links caste inequality with personal merit: one's current caste is the result of compliance or violation of *Dharma* in a previous life. For the same reason a person who observes the rules of Dharma "will be born in his next incarnation in a high caste, rich, whole and well endowed. If he does not observe them he will be born in a low caste, poor, deformed, and ill endowed" (Srinivas 1969: 267). Past behavior explains one's present status and determines one's prospects in the next life. Misery and suffering are not random.

> What appears to be a gratuitous distribution of good fortune and misery becomes intelligible, when seen in terms of the ideas of transmigration and the karmic conservation of the moral consequences of individual actions.... The theory of Karma seals status boundaries, just as the idea of the presence of God in each person tends to make them permeable.
>
> (Parish 1996: 52)

The combination of *Dharma* and *Karma* must rank as one of the most ingenious and effective legitimations of any structure of inequality. Linking past to present and present to future while making it impossible to verify the causal nexus reduces the likelihood of resistance and conflict. Such an inequality-maintaining belief system had distinct advantages over feudal and early industrial ideologies which promised at least some tangible rewards in this life for virtuous conduct and were therefore vulnerable to disaffection if apparently exemplary behavior led to suffering or poverty. Caste ideology neatly sidestepped that problem.

Nonetheless, the reality of caste perceptions is more complex. Whereas basic ideas of purity and pollution may be widely shared by members of all castes, including untouchables, they are also negotiated, reinterpreted, resisted or taken advantage of in everyday relations between castes. Concern with pollution and purity tends to be highest among *Brahmin*, but even they might observe caste rules more in public than in private. Among lower castes outward deference can be motivated by a genuine belief in polluting consequences, serve as a means to gain favors, or take an exaggerated form which ridicule upper caste individuals. Lower caste people appear more skeptical of the connection between *Dharma* morality and one's station in life and see caste more as a structure of mutual exchange, opportunity and patronage (Sharma 1999: 38). They understand their economic dependence on higher caste land-owners for share-cropping, or their inability to escape cheating and exploitation by wealthy but miserly employers (Freeman 1979: 324–353). Not heeding caste obligations may mean hunger and suffering, whereas open opposition may provoke collective violence from members of higher castes (Fruzetti et al. 1982). Actual caste life is therefore full of nuances and ambiguities, and acceptance and rejection of caste limits often appear in the statements of the same person. *Shudra* and even untouchables claim superiority over other low castes and treat them accordingly, though both face the same stigma. Hierarchy tends to disappear when looking upward but is maintained when looking down (Parish 1996: 46; Sharma 1999: 37). Lower-caste individuals may try to escape caste limits altogether by converting to Buddhism or by moving to the anonymity of urban life. Just like feudal peasants, lower castes invent their own complex social and cultural responses to their position. These are often far less visible than formal legitimations but play a crucial role in the maintenance of caste structures.

Slavery

Slavery is probably the oldest, most variable and, until the arrival of industrial capitalism the most widespread form of inequality in human societies. There is evidence of slavery in Sumerian society as early as 3200 BC. Hammurabi's legal code, written about 1750 BC, allowed a free person to be sold into slavery to redeem a debt, defined slaves as the lowest of three categories of persons, forced them to wear a distinctive haircut, and specified a variety of penalties for slaves and for people who harbored fugitive slaves (Klein 2002: 165). People could be turned into slaves by conquest, as collateral for a loan, as payment for goods and services, as a means to collect ransom, or as a gift of children to temples or priests. Slaves could be used as domestic servants, common laborers, messengers and officials, kept for sexual favors or sold for profit. Slave labor and slave trade became essential parts of the economies of ancient Athens, Rome and the *ante bellum* American south. Slaves could be treated with cruelty or benign paternalism, could be physically marked and stigmatized or integrated to a degree that made them virtually indistinguishable from their owner. They could, on occasion, rise to considerable prominence and wealth. No matter how variable their status, however, their movements and conduct were subject to the whims or the calculated economic interest of those who owned them. What legal protection they had stemmed from religious or moral beliefs of their owners or from the fear that excessive brutality might lead to slave revolts. Manumission, the granting of freedom, was invariably the prerogative of slave-owners, not a right of the slave, except where laws gave the child of a slave concubine the free status of its father (Klein 2002: 5). The overriding interest of owners lay in the labor of their slaves: they were worth keeping as long as they produced more than it cost to maintain them.

Slavery in Borgu: Origins

Slavery in the Borgu area of what is today Benin in West Africa (Baldus 1977) illustrates the extraordinary variety of slave systems. It was an indigenous institution, and although abolished during the French colonial administration it continued informally. The Borgu was originally inhabited by an ethnically homogeneous population, the *Batomba*, and was politically divided into fiefdoms ruled by aristocratic families. Endemic warfare between them aimed primarily at capturing and removing people from invaded areas. A few of these captives became officials at the ruler's court. The majority were settled in slave villages to produce food for the ruler's family and retainers and for military campaigns. A substantial number were sold or given away as domestic slaves to free *Batomba*. Slavery was thus already an established practice when the pastoral *Fulbe* peacefully moved into the thinly populated Borgu area in the late eighteenth and early nineteenth century. The *Fulbe* soon began to buy slaves from the agricultural *Batomba* in exchange for their own cattle. But there was a second, more fortuitous source of slaves: the belief, fairly widespread in West Africa, that children whose first teeth appeared in the upper jaw brought misfortune to their family. The *Batomba* went beyond the ritual purification which most West African cultures considered sufficient to avert these consequences. They abandoned such children to die of exposure. The Muslim *Fulbe* who did not share this belief adopted them and raised them as slaves. Regardless whether they were former captives of war or abandoned children, the slaves of the *Fulbe* constituted a separate slave group, the *Machube*. They assumed *Fulbe* culture and language and were the property of individual *Fulbe* families.

The Distribution of Costs and Benefits

The slaves of the *Batomba* provided a typical range of services for their owners. As messengers and court officials, recognizable by special dress and haircut, they could gain a measure of influence and derived authority. As family slaves, women did household chores while men worked the land of their owners. A third group, living in large slave settlements, produced agricultural surplus for aristocratic courts and armies. Their lives were perhaps the harshest of the three slave groups. Demands were particularly heavy prior to military raids, and their ranks were easily replenished by new captives of war.

The work of the *Machube* was shaped by the pastoral life of their *Fulbe* owners who derived their livelihood from their herds. Apart from farming, which the *Fulbe* avoided, male slaves aided in herding cattle while women did the heavy work of the household and became on occasion a concubine or, more rarely, a second or third wife of their owner. No matter what their duties, both groups of slaves experienced a dramatic loss of social standing. They often became targets of derision and contempt by free *Batomba* and *Fulbe*. Apart from being required to work, their movements were curtailed. Sexual unions were restricted to slaves of the same owner or led to haggling among different owners over compensation for the loss of a slave's labor through marriage, pregnancy or childbirth.

Maintenance and Social Control

Slave rebellions occurred throughout history, ranging from personal resistance to large organized uprisings such as Toussaint L'Ouverture's rebellion between 1791 and 1803 against French plantation owners in Haiti, one of the few that were successful. The most remarkable aspect of slavery in Borgu is the virtual absence of conflict between owners and slaves. The *Fulbe* took no formal precautions and created no sanctions in anticipation of slave resistance. In part this was due to the social disorganization among the slaves. The loss of kinship ties, the drop in status, and their isolation and frequent migration with *Fulbe* owners made contact and organized action among the *Machube* difficult. But there were more subtle and more effective reasons for their acquiescence. Although they did no longer abandon their own children, which at any rate would have interfered with the interests of their owners, the *Machube* accepted the myth of the fateful birth and felt a sense of gratitude for having been saved from certain death by their *Fulbe* family. Shame and self-blame mingled with the belief that Muslim culture and the superior magic of the *Fulbe* removed the damaging effects of their birth. What was for the *Fulbe* an act of self-interest established for the slaves a moral obligation to stay with and work for their owner.

> *Fulbe* rank higher than *Machube* because they have taken over the task of raising them. The *Machube* come from a *Batomba* child who has the first teeth in the upper jaw. The *Batomba* can abandon it and the *Fulbe* can take it, or the *Batomba* can give it to the *Fulbe* as a gift. They cannot keep the child. The *Fulbe* raise and provide food for the child until it grows up. We carry out their commands. The *Machube* do what the *Fulbe* demand because they have grown up with the *Fulbe*, and our ancestors were already slaves of the *Fulbe*. The *Fulbe* own us, therefore we work for them ... even if it was at night and the *Fulbe* woke us up to ask for something.
> (Cited in Baldus 1977: 444)

The master-slave relationship was further justified by a variety of *Fulbe* cultural concepts which depicted inequality as a natural or God-given fate. As well, the integration into *Fulbe* culture allowed the *Machube* to imitate their owners' customs and dress and to benefit at least vicariously from the superior cultural status of *Fulbe* religion and literacy. Although they fooled neither *Fulbe* nor *Batomba*, this imagined reduction of social distance meant much to the slaves. Strategies by lower groups to narrow status differences by imitating the dress, speech or manners of their superiors can be found in many other inequality structures.

There was one more aspect of *Machube* culture which stabilized the master-slave relationship. *Fulbe* treated their slaves the same, regardless of whether they had found or bought them. But for the *Machube* these differences assumed a disproportionate importance and led to major internal divisions. Not only did each group rank itself above the other, but invidious distinctions led to a high level of strife among the *Machube* themselves. This internal disorganization of the slaves gave the *Fulbe* an added measure of security.

The subjective reconstruction of their slave existence by the *Machube* is all the more remarkable because it was not imposed by the *Fulbe*. Whereas the latter's interests are reflected in the *Machube's* world view, *Machube* culture was largely their own invention and their way of making sense of their situation. At the same time, and unintentionally, it also maintained the very relationship of inequality that was at its root. Occasionally, the ideological reversal of the world became complete. Asked what would happen if the orders of the *Fulbe* were not carried out, a slave responded:

> Nothing happened, because the *Machube* did carry out all orders. Their grandparents had already carried out orders, and nobody has refused. I am happy to be with the *Fulbe* because (they) do not take my possessions away ... and let me make my own fields ... let me weave and make my own cloths, and if I make them I make them for their children, too. Being with the *Fulbe* I feel free. That is why I am satisfied with my life.
>
> (Cited in Baldus 1977: 455)

Central Problems for the Study of Inequality

Feudal, caste and slave inequality structures reveal common empirical traits. First, contingent, historically unique causes played a major role in the evolution of each of these systems. Feudal rulers did not invent the ideology of the three orders, the stirrup or the motte and bailey castle. They merely forged a new system of inequality from materials and ideas they found at hand (Duby 1980: 63). We see the same creative adaptation of contingent, pre-existing elements in the rise of caste systems and in the historical accident that matched the customs of the *Batomba* with the interests of the *Fulbe*. In each case, contingency opened opportunities which eventually concentrated large shares of jointly produced strategic resources in the hands of a few people while imposing severe direct and opportunity costs on the rest.

Second, these divisions produced no parallel polarization of subjective responses. The three systems remained stable although peasants, untouchables and slaves were clearly worse off than those they served. Inequality seems to be able to endure even if it is harmful for the majority of those affected, but it required additional measures of social control which turned feudal rule into a divine order, portrayed the burdens of lower caste as a punishment for past sins, and transformed slavery into a form of freedom. Feudal power relied much on the deliberate construction of such legitimating images and on the calculated use of coercion and fear. The Indian caste system and the relations between *Fulbe* and *Machube* rested on more internalized forms of social control. The case of the *Machube*, in particular, shows that the dynamics that maintain an inequality structure can originate to a substantial extent among the very people who carry the bulk of its burdens. These dynamics differ from the causes that gave rise to inequality in the first place, and appear often only after it has established itself.

Third, although each endured for a long time, these three inequality systems show no inherent logic which suggests that they were biologically advantageous, socially beneficial or followed predictable developmental paths. Feudal inequality eventually succumbed, the caste systems weakened and change even reached the *Machube*: slaves have formed political parties for municipal elections and have taken control of some municipal councils in Northern Benin (Hahanou 2009).

These case studies provide an initial scope for the study of social inequality. A theory of inequality must be able to account for the complexity of its causes, the wide variety of subjective responses to inequality structures, and the reasons for their long-term stability and change.

Notes

1 All English translations from German and French sources in this book are the author's.
2 In a striking parallel the disbanding of peasant levies by the Kammu emperor in Japan at the end of the eighth century encouraged gangs of peasants to plunder wide areas of the country. By the end of the twelfth century some had established themselves as a hereditary *samurai* aristocracy with landed property, special privileges and their own code of honor and duty. Their decline began with the rise of the Tokugawa dynasty in the sixteenth century.

Bibliography

Atkinson, Anthony B., Thomas Piketty and Emmanuel Saez. "Top Incomes in the Long Run of History." *NBER Working Paper w15408*. Berkeley: National Bureau of Economic Research, 2009.

Baldus, Bernd. "Responses to Dependence in a Servile Group: The Machube of Northern Benin." In Susan Miers and Igor Kopytoff (eds) *Slavery in Africa. Historical and Anthropological Perspectives*, 435–458. Madison: University of Wisconsin Press, 1977.

Baldus, Bernd. "...to Race and Gender, Everyone? Some Thoughts on the Future of Research on Social Inequality." *Canadian Journal of Sociology* 29 (2004) 4: 577–582.

Bartlett, Robert C. *The Making of Europe: Conquest. Colonization and Cultural Change*. Princeton: Princeton University Press, 1993.

Bennett, H.S. *Life on the English Manor*. Cambridge: Cambridge University Press, 1971.

Bergreen, Laurence. *Over the Edge of the World*. New York: Harper Collins, 2003.

Bétaille, André. *Social Inequality*. Harmondsworth: Penguin, 1969.

Bloch, Marc. *Feudal Society*. Chicago: University of Chicago Press, 1961.

Boudon, Raymond. *Theories of Social Change: A Critical Appraisal*. London: Polity Press, 1986.

Brackert, Helmut. *Bauernkrieg und Literatur*. Frankfurt: Edition Suhrkamp, 1975.

Brady, David. *Rich Democracies, Poor People*. New York: Oxford University Press, 2009.

Bur, Michael. "The Social Influence of the Motte-and-Bailey Castle." *Scientific American* (1983): 132–140.

Coelho, Philip, Frederick Worken-Eley and James McClure. "Decline in Critical Commentary, 1963–2004." *Econ Journal Watch* 2 (2005) 2: 355–361.

Davis, Kingsley and Wilbert Moore. "Some Principles of Stratification." In Reinhard Bendix and Seymour M. Lipset (eds) *Class, Status, and Power*, 47–53. New York: Free Press, 1966 [1945].

Dollery, Brian, Joel Byrnes and Galia Akimova. "The Curtailment of Critical Commentary in Australian Economics." *Econ Journal Watch* 5 (2008) 3: 349–351.

Duby, Georges. *The Three Orders*. Chicago: University of Chicago Press, 1980.

Dumont, Louis. *Homo Hierarchicus*. Chicago: University of Chicago Press, 1970.

Dutt, Nripendra Kumar. *Origin and Growth of Caste in India*. Calcutta: Firma K.L. Mukhopadhyay, 1968.

Fichtenau, Heinrich. *Lebensordnungen des 10. Jahrhunderts*. München: Deutscher Taschenbuch Verlag, 1992.

24 Dimensions of Inequality

Flannery, Kent and Joyce Marcus. *The Creation of Inequality*. Cambridge: Harvard University Press, 2012.

Freedman, Paul. *Images of the Medieval Peasant*. Stanford: Stanford University Press, 1999.

Freeman, James M. *Untouchable. An Indian Life History*. Stanford: Stanford University Press, 1979.

Fruzetti, Lina, Akos Östör and Steve Barnett. "The Cultural Construction of the Person in Bengal and Tamilnadu." In Akos Östör, Lina Fruzzetti and Steve Barnett (eds) *Concepts of Person: Kinship, Caste and Marriage in India*, 8–30. Delhi: Oxford University Press, 1982.

Giddens, Anthony. *Central Problems in Sociological Theory*. London: Macmillan, 1979.

Goldthorpe, John H. "Causation, Statistics, and Sociology." *European Sociological Review* 17 (2001): 1–20.

Hacker, Jacob S. and Paul Pierson. *Winner-Take-All Politics: How Washington Made the Rich Richer – and Turned Its Back on the Middle Class*. New York: Simon & Schuster, 2010.

Hahanou, Eric Komlavi. "Debating Slavery in Contemporary Benin. From Discourses to Practices of Subordination, Emancipation and Alliances." Paper presented at the *Tales of Slavery: Narratives of Slavery, the Slave Trade and Enslavement in Africa* conference, University of Toronto, May 20–23, 2009.

Heer, Friedrich. *The Medieval World. Europe 1100–1350*. New York: New American Library, 1962.

Isaac, Larry W. and Paul F. Lipold. "Toward Bridging Analytics and Dialectics: Nonergodic Processes and Turning Points in Dynamic Models of Social Change with Illustrations from Labour Movement History." In Harry F. Dahms and Lawrence Hazelrigg (eds) *Theorizing Modern Society as a Dynamic Process*, 3–33. Bingleu: Emerald Group Publishing, 2012.

Kalckhoff, Andreas. *Karl der Grosse. Profile eines Herrschers*. München: Piper, 1987.

Klein, Martin. *The A to Z of Slavery and Abolition*. Lanham: Scarecrow Press, 2002.

Meillassoux, Claude. "Are There Castes in India?" *Economy and Society* 3 (1973) 1: 89–111.

Mervis, Jeffrey. "Research Transparency – Why Null Results Rarely See the Light of day." *Science* 345 (2014) 6200: 992.

Milanovic, Branko. *Worlds Apart*. Princeton: Princeton University Press, 2005.

Milanovic, Branko. "The Inequality Possibility Frontier: Extensions and New Applications." Policy Research Working Paper Series 6449. *The World Bank*, 2013.

Moorjani, Priya, Kumarasamy Thangaraj, Nick Patterson, Mark Lipson, Po-Ru Loh, Periyasamy Govindaraj, Bonnie Berger, David Reich and Lalji Singh. "Genetic Evidence for Recent Population Mixture in India." *American Journal of Human Genetics* 93 (2013) 3: 422–438.

Mundy, John H. *Europe in the High Middle Ages 1150–1309*. New York: Basic Books, 1973.

Myles, John. "Where Have All the Sociologists Gone?" *Canadian Journal of Sociology* 28 (2003) 4: 551–559.

O'Hanlon, Rosalind. *Caste, Conflict, and Ideology*. Cambridge: Cambridge University Press, 1985.

Organisation for Economic Co-operation and Development (OECD) "Growing Unequal? Income Distribution and Poverty in OECD Countries." *OECD Publishing*, 2008. Available online at: www.oecd-ilibrary.org/social-issues-migration-health/growing-unequal_9789264044197-en

Parish, Steven M. *Hierarchy and its Discontents. Culture and the Politics of Consciousness in Caste Society*. Philadelphia: University of Pennsylvania Press, 1996.
Piketty, Thomas. *Capital in the Twenty-First Century.* Cambridge, MA: Belknap Press, 2014.
Piketty, Thomas and Emmanuel Saez. "Income Inequality in the United States, 1913–1998." *Quarterly Journal of Economics* 118 (2010) 1: 1–39.
Roscigno, Vincent. "Power, Revisited." *Social Forces* 90 (2011) 2: 349–374.
Sharma, Ursula. *Caste*. Buckingham: Open University Press, 1999.
Srinivas, M.N. "The Caste System in India." In Andrew Bétaille (ed.) *Social Inequality*, 265–272. Harmondsworth: Penguin, 1969 [1952].
Stiglitz, Joseph. *The Price of Inequality*. New York: W.W. Norton, 2012.
United States Congressional Budget Office, 2011. "Trends in the Distribution of House Income Between 1979 and 2007." Available online at: www.cbo.gov/publication/42729
Wilson, Edward O. *Sociobiology*. Cambridge: Harvard University Press, 1975.

2 Contested Terrain
The Rise of Modern Theories of Social Inequality

Theories always build on already existing ideas and are influenced by wider social problems and political debates of their time. The topics that dominated early sociological explanations of inequality – the search for social order, social harmony and social progress – responded to the turbulence of the nineteenth century societies by recasting older concepts into the language of modern social science.

The tremors of social change which ruptured the static ties between lord and peasant had been felt long before the onset of industrialization. Rural people had begun to move to the cities, cities began to avoid feudal strictures, and increasing trade and manufacturing brought prosperity to a growing bourgeoisie. On the ideological level, the idea of a providential social order that assigned aristocracy, church and peasantry specific social duties had begun to erode. Renaissance and Reformation expanded the sphere of human autonomy, the former by enhancing the interest in the practical understanding and transformation of the world, the latter by giving the individual greater responsibility for salvation. The focus of human life began to shift from the hope for redemption after death towards happiness in this world. As so often, popular belief sensed these changes long before the established classes of society became aware of them. In 1705, Bernard de Mandeville (1670–1733) published a satirical pamphlet in London which became known as *The Fable of the Bees*. Here, British society, thinly disguised as a hive of bees, happily conducted its life on the basis of unrestrained selfishness, fraud, bribery and a craving for luxury. But these vices also created employment and ensured the prosperity of the hive as a whole.

> Thus every Part was full of vice,
> yet the whole Mass a Paradice ...
> Such were the Blessings of that State
> Their Crimes conspir'd to make them Great ...
> The Worst of all the Multitude
> Did something for the common Good.
>
> (Mandeville 1924, Vol. I: 24)

This beneficial arrangement came to an end only when the bees opted for "honesty" and the curtailment of vice and crime. As a result trade and commerce suffered, unemployment increased, and the hive declined. Mandeville also pointed out that the enjoyment of property required a large class of impoverished people forced to work for others; "in a free Nation where Slaves are not allow'd of, the surest Wealth consists in a multitude of laborious Poor" (Mandeville 1924, Vol. I: 286, 287). That was fine with him. He mocked any idea of redistribution – it was neither in the interest of well-off individuals nor of the nation as a whole. The state should instead turn the poor into domesticated subjects who, accustomed to their situation, would learn to turn their servitude to their own advantage (Mandeville 1924, Vol. II: 184).

Mandeville's shopkeeper morality caused a storm of indignation among the British establishment. But it was also wildly popular. Mandeville had sensed a tectonic shift in his society's social structure towards the free-wheeling practices of a new capitalist market. *The Fable of the Bees* contains many themes which appear in the work of political philosophers such as Hobbes and Mill, economists such as Adam Smith, and nineteenth century sociologists such as Spencer and Sumner: the "hidden hand" that reconciles self-interest with the common good, hostility to state intervention in the economy and support for state protection of private wealth. But Mandeville's doggerels also revealed what looked like a dangerous flaw in this new *laissez faire* thinking. In order to function, markets required that all participants, including the new industrial working class, should be free to contract and sell their products and services. This increased personal freedom seemed to open a Pandora's Box of claims for a more equitable distribution of collectively achieved wealth, and of the threat of social conflict.

Alexis de Tocqueville (1805–1859) observed the corrosive potential of that dilemma during his visit to America. In aristocratic societies, people were bound together by clear hierarchical relations. In the new social order

> new families are constantly springing up, others are constantly falling away, and all that remain change their condition; the woof of time is every instant broken and the track of generations effaced. Those who went before are soon forgotten; of those who come after, no one has any idea: the interest of man is confined to those in close propinquity to himself. As each class gradually approaches others and mingles with them, its members become undifferentiated and lose their class identity for each other. Aristocracy had made a chain of all members of the community, from the peasant to the king; democracy breaks that chain and severs every link of it.
>
> (Tocqueville 1954: 105)

The disintegration and soullessness of the new society was most obvious in the changed relations between owners and workers. Industrial manufacture raised one to great wealth and pushed the other into poverty. But their relationship was impersonal. The goal of the new aristocracy of business was not to govern the working population but to use it, whereas the laborer was dependent on employers, but not on any particular one. Susanna Moodie, an upper class immigrant from England, observed the same breakdown of customary social relations in Canada. Her servants no sooner set foot upon Canadian shores than they become possessed with this ultra-republican spirit. All respect for their employers, all subordination is at an end; the very air of Canada severs the tie of mutual obligation which bound you together. They fancy themselves not only equal to you in rank, but ... demand the highest wages, and grumble at doing half the work ... and if you refuse to listen to their dishonest and extravagant claims, they tell you that "they are free."

She also saw the reason for this behavior. The customary deference of her servants

is repugnant to their feelings, and is thrust upon them by the dependent circumstances in which they are placed. This homage to rank and education is not sincere. Hatred and envy lie rankling at their heart, although hidden by outward obsequiousness. Necessity compels their obedience; they fawn and cringe, and flatter the wealth on which they depend for bread. But let them once emigrate, the clog which fettered them is suddenly removed; they are free; and the dearest privilege of this freedom is to wreak upon their superiors the long-locked-up hatred of their hearts.

(Moodie 1913: 248, 247)

The Search for Order

Three catalysts heightened the fears caused by the apparent crisis in social cohesion and the problem of how to distribute the wealth created by combining labor with steam engines and mechanical looms. The first was the trauma caused by the French Revolution. Its images of aristocrats ending their days under the guillotine or strung up on lanterns unnerved Europe's upper classes. The export of republican ideas by Napoleon deepened their fears. As late as 1859, 70 years after the storming of the Bastille, Dickens' *Tale of Two Cities* still chilled large audiences with its image of revolutionary women knitting while counting out the steps of prisoners climbing the scaffold on their way to the guillotine. To many readers it must have looked as if they were knitting the shroud of civilized society. The French Revolution had let a genie out of the bottle which quickly grew to menacing proportions. The bourgeoisie had used demands for liberty and equality to break down the constraints imposed on them by aristocratic privilege. For better effect and to gain allies, they had portrayed their interests as a struggle for the universal rights of man. Few of them had anticipated that these rights would then be claimed by people for whom they had never been intended: the urban poor and the growing working class. The very vagueness of the slogans *liberté, égalité, fraternité*, invited interpretations that were far more radical than what industry owners and governments were willing to concede. The French Revolution openly politicized the distribution of wealth and power. Whereas Article 2 of the 1789 Declaration of the Rights of Man listed property among the "natural rights," Article 1 made the common good the sole source of social distinctions. Wage, price and profit controls, the taxation of inheritance, a centrally planned economy, public education, and a social security system which provided annual payments and free health care for the old, sick, single mothers and widows with children, were among the many concrete redistributive policies initiated between 1789 and 1794.

The impact of the revolution did not end there. Questioning authority became a legitimate pursuit. If conservatives such as Edmund Burke in his 1790 *Reflections on the French Revolution* had only contempt for the "swinish multitude" of common people, radicals like Thomas Paine and Thomas Spence portrayed aristocrats as corrupt, useless and idle, and called for the expropriation and nationalization of private land and for a cooperative agrarian socialism. Paine's 1797 pamphlet, *Agrarian Justice*, proposed an inheritance tax on landed property to pay for old age and disability pensions for the landless population, and for an equal capital grant or "basic income" which all citizens should receive at the "age of majority" and use in any way they wanted. The response was heavy-handed suppression. Paine's *Rights of Man* was outlawed and he was exiled in 1793. Spence was imprisoned for treason. Paine's publisher, Daniel Isaac Eaton, suffered repeated prosecution for reprinting Paine's book, the last time at the age of 60 when he was sentenced to the pillory and 18 months in prison. Matters were made worse by the fact that the spirit of unrest, helped by increasing literacy and the rapid growth of printed mass media, spread to other parts of the world. In a prelude to the 1837 rebellions in Upper and Lower Canada, the London Workingmen's Association sent a message of solidarity to a meeting of Quebec workers which read:

> It is then today or never that the working class must strike a decisive blow for their complete emancipation.... A parliament which represents only capitalist property owners of money or land, will never protect the working classes; its object is to make money dear; and work cheap; yours on the other hand is to lower the cost of money and to raise the price of labor; between these opposing interests peace is impossible. (Bring the) bourgeois parliament face to face with a democratic assembly, and you will soon overthrow the men of wealth.
>
> (Cited in Ryerson 1968: 64)

This was strong stuff, and it brought forth the customary reaction: the colonial government banned all public meetings, and the bishop of Montreal ordered priests to refuse absolution to anyone who preached resistance to "the government under which we have the happiness to live." But neither repression nor ideological defenses of privilege could stem the tide of growing dissent.

The second source of political fears was the appalling social conditions and the high visibility of social differences in industrializing societies. Working days were as long as 17 hours; 12 to 14 hours were the norm. Child labor, a common feature of pre-industrial domestic production, became now widespread in cotton mills and mines. Urban housing, built by employers or by unscrupulous speculators, was cramped, unsanitary, and available only at high rents. Public parks and gardens were non-existent. A truck system forced workers to buy from company stores and even taverns, often at above-market prices. Their purchases were deducted from their wages, and they received only the balance in cash. Epidemics of typhoid, cholera and tuberculosis were common, and mortality rates, especially for young children, were high. Construction of sewers began in most industrial cities only around the middle of the nineteenth century on the assumption that illness was caused by "miasma," the stink coming from the polluted creeks and cesspools in urban neighborhoods.

By contrast, the material situation of the old and new gentry improved. The late eighteenth and early nineteenth century was a golden era for the landowning aristocracy (Hobsbawm 1969: 80). Many of its members benefited from higher prices for land and agricultural products caused by the growth of cities and of a landless industrial working class. At the same time they retained their political power, joined now by self-made industrialists, merchants and bankers who voiced their contempt for the effortless advantage of the old feudal order but also aspired to aristocratic lifestyles, country houses and marriages into the old nobility.

At the same time, however, the new inequality made "the city ... a volcano, to whose rumblings the rich and powerful listened with fear, and whose eruptions they dreaded." For the poor "it was ... a standing reminder of their exclusion from human society. It was a stony desert, which they had to make habitable by their own efforts" (Hobsbawm 1969: 87). These differences were plainly visible to both sides. Both lived close to the factories, one to keep an eye on machines and workers, the other because they had to walk to and from work. In nineteenth century cities the ostentatious homes of owners often stood mere steps away from the slums of working people.

Such glaring inequality provoked social unrest. In England, the 1840s were the politically most unstable years of the nineteenth century: an economic depression from 1837 to 1842 with massive unemployment and starvation was accompanied by political radicalism and riots. Depressions continued through the century, exacerbated by the failure of industrialists to understand that the purchasing power of working class people could create markets for the goods which their factories produced. Instead, the prevailing view was that wages reduced profits and had to be kept as low as possible. The resulting periodic economic crises of overproduction imposed large-scale layoffs and unemployment. Across Europe, the 1848 rebellions and the repressions that followed deepened the rift between working class radicals, reformers and conservatives. Every inch of the distributive landscape became contested terrain and was fought over by force or by ideological sophistry. Was the 10 hour day a step towards more humane working conditions or a tyrannical piece of state intervention which deprived the workers of choice and of the right to work as many hours as they wanted? Should property qualifications be lowered to allow more people to vote or would this merely hand political power to the poor whose lack of property made them irresponsible and uninterested in social stability? Would a public, tax-financed school system benefit lower class children and offer employers insurance against class conflict, or would educating the laboring classes

be prejudicial to their morals and happiness ... teach them to despise their lot in life, instead of making them good servants in agriculture, and other laborious employments to which their rank in society had destined them; instead of teaching them subordination, ... render them factious and refractory ... enable them to read seditious pamphlets, vicious books, and publications against Christianity; (and) ... render them insolent to their superiors.
(Cited in Hammond and Hammond 1968: 48, 49)

The fear that the spirit of insubordination might infect "the honest independence of the working and laboring classes" (Bonnycastle 1849: 106) was widely shared by conservative sections of industrializing societies and created a defensive and at times paranoid mentality intent on creating bulwarks against political change.

The third reason for the fear generated by the new industrial inequality was the lack of any obvious legitimation for the new distribution of wealth. The aristocracy which had claimed for centuries to be indispensable to the well-being of society seemed to have collapsed almost overnight. Now that it was gone, few people missed it. Saint-Simon, with his tongue firmly in his cheek, wrote in 1819 that if France was to lose a good portion of its first-class doctors, chemists, farmers and ironmasters, "the nation will degenerate into a mere soulless body and fall into a state of despicable weakness." But if it lost on the same day the king's brother and the cream of the French nobility employed in state, church and judicial administration, as well as a hundred thousand landed proprietors,

> such an overwhelming catastrophe would certainly grieve the French, for they are a kindly disposed nation. But the loss of a hundred and thirty thousand of the best-reputed individuals in the State would give rise to sorrow of a purely sentimental kind. It would not cause the community the least inconvenience.
> (Cited in Gordon 1991: 278, 279)

The role of chance and luck, of inheritance and speculation in factory owners' rise to wealth was often plainly evident to them and their workers. Large sums of money were made and lost quickly, and spectacular scandals and financial bubbles were common. Stock and commodity exchanges had few rules, and investments fed on gossip and rumor. Neither divine providence nor inherited nobility could any longer justify newly acquired wealth. An equally serious legitimation deficit arose on the factory floor. Early industrial management consisted of the owner and a small accounting staff, often limited to family members, a legacy of earlier merchant traditions to entrust only one's own kin with goods and money sent on long journeys to distant places. Many early industry owners were more familiar with raising capital and marketing goods than with production. Even if they came from an artisan background, their entrepreneurial role was usually supervisory.

Workers on the factory floor, on the other hand, were often downwardly mobile craftspeople who could no longer compete with cheaper manufactured goods. Their experience as independent artisans did not sit well with repetitive, machine-driven and often undemanding industrial work. In contrast to many owners they had a perfectly good understanding of the production process and could have managed it on their own, save for the lack of money to buy machines and buildings. Everywhere in industrializing countries former artisans were the most vocal leaders of the labor movement and made up the majority of those arrested in political protests (Lipton 1968: 12–15). In a message sent to British Chartists in 1837, Canadian artisans compared their own labor on which "nearly our whole population is dependent for subsistence" with "the idler" whose wealth came from the work of others, and who was "a mere consumer of what other men produce" (Lipton 1968: 12). Here was the core of the legitimacy problem of the new industrial order: who really created industrial wealth, owner or worker? What share of the wealth should each receive? Who should control industrial production?

The search for answers proceeded along ideological, organizational and scientific lines. The ideological priority was to defuse tensions between social classes. The organizational priority was to find appropriate roles for capital and labor in industrial production. The scientific priority was to find acceptable guidelines for the distribution of industrial wealth. Eighteenth and nineteenth century political philosophers tried to resolve the contradiction between property rights and their freedom-curtailing social consequences. Economists looked for ways of sharing the value created by industrial production between capital and labor. Sociologists were concerned with the consequences of inequality for social relations and social harmony.

The Ideological Problem: The Taming of Ambition

By the late nineteenth century, working classes in all industrial countries became organized, and socialist parties were now a major factor in political life. Working conditions such as child labor and the length of the working day were subject to basic regulations, and in the 1880s Germany created the first rudimentary social security system protecting workers from the worst hazards of their life: illness, industrial accidents and old age. These were hard-fought gains, conceded in order to slow the growth of labor movements and wrested from industrialists who argued that long working hours kept workers away from idleness and vice, that low wages strengthened the willingness to work and reduced alcoholism and that education encouraged unrealistic ambitions in the minds of working class children.

Concessions to working class interests were combined with a broader ideological reconstruction of the nature of inequality. This effort proceeded along many different routes, was often uncoordinated and was fraught with errors and misconceptions. It found support not only in its natural constituency – the upper classes and those who had most to gain – but also among ordinary people to whose detriment it worked. It manifested itself in arguments by business leaders that their wealth was really a "living profit," equivalent to the living wage of their workers (Bliss 1974). It emerged in the distinction between the good and the bad poor in Victorian fiction (Keating 1971) and in the portrayal of social mobility and class relations in the popular novels by Horatio Alger. Samuel Smiles' self-help movement introduced workers to the idea that

All life is struggle. Amongst workmen, competition is a struggle to advance towards high wages. Amongst masters, to make the highest profits.... Stop competition, and you stop the struggle of individualism.... Under competition, the lazy man is put under the necessity of exerting himself; and if he will not exert himself, he must fall behind. If he does not work, neither shall he eat.... There is enough for all, but do your own share of work you must.

(Cited in Briggs 1996: 112)

Such imagery surfaced in the Sunday Schools and the Methodist churches which taught the value of discipline, frugality and good character, and inspired the replacement of "Saint Monday" with the Saturday half-holiday as the mark of a new working class respectability (Reid 1976). It motivated public school promoters to educate the poor "in order ... to elevate their character rather than their station" (cited in Baldus and Kassam 1996: 335). Such ideological re-casting of inequality occurred in churches and taverns, sermons and parliamentary debates, schoolbooks and newspapers. Marx had suspected early on that the "empire of reason" of the French Revolution

> was nothing more than the idealized empire of the bourgeoisie; that eternal justice became in reality bourgeois justice, that equality amounted to the bourgeois equality before the law; that the bourgeois property was proclaimed as one of the most fundamental rights of man; and that the state of reason ... Rousseau's social contract ... could only come into reality as the bourgeois republic.
>
> (MEW 19: 190)

As the nineteenth century progressed, all of the iconic principles of the French Revolution were redefined and narrowed. Equality was gradually reduced to equality of judicial procedure, liberty to the right to property and to the right to vote, and fraternity to the organic solidarity of an industrial division of labor. These were still significant advances, but they were also a far cry from the more radical visions of the French and American Revolutions for a more egalitarian, cooperative society.

The Organizational Problem: The Social Construction of the Division of Labor

The gain in efficiency made possible by cooperative divisions of labor was one of the earliest human discoveries, but so was their potential use as a vehicle for the inflation of rank and the legitimation of power. Aristocrats posed as guarantors of security to which they were the biggest threat. Medieval guilds artificially prolonged the training of apprentices and journeymen and surrounded their craft with ritual mumbo-jumbo in order to lessen competition. Industrial production, too, required new forms of legitimation. The contrast between the technical expertise of many factory workers and the comparative ignorance of the employer who merely supplied the capital left the role of the "boss" undefined and made it imperative to put it on a more solid organizational footing. The new industrial division of labor offered an opportunity to create a legitimate managerial function for the capitalist.

Both technical and social aspects of the industrial division of labor were discussed in Adam Smith's (1723–1790) *Wealth of Nations*. His famous example of the manufacture of pins, used in his day as universal fasteners for anything from loose sheets of paper to wayward garments, showed that by dividing production into separate tasks one worker was able "to do the work of many." A single laborer could make at most 20 pins in a day. Splitting the different production steps among 10 workers allowed them to produce together up to 48,000 pins a day. This increase in productivity was possible because performing limited and repetitive tasks improved dexterity, because workers could stay in the same place instead of moving from one task to another and because it became easier to combine human labor with machines. The first two advantages had been known long before. Machines merely enhanced their effect.

Smith also discussed two social consequences of industrial divisions of labor. Increased productivity came at a price: work became more repetitive and monotonous, skills were reduced, and the life of workers and ultimately the working class became desensitized and stultified. These social costs could reduce or outweigh any efficiency gained by the division of labor. Moreover they were likely to incite social conflict which could only be prevented through social control.

> Wherever there is great property, there is great inequality.... The affluence of the rich excites the indignation of the poor, who are often both driven by want, and prompted by envy, to invade his possessions. It is only under the shelter of the civil magistrate that the owner of that valuable property, which is acquired by the labor of many years, or perhaps of many successive generations, can sleep a single night in security. He is at all times surrounded by unknown enemies, whom, though he never provoked, he can never appease, and from whose injustice he can be protected only by the powerful arm of the civil magistrate continually held up to chastise it. The acquisition of valuable and extensive property, therefore, necessarily requires the establishment of civil government. Where there is no property, or at least none that exceeds the value of two or three days labor, civil government is not so necessary.
> (Smith 1896: 670)

The British government heeded Smith's advice. It covered industrial areas with a net of spies, informers and *agents provocateurs*, and its 1799 Combination Acts, an "odious piece of class legislation" (Thompson 1980: 551), gave it almost unlimited power to arrest workers whose association was deemed "criminal" or "conspiratorial."

Missing from Smith's analysis was the question how the added value achieved by the division of labor was to be distributed. Just as he showed that it increased the average number of pins produced by each worker, he could have divided the proceeds from their sale equally. He avoided this question, although it entered his argument implicitly. His calculation of the advantages of the division of labor relied crucially on the fact that breaking up production into different tasks made it possible to purchase work at different wage rates. When pins were produced by single workers, their wage had to reflect the most expensive skill component of their work. A division of labor allowed some tasks to be given to children and women at far lower wages. The increase in output was a technical matter. The increase in the factory owner's profit presupposed already existing wage inequalities in the market, and these reflected social differences in bargaining power. This fact did not escape employers. Dr. Ure, whose 1835 *Philosophy of Manufacturers* became the ideological bible of early nineteenth century capitalism, observed that

> It is ... the constant aim and tendency of every improvement in machinery to supersede human labor altogether, or to diminish its cost, by substituting the industry of women and children for that of men; or that of ordinary laborers, for trained artisans.
>
> (Cited in Thompson 1980: 396)

Ure also noted that most capitalists had no knowledge of the production process from which they drew their profits. Here lay the second problem. Smith's model suggested, at least implicitly, a hierarchical work structure. But industrial divisions of labor could be organized in many different ways: as cooperative teams or hierarchical work groups, as consultative or command systems and with flexible or rigid lines of authority. What form they took depended first and foremost on who owned the machines and who controlled the work process. At the beginning of industrialization there were at least three possible models for organizing industrial production: the state-owned and centrally planned manufacturing establishments typical of the mercantilist economy of pre-revolutionary France, worker cooperatives whose prototypes emerged early in industrial areas of Europe, and privately owned capitalist firms (Sabel and Zeitlin 1985). Each was capable of using machine-based industrial divisions of labor, but the profits would have gone respectively to the state, to workers, or to capitalists.

Capitalism prevailed, but the individual capitalist had no natural role in the process of production. He contributed money which was inherited, borrowed or secured from shareholders. Production was carried out by a skilled labor force whose understanding of industrial manufacture often exceeded the owner's. Many workers felt that they could dispense with owners and retain the full value of what they produced if only they could afford to buy buildings and machines. In 1866, the London *Spectator* noted that cooperative factories in Manchester were more productive because workers had a stake in ownership and production. The same paper observed that the Rochdale cooperative experiment "showed that associations of workmen could manage shops, mills, and almost all forms of industry with success, and they immensely improved the condition of the men, but then they did not leave a clear place for the masters" (cited in MEW 23: 351).

The industrial division of labor gave owners of capital an opportunity to insert themselves into the production process and to deal with the legitimation deficit where it was most pressing: on the factory floor.

without specialization, the capitalist had no essential role to play in the production process.... Separating the tasks assigned to each workman was the sole means by which the capitalist could, in the days preceding costly machinery, ensure that he would remain essential to the production process as integrator of these separate operations into a product for which a market existed.

(Marglin 1974: 38)

The breaking up of industrial production into ever smaller processes thus created new and ideologically more defensible managerial functions for the capitalist. The division of labor increased productivity, but it also made the production process less transparent and more confusing, whereas assigning work to women and children reduced not only the cost but the political power of skilled labor.

> The more skilled a workman, the more intractable to discipline he became, "the more self-willed and ... the less fit a component of a mechanical system, in which, by occasional irregularities, he may do great damage to the whole." Thus the manufacturers aimed at withdrawing any process which required "peculiar dexterity and steadiness of hand ... from the *cunning* workman" and placing it in charge of a "mechanism, so self-regulating, that a child may superintend it."
>
> (Ure cited in Thompson 1980: 396)

Owners of industry could now demonstrate that they were needed to put together what the division of labor had taken apart and were therefore entitled to a major share of the wealth produced in their factories. They could define skill and wage hierarchies and fend off any idea of worker participation in management by claiming a monopoly of coordinating expertise. Only later did sociologists such as Mosca and Michels point out that organizational work roles were social creations and could be inflated in number and scope far beyond what technical or administrative efficiency required.

The Scientific Problem: The Political Philosophy of Property

Political philosophers such as Hobbes (1588–1679), Locke (1632–1704) and Rousseau (1712–1778) shared the premise that social order, instead of being divinely ordained, was a contract negotiated between free individuals who enjoyed fundamental human rights. These rights included the right to own property. The conundrum was that the accumulation of property in the hands of a few was likely to diminish the rights of others, forcing those without property to sell their labor under conditions dictated to them.

In Hobbes' original "state of nature" people were governed by internal "appetites and aversions," but though some were stronger or quicker of mind than others, such differences were not enough to create a natural social hierarchy. The state of war of all against all and the emergence of inequality were due to the fact that the clash of appetites created an atmosphere of general distrust and mutual dread where even those not interested in power were forced to defend themselves against the covetousness of their fellows. Nowhere was this more obvious than in competitive markets where greed and general distrust made it unlikely that competition could be curtailed either by individual wisdom or voluntary agreements. Pervasive insecurity could be reduced only by a covenant by which citizens surrendered part of their freedom to a collective sovereign whose ability to inspire fear and awe prevented the most destructive consequences of mutual suspicion. What form this "Leviathan" took did not matter as long as it civilized competition by imposing impartial laws which guaranteed contracts, protected property, and allowed citizens to live a "commodious life." The state as sovereign did not eliminate inequality and the accumulation of property, but blunted its exploitative edge. Hobbes' recognition of the conflict between individual freedom and inequality and his focus on individual motivations and trust were important achievements. What he did not see was that markets could create powerful coalitions of interests which could buy the Leviathan's services, impair its role as an impartial arbiter and manufacture illusions of the "commodious life" which satisfied the poor and rendered them harmless.

The distribution of collectively achieved wealth was also a central concern of Locke. He, too, began with a state of nature where the earth and its products were given in common to a humanity whose members enjoyed a fundamental equality of opportunities and faculties. Human labor transformed natural materials into possessions and private property. The problem Locke set out to solve was how the accumulation of property by one person could be prevented from harming the life, health, liberty, or possessions of another. His answer was that equality could be maintained if private property was subject to three conditions. First, an individual's use of property must leave "enough and as good" for others in order not to interfere with their rights. Second, people should acquire only as much as they needed; nothing should be destroyed, spoiled, or permitted to go to waste. Third, since property was the direct fruit of work it should be limited to the amount which could be gained by a person's labor.

These conditions placed severe limits on the accumulation of property. Locke solved this problem with the ingenious argument that the invention of money removed these limitations. First, it did not spoil or deteriorate. There was therefore no longer a natural limit on how much one could hoard or use. Money also made it possible to earn interest and profit, and therefore to enlarge one's possession of land and capital beyond one's personal needs. Finally, although the accumulation of property could leave some people without any property except their labor, the subsistence wages they were paid by the owners of capital and land were proof that "enough and as good" had been left for them.

What Locke ignored was that the accumulation of money and property gave its owners the power to define how much was "enough and as good" for the "owners" of labor. Locke imposed some restrictions: the state acted as the guarantor of life, freedom and property but unlike Hobbes' absolute sovereign it came under closer civic scrutiny. Should it be abused by vested interests or assume arbitrary powers, citizens had the right to rebel. However, Locke did not include the laboring classes in the respectable citizenry. Their precarious life and lack of manners made them prone to lose respect, resort to armed force and "break in upon the rich and sweep all like a deluge." Governments therefore had to be prepared to employ a combination of threat, indoctrination and charity to prevent periodic rebellions by the poor. The transformative power of money thus also changed the nature of civic society by creating "a natural right of *unlimited* appropriation, by which the more industrious could rightfully acquire all the land, leaving others with no way to live except by selling the disposal of their labor" (Macpherson 1962: 231).

Rousseau took a much more critical view of inequality. His state of nature was a lost ideal where early people, equipped only with simple tools and facing an often hostile nature, formed egalitarian, cooperative communities and had neither the opportunity nor the inclination to use others as tools for their own ends. As population density increased and resources became scarcer, conquest and seizure of resources became more common. Like Locke, Rousseau derived the right to property from an individual's labor and cultivation, "the true foundation of civil society." But he saw more clearly that it could turn into a tool for the exploitation of the labor of others: the first man who fenced in land and found people gullible enough to accept it laid the foundation of all subsequent inequality and the misery it inflicted on human history. For Rousseau, the origin of states and laws lay in supporting and safeguarding such claims. This could be achieved by force, but it was much more effective to transform "might into right and obedience into duty" by making laws which ostensibly protected the deprived and oppressed but in reality

> gave new fetters to the weak and new powers to the rich, irretrievably destroyed natural liberty, established forever the law of property and inequality, made clever usurpation into an irrevocable right, and, for the benefit of a few ambitious individuals, henceforth subjected the whole human race to labor, servitude, and misery.
>
> (Rousseau 1988: 44, 45)

The loss of freedom and equality could be reversed only by creating a General Will which combined the guarantee of freedom with the burden of civic obligations, asked individuals to subordinate personal desires to the common good and to accept a moderation of want which limited enrichment and exploitation. It was enforced by laws which were obeyed because they reflected the collective decision of citizens. Material equality was an essential prerequisite for political freedom. This did not mean that all citizens had to be equal. Instead, society should devise legal controls which blunted the greed of the rich and the envy of the poor, and where political equality ensured the pursuit of the common good while moderate material differences rewarded individual ability and effort. Similar visions of a society were entertained by the British Levelers a century before, and by Thomas Jefferson in the US half a century later.

Early Economic Theories of Distribution

If philosophers were preoccupied with the question how property claims could be reconciled with individual freedom, early economists confronted the problem that the new industrial production produced wealth on a scale unprecedented in human history, but that the rules which had for centuries governed its distribution were quickly unraveling. They came to widely different conclusions about how that wealth should be divided. Some replaced older notions of divine providence with iron laws of the market which assigned fixed shares of collectively achieved wealth to the participants in production. For others, labor was the ultimate source of all economic value, and property rights and political power deprived workers of what was rightfully theirs.

In the *tableau économique* constructed by Francois Quesnay (1694–1774), Louis XV's personal physician, wealth flowed through society much like nutrients and blood circulated through the body. Land was the source of all wealth available for distribution. A fixed share went to the "productive class" of peasants as a "natural price" which covered farm expenditures, seeds and subsistence wages. The surplus derived from the sale of agricultural produce flowed as rent to a second, "distributive" class of landowners because they made their land, a "gift of nature," available for cultivation. They used their profit to buy goods and services from a third, "sterile" class of merchants and artisans who traded but did not produce wealth. A fourth class, the *petit peuple* without property, was a residual, unproductive part of society who participated in circulation only as petty criminals, recipients of charity, and providers of menial services.

Quesnay's economic system was static, and the shares going to different classes could be increased only by more agricultural production. Adam Smith offered a more dynamic model of distribution. In early societies there had been no private property and labor was the source of all value. But as markets emerged, land, labor and capital acquired their own prices based on supply and demand and the rise and fall of national wealth. The income of different classes varied accordingly – growing wealth increased competition between capitalists and reduced their profits, while an increased demand for labor raised wage levels. If markets were not disturbed by government taxation or monopolistic industries, the shares of income going to land, labor and capital gravitated toward "natural rates." The "hidden hand" of the market gave each group its due while increasing the prosperity of all.

Although Smith's model of income distribution still followed mechanical laws he understood that social and historical factors also influenced the distribution of collective achievements. In a propertyless society, workers received the full value of what they produced. Private property of land and capital fundamentally changed this situation. Wages became a residual income: the worker received what was left over after the owners of land and capital deducted rent and profit from the yield of their fields and machines. Smith's view that profit diverted part of the value created by labor became a foundation of Marx's theory of surplus value.

Smith also described with surprising realism the social impact of markets. Merchants and manufacturers often lacked concern for the common good which was so important for social harmony. "The ... mean rapacity, the monopolizing spirit of merchants and manufacturers, who neither are, nor ought to be, the rulers of mankind" led them in "every country to secure to themselves the monopoly of the home market" (Smith 1896, Vol. I: 497, 498). Public interest demanded that people should be able to buy goods as cheaply as possible. The "interested sophistry of merchants and manufacturers" aimed for the opposite: to portray "their interest ... (as) the interest of the public."[1] Any legislation purporting to serve the common good was therefore likely to come from a class of people "who have generally an interest to deceive and even to oppress the public, and who (have done so) upon many occasions" (Smith 1896, Vol. I: 264, 265). Nowhere was this deception more evident than in the market for labor. No matter how much employers competed, they were always ready to conspire to lower wages, or at least to keep them from rising. They did so in secret, counting on surprise and confusion to make workers accept the change. Should workers protest, the superior organization of employers, government repression and the poverty of servants, laborers or journeymen made it likely that protests "generally end in nothing, but in the punishment or ruin of the ringleaders" (Smith 1896, Vol. I: 68). The actual as opposed to the natural wage rate was thus strongly influenced by political power.

Smith also noted that the industrial division of labor profoundly affected the personal lives of workers. The monotony of industrial production reduced work to a few repetitive operations, prevented workers from developing their talents, from enjoying their private lives and from participating in public affairs. As a result, they became "as much mutilated and deformed in mind as ... in body" (Smith 1896, Vol. II: 307, 308). Unlike Marx whose writing on alienation owed much to these passages, Smith saw the deterioration of working lives as a regrettable but inevitable by-product of economic growth which could be alleviated only through state-sponsored education.

Smith's confidence that the "hidden hand" would solve distributive problems was not shared by everyone. The large-scale migration of rural labor to English cities and the availability of demographic data after 1760 led Robert Malthus (1766–1834) to argue that population growth always exceeded "the power in the earth to produce subsistence for man," leading to recurrent natural corrections through epidemics, wars and starvation which re-established a "subsistence" equilibrium between procreation and food production. This universal law seemed particularly relevant to the social conditions of industrializing England. Uneducated and given to impulse, the growing urban underclass seemed to respond to any improvement in their situation by having more children, thereby lowering real wages and becoming vulnerable to "preventive checks" such as illness, hunger and violence. "Moral restraint" through sexual abstinence and postponement of marriage could alleviate these effects, but could not fundamentally alter the law that kept working-class standards of living at the survival minimum.

David Ricardo (1772–1823), a close friend of Malthus, refined this scenario. He too saw the combination of land with labor as the ultimate but also finite source of all wealth. But this wealth flowed in different measure to landowners, workers and capitalists. Population growth and the limited supply of land forced agriculture to expand into ever more marginal land. Yields declined while the cost of labor and the price of food increased. The only beneficiaries of this trend were landlords because rising food prices steadily increased their returns, except for those who owned the most marginal land. Labor did not benefit because higher wages were cancelled out by higher food prices, and real wages therefore stagnated at subsistence levels. Capitalists' profits were also reduced by increasing wage levels. As laborers were too poor to save, landowners spent their wealth on consumption rather than investment, and capitalists, the only group to save and invest, faced declining rates of profit, economies tended to stagnate in the long term. Nations could improve their situation through international trade, but that did not change the fundamental trends in the distribution of the wealth. However, like Smith, Ricardo understood that social conditions had a profound impact on distribution, and that landowners owed their wealth to their property rights, not their effort. Rent was "not a creation but merely a transfer of wealth" from its true creator, agricultural labor. This, and the view, shared with Smith, that labor was the source of all value, did not escape the notice of Karl Marx.

John Stuart Mill (1806–1873) gave political and social factors an even greater role in the distribution of jointly achieved wealth. His *Principles of Economy*, published in 1848, the same year as Marx's *Communist Manifesto*, treated production and distribution as separate spheres. The laws of production were "as much a subject for scientific enquiry as any of the physical laws of nature." There was nothing arbitrary about them. The distribution of wealth, by contrast, was subject to social decisions, whether by common consent or by power.

> The rules by which (the distribution of wealth) is determined, are what the opinions and feelings of the ruling portion of the community make them, and are very different in different ages and countries; and might be still more different, if mankind so chose.
>
> (Mill 1852, Vol. 1: 244)

Private ownership of capital allowed the capitalist to appropriate that portion of the value of workers' product which exceeded the cost of the reproduction of labor.

Distributive inequality was thus negotiable and could be corrected by political intervention. Accordingly, Mill supported social policies such as a land tax to siphon off part of the income of landowners, an inheritance tax to reduce inequities in economic starting conditions, and the formation of industrial cooperatives to improve wage levels. He began as a staunch defender of laissez-faire capitalism, but called himself a socialist toward the end of his life. His work marked the transition from classical economics which abhorred state intervention, to a welfare-liberalism which advocated a role for government in the redistribution of wealth.

There were more radical voices. Jean de Sismondi (1773–1842) argued that competition increased production but did not guarantee a natural or fair distribution of the results. Wealth, once in private hands, enabled its owners to pocket gains in productivity while the working population remained poor. The profit of the entrepreneur came at the expense of the worker. A more equitable distribution of land and industrial property could increase the number of independent producers while greater income equality increased overall consumption. Sismondi was one of the first to see that higher wages created a market for industrial goods which could counteract the crises of unsold goods caused by improved industrial productivity. Fourier (1772–1837), Pecqueur (1801–1887) and Blanc (1813–1882) suggested practical ways of achieving a more egalitarian distribution, ranging from producer and consumer cooperatives which allowed workers to retain the value they created, to the take-over of industrial capital by the state, a centrally planned economy and a centrally regulated distribution of income. The industrialist Robert Owen (1771–1858) established model working conditions with shorter hours, higher wages and reduction of child labor at his factory at New Lanark in England. Paine's *Rights of Man* (1792) and Condorcet's *Sketch for a Historical Picture of the Progress of the Human Mind* (1793) proposed state-sponsored systems of redistribution. Both were helped by the discovery of statistics which allowed actuarial calculations of life risks such as illness and old age. Differences between rich and poor were "present imperfections of the social art" which could be remedied by universal pensions and public schooling, inheritance duties and tax-financed social insurance. 250,000 copies of Paine's book were sold in the year after its publication, but he also became a target of government repression and was burned in effigy in many towns and villages in 1792–1793 as part of the political paranoia which seized the British establishment after the French Revolution. Condorcet's proposals received a more sympathetic reaction in France, but wars and inflation stopped their implementation.

In the late nineteenth and the twentieth centuries, divisions among economists over the distribution of wealth continued. Neo-classical theorists such as Cairnes (1823–1875) and Jevons (1835–1882) argued that "laws of exchange" allocated shares of income to labor and capital based on the marginal price paid for them in competitive markets. Institutional and historical influences were excluded as "externalities," and individual behavior was reduced to rational utility comparisons. Profit was explained as compensation for risk-taking and innovation, for abstinence from consumption in order to save capital, or as rents resulting from market imperfections. It remained the most elusive element of modern economic theories. On the other side of the debate, the historical school of economics in Germany and Austria after 1870, and institutional and behavioral economics in the US in the twentieth century argued that economic processes such as distribution were products of specific historical choices and complex human motives and could therefore be changed. The question how jointly produced wealth should be distributed among the participants remained unresolved.

The Rise of Sociological Theories of Inequality

Sociologists were latecomers to the debate over social inequality. Their focus was the social turmoil emanating from the new forms of inequality. Marx and Engels welcomed it as a harbinger of social change. To others such as Comte

(1798–1857) it seemed to destroy the very bases of social order. From his point of view the sociologist's task was

> to sufficiently contain and prevent as much as possible this fatal disposition for the fundamental breaking up of ideas, sentiments and interests ... which, if it could follow its natural course without hindrance, would in the end inevitably halt social progress.
> (Comte 1908, Vol. 4: 319)

As late as 1893, Durkheim was still troubled by the

> incessantly recurrent conflicts, and the multifarious disorders of which the economic world exhibits so sad a spectacle. For, as nothing restrains the active forces and assigns them limits they are bound to respect, they tend to develop haphazardly, and come into collision with one another, battling and weakening themselves. To be sure, the strongest succeed in completely demolishing the weakest, or in subordinating them. But ... the conquered ... do not consent to it, and consequently this cannot constitute a stable equilibrium. Truces, arrived at after violence, are never anything but provisional, and satisfy no one.... If all authority ... is wanting, the law of the strongest prevails, and latent or active, the state of war is necessarily chronic.
> (Durkheim 1964: 2, 3)

In examining this threat, sociologists drew on a variety of already existing ideas. The most influential of these was Darwin's theory of evolution. Although the *Origin of Species*, published in 1859, mentioned human evolution only in the single sentence that the theory of natural selection would shed "much light ... on the origin of man and his history," evolutionary concepts quickly entered the language of sociologists although their understanding of Darwin's theory was highly selective.

Darwin's work ran counter to the search for order and predictability that dominated nineteenth century science. Evolution led to diversity but not hierarchy, was driven by random variations instead of universal laws and followed no predetermined path. Such ideas did not fit into the ideological landscape of the nineteenth century. For social scientists the mystery of mysteries was not the evolution of species but the emergence of new forms of social inequality and the apparent threat of social disintegration. They looked for laws that promised stability and predictability in a troubled time. Darwin's ideas were soon hitched to these priorities and were often changed beyond recognition. Sociologists probed them for anything that could explain wealth and poverty and predict, depending on one's political preferences, gradual progress or radical political change. Spencer turned the struggle for existence into a universal law of competition which created a natural hierarchy from the "fittest" down to the useless and expendable. This allowed the rich to see their success as proof of their superior qualities while holding the poor responsible for their fate. For their part, those who lived in the slums of the industrial cities and toiled in factories for long hours and low wages found in Darwin's theory scientific support for revolutionary change: if even the most humble species could evolve, then surely the working class could rise from poverty to a better life. Marx wrote in 1861 that he saw in Darwin's book the natural-scientific basis for the class struggle in history. More conservative sociologists agreed with the historian Leopold von Ranke (1795–1886) that the predominant task of the time was "to distinguish law-like progress from impatiently destructive innovation," and found comfort in Darwin's suggestion that evolution was a slow, incremental process. The physiology of the body supplied a tempting model for a harmonious class structure: Comte and Durkheim portrayed societies as natural organisms in which classes, like heart or liver, had mutually interdependent functions. The zoologist Lamarck's (1744–1829) idea that acquired characteristics could be inherited confirmed upper classes' belief in their natural superiority, but also implied that lower classes could gradually and peacefully improve their lot through self-improvement and education. The geologist Lyell's (1797–1875) argument that the earth was formed by uniform timeless laws seemed to indicate that social inequality, too, was a natural process of stratification, laid down like so many layers of sedimentary rock. As for the direction of history, Karl Ernst von Baer's (1792–1876) work on the growth of embryos suggested that the history of societies progressed along a predefined path of advancement. Such "evolutionary" ideas bore little resemblance to Darwin's theory but had a powerful impact on the new field of sociology. They allowed older religious notions to be dressed in new scientific garb. Divine providence now resurfaced as a social order governed by invariant social laws. The notion of righteous religious conduct turned into functional behavior and rational choice. The fear of sin survived in the deep ambiguity towards agency and change. The eschatological idea of redemption reappeared in the many sociological models of progressive historical development, from theological to metaphysical to scientific knowledge (Comte), from militant to industrial societies (Spencer) or from mechanical to organic solidarity (Durkheim).

Instead of Darwin, sociologists turned to Newton to find the theoretical foundations for their field and to identify the social laws which explained the universal necessity of social inequality. Montesquieu (1689–1755) was one of the first to dismiss the role of chance in social life:

> It is not Fortune who governs the world.... There are general causes, some moral, some physical, which operate in every monarchy, raise it, maintain it, or overthrow it; all such events are subject to these causes; and if a particular cause such as the accidental result of a battle, has ruined a state, there was a general cause that made it necessary that this state perished by a single battle. In a word, the principal movement drags along all the particular occurrences.
>
> (Montesquieu 1968: 145)[2]

The discovery by Gauss (1777–1855), Laplace (1749–1827), Buckle (1821–1862) and Quetelet (1796–1874) of probability, the fact that multiple measurements of natural and social phenomena arranged themselves around central values, encouraged the hope that further research would find general laws behind the surface variation of social behavior. Working independent of time, context and human intent, they suggested a new "science of society" which could

> accomplish for the history of man something equivalent, or at all events analogous, to what has been effected by ... different branches of the natural sciences. In regard to nature, events apparently the most irregular and capricious have been explained, and have been shown to be in accordance with certain fixed and universal laws ... if human events were subjected to similar treatment, we have every right to expect similar results.... Indeed, the progress of inquiry is becoming so rapid and so earnest, that I entertain little doubt that before another century has elapsed, the chain of evidence will be complete, and it will be as rare to find a historian who denies the undeviating regularity of the mortal world, as it is now to find a philosopher who denies the regularity of the material world.
>
> (Buckle 1871: 6, 33)

From here it was only a step toward confounding the normal with the normative. Comte defined the central region of normal distributions as the common, desirable range of social behavior, purged of deviations and extremes. It promised "a resolution of the intellectual and moral anarchy that above all characterizes the great crisis of our time" (Comte cited in Hacking 1990: 168). Durkheim, too, saw behind statistical tendencies the working of "cosmic forces" (Durkheim 1952: 309) which could offer an antidote to the unrest caused by industrialization and could immunize the lower classes against social disorder.

The "taming of chance" (Hacking 1990) by the social sciences was accompanied by the taming of "free will" and its most dreaded manifestations: creativity, innovation and the accompanying specter of "fraternity" and revolutionary collective action. The fear of unfettered human agency had a long history. The Book of Genesis linked free will directly to the challenge of authority: God forbade Adam to eat from the forbidden fruit because it would make him "like one of us." Uncontrolled freedom threatened established order, the more so because Satan seemed to avail himself most often of peasants and other common folk to foment unpredictable outbreaks of passion, vice, and rebellion. Their ignorance could lead them to misinterpret biblical passages that the meek would inherit the earth and that it was easier for a camel to pass through the eye of a needle than for a rich man to enter heaven.

Such fears waxed and waned, closely tracking levels of social conflict. In the relatively benign political and economic climate of England prior to the French Revolution, the economies of Smith and Ricardo were still populated by landowners, merchants and laborers who fought each other in the political arena and displayed complex emotions such as greed, misery and compassion. Smith even argued that the personal pursuit of wealth was a grotesque and wasteful aberration.

> With the greater part of rich people, the chief enjoyment consists in the parade of riches, which in their eye is never so complete as when they

appear to possess those decisive marks of opulence which nobody can possess but themselves.

(Smith 1896: 160)

The impersonal "hidden hand" acted only as an unintended economic consequence: the money spent by the rich on "baubles and trinkets" trickled down to the silversmiths who made their spoons, the masons who built their mansions, and the servants who emptied their chamber pots.

During the course of the nineteenth century, the social sciences brought independent human agency increasingly under the control of external laws, functional/rational or biological needs. Statistical distributions seemed to render individual actions irrelevant. The more actors there were, "the more individual will fades out, and allows the series of general facts to predominate, the facts which depend on general causes, and in virtue of which society exists and is conserved" (Quetelet cited in Hacking 1990: 123). By the late nineteenth century, market participants had become caricatures, automata with fixed preferences and perfect information that were driven by an innate desire to maximize their utility. Sociologists conceived their own version of *homo sociologicus* who rationally met given needs with given resources. Social processes and structures were considered legitimate objects of scientific inquiry only if they were orderly and measurable. Determinism, summed up succinctly in Skinner's dictum that one "can't have a science about a subject matter that hops capriciously about" (Skinner 1962: 257), discounted all forms of contingency. Operationalism rejected internal, cognitive processes because they could not be quantified. Sociologists developed a deeply ambivalent attitude toward consciousness. They celebrated it as the distinguishing feature of the human species but refrained from studying its actual consequences:

> Every time that a social phenomenon is directly explained by a psychological phenomenon, we may be sure that the explanation is false.... The determining cause of a social fact should be sought among the social facts preceding it and not among the states of individual consciousness.
>
> (Durkheim 1938: 104, 110)

These views swept across the social sciences. Behaviorism turned human actions into stimulus-response sequences and banished the study of cognition from psychological research. Neoclassical economics posed as a "positive science" which revealed the economic laws which gave various classes their due share of wealth and guided economies toward prosperity. Neo-Darwinism reduced evolution to an entirely external selection process in which organisms played no independent role.

Having expelled chance and agency from their theories, sociologists were supremely confident that they could not only explain inequality but find practical solutions for the conflicts it seemed to cause. Henri Saint-Simon (1760–1825), who had barely escaped the guillotine during the French Revolution, recommended the creation of a "Council of Newton," 21 scholars who would enforce "scientific" rules of social and political conduct with unrestricted authority. The idea was taken up by his disciple Comte. "Social physics," which he later renamed sociology, would reveal social laws which an elite corps of philosopher-sociologists could then apply to guide social life and avoid social conflict. Comte's *Plan of Scientific Work Necessary for Reorganizing Society* (1822) laid out how this should be done. A strong state enforced the guiding principles, capitalists secured the material means necessary to realize them, and the working class did its work and "neither aim(ed) for wealth nor for political mandates" (Comte 1907: 204). Disparities of wealth would be relieved by the cultivation of a "spirit of community" informed by the knowledge of the "real laws" of social processes (Comte 1908, Vol. 4: 195). Chief among these was the belief that social inequality was a universal and necessary feature of human societies.

Notes

1 Employers testifying in 1816 before a parliamentary committee investigating child labor in factories claimed that children working for 13 to 15 hours a day were healthier, more intelligent, more moral than others and less tired than adults. Long hours encouraged "habits of early subordination, industry, and regularity." Legislation to protect children "would spell ruin to the country and put money into foreigners' pockets" (Hammond and Hammond 1968: 142).
2 His contemporary, the Prussian King Frederic II (1712–1786) who knew how little separated military victory from defeat, came to different conclusions: "Chance makes a mockery of all wisdom and greatness of men. Small and sometimes ridiculous causes change all too often the happiness of entire states and monarchies" (cited in Kunisch 2004: 131).

Bibliography

Baldus, Bernd and Meenaz Kassam. "Make Me Truthful, Good and Mild: Values in Nineteenth Century Ontario Schoolbooks." *Canadian Journal of Sociology* 21 (1996) 3: 327–358.
Bliss, Michael. *A Living Profit*. Toronto: McClelland and Stewart, 1974.
Bonnycastle, Richard H. *Canada and the Canadians*. London: Colburn, 1849.
Briggs, Asa. *Victorian People: A Reassessment of Persons and Themes 1851–67*. Chicago: University of Chicago Press, 1996.
Buckle, Henry Thomas. *The History of Civilization in England*. Vol. 1. London: Longmans, Green, and Co, 1871 [1857].
Comte, Auguste. *Discours sur l'ensemble du positivisme*. Paris: Société positiviste internationale, 1907.
Comte, Auguste. *Cours de philosophie positive*. Vol. 4, 5th edition. Paris: Librairie C. Reinwald, 1908 [1830].
Durkheim, Emile. *The Rules of Sociological Method*. Chicago: University of Chicago Press, 1938 [1895].
Durkheim, Emile. *Suicide*. Translated by John A. Spaulding and George Simpson. London: Routledge and Kegan Paul, 1952 [1897].
Durkheim, Emile. *The Division of Labour in Society*. New York: Free Press, 1964 [1893].
Gordon, Scott. *The History and Philosophy of Social Science*. London: Routledge, 1991.
Hacking, Ian. *The Taming of Chance*. Cambridge: Cambridge University Press, 1990.

Hammond, John L. and Barbara Hammond. *The Town Labourer*. Garden City: Doubleday, 1968.
Hobsbawm, Eric J. *Industry and Empire*. Harmondsworth: Penguin, 1969.
Keating, P.J. *The Working Classes in Victorian Fiction*. London: Routledge, 1971.
Kunisch, Johannes. *Friedrich der Grosse*. München: C.H. Beck, 2004.
Lipton, Charles. *The Trade Union Movement of Canada 1827–1959*. Montreal: Canadian Social Publications, 1968.
Macpherson, Crawford B. *The Political Theory of Possessive Individualism. Hobbes to Locke*. London: Oxford University Press, 1962.
Mandeville, Bernard de. *The Fable of the Bees; or, Private Vices, Publick Benefit*. Two volumes. Oxford: Clarendon Press, 1924 [1723].
Marglin, Stephen A. "What Do Bosses Do? The Origins and Functions of Hierarchy in Capitalist Production." *Review of Radical Political Economics* 7 (1975) 1: 20–37.
MEW (Karl Marx, Friedrich Engels, *Werke*). Forty volumes, two supplementary volumes. Berlin: Dietz Verlag, 1957–1985. Vols. II and III of *Das Kapital* republished by Europäische Verlagsanstalt: Frankfurt, 1968.
Mill, John Stuart. *Principles of Political Economy*. Two volumes. London: John W. Parker and Son, 1852.
Montesquieu, Charles-Louis. *Considérations sur les causes de la grandeur des Romains et de leur décadence*. Paris: Garnier-Flammarion, 1968 [1734].
Moodie, Susanna. *Roughing it in the Bush*. Toronto: Bell & Cockburn, 1913.
Reid, Douglas A. "The Decline of Saint Monday 1766–1876." *Past and Present* 71 (1976) 1: 76–101.
Rousseau, Jean Jacques "On Social Contract or Principles of Political Right." In Alan Ritter and Julia Conaway Bondanella (eds) *Rousseau's Political Writings*, 84–173. New York: W.W. Norton, 1988 [1762].
Ryerson, Stanley B. *Unequal Union*. New York: International Publishers, 1968.
Sabel, Charles and Jonathan Zeitlin. "Historical Alternatives to Mass Production: Politics, Markets and Technology in Nineteenth Century Industrialization." *Past and Present* 108 (1985) August: 133–176.
Skinner, Burrhus F. *Walden Two*. New York: Macmillan, 1968.
Smith, Adam. *An Inquiry Into the Nature and Causes of the Wealth of Nations*. Two volumes. London: George Bell & Sons, 1896 [1776].
Thompson, Edward P. *The Making of the English Working Class*. London: Penguin, 1980 [1963].
Tocqueville, Alexis de. *Democracy in America*. New York: Vintage Books, 1954 [1840].

3 Theories of Social Inequality
Classical Paradigms

Biological Theories of Inequality: Darwin and Social Darwinism

When Darwin's *Origin of Species* appeared in 1859, the basic ideas of Social Darwinism had been in place for some time. Malthus had already suggested that if population and food supply had increased at the same rate, "man might never have emerged from the savage state" (Malthus 1959: 127). Seven years before the publication of the *Origin of Species*, Herbert Spencer (1820–1903) had given the "struggle for existence" a central role in maintaining the "vigor" of a society by eliminating its weak and diseased individuals. Darwin was not immune to such ideas. Some passages in the *Origin of Species* and *The Descent of Man* have a distinctly Social Darwinist flavor, leading Marx to comment that it was "remarkable how Darwin rediscovers among beast and plants his English society with its division of labor, competition, opening-up of new markets, 'inventions', and the Malthusian 'struggle for existence'" (MEW 41: 380).

There were, however, key differences between Darwin's theory of evolution and the nineteenth century Social Darwinism which appropriated his name. The first concerned the causes of evolution. Darwin knew that the raw material for natural selection came from the numerous heritable variations around the "average type" of each species. Although he knew nothing about their genetic origin he understood that they appeared "accidentally," unrelated to their eventual use. Social Darwinists, on the other hand, looked for ultimate, determining causes which explained social inequality as a necessary and beneficial feature of all human societies.

Second, Darwin's evolution proceeded slowly over many generations and in all directions and produced an abundant variety of new organic forms. He saw "no evidence of the existence of any law of necessary development" in organic or human evolution (Darwin 1958: 39). By contrast, for Social Darwinists evolution was a developmental process which "could not possibly have been other than it has been" (Spencer 1897: 233, 234) and converged toward a desirable end state.

Third, Darwin's theory had little to say on the subject of social inequality. Fitness was not a one-dimensional property. Adaptation always occurred in relation to specific environments and could involve violent struggle, but also cooperation or the peaceful penetration of hitherto unoccupied environments.

It could produce admirable specialization, but to look for hierarchy in nature was "hopeless; who will decide whether a cuttle-fish be higher than a bee" (Darwin 1958: 331). Social Darwinists were not interested in diversification but in the consolidation of rank and social class in the new industrial societies.

The Survival of the Fittest and the Law of Progress

Spencer's ideas were shaped by his early involvement in radical (liberal) politics. His individualism reflected the self-confidence of a rising middle class which saw itself, rather than the British establishment, as the true creator of the industrial revolution. His opposition to state intervention stemmed from his rejection of the control of English society by a corrupt government dominated by aristocracy and the Church of England. He opposed all forms of "statism," whether it was the Corn Laws passed in 1815 to protect landowners against cheap imported corn, or the New Poor Laws which seemed to support the indigent and idle at the expense of the industrious and wealthy. Where British conservatives were preoccupied with the defense of a providential order, he believed in the perfectibility of human nature.

Spencer's theory drew on an eclectic assembly of sources. The discovery of laws by the natural sciences convinced him that a "law of progress" governed the development of human societies. Over time, human culture became more diverse because every force produced more than one change. But just as the first law of thermodynamics proved that no energy was lost in the transformation of motion into heat or solids into gases, Spencer deduced that a similar "persistence of force" assured that human history, for all its variations and conflicts, possessed a universal causal continuity: the struggle for existence. Proof seemed to come from the work of Karl Ernst von Baer, Spencer's fellow correspondent at the London *Economist*, whose studies of embryos seemed to suggest that societies developed along a fixed path from primitive beginnings to higher, more complex forms while retaining their functional unity.

For the dynamics which drove this process, Spencer borrowed from Lamarck whose view of evolution as an inheritance of characteristics acquired during one's lifetime recommended itself because it made it possible to link wealth and poverty to personal effort and ambition. This provided a ready legitimation of wealth and a justification for leaving it to one's descendants. It also implied that the poor could improve their lot by personal effort, a far more acceptable solution of the problem of poverty than violent revolution. To account for any persistent poverty, Spencer borrowed from Malthus and Darwin to argue that the winnowing power of natural selection always left behind a residue of individuals too weak or too idle to survive.

Spencer combined these ideas to argue that the social conditions in the nineteenth century were only the latest manifestations of a universal process which began at the dawn of human history. Early societies were homogenous and unstable. Divisions of labor did not exist. Individuals were self-sufficient; "every part fulfills for itself all needs" (Spencer 1897: I-2: 452). Social structures were incoherent: when disturbed by violent competition, they fractured easily because their parts could live on their own. What kept them together was the fear of human aggressors, predatory animals and imagined supernatural threats. In response, they formed "militant societies" where social hierarchy was pronounced, regimentation and subordination were common, and courage, strength and obedience were highly valued. Failure was met with contempt and harsh punishment. Private possessions could be confiscated by rulers or tribe, and economic productivity was low. Even here, however, the power of progress was already at work, clearing the earth of inferior people and leaving scarce resources in the hands of stronger survivors.

As societies advanced, the struggle for existence gradually became more peaceful. Commercial and intellectual competition prevailed over violent conflict, and divisions of labor replaced the hierarchical structures of militant societies. A new "industrial society" developed where private associations increasingly assumed the functions of the state, and democracy opened governments to pressure from citizens. States limited themselves to the defense of individual rights and the protection of private property, especially against any redistribution of wealth which "takes from some men part of the advantages they have earned, and awards to other men advantages they have not earned" (Spencer 1897: 610).

The transition from militant to industrial societies led to greater occupational differentiation and social inequality, but also to greater functional interdependence and social coherence. The driving force of this transformation remained the struggle for existence which eliminated the deficient and favored the capable whose actions ensured not only their own survival but the long-term progress of the human race. This process was not perfect, but although "much chaff is left behind which should be winnowed out, and much grain is taken away which should be left behind ... the *average* effect is to purify society from those who are, *in some respect or other*, essentially faulty" (Spencer 1868: 415). Spencer sidestepped Hobbes' war of all against all and the consequent need for a strong state by assuming that competitive self-interest was mitigated by a "moral sense," reminiscent of Adam Smith's "fellow feeling," which gave rise to sentiments of justice, guilt and compassion. Struggle did not disappear, but in industrial societies it came increasingly under mental control which softened desires and improved intellectual faculties. Those who fared well became the rightful owners of what they had gained.

> If ... out of many starting with like fields of activity, one obtains, by his greater strength, greater ingenuity, or greater application, more gratifications and sources of gratifications than the rest, and does this without trenching upon the equal freedoms of the rest, the moral law assigns him an exclusive right to all those extra gratifications and sources of gratifications; nor can the rest take them from him without ... violating that law.
>
> (Spencer 1897: 66)

The separation of fit from unfit individuals led to a parallel functional differentiation between governing and governed. In early societies power soon became hereditary. Eventually, "regulating classes" took control of religion, industry and government. Inferior classes meanwhile produced the necessities of life. Inequality thus increased economic efficiency and social progress. That was its only justification. "Ethically considered, there has never been any warrant for the subjugation of the many to the few, except that it has furthered the welfare of the many; and, at the present time, furtherance of the welfare of the many is the only warrant for that degree of class-subordination which continues" (Spencer 1887: 255, 256).

The collective benefits of management of social affairs by superior individuals were as self-evident as the inevitable pain and suffering which the struggle of existence imposed on the poor.

> It seems hard that an unskilfulness which with all his efforts he cannot overcome should entail hunger upon the artisan. It seems hard that a laborer incapacitated by sickness from competing with his stronger fellows, should have to bear the resulting privations. It seems hard that widows and orphans should be left to struggle for life or death. Nevertheless, when regarded not separately, but in connection with the interests of universal humanity, these harsh fatalities are seen to be full of the highest beneficence – the same beneficence which brings to early graves the children of diseased parents, and singles out the low-spirited, the intemperate, and the debilitated as the victims of an epidemic.
>
> (Spencer 1868: 353, 354)

Such natural costs of competition had to be distinguished from preventable social conflict caused by the fact that the adaptation of societies often lagged behind the changing conditions of life. Obsolete remnants of primitive militant societies still surfaced in industrial societies.

> The attributes of the original man have not yet died out.... Our savage selfishness is seen in commerce, in legislation, in social arrangements, in amusements.... Classes quarrel about their respective "interests"; and corruption is defended by those who profit from it.... Gamblers pocket their gains with unconcern; and your share-speculator cares not who loses, so that he gets his premium. No matter what their rank, no matter in what they are engaged ... men show themselves as yet, little else than barbarians in broadcloth.
>
> (Spencer 1868: 221, 222)

In his early writings Spencer expressed confidence that such anachronisms would soon disappear. Later he became increasingly concerned that class divisions, helped by modern organization and communication, would lead to a "rebarbarization" of society.

Where Spencer painted the struggle for survival in bold theoretical strokes, the other founder of nineteenth-century Social Darwinism, William Graham Sumner (1840–1910), filled in the details. Like Spencer, Sumner saw competition as an unchangeable law of nature, an "iron spur" which pitted human wants and needs against hostile natural and social environments and separated the fit from the weak, a consequence which "can no more be done away with than gravitation" (Sumner 1914: 68). Its destructive aspects were mitigated by the ability to seek the help of others in pursuing a common purpose. This was not altruism – sacrifice for one's kin was the only example of that in nature – but "antagonistic cooperation" which allowed individuals to compete with each other for their mutual benefit.

Inequality was the natural result of competition. At the bottom of industrial societies stood the paupers who took more from society than they contributed and were a dead-weight on a society's struggle for improvement (Sumner 1972: 20, 21). At the top were the great captains of industry, individuals of "judgment, courage and perseverance." The few who possessed these gifts deserved therefore "excessive and constantly advancing rates of remuneration" (Sumner 1992: 254). Without the incentive of luxury and leisure they would never accept the responsibility of leadership and use their wealth to create new capital. Capital formation, from primitive stone tools to modern machines, was the driving force of human progress. Its benefits trickled down the social hierarchy, culturally because lower classes imitated the customs of their superiors and thus gradually improved their manners and interests, and economically because profits, the "wages of superintendence" (Sumner 1972: 52), increased the wealth of society.

> No man can acquire a million without helping a million men to increase their little fortunes all the way down through all the social grades.... The millionaires are a product of natural selection, acting on the whole body of men to pick out those who can meet the requirement of certain work to be done.... They get high wages and live in luxury, but the bargain is a good one for society.
>
> (Sumner 1992: 155)

Sumner's *Folkways and Mores* (1906) drew a more detailed picture of the inequality produced by the struggle for existence. The top consisted of people of "genius" and "talent." Next came the vast majority of the population, "the masses," arranged around an average of "mediocrity." Below them stood the "unskilled and illiterate," the "proletariat," whose members had abandoned the struggle of existence in favor of vulgar enjoyments and passions which "recklessly increase their numbers." The "defective, dependent and delinquent" were at the very bottom of the hierarchy (Sumner 1979: 40). Frugality, industry, temperance and perseverance aided in the struggle for self-preservation. Negligence, shiftlessness, imprudence and inefficiency led to defeat. These traits could be lost through indifference and laziness, or improved through learning and self-discipline. Because they were inherited by one's children, they could keep property in the hands of the most capable but could also lay down lineages of indigence and failure.

Folkways and Mores avoided the strident tone of Sumner's earlier work. Spencer had argued that culture mirrored inequality more or less directly.

Militant societies valued hero-worship and obedience, whereas industrial societies valued individualism, honesty in contracts, and regard for the rights of others. For Sumner, the relationship between culture and social evolution was more complex. What was deemed right in one culture was judged wrong in another, and the "aleatory element" of unanticipated opportunities and risks ensured that "luck is always present in the struggle for existence" (Sumner 1979: 7). The culture of the fittest did not necessarily produce the fittest culture. The upper classes could impose undesirable values and practices on those below them, taking advantage of the fact that masses were instinctively conservative, "disinterested in politics, shallow, narrow-minded, and prejudiced" and therefore easily manipulated. Overall, however, cultural innovation by the upper classes benefited society in the long run. The broad mass of the population adapted features of higher class culture to their own conservative tastes while its most capable members were constantly co-opted into the upper class, preempting their potential role as leaders of social protest. Here, as everywhere else in the struggle for life, any interference was unwarranted. History was "full of error, folly, selfishness, violence, and craft" (Sumner 1979: 49), but that did not derail the path of societal progress.

Social Darwinism and Social Policy

Like many early sociologists, Spencer and Sumner saw their role not just in explaining social inequality but in showing governments that social life was "fixed by laws of nature precisely analogous to those of the physical order" (Sumner 1992: 172). Knowledge of these laws and their consequences could add "oil to the movement – to remove friction" (Spencer 1908: 367) and prevent policies "which lead to pathological states and accompanying degradations" (Spencer 1908: 367).

Spencer took aim at two controversial issues of his time: the demand for equality and the problem of poverty. He solved the first by reducing the scope of equality to opportunities rather than outcomes. Social equality did not mean that "all shall have like shares of ... things ... but that all shall have like freedom to pursue these things" (Spencer 1897: 65). Sumner agreed; instead of eliminating the differences between existing classes, "our aim should be to *increase, multiply, and extend the chances.* Such is the work of civilization" (Sumner 1972: 168). As for poverty, it was essential to distinguish between the natural misery resulting from the struggle for existence, and suffering caused by artificial limits placed on the ability to participate in the struggle. Here, Spencer advocated much that was progressive for his time: he favored free trade and opposed price-fixing monopolies and the concentration of land ownership. He rejected slavery, advocated (but later opposed) allowing women to vote, opposed child labor, criticized inherited rank and rejected colonialism as serving neither colonizers nor colonized. Sumner, too, saw that throughout human history "chiefs, kings, priests, warriors, statesmen, and other functionaries have put their own interests in the place of group interests, and have used the authority they possessed to force the societal organization to work and fight for their interests" (Sumner 1979: 64). Industrial societies, in particular, were threatened by a "plutocracy" of business owners who used their economic and political power to gain political influence.

> Modern plutocrats buy their way through elections and legislatures, in the confidence of being able to get powers which will recoup them for all the outlay and yield an ample surplus besides.... Democracy especially dreads plutocracy, and with good reason. (Plutocracy) is very largely operated in secret, it has a large but undefined field of legitimate, or quasi-legitimate, expenditure, for which there is no audit. As the operations of this apparatus are extra-legal they are irresponsible, yet they reach out to, and control, the public and civil functions. Even on the field of constitutional institutions, plutocracy always comes into the contest with a small body, a strong organization, a powerful motive, a definite purpose, and a strict discipline, while on the other side is a large and unorganized body, without discipline, with its ideas undefined, its interests ill understood, with an indefinite good intention.
>
> (Sumner 1992: 144, 147)

Such shortcomings were, however, not systemic consequences of inequality, but remnants of earlier and now imperfect adaptations. The removal of the weak and useless remained a "natural process of elimination by which a society continually purifies itself" (Spencer 1887: 346). Efforts to lessen inequality through redistribution wasted resources which middle and upper classes could put to more productive use, and removed incentives for the poor to improve themselves. Private charity should distinguish between victims of misfortune and dishonest cheaters out to exploit the benevolence of others. Education should be private rather than public because parental ambition was the best incentive to give children a good start in life. Spencer even asserted that public education increased crime, citing evidence that the least educated had the lowest crime rates (Spencer 1868: 380). Postal services, banks and municipal services such as sewage or lighting should be privatized to discourage the growth of governmental bureaucracies. Sanitation, vaccination and medical care should be private to allow the natural depletion of the unfit. Markets encouraged self-reliance and delivered services and goods more efficiently than governments. Sumner categorically rejected any political action for social change. Capital was akin to a vital "energy" or "force" and should be allowed to flow to its most efficient use. True hardship deserved compassion, but the majority of the poor who "constantly arouse the pity of the humanitarians and philanthropists" were in fact "simply good-for-nothings, who in one way or another live on the good-for-somethings" (Spencer 1887: 122). The cost of supporting them was borne by the hardworking and frugal "forgotten man" who generated capital only to have it taken away through taxation and wasteful government expenditure. "Let every man be sober, industrious, prudent and wise, and poverty will be abolished in a few generations" (Sumner 1934, Vol. I: 109).

By 1920, Social Darwinism had been weakened by the rejection of Lamarck's theory of inheritance, by more critical attitudes towards business and competition, and by the growing voice which unions and working class parties gave to the "unfit." Its political and ideological legacy survived in modern neo-liberal and conservative policies. Social Darwinism put sociological flesh on the bones of classical economic liberalism and offered seemingly scientific solutions to key problems of industrializing societies. It celebrated private property, legitimated the distribution of wealth and projected a bright future. It disposed of the problem of poverty by linking it to personal rather than structural faults. Inequality, far from exploiting the poor, promoted their long-term prosperity. For the rich, unsettled by social unrest and uncertain in the justification of their wealth, Spencer's vision brought relief from anxiety and a troubled conscience.

> Spencer's message that, despite appearances, order existed and change was necessarily progress (a view he later revised) must have been like a balm to a generation which had undergone an unprecedented explosion both of their social world and of their vision of nature.... Christian providence lay behind Spencer's evolutionary progress and predestination behind his smiling secular necessity.
>
> (Peel 1972: xxiv)

Modern Biological Explanations of Social Inequality

After Spencer and Sumner, biological explanations of social inequality went in two different directions. One, following the Social-Darwinist tradition, looked for more precise evidence of inherited traits which could explain observable differential success in the lifetime competition for wealth or status. Intelligence, a seemingly all-purpose adaptive (and presumably heritable) trait, was an obvious candidate, leading to research on individual, sex- and race-related differences in cognitive ability. The second route followed Darwin's theory more closely and used speculative reconstructions of past "environments of evolutionary adaptedness" which could explain how natural selection could have entrenched heritable inequality-inducing behaviors in human societies.

As for the first of these efforts, Darwin shared the concern that in civilized societies medical advances and charity might interfere with the tendency of natural selection to eliminate the mentally or physically defective. But perhaps mindful that his own modest academic success did not foretell his eventual achievements, he was also hesitant to classify people on the basis of hereditary characteristics: "I have always maintained that, excepting fools, men did not differ much in intellect, only in zeal and hard work" (cited in Gould 1981: 77). That did not prevent Darwin's cousin Francis Galton (1822–1911) from arguing that a "science of eugenics" could offer a solution to social and political problems by creating state-sponsored scientific programs of "breeding the best." The eugenics movement quickly gained popularity. Sterilization of the "feebleminded" began in the US in 1907 and ended there and in Canada only in the early 1970s.[1] European countries such as Switzerland, Sweden and Norway passed sterilization laws between 1928 and 1934. The Nazi regime first sterilized the "hereditary inferior." The policy was soon extended to the "morally feeble-minded" such as vagrants and beggars and led eventually to the large-scale murder of people considered racially inferior.

The eugenics movement never managed to isolate inherited traits from social and environmental influences. Reliable quantitative indicators which could be used to distinguish "normal" from "inferior" populations and to regulate reproduction proved elusive. Eugenicists were primarily preoccupied with the extreme ends of the social scale, namely the comparatively low reproductive rate of people of "genius" and the proliferation of the "unfit." But their aims broadly aligned with the basic Social Darwinist assumption that social inequality represented a natural ordering of people on the basis of their inherited ability. Pearson (1857–1936), the founder of statistical correlation methods in sociology, argued that if we looked at societies as a whole, class distinctions followed differences in aptitude. Working classes were on average not as intelligent as professional classes, and the difference was at least partly inherited (Hawkins 1997: 228). Early proponents of IQ measurements such as Binet, Goddard and Terman saw intelligence as a largely inherited, measurable quantity which could be used to assign people to unskilled, skilled and professional employment. Controversies continue over whether intelligence is a uniform or diversified trait, and so do efforts to link intelligence to individual (Jensen 1998), class (Herrnstein and Murray 1994; Murray 1999), and gender, racial and ethnic inequality (MacDonald 1994; Rushton 1997; Entine 2007; Murray 2007).

The second branch of biological explanations of social inequality looked at its effects on long-term reproductive success. During the early twentieth century, Neo-Darwinism began to combine an improved understanding of genetics with hypothetical selection environments in order to explain how evolution could have favored behavioral traits which gave adaptive advantages to early humans and gradually spread across populations through inheritance. Human culture, including inequality," whatever else it was, must have been adaptive ... in terms of survival and reproduction" (Durham 1978: 429). Sociobiologists were confident that a "biogrammar" of human behavior could reveal the deep genetic structure behind cultural practices. Selection scenarios for cultural traits often went back to the long Pleistocene period during which most human behavior was thought to have evolved. Their speculative character was not seen as a problem because "the elegant (adaptive) logic of evolutionary analysis often lets us figure out the role of genes without worrying about the nuts and bolts of their influence" (Wright 1995: 244).

The consequence was a proliferation of adaptive rationales for the evolution of inequality in human societies. Inequality was seen as an extension of dominance, aggression or territoriality found among animal species. The adaptive advantage of such behaviors was obvious:

> with rare exception, the aggressively superior animal displaces the subordinate from food, from mates, and from nest sites. It only remains to be established that this power actually raises the genetic fitness of the animals possessing it. On this point the evidence is completely clear.
>
> (Wilson 1975: 287)

58 Theories of Social Inequality

In human cultures, dominance regulated access to scarce resources, whereas territoriality and private property discouraged ruinous competition. The advent of agriculture and the production of surplus beyond subsistence allowed dominant individuals to bequeath rank and wealth to their offspring (Barkow 2006: 37), favoring the emergence of "coherent, self-interested elites or upper classes" (Barkow et al. 1992: 634).

The many historical forms of social inequality were shoehorned into adaptive "uniformities" such as a "predisposition for self-enhancement" (Lopreato 1984: Chapter 4) which evolved to intimidate sexual and social rivals. Hierarchies were claimed to bring adaptive "advantages in terms of coordination and cohesion" and opportunities to "learn advantageously from the more successful" (Hodgson and Knudsen 2010: 194, 185). Redundant or harmful consequences were given "latent" fitness properties,[2] were seen as mismatches between stone-age adaptations and modern social environments, or were dismissed as temporary "destructive" behavior which was unlikely to be selected (Hodgson and Knudsen 2010: 122). The costs of nepotism and unearned privilege paled in comparison with their benefits because without leaders social life "would be chaotic; there would be no coordination and effective task implementation" (Mazur 2005: 9). Not all authors were oblivious of the costs of inequality. Durham's study of cultural evolution conceded that powerful groups could impose values on others for their own benefit, and that this could cause the persistence of sub-optimal traits, although in the end "genetic selection and cultural selection have generally harmonious, parallel influences in guiding the evolution of human diversity" (Durham 1991: 419). Barkow admitted that cultural symbols could be "stretched" to help elites to accumulate advantages, but argued that such costs were always outweighed by the adaptive benefit of learning from "the high in status and power" (Barkow 1989: 312).

The overall view was that inequality evolved because "to recognize good performance and to defer to individuals who achieve it is a cross-culturally stable tendency which would have a clear adaptive advantage in promoting the learning of effective behavior and in structuring groups around effective individuals" (Erdal and Whiten 1994: 177). The long human history of despots, exploiters and corrupt elites who inflicted prolonged harm on large numbers of people of equal or greater ability was ignored. Only rarely did authors who argued for an adaptive "need for more powerful and formal leaders to manage complex intra- and intergroup relations – the chiefs, kings, presidents, and CEOs" also concede that elites "at best provide important public services and at worst abuse their position of power to dominate and exploit followers" (King et al. 2009: 915).

Forms of legitimation such as religion evolved to maintain relations with powerful agents, whether gods, heroes or dominant groups, and facilitated the functioning of hierarchies (Boyer 2008). Status and deference had similar causes: high status signaled physical strength and the capacity to accumulate resources, and therefore discouraged others from potentially harmful competition. Submission and deference protected subordinates from "the tensions that accompany the assertion of dominance" (Mazur 2005: 61) and allowed them to share in their superiors' prestige and learn the secrets of their success. Residual opposition by low-ranked members could be reduced by splitting society into so many status-seeking groups that competition was diffused, or by "encapsulating" lower groups so that they considered "those with demonstrably higher power and control of resources ... as members of a higher species" (Barkow 1989: 384) and stopped competing with them. Low-ranked individuals could also satisfy the biological need "to maintain an evaluation of self as superior to at least some others" (Barkow 1989: 180) by finding surrogate arenas of competition such as sports, fashion or the acquisition of status symbols. All such behaviors were favored by natural selection because they were reproductively advantageous to their carriers.

Status competition also shaped relations between men and women. Females selected males on the basis of physical or social indicators of their capacity as a provider and parent, an important indirect contributor to the female's reproductive success. For men, the adaptive advantage of status and social inequality lay in regulating potentially destructive competition for females. As well, it was in the fitness interest of males that their female children pair with prestigious, resource-controlling males. Both men and women should "find it easy to like, admire, and defer to those who demonstrate greater ability to control resources (Barkow 1989: 188). Evidence of higher reproductive rates among upper class individuals or of the frequency-dependence of female orgasms on the wealth of their male partners (Pollett and Nettle 2009) was seen as proof of the adaptive nature of social inequality.

Inequality as Domination: Marx and Engels

Karl Marx (1818–1883) and Friedrich Engels (1820–1895) readily acknowledged the intellectual debts they owed to the economic theories of Smith and Ricardo, to the philosophy of Hegel (1770–1831) and to Darwin's theory of evolution. When Marx referred to the "human species" and "species being," he used language that had become fashionable with the decline of creationist views of human descent. His belief that natural science and the "science of man" would merge into a single field was also held by Comte, Spencer and later by Durkheim. The conviction that human history was guided by laws informed Hegel's "Weltgeist" as much as Spencer's "persistence of force." The stunning advances of science and industry which made Marx marvel at "the conquest of the forces of nature, machines, the use of chemistry in industry and agriculture, steamships, railways, the electric telegraph, the cultivation of entire continents, the canalization of rivers" (MEW 4: 467), inspired widespread hope for social and political progress. As for class struggle, Marx pointed out that historians and economists had discovered it long before him, but the revolutionary events which swept European countries between 1830 and 1848 seemed to bring it to a climax, uniting large segments of the population in the fight for voting rights, republican government, a free press, national unification and socialism. History placed Marx in the thick of these events. His agitation led the reactionary Prussian government in 1843 to close the radical-liberal *Rheinische Zeitung* which he edited, and to pressure the French government to expel him from Paris in 1845. He moved to Brussels where the Belgian government, worried that the 1848 revolution in France would spill across the border, expelled him in the same year. Back in Paris and then in Cologne, he was tried for subversion and acquitted, but was expelled again in 1849, forcing him to his final refuge, England. For a young activist still unaware of the financial and personal costs which his views would exact from him and his family, these were heady times. He was not alone. Alexander Herzen, a member of the Russian gentry and a socialist who had fled Russia, expressed feelings that were shared by reformers and radicals across Europe.

> I ... was carried away again by the events that seethed around me ... the whirlwind which set everything in movement carried me, too, off my feet; all Europe took up its bed and walked – in a fit of somnambulism which we took for awakening. And was all that ... intoxication, delirium? Perhaps – but I do not envy those who were not carried away by that exquisite dream.
> (Cited in Rapport 2008: 41)

Between the publication of the *Communist Manifesto* in 1848 and the first volume of *Das Kapital* in 1867 everything pointed toward an increasing polarization of the class structures in Europe's leading industrial countries. Capitalism seemed to divide societies into two hostile camps, the bourgeoisie and proletariat, implacable enemies except for the latter's occasional tactical cooperation with the bourgeoisie's "most progressive elements."

Unbeknownst to Marx and Engels, this relationship was about to undergo profound changes. By the late nineteenth century, capital ownership, instead of becoming more monopolized because "one capitalist always kills many" (MEW 23: 790), had been diversified by the rapid growth of markets for an ever greater range of goods. As for workers, machines did not obliterate all distinctions of labor. In Marx's time, occupational differentiation had barely begun. By the end of the nineteenth century, occupational divisions had multiplied and created new social identities which cut across class lines. Workers formed unions and political parties and fought for the 10-hour day, but also advocated temperance and strove for bourgeois respectability.

Labor and the Emergence of the Human Species

Marx rarely missed a chance to pour sarcasm on ideas he did not like. One of these was the story of the origins of social inequality as told by classical economists: once upon a time there were people who were industrious, intelligent and thrifty, and others who were lazy and wasteful scoundrels.

> So it came to pass that the former accumulated wealth, while the latter ended up having nothing to sell but their own skins. And from this original sin dates the poverty of the great mass of people who, in spite of all their work, still have nothing to sell but themselves, as well as the wealth of the few which keeps growing, although they long ago stopped working.... In real history it is well-known that conquest, subjugation, robbery and murder, in short,

violence, play the major role. In the sheltered world of political economy more idyllic conditions have always prevailed.

(MEW 23: 741, 742)

By turning private property into a universal right, by making self-interest the essence of human nature and by deriving wealth and poverty from natural laws, economists had dressed up human creations as eternal truths. To look behind this fiction required the study of the actual historical separation of labor from the value it produced and to decipher the "social hieroglyphics" of ideology which concealed the domination of one class over another.

Such an analysis had to start with labor, the transformation of natural and social environments by the uniquely human ability to imagine goals prior to putting them into practice. Labor was more than a tool for survival. It was a process so basic that "we can say that labor has created man." It was a "force of production," a sphere of self-realization and a source of creativity and discovery. At the same time, however, labor always operated within natural and social constraints. Robinson Crusoe lived only in literary fiction, just as the *homo oeconomicus* resided only in the minds of economists. Specific historical conditions determined the actual forms of work and the distribution of its result. Africans were not born slaves; they became slaves only when the plantation economies of the Caribbean and America forced them to work in cane and cotton fields. Spinning machines were mechanical inventions; only under particular social conditions did they became capital and produced private profit. It was not "what is made, but how and with what tools it is made, that distinguishes different economic epochs" (MEW 23: 194, 195). Means of production – available materials, tools and technology – and relations of production – whether labor was communally organized or controlled by slave owner or a feudal lord – together created a mode of production typical for a particular historical time, and in turn gave rise to a characteristic superstructure of laws, political and philosophical thought, cultural preferences and scientific ideas. New modes of production were always built on the remnants of earlier ones. Understanding them therefore required reconstructing their historical descent lines.

Engels argued that the decisive step in the evolution of humans occurred when primates moved from an arboreal habitat to life on the ground, adopted upright walk, freed their hands for new activities and developed language, all of which increased their ability to discover hitherto unknown properties of natural objects (Engels 1962: 445–447). Early humans lived as hunter-gatherers or herders, and their primitive tools meant that all available time was taken up by securing their survival. Their societies tended to be egalitarian by necessity as much as by choice because there was little to distribute. Differences of authority were minor and transient. More recent anthropological research has revised this picture, showing that early hunter-gatherer societies developed sophisticated skills which allowed them to secure their necessities of life with relatively little labor, leaving them with considerable spare time and allowing them to cross subsistence thresholds much earlier than Marx and Engels thought.

From such "primitive communism," inventions of new forces of production such as agriculture and herding increased the productivity of labor to the point where it yielded more than was required for mere subsistence. For Marx, the production of surplus was a crucial point in the historical development of social inequality. On one hand, it became a lever for human creativity, making it possible to store food as an insurance against famine, to free labor for common projects such as irrigation and to produce more goods for exchange. Spare time allowed people to think, to invent and to develop visions of their future. The presence of surplus thus greatly accelerated the evolution of human culture.

However, surplus also had a darker side: it raised the question who should own it. Surplus made a tempting target: taking it away from its producer yielded a ready return for little or no effort. That was made easier because new divisions of labor and markets for products made egalitarian social relations less intuitive. Surplus therefore opened the possibility that society divided into classes.

> The specific economic form in which unpaid surplus labor is pumped out of the direct producers, determines the relation of domination and servitude.... It is always the direct relation between the masters of the conditions of production and the direct producers which reveals the inner secret, the hidden foundation of the entire social edifice and therefore also of the political form of the relation between sovereignty and dependence, in short, of the particular form of the state.
>
> (MEW, Das Kapital, Vol. III: 799)

The Expropriation of Surplus and the Growth of Inequality

In the *Grundrisse*, Marx advanced two scenarios for the way the expropriation of surplus could have replaced original "naturally grown" forms of property where producers simply took possession of what they created. In one, exploitation and inequality took root in early egalitarian societies almost haphazardly as a consequence of chance events such as soil exhaustion, fortuitous differences in the productivity of land farmed by different families, captivity or enslavement as a result of warfare or conquest, or because existing forms of communal production and distribution were accidentally or deliberately undermined (Marx 1939–1941: 386). In this view, social inequality arose through a combination of historical contingency and human opportunism. Surplus created the chance – but not the necessity – for its appropriation by more powerful non-productive groups.

In Marx's later work, the dissolution of natural property and the expropriation of surplus by non-producers became a more mechanistic process. Communal relations of production already contained the seeds of their own destruction. Advances in productive technology inevitably required new forms of social organization. Changes in productive forces created their own typical relations of production, and with them characteristic forms of expropriation. Marx never resolved this ambiguity between the role of contingent forces in the evolution of inequality, and the view that class structures unfolded with the "iron necessity" of a "natural process" (MEW 23: 791).

Whatever the cause of the expropriation of surplus, it always involved the transformation of free into dependent labor. The expropriator's interest was to keep the price of labor as close to what was needed to ensure its physical reproduction and continued supply. This portion was variable: there were kind and brutal slave masters, generous and avaricious capitalists. The perceptive master would know that treating subordinates generously increased their productivity. In capitalism, in particular, worker resistance, the formation of unions, or competition among capitalists for labor could raise the subsistence portion of the average wage above the minimum needed for physical survival. But these absolute gains did not change the position of the worker relative to that of the capitalist.

> Even the *most favorable situation* for the working class, *the most rapid possible growth of capital*, however much it may improve the material existence of the worker, does not remove the antagonism between his interests and the interests of the bourgeoisie, the interests of the capitalists. *Profit and wages remain as before in inverse proportion.* If capital is growing rapidly, wages may rise; the profit of capital rises incomparably more rapidly. The material position of the worker has improved, but at the cost of his social position. The social gulf that divides him from the capitalist has widened.
>
> (MEW 6: 416)

The value which workers created over and above their subsistence portion was available for expropriation. In early societies, this could be done through sporadic warfare or raids, through tribute payments or through debt, marriage or slavery. The most effective way, however, was to separate the producer altogether from the means of production. The feudal system, for example, concentrated all arable land in the hands of the aristocracy. The feudal lord was now in a position to readmit peasants to a piece of land, their sole source of livelihood, allow them to retain enough produce for their families' subsistence, and force them to hand over the rest.

Private property of factories, machines and finance capital gave early capitalists the same leverage which landed property gave to the aristocracy. They offered employment to the mass of landless labor on the proprietor's terms, namely the surrender of the surplus which their work generated during industrial production. Just like land was useless to the feudal lord without peasants, the capitalist's machines were useless without workers. Moreover, machines and buildings were "constant" capital which depreciated until their rusting or crumbling remains were discarded. Labor did not depreciate. As "variable" capital it reproduced and renewed itself as a continuous source of "labor power," both in the sense of being always available as long as it was paid subsistence wages, and in the sense of being a flexible resource which could be put to many different uses. The capitalist used the full labor power but paid only a wage which ensured the continuing availability of workers. He kept the difference, minus the depreciation costs of constant capital, as profit. Profit could be increased by raising the price of products, by lengthening the work day, or by increasing the productivity of labor by adding more constant capital. The first strategy ran into the obstacle of competition, the second into increased worker resistance, leaving the third as the most likely option. In the long term, capitalist production therefore required less labor and became more capital-intensive. The consequences of this changing composition of capital were dire for both sides, creating on one hand a reserve army of impoverished workers while the ever-increasing costs of constant capital led to a long-term decline of the rate of profit. Both would eventually contribute to the demise of capitalism.

Alienation, Reification, Ideology and Change

Neither capitalist nor worker were likely aware of the history and true nature of their relationship. To the workers, the organization of work appeared as a rational plan imposed by the authority of the capitalist. Their wage looked like pay for a full day's work and extinguished "every trace of the division of the work day into necessary and surplus labor, paid and unpaid work" (MEW 23: 562). Capitalists, on their side, had long forgotten that their first use of surplus labor was to free themselves from manual work. Marx recognized that large organizations required functional, administrative hierarchies (MEW 23: 350) but there was no need for these to be run by capitalists. The latter involved themselves in the production process only to control and discipline an antagonistic work force, aided by coercive layers of foremen and supervisors. Capitalists posed as "captains of industry" but had no essential function. Their power was a socially constructed artificial "attribute of capital, just as during the feudal time the supreme command of war and law courts was an attribute of the landowner" (MEW 23: 352).

The privatization of the means of production had psychological consequences. It distanced and alienated the worker from the process of production. Instead of being creative and self-directed, labor became an enforced activity controlled by others. Self-expression shifted to the time after work and to the sphere of consumption. Similarly, the value of products was no longer visibly linked to the labor required to produce them. Instead they appeared to be independent, "reified" commodities whose value was measured in money. Much like the supernatural beings which populated the "foggy terrain of the religious world" they turned into fetish-like objects of fantasy, desire and prestige which could transform the social appearance of people and relationships.

> What exists for me through money, what I can pay for, i.e. what money can buy, that *I am*.... The power of my money is my power. The properties of money are my – the owner's – properties and faculties. What I am and can do is, therefore, not at all determined by my individuality. I *am* ugly, but I can buy the *most beautiful* woman. Therefore I am not ugly, for the effect of ugliness, its power to repel, is eliminated by money. As an individual I am lame, but money gives me 24 legs.... I am a despicable, dishonest, unscrupulous, stupid person, but since money is honored, so is its owner.... I who can have, through money, everything which the human heart desires, do I not possess all human abilities? Does not my money, therefore, transform all my failings into their opposite?
>
> (MEW, Supplementary Vol. I: 564)

Alienation and reification created opportunities for a more general mystification of the world. The social and political world appeared no longer as a creation by living people but as a product of impersonal forces. This transformation opened the door for ideological images and myths which obscured the real historical origins of social inequality and made it look permanent and beyond human control. Ruling classes could now more easily represent their own interests as the common interest of society. Alienation and reification made it easier to blur class lines, justify inequality and make demands for greater equality appear sinful, utopian and destructive.

Powerful as such ideological obfuscation was, it could not permanently prevent social change. Forces of production grew at a relatively independent pace and continued to open new technical, social and political possibilities. Dominant modes of production, on the other hand, relied on particular ways of producing and appropriating surplus which dictated *specific* uses of knowledge and technology. Immediately after coming to power, ruling classes were open to new ideas. The pent-up desires of preceding periods were set free, and the resulting growth in production benefited in some measure all classes in society. Soon, however, ruling classes asserted their interests more forcefully. They favored ideas which justified their position and technologies which increased their profits. A growing gap emerged between what was possible and what the existing class relations allowed. For a while, this discrepancy could be concealed by ideology, but eventually it led to growing social tensions. Lower classes became conscious of their interests and actively pursued their visions for the future through political struggle. Class structures reached the breaking point. Toward the end of feudal rule in Europe, for instance, the limitations it imposed on economy and trade were increasingly resented by a bourgeoisie aware of the profitable potential of markets and technologies such as the steam engine or the mechanical loom. Eventually, they broke the chains of aristocratic power. Then the process started anew: after a brief flowering of liberalism and technology, contradictions grew between a retrograde capitalism and a working class which saw a better future. The tension between forces and relations of production, the driving force of all revolutionary change, led to the expropriation of the expropriators and to a new communist society based on cooperation and common ownership of the means of production.

Functional Theories of Social Inequality: Durkheim and Parsons

Functional arguments reflected some of the oldest explanations of social inequality, many of which used organic analogies. The Roman historian Livius, for instance, related a fable describing how Roman patricians deflected plebeian protests against rising inequality. The organs of the body (representing the people) thought the stomach (the patricians) was getting a free ride. They therefore decided to starve it, only to find themselves soon fatigued and ill. They thus realized the importance of the stomach and their dependence on it. The medieval tripartite division of society invoked a similarly organic image to explain the mutual benefits of a relationship where peasants provided nourishment for nobility and church, the aristocracy "protected" the peasants, and the church prayed for both and prepared them for God's judgment after they died.

Modern functionalism, too, understood society as composed of interdependent and mutually supportive parts. Émile Durkheim (1858–1917) shared the anxiety of many nineteenth century observers that social tensions and conflict threatened the new industrial societies. The first pages of his *Division of Labor* (1893) express his fear that the violence of the Paris uprising of the *commune* of 1871 was a symptom of the "anomic state," the "juridical and moral anomy" and the "exceptional gravity" of class relations. Durkheim agreed with Spencer that societies became increasingly heterogeneous in the course of their historical development, but he rejected Spencer's suggestion that contractual relations between individuals were sufficient guarantees for the stability of industrial societies. And while he shared Comte's conviction that social disorder was the greatest of all evils, he disagreed with his proposal that the solution lay in an authoritarian state. In the *Division of Labor* Durkheim argued instead that structural differentiation and greater individual freedom, rather than leading to social disintegration, produced new forms of social cohesion which could reduce social conflict and ensure harmonious social relations.

Durkheim thought that the functional relations between different social institutions and the resulting inequality were merely a particular form of the physiological interdependence of organs in the body. Both reflected general principles of biological organization (Durkheim 1964: 41). Just as illness threatened the healthy body, social conflict and class divisions disturbed social equilibrium. The analogy was completed by using the development of the embryo as a model for the long-term development of societies. Early anthropologists such as Morgan (1810–1881) and Tylor (1832–1917) had collected ethnographic information which seemed to support the existence of "cultural universals" such as incest taboos which Morgan explained as a biological defense against inbreeding, whereas Tylor saw its functional value in forcing people to marry outside their family which broadened their social networks and improved their chances of survival. Functional explanations soon proliferated. Universal "human needs" for food, shelter, sex and protection seemed to create similar social institutions in all societies. Property relations, inheritance and rules of succession regulated access to scarce goods. Religion alleviated anxiety and the fear of the unknown. What was now called "social stratification" rewarded individuals for their contributions to society.

Durkheim gave these ideas a coherent theoretical form. Social institutions such as inequality were supra-individual phenomena and not simply reflections of individual interests. If they served such interests, that was a happy coincidence, but their true causes always lay in the social need they satisfied (Durkheim 1950: 109). Similarly, what made people participate in these structures were not individual utility calculations but a deeper "collective conscience." Individual motives revealed nothing about the emotional bonds between individual and society. These were a reality of their own, a "social solidarity" of feelings of belonging, of trust and mutual support, a "warmth which animates its members, making them intensely human, destroying their egoism" (Durkheim

1964: 26). Solidarity went far beyond the pleasure derived from self-interested actions. The surrender of self to a common cause could manifest itself in religious experiences, could be inspired by charismatic leaders or rally people around symbols of tribe and nation. Solidarity also underpinned modern divisions of labor whose "coordination can be produced only in the midst of a society, and under the pressure of social sentiments and social needs" (Durkheim 1964: 277).

In archaic societies collective conscience overwhelmed individuality. People were held together by a "mechanical solidarity," a "more or less organized totality of beliefs and sentiments common to all members of the group" (Durkheim 1964: 129). Individuals were absorbed into the collectivity and merely followed its movements. Conformity was paramount; dissimilarity caused moral outrage and was punished by priests or chiefs. A division of labor existed only periodically and in a rudimentary form, such as during war or the construction of monumental buildings. Despotism directed and intensified collective sentiments and was the functionally appropriate form of inequality (Durkheim 1964: 196).

As societies advanced, population growth and improvements in technology and communication led to an increasing differentiation of society and dissolved earlier centralized structures. Durkheim's central argument was that the resulting increase in individualism did not weaken the bond between individual and society. Instead, social cohesion now arose from the recognition of the functional interdependence of different social tasks performed by different parts of the society. This new "organic" solidarity provided more room for individual initiative, but also increased the ability to pursue common goals. Rather than being an obstacle to social integration, the rapid growth of specialized skills and varied interests was an essential part of the industrial division of labor. Instead of enforcing rules and punishing violators, the coordination of the civil and commercial processes now became the primary role of governments.

Organic solidarity derived its strength neither from an increase of individual happiness nor from the greater supply of consumer goods but from the emotional interdependence of individual and collectivity.

> Because the individual is not sufficient unto himself, it is from society that he receives everything necessary to him, as it is for society that he works. Thus is formed a very strong sentiment of the state of dependence in which he finds himself.... On its side, society learns to regard its members no longer as things over which it has rights, but as co-operators whom it cannot neglect and towards whom it owes duties.
> (Durkheim 1964: 228)

This did not require a detailed knowledge of "vast portions of the social horizon." It was enough that individuals knew that their own actions, no matter how specialized, were linked to a greater good. Nor did it require a detailed accounting of what one was owed by society. It sufficed that each member of the society trusted that they received what they deserved, just as each organ of the body demanded only as much nutrition as it needed to function (Durkheim 1964:

68   Theories of Social Inequality

376). Social stratification mediated between individual and society. On one hand it offered opportunities for career choices, social mobility and self-improvement. On the other, it matched talents with societal needs, motivated people to contribute to collective goals, and made them accept incomes commensurate to their contribution. Social harmony required mutual moderation and the creation of an internalized "normal intensity of need."

> When (the individual) respects the rules and recognizes collective authority, that is if he has a healthy moral constitution, he feels that it is not good to ask for more. A goal and a limit is thus created for passion.... Everyone, at least in general, is then in harmony with his condition and only wants what he can legitimately expect as the normal price for his activity.
>
> (Durkheim 1960: 277)

In a healthy society, wealth was neither considered immoral nor did it become an obsession. Exploitation and unbridled greed could occur, "but these are exceptional and, one may say, morbid cases. Normally, man finds happiness in realizing his nature; his needs are in relation to his means" (Durkheim 1964: 376). The role of the state was to make sure that the market price paid for labor reflected the natural inequality of merit, and that education helped each person to "like the idea of circumscribed tasks and limited horizons" (Durkheim 1964: 402).

Inequality, Anomie and Social Conflict

If the emergence of organic solidarity was a "historical law" (Durkheim 1964: 378), why did social inequality cause so much disunity? What were the reasons for the "chaotic" state of his time, and for the "real crisis of morality" and the "sick conditions" of which Durkheim warned in the conclusion of the *Division of Labor?* His answer was that the causes of social tensions lay not in the division of labor but in its pathological distortions. Anomic divisions of labor resulted from breakdowns in solidarity caused by economic crises, rapid industrial growth, and an increasingly mechanized production. Bankruptcies and loss of employment destroyed habitual rights and obligations. The anonymity and mechanization of factory work made work meaningless and boring. If there was no purpose to his effort, the worker

> can only continue to work through routine. Every day he repeats the same movements with monotonous regularity, but without being interested in them, and without understanding them. He is no longer a living cell of a living organism which unceasingly vibrates with neighboring cells, which acts upon them, and to whose actions it responds and with whose needs and circumstances it changes. He is no longer anything but an inert piece of machinery, driven by an external force which always moves in the same direction and in the same way. Surely, no matter how one may represent the moral ideal, one cannot remain indifferent to such debasement of human nature.
>
> (Durkheim 1964: 371)

Tensions could also arise where work rules were enforced without regard to their functions, where workers worked below their ability, or where market power or inheritance created unjust advantages and distorted the relationship between merit and compensation (Durkheim 1964: 384).

Anomic divisions of labor were not chronic features of social inequality but an "abnormal circumstance" (Durkheim 1964: 372), remnants of pre-industrial societies or consequences of the "extreme rapidity" of industrialization which had not yet found its equilibrium. Social unrest could be avoided by creating employer and worker associations in different branches of industry which educated their members about their responsibilities and obligations.

> By forcing the stronger to use their power only in moderation, and by preventing the weaker to extend their demands endlessly, by reminding both of their mutual obligations and the general interest, by regulating, in certain cases, production to prevent it from degenerating into a feverish illness, it would moderate one set of passions through another and, by setting limits, allow their peaceful resolution.
>
> (Durkheim 1960: 440)

Such syndicalist associations could allow individuals to identify with familiar groups without having to comprehend the entire complex industrial structure. Durkheim's corporatism reflected a life-long commitment to a socialism not of the class struggle but of a solidarity which required "that we be thoughtful of our fellows and that we be just, that we fulfill our duty, that we work at the function we can best execute, and receive the just reward for our services" (Durkheim 1964: 407, 408).

Durkheim Updated: Parsons' General Theory of Social Systems

Talcott Parsons' (1902–1979) most influential work was published between 1949 and 1960 in a post-war social climate in the United States characterized by general economic optimism and prosperity and by a remarkable homogeneity of political values. The McCarthy hearings during the early 1950s, the war in Korea and the Cold War had narrowed the collective political vision. Social divisions between classes appeared to be a thing of the past. The "end of ideologies" seemed to have dawned; they were no longer needed because basic distributive problems seemed to have been solved and calls for social and political change had run their course. Class divisions had given way to "social stratification," the technical allocation of rank on the basis of system needs and human skills. American society was seen as a beacon for the rest of the world. "Developing countries" which had not yet reached this advanced state were poised for the "take-off to economic growth." This political climate also seemed to bode well for the sociologist: if Durkheim's functional division of labor had become a reality, so had Comte's vision of a society guided by a caste of philosopher-sociologists:

In a functional and rationalistic universe, the scientists and social scientists are accorded an increasing monitor role in political life.... Human mysteries have become technical problems. In the modern development communities, (the social scientist) is asked to apply his knowledge. He displaces the physician as a new symbol of aloofness.... Social science is becoming accepted as scientific, and scientific norms are increasingly accepted as guides to social conduct. There is a universal trend toward planning, calculation, and rationalistic goals concerned with the future in both the developing and the developed areas.... Both science and technology are, in application, intertwined with social sciences. In modern scientific communities, governments are the greatest single consumers of social science. They not only stimulate policy research but consume the product.

(Apter 1964: 40–41)

This heady atmosphere provided the setting for Parsons' elaboration of Durkheim's theory.

In Parsons' view, stratification arose historically as a response to the functional "need for centralization of responsibility" in the face of growing societal complexity. Decentralized kinship units in early societies could no longer cope when population growth and territorial expansion increased the problem of maintaining internal order and external defense. An intensification of hierarchy brought clear functional advantages. Prestige positions allowed elites to "stick their necks out" and gain "a secure enough position that they can accept certain risks in undertaking collective leadership" (Parsons 1969: 693, 694). Increased stratification also permitted new forms of legitimation which went beyond simple appeals to family or ethnic loyalty and offered more general justifications of the social advantages and burdens of inequality. Together, these changes created the conditions for "breaking out of what may be called the 'primitive' stage of societal evolution ... without both stratification and legitimation no major advances beyond the level of primitive society can be made" (Parsons 1969: 693).

Stratification and legitimation formed around a normative and emotional core of shared collective goals. Their role was akin to Durkheim's solidarity, but Parsons was neither interested in their historical origins nor their actual content. The task of looking into the "black box" of personal motives could be left to psychologists and historians, and Parsons' voluminous work contains few empirical examples. Instead he set out to develop a general theory which could explain the functional interaction of central societal institutions in all social systems. That included stratification.

The "general theory of action" began with a hypothetical "interaction paradigm" which imagined a first encounter between two individuals who brought to their relationship their personal needs and sensitivity to the other person's behavior. If their needs were incompatible, or if they found each other's behavior objectionable, the interaction would end. If, on the other hand, they had common interests and found their cooperation rewarding, they would continue to interact. Individual differences did not disappear, but the interests they shared turned into more stable "object orientations" which encouraged continued cooperation, whereas initial reactions to each other became more permanent "partner expectations." As societies grew, these eventually consolidated into stable societal goals and role expectations. Goals were collective visions of what a society considered important. Role expectations were generalized anticipations of the behaviors associated with social positions required to reach these goals. Both were deliberately chosen, supported and remembered by members of a social system. Because they were derived from individual wants, "the interest of the collectivity and the private interest of its constituent members (can) be said to reach coincidence" (Parsons 1964a: 42). Consensus and equilibrium rather than conflict were therefore the normal state of social systems.

Goal and role expectations shaped social systems in different ways. On the institutional level they became blueprints for the organization of society. On the cultural level they became the bases for norms, values, beliefs and symbols. On the personal level they motivated individuals to identify with their society. The institutionalization of goals therefore went hand in hand with their internalization by the individual. The acceptance of societal institutions rested on a generalized trust that the obligations and duties they imposed reflected shared – and therefore also individual – goals.

Spheres and Media of Exchange

All societies had to create four basic institutions in order to meet their goals, whatever they were. Economic institutions were needed to "adapt" social systems to changes in its external environment. Governments mobilized and coordinated the means required for "goal attainment." Societies also had to resolve potentially destructive conflicts between self- and collectivity interest. The need for "integration" was met by social stratification. Finally, there had to be institutions which maintained and reinforced each member's commitment to the society's goals. This function – "latent pattern maintenance" – was performed by family, church, schools, courts and prisons which introduced new members such as children or immigrants to shared values, and punished and reintegrated those who, for whatever reason, deviated from them. Adaptation, goal attainment, integration and latent pattern maintenance (AGIL) were the universal functional prerequisites of all social systems.

In each of these four sub-systems individuals were linked to society through transactions which used specific media of exchange. In the economy, that medium was money. By spending it, individuals gave up solvency in return for receiving utility from the economic subsystem. In the sphere of goal realization the medium of exchange was power, defined by Parsons as "the capacity to get things done in the collective interest." Here, the members of a society accepted resource-mobilizing obligations such as taxes in return for goal-realizing services by governments. In the sphere of stratification, the exchange media were influence, prestige, status and material rewards which members of social systems granted to individuals with superior skills or talents in return for their promise to use these resources to promote the society's goals. Finally, institutions in the area of latent pattern maintenance encouraged trust in exchange for the general promise that all spheres of exchange remained committed to shared goals even if members saw no immediate or visible return. In extreme cases, however, trust could degenerate. Inflation could lead to blind confidence in a leader, such as in the case of Fascism in Germany and Italy and McCarthyism in the United States, while deflation or loss of trust forced people to return to barter with others for goods and services.

Stratification as a System of Exchange

Stratification arose from the functional need to assign people of different skills and abilities to the tasks needed to reach the goals of a social system. This meant that "those who take responsibility for coordinating the actions of many others must have a different status in important respects from those who are essentially in the role of carrying out specifications laid down by others" (Parsons 1954b: 327). The question was why this potentially divisive distinction should be accepted rather than cause dissent and conflict. The solution lay in the nature of the medium of influence.

Influence meant that one accepted demands for professional, economic or administrative autonomy because they were "made by someone with a high reputation for competence, for reliability, for good judgment, etc., (rather) than by someone without this reputation or with a reputation for unreliability" (Parsons 1963: 50). The recipients could act without having to justify each and every decision in terms of the dominant values. In exchange, they agreed to honor the trust placed in them by abstaining from malfeasance, fraud or professional misconduct. The integrative strength of stratification arose from this "fiduciary arrangement" which assumed that talented members of society used the influence given to them for common purposes rather than their own.

The historical origins of private property lay in such a fiduciary consensus: originally tribal property was voluntarily surrendered to competent leaders when it was felt that they could use it more productively for the collective good. Stratification thus reflected a complex give and take which ensured the society's welfare because it was grounded in a consensus of common interests. As in Durkheim's work, conflict was exceptional, not system-immanent or chronic. Actual "rewards" for fiduciary duties were settled by markets which matched the functional importance of positions with appropriate skills (Davis and Moore 1966). The overall effect of stratification was to create harmony rather than division:

> Men have a sense of justice fulfilled and of virtue rewarded when they feel that they are fairly ranked as superior and inferior by the value standards of their own moral community. This sense of justice is an important element in the integration of society.
>
> (Barber 1957: 7)

Durkheim's and Parsons' consensual social system bore an unintended similarity to Marx's vision of a socialist society. There, too, individuals contributed according to their abilities, received according to their performance, and acted out of an internalized sense of social duty. The state was no longer an executive organ of the bourgeoisie but a functional institution which planned, coordinated, and delegated power to self-administering corporate units pursuing collective goods. Marx predicted such a society for the future. Durkheim felt it was within reach. Parsons thought it was here. History turned out to be more complicated.

Social Inequality and the Dynamics of Organizations: Pareto, Mosca, Michels and Weber

The second half of the nineteenth century saw a rapid expansion of bureaucracies in industry and governments which inserted new, intermediate layers of administrative and professional groups between capital and labor. At the same time, more fluid group identities emerged which cut across class divisions. Clerical occupations in banks, insurances and businesses could aspire to a "gentlemanly" life, an inexpensive luxury which set them apart from the laborer even although their salary was barely higher than that of a skilled worker (Lockwood 1958: 29). Their pretensions were neither discouraged by their dependence on their employer's whims (having rejected the protection of unions as unsuitable to the clerkly estate), nor by the contempt and the derision in which the "poor, sad snob of a clerk" was held by those below and above him. Such new identities blunted the distinctions between factory owner and worker, rich and poor that characterized the first part of the nineteenth century. Now, workers supported and opposed the union movement and voted for parties of the left and the right. Class divisions did not disappear, but they were overlaid by more complex and shifting social affiliations.

Neither Spencer nor Marx had anticipated these changes. Marx dismissed governments as mere tools of the bourgeoisie, whereas Spencer saw them as an obstacle to the struggle for survival. Neither of them realized their future importance, nor did they anticipate that public opinion was no longer tied to structural position. After centuries during which the voices of the mass of the population rarely received attention, the emergence of public opinion was one of the most striking developments of the late nineteenth century. Public education increased literacy, and newspapers and popular literature drew attention to wider social and political issues. Competition for public opinion became increasingly important, and so did the need to understand "the constant psychological tendencies determining the behavior of the human masses" (Mosca 1939: 1).

In the late nineteenth and early twentieth century, four authors tried to make sense of these changes. They explored new forms of inequality: the emergence and circulation of elites, the growth of parties and bureaucracies and the role of collective beliefs and identities in maintaining inequality structures. Wilfredo Pareto (1848–1923) offered a theory of the circulation of elites which resembled Marx's chronology of the rise and decay of ruling classes. As elites rose to power they brought fresh ideas into societies and caused a surge of economic and social development. In later stages, however, their interests became increasingly narrow, restricting technical and social development and leading eventually to revolutionary change. Pareto even agreed that "the 'class struggle' ... is the great dominant fact in history" (Pareto 1966: 117), but his views of the causes, nature and outcome of this struggle differed from those of Marx.

Natural differences in rank arose everywhere in social life – among thieves and engineers, prostitutes and scientists, workers and capitalists – but there was no guarantee that this brought the fittest and best to the top, nor that elites ensured that societies followed a path of progressive advancement. Such outcomes would require rational choice and rational planning. In reality, non-rational rather than logical behavior dominated social life. Throughout human history people had enlivened inanimate objects, attributed accidents to divine wisdom and blamed misfortune on their own sins or the influence of witches. Such rationalizations were not just born of ignorance but revealed a general tendency of social actors to "cover their behavior with a veneer of logic" (Pareto 1966: 185). Non-rational behavior was as common in modern societies as in ancient ones: what felt like conscious deliberation was most often rationalization after the fact. Most people did not act because they thought but thought because they had acted. Religious beliefs, political symbols and slogans, and claims by vested interests to serve the common good were distortions, much like an object seen in a curved mirror.

Behind these distortions lay deeper instinctive predispositions present to different degrees in different people. These "residues" were the true sources of social behavior, although Pareto never clarified whether they were inherited or learned. Two of them were particularly important in the rise and circulation of elites throughout human history. The first was a "propensity for combining" which encouraged innovation, speculation, opportunism and compromise. The second was the "persistence of aggregates," a force similar to mechanical inertia which made people conservative, attached to the past and obedient to rules and conventions. It encouraged patriotism and nationalism and the identification with family, ethnicity, religion or tradition.

Residues usually remained hidden behind "derivations," visible and ever-changing rationalizations such as taboos, superstitions, appeals to "truths" and "higher principles," or political myths and ideologies which helped people to justify and make sense of what they did. Such constructions usually had no basis in fact. Their appeal was sentimental and affective, but often strong enough to make people defend them by force. They were the common language of social life, used by elites and non-elites alike to rationalize their interests and actions.

Elites formed among both innovators and traditionalists. Each had its own distinctive style of rule. The first relied on cunning and clever opportunism, the second on force and appeals to fundamental religious or political feelings. In practice, type one and type two elites became respectively liberals and conservatives, speculators and rentiers, Machiavelli's "foxes" and "lions," the demagogues of Athens and the tyrants of Rome, the parliamentary liberals and the socialists and fascists of Pareto's time.

Why, then, did elites not gain permanent control of societies? Why did history appear like a series of cyclical ups and downs with no discernible direction, a graveyard of failed elites and aristocracies? Pareto offered two reasons. The first was functional: governments needed a "circulation of the blood" (Pareto 1966: 112). Innovation and conservatism, democracy and the willingness to use force were all required to give governments the flexibility to adapt to changing circumstances. Ideally, this could be achieved by recruiting capable individuals from both types of elites and dismissing those who proved incompetent. In real political life nepotism prevailed. Whichever elite ascended to power was likely to hire its own descendants and supporters. Because Pareto did not believe in the inheritance of acquired characteristics, nepotism did not improve an elite but diluted its quality: by promoting their own sons and daughters regardless of their ability and by protecting them from competition, a ruling elite also prevented new talent from joining its ranks and thereby acquired an ever-increasing number of useless hangers-on. Styles of rule changed, too. Speculators and opportunists were increasingly open to any deal that helped them to cling to power. Conservatives became increasingly authoritarian and willing to use force to defend their goals. Meanwhile, the excluded non-governing elite became impoverished and resentful. Social tensions increased until the elites in power were overthrown.

The second cause for the circulation of elites lay in the distorting power of derivations. In an ideal world a governing elite would be replaced when concern for its own members outweighed the utility of its policies for the society as a whole. The problem was that appearances were susceptible to irrational judgment and manipulation, and governing elites were in a position to use that to their advantage. Elites soon developed an intuitive grasp for opportunities to influence public opinion through bribery, vote-buying and by persuading people "that sound and enlightened patriotism calls for the success of their modest proposals."

> Those who hope to gain a million a year will know no rest by day or night. They will win newspapers over to their interest by financial inducements and drum up support from all quarters. A discreet hand will warm the palms of needy legislators, even of ministers. In the United States there is no necessity to resort to such underhand methods; there deals are made in the open: there is an open market in votes just as there are open markets in cotton and grain.
>
> (Pareto 1966 115, 116)

By such means elites could conceal the harm they caused and stay in power long after they had outlived their usefulness to society. Non-elites used the same tools: calls for the overthrow of ruling classes merely exploited the fact that "people everywhere love to find some scapegoat on which to unload all their faults. But this is nothing more than a pure illusion" (Pareto 1966: 117). The result was that elites were overthrown in irregular, unpredictable cycles.

Gaetano Mosca (1858–1941) shared Pareto's conviction that governing classes, whether religious, military or aristocratic, were an enduring feature of human history. Neither Rousseau's *volonté générale* nor Marx's classless society could ever work. There could be "no human organization without rankings and subordination" because it was "in the nature of the human being that many men should love to command and that almost all men can be brought to obey" (Mosca 1939: 397).

One class always controlled political processes, monopolized power and enjoyed its benefits. The second, larger one was induced by ideology or force to provide for the basic needs of society. Even in modern democratic societies elites organized party programs and elections, chose candidates and issues and manipulated ordinary people into believing in the power of the popular will. Heredity, learning and education, family background, financial means and fortuitous opportunities all played a role in the "struggle for pre-eminence," the "determination to rise in the world and to cling to one's place at the top when one gets there" (Mosca 1939: 434).

Whereas the struggle for survival eliminated the losers, the object of the struggle for pre-eminence was the conspicuous display of wealth and social status. It therefore needed an audience, a lower class which could admire elites while at the same time deriving modest benefits from their rule. Success in this struggle required no superior ability or character, nor did it assure the progress of society. Otherwise

> we should not, as is frequently the case in history, see a people take a great many steps forward, or sometimes a great many steps backward, in the course of two or three generations. Examples of such rapid advances and giddy declines are so common as scarcely to require mention.
> (Mosca 1939: 31)

The real strength of elites came from the organizational advantages they enjoyed. Their small size made it easy to establish effective social support networks and form the connections which allowed one to "avoid the gropings and blunders that are inevitable when one enters unfamiliar environment without any guidance or support" (Mosca 1939: 61). Ruling elites could use such advantages to gain economic, religious and military influence. As a result, they tended to become hereditary in fact, if not in law, although the dynamics that made them so were social rather than biological.

Organizational leverage also allowed governing classes to manipulate public opinion through "political formulas": flags to rally behind, tunes to march to, ranks and distinctions which satisfied the vain, and populist appeals which "flatter passions, satisfy whims and appetites, and inspire fear" (Mosca 1939: 193, 194). A political formula

> must promise that justice and equality will reign in this world, or in some other, or it must proclaim that the good will be rewarded and the wicked punished. At the same time it will not go far wrong if it yields some small satisfaction to the envy and rancor that are generally felt toward the powerful and the fortunate, and intimates that, in this life or in some other, there will come a time when the last shall be first and the first last.
> (Mosca 1939: 176)

Such myths arose in every society to justify inequality. In contrast to Pareto there was no mechanism which periodically replaced elites or prevented them from abusing their powers. As long as elites created the rules, neither elected representatives nor an appointed judiciary could be considered impartial. Under such circumstances,

> to proclaim universal suffrage, or the rights of man, or the maxim that all are equal before the law, is merely ironical; and just as ironical is it to say that every man carries a marshal's baton in his knapsack, or that he is free someday to become a capitalist himself. Even granting that some few individuals do realize those high possibilities, they will not necessarily be the best individuals, either in intelligence or in morals. They may be the most persistent, the most fortunate or, perhaps, the most crooked. Meanwhile the mass of the people will still remain just as much subject to those on high.
> (Mosca 1939: 143)

The only antidote was a system of institutional safeguards which could guarantee individual rights and dilute the power of elites. A large middle class of professionals, scientists and independent businesses could offer additional support for a relatively equitable distribution of wealth, freedom of the press and a parliamentary system. Even then, Mosca doubted that parliamentary democracies could resist the danger of unrestrained patronage, lobbying and electioneering, the onslaught of ideologies and the danger that short-lived and unstable parliamentary governments increased the power of standing bureaucracies. Democracy degenerated into an effort "to flatter, wheedle and obtain the good will of the voters" (Mosca 1939: 155). In a passage as applicable to his own time as to modern neo-liberal tax-cut policies Mosca observed that "in many countries ... if increases in taxes were submitted to referendum, they would always be rejected, even though they were of the most unqualified urgency and would be of the most obvious benefit to the public" (Mosca 1939: 158).

Robert Michels (1876–1936) also considered the rise of administrative and political leadership inevitable, but where Pareto focused on the motivational bases of elite rule and Mosca on the resources which strengthened elite power, Michels provided an intimate, detailed picture of the inner dynamics of organizations. He was a student, collaborator and friend of Max Weber and taught sociology in several German and Italian universities. He was active in the German socialist movement and had an inside knowledge of Italian, French and German socialist organizations. Politically, Michels was closer to Marx than either Mosca or Pareto. His main critique was that Marx considered the abolition of private capital and the redistribution of wealth sufficient for the establishment of socialism. After that, and after a brief interlude of a dictatorship of the proletariat, the bourgeois state would wither away. Only a technical administration would remain to serve the goals of a classless society.

In Michels' view, this underestimated the fact that all organization was susceptible to the emergence of expert leaders who may have initially carried out the collective will but soon concentrated power in their own hands. These inequality-generating dynamics could become as tenacious a source of social inequality as the private ownership of capital, and they were the focus of Michels' work. He chose to study them where one would least expect to find them: in socialist parties which struggled against domination in all its forms. If inequality appeared even here, it was likely to reveal the true causes of hierarchical structures.

Michels' *Political Parties*, published in 1911, looked for "an unprejudiced analytical answer to this question." Technical and practical necessity was the most important cause of internal inequality. As organizations increased in size, they reached a point which required a concentration of functions. Party business could not be transacted by meetings of thousands of people. Experience and knowledge of duties accumulated in the hands of administrators, and skills such as the ability to speak in public propelled functionaries into prominent positions. As a result,

> the gulf between leaders and the rest of the party becomes ever wider, until the moment arrives in which the leaders lose all true sense of solidarity with the class from which they have sprung, and there ensues a new class-division between ex-proletarian captains and proletarian common soldiers.
> (Michels 1962: 108, 109)

These divisions received unintended support from changes among the rank and file. Political movements were unlikely to sustain the continued interest and participation of their members. Except for times of political unrest, personal and family concerns prevailed over party affairs. Younger workers were more interested in leisure and amorous pursuits, whereas older workers were often tired or disillusioned. The social democratic party therefore lacked the "force of control of ardent and irreverent youth and also that of experienced maturity, making it easier for leaders to establish and maintain their control" (Michels 1962: 105).

In party meetings, self-selected minorities set up agendas and wrote minutes. Sparse attendance made party leaders the most constant element of the organization, and incumbents were often routinely confirmed in their offices and nominated their successors. Functionaries began to regard their prerogatives as their right and expanded the scope and budgets of their office. The servants of the masses turned into their lords, although

> the despotism of the leaders does not arise solely from a vulgar lust of power or from uncontrolled egoism, but is often the outcome of a profound and sincere conviction of their own value and the services which they have rendered to the common cause.
> (Michels 1962: 85)

In the end, however, increasing distance from the rank and file encouraged typical organizational traits. "In every bureaucracy we may observe place-hunting, a mania for promotion, and obsequiousness towards those upon whom promotion depends; there is arrogance towards inferiors and servility towards superiors" (Michels 1962: 191). Leaders might feign closeness to the masses, but behind the veil of selfless devotion "the revolutionaries of today become the reactionaries of tomorrow" (Michels 1962: 187).

The fourth author who devoted a major part of his work to the growth of bureaucratic power was Max Weber (1864–1920). Like Pareto, Mosca and Michels, Weber saw the increasing importance of bureaucratic structures as an independent inequality-creating force, separate from inequalities of class and political power although they could become intertwined. Bureaucratic power was indispensable for the efficient administration of industry and government, but could also grow into a self-serving, powerful institution.

Pre-modern bureaucracies consisted of councils of elders or trusted retainers with ties of personal dependence and loyalty to chiefs, lords or kings. Modern bureaucracies separated administrative from executive functions. Faceless and competent, they could serve monarchies or democracies, governments of the left and the right. They penetrated all spheres of administration, from governments, churches and military to capitalist business whose need for efficient accounting and legal protection of contracts made it "the pacemaker of modern bureaucracy."

The revolutionary advantage of these new forms of administration lay in their efficiency and their permanence.

> A fully developed bureaucratic mechanism compares to other organizational forms exactly as a machine does to non-mechanical ways of producing goods. Precision, speed, clarity, knowledge of the files, continuity, discretion, uniformity, strict subordination, reduced friction, and savings in material and personal costs are brought to a optimum by a strictly bureaucratic, especially centralized, administration by well-trained individual officials, compared to collegial, honorific or part-time administrative forms.
> (Weber 1922: 660)

New bureaucratic structures created new forms of legitimacy. Pre-modern traditional authority rested "on an established belief in the sanctity of immemorial traditions and powers of rulers" (Weber 1922: 130), whereas charismatic authority depended on the affective devotion to a prophet, war hero or demagogue. Both usually ended with the death of a leader or the disaffection of followers. Modern bureaucracies established a more permanent rational-legal authority based on the appearance of an impartial application of rational administrative procedures. They leveled social and economic differences because of their meritocratic standards of recruitment and promotion, and because bureaucratic rules were based on the principle of equality before the law. At the same time, however, their efficiency made them indispensable. Once established, bureaucracies were almost impossible to destroy. Modern government officials, university professors or hospital nurses all worked in environments which they no longer owned or controlled. Bureaucracies separated them from their means of production in the same way as capitalist enterprise separated the workers from theirs (Weber 1922: 666). The effects were reminiscent of Marx's alienation: chains of command encouraged mindless obedience and employees became cogs in a bureaucratic machine. Towards the outside, bureaucracies formed a "community of functionaries" with a strong *esprit de corps* and a common interest in protecting and expanding bureaucratic operations and surrounding them with secrecy. Those who depended on their services confronted a monopoly of administrative expertise which was dispensed with haughtiness and pedantry. As well, the apparent bureaucratic impartiality could disguise "the direction which the powers using the apparatus give to it. Very frequently a crypto-plutocratic distribution of power has been the result" (Weber 1922: 670).

Weber did not deny that ownership and non-ownership of capital remained a basic cause of class divisions. His argument was that the emergence of cohesive bureaucratic *Stände* or "estates" exemplified the increasing structural and subjective differentiation of inequality structures. Half a century after Marx's death, industrial societies had not been torn apart by the apocalyptic conflict between labor and capital which Marx had predicted. Taking a swipe at "the claim of a talented author that the individual may be mistaken about what is good for him, but that the 'class' is 'infallible' about its interests" (Weber 1922: 634), Weber defined class interest more cautiously as "the probability that the 'average' of the people subject to a class situation share a direction of interests as a consequence of their position." People could respond to the same class situation in many different ways. Whether a particular inequality structure was accepted or opposed depended on "the *transparency* of the connections between the causes and consequences of the "class situation" (Weber 1922: 633). Power and ideology could obscure that connection and affect the level of stability and conflict in societies. Classes could develop emotional cohesion and a common political purpose or remain amorphous pluralities united by little else but their similar market position. Class and *Stände* interests could be pursued by political parties, but even here internal divisions and changing programs blurred the connections.

Weber's objective in his analysis of class, *Stände* and party was to show the fluidity and unpredictability of subjective and political reactions to structural market and class positions. Where subjective identities did consolidate they could increase social distance and social closure and facilitate the control of strategic resources such as material goods and knowledge, a common historical starting point for the evolution of social inequality.

> This process of "closure" of a community is an event which frequently repeats itself, and is the source of "property" of land as well as of all guild and other group monopolies.... The goal is to some extent always the "closure" of social and economic chances for outsiders.... Without exception all "property" of natural goods arose historically from the gradual appropriation of shares in an already monopolized communal ownership. Unlike today, the object of this appropriation consisted not only of concrete material goods, but also social and economic chances of all conceivable kinds.
>
> (Weber 1922: 184)

The Psychology of Inequality: Le Bon, Nietzsche, Veblen and Weber

Theories which saw individuals as pawns in predetermined social processes had little interest in the psychological state of the participants. Scattered observations of subjective motives and reactions related to inequality are spread through the work of Marx, Engels, Sumner and Durkheim, but they were usually harnessed to their authors' convictions.

Gustave Le Bon (1841–1931) and Friedrich Nietzsche (1844–1900) shared the widespread nineteenth century fear of social and cultural disintegration caused by the growth of the working class and the decline of traditional elites. Nietzsche was intensely troubled by "this decaying, self-doubting present" (GdM II, 24)[3] which was in his eyes "essentially the consequence of a senseless sudden mixing of classes" (GdM III, 17). Le Bon worried that society was entering an "era of crowds" where "the advent to power of the masses marks one of the last stages of Western civilisation" and where their claims "are becoming more and more sharply defined, and amount to nothing less than a determination to utterly destroy society as it now exists" (Le Bon 1926: 6).

Nietzsche drew a polarized picture of a world populated by "the solitary predator species man" (GdM III, 18) governed by instinct and passion, not intellect and reason. Biological differences made some people "hard" and others "soft." Struggle and competition created natural hierarchies where "the strongest and most evil spirits" assumed political and cultural power. Like Spencer, Nietzsche overlooked Darwin's nuanced view of survival strategies, opting instead for a coarser process that left behind only the masters and the "herd."

The "higher specimens" prevailed in this struggle through their "will for power," a desire to rule and dominate that evolved in responses to the cruelty and senselessness of nature. They stood above duty and conventions, confident that "at all times the aggressive man, as the stronger, more courageous, more noble, has also had the clearer eye, the better conscience on his side" (GdM II, 11). They were physically strong and resilient, treated others as means to an end, sought out challenges and pain, and delighted in the "pathos of distance" that separated them from those below. But they could also inspire social renewal and historical progress; "the strongest and most evil spirits have so far done the most to advance humanity" (DfW, 4).

Far below the "higher type" stood the great mass of humanity, "slaves in one sense or another." Resentment dominated the minds of the herd, the losers to whom both dominance and revenge were denied and who therefore turned their hatred against everything that was strong. Once provoked it concocted a witches' brew of hate which depicted the noble and powerful as evil and cruel, "you who will be forever the unblessed, cursed and damned" (GdM I, 7). At the same time it transformed its own weakness into a virtue, and its impotent envy into the promise of future justice. The slave's soul was insincere, "his spirit needs subterfuges, back alleys and back doors, everything that is hidden appears to him as *his* world, *his* security, *his* nourishment; he knows how to be silent, how not to forget, how to wait, how to make himself small for a while, how to humiliate himself" (GdM 10, 29).

The slave morality did not just vilify the strong but inverted their ideas. It turned the right of the strong to inflict harm into the celebration of the persecution of the weak, of the blood of martyrs, of Christ nailed to the cross. The spontaneous display of mercy by the strong turned in the mind of the slaves into the claim that the poor and the helpless were blessed by God and certain to enter heaven. Where the natural instinct of the strong was to remain solitary, the weak naturally formed crowds willing to be led and to obey, and filled modern parliamentary systems with people of their own kind. The prophets of secular salvation, the "socialist fools and morons," promised equality and social justice.[4] They posed as servants of the people and defenders of the common wheal and preached the values of the herd: respect, moderation and compassion. The "dark workshop" of modern mass culture celebrated ordinary people and taught them to accept industrial work with its monotonous regularity, its numbing obedience and its short-range life goals (GdM III, 18). Granting them small pleasures and creating the illusion of community sufficed to "wake man up from his slow sadness (and) put to flight at least for a time his dull pain, his hesitant misery" (GdM III, 20). The masters' careless confidence and dismissive contempt for lower classes allowed the herd mentality to fester and to infect eventually the morality of the strong. That was Nietzsche's great fear for his time.

That fear stood also behind Le Bon's psychology of the crowd. While in earlier societies the opinions of the mass of the population did not count, "the substitution of the unconscious action of crowds for the conscious activity of individuals is one of the principal characteristics of the present age" (Le Bon 1926: 2). The masses were now forming unions "which in spite of all economic laws tend to regulate the conditions of labour and wages" and were intent on "the elimination of all the upper classes for the benefit of the popular classes" (Le Bon 1926: 5, 14).

Mass behavior tapped into inherited layers of the unconscious, dormant in civilized society but freed when individuals were hidden in the anonymity of the crowd and knew that they could act with impunity. Le Bon admired Spencer but rejected his view of societies as aggregates of individuals. Crowds were new organisms whose members became automata, "a grain of sand amid other grains of sand, which the wind stirs up at will" (Le Bon 1926: 14). They responded to ideas that were simple, startling and clear, and were rooted in extreme sentiments. Crowd behavior was not influenced by reason but by rough and ready beliefs. Their members were instinctively driven to leaders whose control of crowds relied on the affirmation of slogans, their frequent repetition, and their spread through the crowd by contagion and imitation. Both Nietzsche and Le Bon acknowledged that the powers of the herd could be rallied to advance human civilization and that crowds were occasionally "capable of great disinterestedness and great devotion" (Le Bon 1926: 26), but that did not diminish their looming menace.

The two other studies of the psychology of inequality focused on its upper segment. Max Weber's well-known essay on the *Protestant Ethic and the Rise of Capitalism*, first published in 1905, explored the coincidental affinity between Calvinist religious principles and early capitalism. In pre-Reformation Catholicism priests, sacraments and confession provided the formal conduits for the believer's dialogue with God and guidance on the path to the Last Judgment. Luther's reformation shifted the responsibility for salvation decisively towards the self. The union with God could only be attained by the individual, counseled by the Bible available for the first time in vernacular languages. God's grace was no longer obtained through obedience to church and priests, but through the intensely personal experience of the "entrance of the divine into the soul of the believer" (Weber 1958: 112).

Calvinism retained Luther's idea of the individual search for salvation, but saw God as a remote and distant figure who ordered every detail of the world in purposeful but unknown ways. That included the spiritual fate of each person. God's grace could neither be lost nor gained, but the lack of any obvious answer to the central existential question whether one was among God's elect left the individual with a "feeling of unprecedented inner loneliness" (Weber 1958: 104). An indication of one's fate could only be obtained through daily conduct based on an unwavering belief in one's own salvation, an absolute confidence that one was among the chosen, and by the rejection of doubt as a temptation by the devil.

Calvinism, like most offshoots of Lutheranism, remained a religion of feeling, but where Luther saw the pursuit of worldly affairs as a distraction from achieving the mystical union with God, Calvinists sought the proof of salvation in doing God's work in this world. It became the duty of both rich and poor to strive for perfection. In practice that required an intense commitment to one's "calling," the pursuit of the work one had been assigned in God's plan, and the faith that God's grace would become visible in the success of one's actions. Second, where Luther had counseled acceptance of the world as it was, Calvinism encouraged the organized, rational stewardship of the world. This meant that time had to be used economically and waste had to be avoided. Profit measured the success of one's efforts. Calvinism's third legacy was to encourage asceticism. Work was an act of faith. Pursuing it for the sake of pleasure or enrichment was reprehensible. Calvinism encouraged the reinvestment of gains and saw the moral justification of wealth in its benefits for the common good.

The unintended consequence was to place Calvinism at the cradle of modern capitalism. The pursuit of a calling strengthened the emergence of divisions of labor. By approving changes in work as long as they were "made for the purpose of pursuing a calling more pleasing to God, which means, on general principles, one more useful" (Weber 1958: 162), it encouraged mobility in capitalist labor markets. The rationalization of conduct encouraged modern accounting and the systematic organization of production. Asceticism facilitated the saving and accumulation of capital.

Calvinist beliefs also laid the foundation of ideologies of liberal economies. They allowed a rising bourgeoisie to berate its aristocratic opponents for their effortless indulgence, setting "the clean and solid comfort of the middle-class home" against "the glitter and ostentation of feudal magnificence which, resting on an unsound economic basis, prefers a sordid elegance to a sober simplicity" (Weber 1958: 171). The mixture of predestination and individual responsibility gave inequality the appearance of a natural order which legitimated economic success while holding the poor accountable for their state, encouraging them to help themselves while stigmatizing those deemed to have succumbed to the sin of slothfulness.

Thorstein Veblen (1857–1929) drew a more detailed picture of the historical origins of upper class motives. He derided conventional economics for reducing economic behavior to a simple utilitarian calculus. In the real world people were "centers of unfolding impulsive activity" (Veblen 1953: 29), adapted to changing environments in creative and often unpredictable ways and were motivated by complex and variable preferences. Unlike the individual utility maximizers which populated traditional economic theories, real economic behavior was collective and cooperative, and participants consciously decided what to produce and how to distribute the results. Private property and social inequality were social conventions which lasted only as long as they were not challenged.

How variable these conventions were was shown by the attitudes to work and wealth in early societies. Most of them had no class differences, and labor was a common obligation performed more or less equably by everybody. If people competed they did so out of pride in their work. Labor was not demeaning and leisure brought no particular prestige. These societies were generally small, peaceable, sedentary and poor and knew little or no private ownership. They were also vulnerable to subversion and cheating; their most notable trait was "a certain amiable inefficiency when confronted with force or fraud" (Veblen 1953: 24).

The change to more unequal social relations was marked by the emergence of a "leisure class" which no longer participated in productive work but gained its wealth and social standing by acquiring goods through seizure or fraud, or by forcing others to work for them. Leisure classes used the conspicuous display of their wealth as a mark of social honor which distinguished them from those who were compelled to engage in what was now seen as vulgar manual work. In time, this led to deeper divisions where "those who work cannot own, and those who own cannot work" (Veblen 1898).

Leisure classes could emerge only when production levels were sufficiently high to allow some people to be freed from work by living off the surplus produced by others. Among the earliest conditions which made that possible was predation in hunt or warfare. It provided opportunities for amassing valued goods and for distinguishing "honorable" exploits such as capturing or killing animals or people from "inferior" work such as planting and harvesting. Differences in temperament, size and strength favored men in such activities, and invidious distinctions soon also valued their labor higher than "the uneventful diligence of the women" (Veblen 1953: 23).

Once such opportunities were seized, they took more permanent cultural forms. Manual work became odious and irksome, and the handling of tools became a mark of low status (Veblen 1953: 31). Initially, what was considered menial work was assigned to women even though they secured the bulk of a group's food. Eventually, manual labor became the exclusive occupation of inferior classes of men, women or slaves. Members of leisure classes were exempt and even debarred by custom from such work. They devoted themselves to "respectable" employments and displayed their superior rank by means of status symbols, titles, liveried retainers, or honorific forms of address. Their wives, initially symbols of prowess and sources of service, were eventually also exempt from vulgar labor. Although she remained her husband's chattel, the "lady of the house" advertised his social standing. The ultimate motive of leisure classes was the psychological gratification gained from conspicuous consumption which displayed one's success, conspicuous waste which demonstrated one's profligate wealth and conspicuous leisure which proved that one derived one's living from "higher" pursuits.

Whereas Spencer's "fittest" never escaped the struggle for survival, the leisure class was mostly sheltered from competition. Its behavior was parasitic, and its primary motive was to secure the means for expansive display. Older customs of predation were adapted to modern markets where predation was peaceful, organized and efficient. "Shrewd practice and chicanery (became) the best approved method of accumulating wealth" (Veblen 1953: 159) and replaced archaic methods of forcible seizure. A gambling mentality strengthened the confidence of modern leisure classes in their superior talents and encouraged them to confuse luck with ability.

New forms of predation led to new forms of consciousness. In modern industrial societies conspicuous consumption was imitated by middle and lower classes. Cheap versions of high-status consumer goods offered lower classes the promise of social approval. The primary function of consumption was no longer to sustain human life. Expensive but useless objects turned into things of beauty, whereas inexpensive objects were devalued even if they were more durable or efficient. For Veblen, the bound feet of Chinese women and the fragile waist and delicate skin of their European counterparts, the grotesque mansions of the rich, the popularity of violent sports, the ceremonial cleanliness of male business apparel, and demonstrative charity all signaled that one had no need to engage in disreputable work and had enough wealth to waste.

These changes were not inevitable. Enjoyment of creative work, the desire for useful possessions and the distaste for waste and unproductive idleness was, and continued to be, the mainstay of people's interaction with their environment. If there was anything natural about human nature it was this "instinct of workmanship." Production in modern industrial societies relied increasingly on technical innovation, economic efficiency and scientific cooperation. This was the world of engineers and scientists, and it was characterized by an absence of self-seeking, a factual interest in cause and effect and a dislike for wasteful activities and unearned prestige. On the other side stood industrial and financial elites whose interests were pecuniary and opportunistic. Their behavior still dominated modern societies, but as the importance of technology in business grew and managerial operations became routine, the leisure class became redundant. Veblen foresaw a future industrial society run on principles of technical efficiency and concern for public welfare. Like Marx, he underestimated the tenacity of the forces he had criticized.

Theories of Inequality: A Critical Assessment

The historical inequality structures examined in Chapter 1 had complex and often fortuitous causes. Human choice played an important role in their consolidation, they endured even though they imposed costs on most participants, and their long-term growth was irregular and subject to change and reversals. The theories examined in this chapter took a much more linear view. They looked for ultimate causes of inequality and attributed its growth to impersonal forces which put its long-term development on predictable and invariant paths. The discrepancy between reality and theory imposed significant limits on the explanatory scope of these theories and was occasionally noticed by their authors. But it can also become a starting point for a new theory of inequality developed in Chapter 4.

The Nature of Causation: Complexity, Contingency and Unanticipated Results

The importance of contingent events in social processes was seen most clearly by Max Weber. He remained a lifelong critic of any notion of general social laws because they ignored the "truly infinite variety of successively or simultaneously appearing and disappearing processes" in social life. Facts which did not fit such "laws" were therefore likely to be ignored "either as a scientifically not yet explained residue which will be incorporated into the 'law-governed' system as it is perfected further, or (as) 'accidental', and for *this very reason* scientifically insignificant and marginal" (Weber 1968: 212, 213). As for prediction, Weber thought it amounted to little more than what "seems probable, so far as our weak eyes can penetrate the dense mist of the future course of human history" (Weber 1958: 62). The complexity of social life could be reduced to heuristic ideal types but social science could offer no certainties. New ideas could acquire their own independent power and like "switchmen" steer history into different directions. On other occasions an accidental confluence of mutually reinforcing circumstances such as the rise of Protestantism and the growth of capitalist markets could accelerate historical change. Even Weber underestimated the force of contingency: in the Renaissance cities of Europe capitalism took root unaffected by Protestant beliefs, while Calvin's theocratic system in Geneva stifled entrepreneurship and innovation, and his ideas brought economic and social stagnation to seventeenth century Calvinist communities of New England (Lucas 1971). Nonetheless, Weber's recognition of the role of contingent events is essential for a better understanding of the evolution of inequality structures.

Sumner, too, saw that "aleatory" factors such as chance and error could affect the course of history but thought they did so primarily in archaic, not in modern enlightened, societies. Marx and Engels recognized the often pivotal role of contingent causes and unintended outcomes as well. The struggle of the bourgeoisie against the feudal aristocracy, for example, had advanced as much by intent as by good fortune. "The knights of industry managed to push aside the knights of the sword only by taking advantage of events for which they were not responsible" (MEW 23: 743), such as the mass of landless labor expelled from feudal land by the enclosures. Similarly, in the sphere of technology,

> Financial capital neither invented nor fabricated spinning wheel and loom. But once separated from their land, spinners and weavers with their looms and wheels fell under the sway of financial capital. The peculiarity of capital is merely that it unites the masses of hands and tools which it finds.
> (Marx 1939–1941: 407)

Engels noted that every human victory over nature might at first bring about the expected result, but was then cancelled out by different, unforeseen consequences.

Such vagaries of history could be brought in line with a deterministic theory only by insisting that "the internal laws which pervade and regulate such chance events ... remain invisible and incomprehensible to the individual agents of production." Laws determined history "only in a very complex and approximate manner, as a moving average of eternal variations" (MEW, Das Kapital, Vol. III: 171, 836). Historical laws only sketched the "general path every people must tread, whatever the historical circumstances," and class differences determined history only "ultimately," "in the long run," "in the last instance" or "more or less."

Similar inconsistencies appear in Marx and Engels' forays into the historical beginnings of social inequality. The first anthropological studies of early societies had revealed a variety of distributive structures based on gender or kinship, communal ownership or property, and egalitarian or autocratic decision-making. Marx and Engels had to fit this rich information into a theory based on historical laws. On one hand they selectively assembled empirical data to construct an idealized "primitive communism" which could serve as a prototype for a later, more advanced form of communism. On the other they had to argue that these early egalitarian social forms contained the seeds of later inequality structures. This raised the obvious question how the idyllic conditions of primitive communism could have given rise to inevitable class struggle. Marx and Engels' suggestions of the beginnings of inequality remained therefore erratic. In the *German Ideology* inequality originated in the family, in *Anti-Dühring* it started in the division of labor, and in Engels' *Origin of the Family* it began with the transition to a herding economy. The "inner secrets" of inequality which they set out to discover ultimately eluded them.

Spencer found a simpler solution for this problem by dividing historical details into "deep-seated and really-important" facts which supported his theory, and "superficial" and "trivial" ones which "hide from us the vital connexions and the vital actions underneath" (Spencer 1887: 96) and could be dismissed as mere variations around an underlying "law of rhythms." He ignored the cooperative features of many early societies because his theory required that they be violent and coercive. He saw the growth of bureaucracy in industry and government but rejected its significance because his theory predicted the decline of the state. He noted the emergence of a new industrial class structure but could accept class conflicts only as anachronisms from an earlier time.

The discrepancy between a predictive theory and a recalcitrant reality also plagued functional theories. Durkheim had elevated solidarity to "a cosmic law" whereas Parsons proclaimed the tendency of social systems to return to equilibrium as "the *first law of social process*" (Parsons 1964a: 205). Social conflict could therefore never be a sign of structural faults but only of episodic periods of *anomie*, external disturbances (Parsons 1964a: 252) or imbalances between goals and means (Merton 1957). Functional theory remained blind to the possibility that common values could be subverted by special interests in order to impose a division of labor which burdened subordinates with heavy and unpleasant work for the benefit of their superiors. Durkheim summarily dismissed such a possibility: social institutions which rested on errors or lies could not last. Parsons agreed: one had to "start with a view that repudiates the idea that any political system that rests *entirely* on self-interest, force, or a combination of them, can be stable over any considerable period of time" (Parsons 1964b: 34).

Because even a cursory look at American society revealed substantial concentrations of wealth and poverty, Parsons had to concede that accumulations of wealth through inheritance, market domination or discrimination based on race or gender could create inequality structures which differed from the ideal functional ranking of individuals based on a common value system. There might even be "a general tendency for the strategically placed, the powerful, to exploit the weaker or less favorably placed" (Parsons 1954b: 330). He wrestled with this contradiction in four separate articles on stratification (1954a, 1954b, 1954c, 1970), convincing himself that such "imperfections" in the distribution of power and wealth, although empirically important, could not invalidate the basic functional character of stratification (Parsons 1954c: 393, 421). In his last article on stratification (now called "inequality"), equality *and* inequality appeared as integral parts of the value system of modern society. The former was enshrined in equality of opportunity and legal and voting rights. In exchange, the "common man" had to sacrifice some egalitarian prerogatives, surrender political power for the sake of effective administration, concede cultural superiority to professions and academic experts, and accept inequalities of wealth for the sake of economic productivity.

Because the logic of functional theories required that all social conflict had its ultimate root in a weakened identification with the collectivity and its goals, conflict between dominant and collective interests could not be resolved by structural change but only by restoring a "strong solidarity with a collective entity which ... which surrounds (the individual) on all sides" (Durkheim 1960: 428, 429). For Parsons, too, poverty was an anomic deviation from the American value of "getting ahead," a personal loss of interest in achievement and a view of work as a necessary evil (Parsons 1954c: 434). Such "abuses" and "imperfections" of inequality structures could be corrected by a leading stratum of business leaders, politicians and social scientists that could restore social cohesion and put the genie of class conflict back into its bottle (Parsons 1960: 247).

The Social Role of Human Agency

Sumner maintained that the stages of social development "follow each other by an inherent necessity, and as if independent of the reason and will of the men affected," although they always achieved a better adjustment ... to the conditions and interests of society (Sumner 1979: 78). Spencer also thought that human action could at most delay the course of progress by failing to adapt or by ignoring its laws. Marx argued that human actors had "the gift of consciousness, act with deliberation or passion, and work towards specific ends; nothing happens without intent, without desired objective. But this difference ... cannot change the fact that the course of history is governed by internal general laws" (MEW 21: 296). "False consciousness" could postpone but not prevent the eventual emergence of a true assessment of working class interests and the inevitable class struggle. Durkheim rejected any explanation based on individual motives whereas Pareto and Parsons relegated them to a psychological "black box." The contribution of social actors to the origin and the maintenance of inequality remained outside the scope of classical theories of inequality.

In spite of the dismissal of independent human agency, more realistic views occasionally appear. Marx's tendency to see all social processes through the lens of class struggle did not prevent him from sometimes describing the complex relationship between structure and action in surprising detail. Being determined consciousness, but in real life the behavior of classes took different forms. Education, tradition and habit made workers accept capitalist production "as self-evident laws of nature ... the silent compulsion of economic relations seals the rule of capitalists over the worker" (MEW 23: 765). That silent compulsion included the subtle psychological appeal of religion, the "opium of the people" which strengthened oppression but also brought hope into joyless lives, offered a refuge from poverty and held up the promise of a justice that was higher than that of the oppressors of this world. The monotony of doing someone else's work not only drove the worker to seek self-fulfillment in the consumption of goods, but allowed the capitalist market to create new wants and artificial pleasures and with them new forms of dependence.

> Every product offers new *potential* for mutual swindle and mutual plunder. Man ... becomes the poorer, the more money he needs to overcome this alien force.... *Excess* and *intemperance* become the true measure of his existence. Subjectively, the expansion of products and needs appear as the *creative* and always *calculating* slave of ever more refined, unnatural and imagined desires.... Every product becomes a bait with which to seduce away the other's very being, his money; every actual or imaginable need is a weakness which will lead the fly to the gluestrip; ... every adversity is an opportunity to approach one's neighbor under the guise of the greatest amiability and say to him: Dear friend, I give you what you need; but you know the conditio sine qua non; you know the ink with which you have to sign yourself over to me; by providing you pleasure, I fleece you. (The capitalist) puts himself at the service of the most depraved fantasies, plays the pimp

between man and his need, excites in him morbid appetites, lies in wait for each of his weaknesses, so that he can then demand cash for this service of love.

(MEW, Supplementary Vol. I: 546, 547)

Consumerism replaced religion. Where people in earlier societies were dominated by the gods created in their own heads, they were now seduced by goods which promised to transform social identities. Conscious thinking was "the material world, translated and transformed by the human mind" (MEW 23: 27). This was no trivial insight. It gave human agents some measure of autonomy: structural constraints and opportunities became socially effective only in the way they were understood and acted upon by the participants.

Pareto, Mosca and Michels also knew that the behavior of the elites and the lower classes corresponded only loosely to their social position. Pareto's most valuable contribution was to see that non-rational behavior was the predominant form of social life. He deplored the fact that "many sociological theories ... either scorn or neglect non-logical behavior, or consider it of little importance" (Pareto 1966: 193), a warning largely ignored by social and economic theories. There was no social mechanism which made logical behavior more common in elites, ensured that collective choices were rational and that individual effort received its proper reward. Power could accumulate in the hands of the capable or the incompetent, and for all kinds of reasons including "the influence of chance, which is far greater than is commonly supposed" (Mosca 1939: 122). Once gained it gave incumbents the means to strengthen their position and become intoxicated by its perks. Mediocre people were promoted because they flattered and fawned on their bosses. Incompetent elites could hide behind a "veneer of honesty" and manipulate people by appealing to their prejudices (Pareto 1966: 53). Weber's criticism was just as harsh. In modern societies the pursuit of a calling was deteriorating into the reckless pursuit of profit which had "the character of a sport." Capitalism was increasingly controlled by "experts without intellect, consumers without heart; and these nonentities fancy themselves to have climbed hitherto unreached heights of humanity" (Weber 1968: 380). Pareto, Mosca and Michels also grasped, however fleetingly, the beginning formalization of politics in liberal societies, the emergence of a political mechanism of left and right which gave the appearance of elite replacement through electoral choice but left the actual distribution of wealth and power intact.

Apart from their contrasting descriptions of the "master mentality" and the leisure class, Nietzsche and Veblen as well as Le Bon shed light on the diversity of lower class culture. Nietzsche's analysis of the "slave morality" showed how the compensatory but impotent resentment of lower classes could turn into a long-term culture of dependence. Veblen also stressed the role of mass culture in habituating people to the shenanigans of the leisure class by imitating its consumption of useless novelty and by transforming its lifestyle into an alluring fantasy world far removed from ordinary lives. For all their insistence that human behavior was driven by necessity rather than choice, some classical theories showed that inequality structures involved complex beliefs and cultural adaptations among both upper and lower classes.

Options for Change

The third area where these theories yield contradictory insights concerned options for distributive change. With the exception of Weber they treated inequality as the only possible or rational form of social organization or, in the case of Marx, as an inevitable stage of historical progress. There was no compelling reason to contemplate alternative forms of distribution. Social justice would eventually arrive through the civilizing influence of the fittest, the persuasive power of collective conscience, or through the revolutionary action of the exploited masses. Injustice was therefore either transient or the natural fate of those who lacked ambition and industry.

Nevertheless, classical theorists were not unaware of ethical problems surrounding the distribution of collectively achieved results. Spencer's "first principle" and Sumner's "antagonistic cooperation" tried, not very successfully, to find guidelines that could prevent one person's pursuit of self-interest from limiting the rights of others. Both realized that inequality could become entrenched around powerful interests and amass an undeserved share of the results of the struggle for existence, although this seemed to conflict with the assumption that the unrestricted accumulation of wealth was the defining feature of this process. Both saw the potential for social harm: governments could commit the "political burglary" of colonialism, professions accumulate unjustified privileges, and military establishments could whip up public fear in order to inflate arms spending. Sumner's fond remembrance of his father as the "forgotten man" whose intelligence and hard work never brought him more than modest success sounded a personal note of resentment against social obstacles to mobility. But their focus on the leading role of the fittest and the heredity of class made them stop short of contemplating redistribution or structural change. The "regulating" role of upper classes could not turn into endemic exploitation (Spencer 1868: 59–61). The evils of industrial society were "not due to any special injustice of the employing class, and can be remedied only ... as fast as human nature improves" (Spencer 1887: 253). Sumner's critique of plutocracy also remained mute. He directed his criticism instead at socialism "whose aim it is to save individuals from any of the difficulties or hardships of the struggle for existence ... by the intervention of the state" (Sumner 1934, Vol. II: 435).

Durkheim and Parson also struggled with the question of whether inequality was a functional institution serving the common good or a tool with which the powerful exploited the weak. Their ambivalence drove them to distinguishing between constructive and destructive social change. Individual crime caused public abhorrence which strengthened social solidarity. It was therefore "a regular agent of social life" (Durkheim 1950: 72). The "antagonism of labor and capital," on the other hand, was pathological and threatened the bond between individual and society. Their interpretation of history was similarly selective. The "constructive" role of Christianity and the Enlightenment differed from "destructive" value systems such as Marxism which "debunk traditional values and ideas" and create a "negative orientation" toward "the symbol of 'capitalism', which in certain circles has come to be considered as all-embracing a key to the understanding of all human ills as Original Sin once was" (Parsons 1954d: 133).

Pareto and Weber understood more clearly that the distribution of collective achievements involved unavoidable utility dilemmas, and therefore also opened opportunities for distributive change. Both saw that standards of distributive fairness and justice were hard to define but easy to manipulate. Weber distinguished normative social goals including the distribution of collectively achieved wealth from the instrumental rationality of pursuing them once they had been chosen. The first was volatile and elusive, the second could have unanticipated consequences. That is why the Protestant ethic could degenerate into the self-interested pursuit of profit, and why the advantages of bureaucracy could turn into a machine in which individuals became little cogs, mesmerized by the need for order, and fearful of innovation.

Michels' work reveals a similar dilemma. Like most social scientists of his time he discerned in the rise of administrative oligarchies a universal "iron law," "an essential characteristic of all human aggregates to constitute cliques and subclasses" (Michels 1962: 6, 364). Inequality appeared to be an unavoidable result of a "natural greed for power" and the "apathy of the masses and their need for guidance" (Michels 1962: 205).

At the same time, Michels recognized that leaders were just as likely to gain power by fortuitous circumstances as by their own superior performance. Personal ambition was largely the product of social conditioning "vigorously nourished by an economic order based upon private property in the means of production" (Michels 1962: 52). Not all leaders of the socialist parties which Michels studied succumbed to the temptations of power. Many worked selflessly and for modest wages to maintain democratic ideals even though they could have earned more elsewhere. At the other end, the apathy of the masses was not just an "atavistic survival of primitive psychology" but the result of efforts by ruling classes to keep working people unaware of the injustice they suffered (Michels 1962: 228).

In light of these observations, Michels' "law of the historic necessity of oligarchy" acquired a more metaphorical meaning designed to correct the "rosy optimism" of socialist movements. The options for change remained open; "it would be an error to abandon the desperate enterprise of endeavoring to discover a social order which will render possible the complete realization of the idea of popular sovereignty." *Political Parties* ends with a statement which reflects the ambivalence of Michels' position:

> The Democratic currents of history resemble successive waves. They break over the same shoal. They are ever renewed. This enduring spectacle is simultaneously encouraging and depressing. When democracies have gained a certain stage of development, they undergo a gradual transformation, adopting the aristocratic spirit, and in many cases also the aristocratic forms,

against which at the outset they struggled so fiercely ... they end by fusing with the old dominant class; whereupon once more they are in their turn attacked by fresh opponents who appeal to the name of democracy. It is probable that this cruel game will continue without end.

(Michels 1962: 371)

Michels did not examine why so many people so often took up the cause of democracy, and why the fight for democracy was "ever renewed." His theoretical contribution was to show that inequality was frequently an unanticipated result of seemingly trivial circumstances, and that it remained open to efforts to counteract recurrent concentrations of power and to establish greater equality.

Most classical theorists did also not hesitate to get actively involved in politics. Spencer preached Social Darwinist policies in his prolific writing and on the lecture circuit, including a trip to the United States in 1882. Sumner was a vocal critic of the Spanish–American war and a defender of a secular social science in a still largely religious academic environment. Weber did not shy from social and political engagement, including an unsuccessful run for parliament. Michels drifted in and out of socialist organizations, ran for parliament and ended up supporting Mussolini because he believed that fascism could represent the proletariat without a party oligarchy. Veblen showed his disdain for wealth and power by thumbing his nose at social and academic conventions. Marx, impecunious but combative, got the worst of it because his ideas went to the very heart of the problem of distribution and therefore provoked an often visceral opposition: he was blamed for misinterpreting the past, misunderstanding the present, and misjudging the future. Spencer and later sociologists whose reconstructions of early societies were less accurate, or Durkheim whose vision of a corporatist society remained as unfulfilled as Marx's hope for a communist one, were rarely measured by the same exacting standards. No matter what cause they took up, however, they all acknowledged that inequality structures were fragile and changeable, and therefore either in need of defense or open to demands for greater fairness and social justice.

Biology and Inequality

Efforts to link social inequality to inherited differences in individual ability or to its adaptive benefits as an institution failed to make a convincing case for biological bases of inequality. During the twentieth century, average IQ results in both wealthy and poorer countries rose faster than what could be accounted for by natural selection, suggesting that cultural factors and social environments play a major role in the rise and decline of both aggregate and comparative intelligence levels (Flynn 2007). Nor is there evidence for a positive association between rank and reproductive success. Demographic evidence for historical reproductive rates among high class populations is mostly anecdotal, whereas comparable data for lower classes are usually missing. Analyses suffer moreover from the typical flaw of ex-post reconstruction. When upper class reproduction is high it is taken as proof of their biological fitness. When it is low it is assumed that reproductive success is increased by providing fewer children with superior qualitative care.

Rather than showing that inequality reflected a natural hierarchy of merit, historical evidence suggests that as early as 1750, elites used biological arguments to justified their social position (Carson 2007: xiii, 277). French and American cultural definitions of ability and merit varied significantly, the former defining it as a way of life whereas the latter saw it as a measurable one-dimensional trait. Both definitions, although intrinsically arbitrary, were used as ideological tools. Similarly, attitudes toward sexuality, marriage and children in countries such as England changed drastically between the sixteenth and the nineteenth century, both among landed aristocracy and propertyless poor, leading to corresponding variations in their reproductive rates (Stone 1979). Modern demographic data since the early nineteenth century show no consistent class-based differences in reproductive success. Even Betzig (1986) who made a case for higher rates of reproduction among upper classes avoided the suggestion that heritable traits could have propelled them to their position. There is no link between genetic fitness and social rank or cultural "competence." Circumstantial evidence from one of the largest historical experiment in selective breeding, the feudal aristocracy, shows that genetic factors were neither a cause of the high social status of the group, nor that they could explain the prolonged aristocratic control of European society. Here as elsewhere external, non-genetic factors outweighed any influence of inherited traits.

Neo-Darwinist biological explanations of social inequality were influenced by the same search for certainty and predictability which motivated positivism and rationalism in the social sciences. They therefore encountered similar problems when trying to force cultural complexity into a narrow adaptive logic. Nonetheless, biological views broke down the barrier which the social sciences had erected between pre-human and human life and treated human culture as an entirely natural evolutionary process. This thread will be taken up in the next chapter.

Notes

1 For a history of the eugenics movement see Hawkins 1997. The idea has not disappeared. "We are justified in considering the preservation of the entire gene pool as a contingent primary value until such time as an almost unimaginably greater knowledge of human heredity provides us with the option of a democratically contrived eugenics" (Wilson 1978: 198).
2 Pinker (1997) suggested, for instance, that the preference of modern CEOs for corner offices originated in Pleistocene needs to occupy high places to survey the savannah for enemies.
3 Nietzsche's *Genealogie der Moral* and *Die fröhliche Wissenschaft* are cited as GdM and DfW. Numbers refer to the numbered sections in each text.
4 Later work by Scheler, Kierkegaard and Schoeck (1969) continued to suggest that resentment and envy lay at the root of socialist policies. Domination and envy were complementary human desires. Envy was the motivational corollary of non-ownership; its natural constituency was therefore the poor, and demands for social justice were merely the covetous longing of the propertyless for the possessions of the rich.

Bibliography

Apter, David. *Ideology and Discontent.* New York: Free Press, 1964.
Barber, Benjamin R. *Strong Democracy.* Berkeley: University of California Press, 1984.
Barkow, Jerome. *Missing the Revolution. Darwinism for Social Scientists.* New York: Oxford University Press, 2006.
Barkow, Jerome, Leda Cosmides and John Tooby. *The Adapted Mind.* New York: Oxford University Press, 1992.
Barkow, Jerome. *Darwin, Sex, and Status.* Toronto: University of Toronto Press, 1989.
Betzig, Laura L. *Despotism and Differential Reproduction: A Darwinian View of History.* Hawthorne: Aldine de Gruyter, 1986.
Boyer, Pascal. "Being Human: Religion: Bound to Believe?" *Nature* 455 (2008): 1038–1039.
Carson, John. *The Measure of Merit: Talents, Intelligence, and Inequality in the French and American Republics, 1750–1940.* Princeton: Princeton University Press, 2007.
Darwin, Charles. *The Origin of Species*, 6th edition. New York: New American Library, 1958 [1872].
Davis, Kingsley and Wilbert Moore. "Some Principles of Stratification." In Reinhard Bendix and Seymour M. Lipset (eds) *Class, Status, and Power*, 47–53. New York: Free Press, 1966 [1945].
Durham, William H. "Toward a Coevolutionary Theory of Human Biology and Culture." In Arthur L. Caplan (ed.) *The Sociobiology Debate*, 428–448. New York: Harper & Row, 1978.
Durham, William H. *Coevolution. Genes, Culture, and Human Diversity..* Stanford: Stanford University Press, 1991.
Durkheim, Emile. *Les règles de la méthode sociologique.* Paris: Presses Universitaires de France, 1950 [1895].
Durkheim, Emile. *Les Formes élémentaires de la vie religieuse* Paris: Presses Universitaires de France, 1960 [1912].
Durkheim, Emile. *The Division of Labour in Society.* New York: Free Press, 1964 [1893].
Engels, Friedrich. 1962 [1873–83]. "Dialektik der Natur." Marx, Karl and Friedrich Engels. *Werke* 20: 307–455. Berlin: Dietz Verlag.
Entine, John. *Abraham's Children. Race, Identity, and the DNA of the Chosen People.* New York: Grand Central Publishing, 2007.
Erdal, David and Andrew Whiten. "On Human Egalitarianism: An Evolutionary Product of Machiavellian Status Escalation?" *Current Anthropology* 35 (1994) 2: 175–183.
Flynn, James. *What is Intelligence?* Cambridge: Cambridge University Press, 2007.
Gould, Stephen J. *The Mismeasure of Man.* New York: W. W. Norton, 1981.
Hawkins, Mike. *Social Darwinism in European and American Thought.* Cambridge: Cambridge University Press, 1997.
Herrnstein, Richard G. and Charles A. Murray. *The Bell Curve. Intelligence and Class Structure in American Life.* New York: Free Press, 1994.
Hodgson, Geoffrey M. and Thorbjørn Knudsen. *Darwin's Conjecture. The Search for General Principles of Social and Economic Evolution.* Chicago: University of Chicago Press, 2010.
Jensen, Arthur R. *The G Factor: The Science of Mental Ability.* Westport: Praeger, 1998.
King, Andrew J., Johnson, Dominic D.P. and Mark van Vugt. "The Origins and Evolution of Leadership." *Current Biology* 19 (2009) 9: 911–916.
Le Bon, Gustave. *The Crowd: A Study of the Popular Mind.* London: T. Fisher Unwin, 1926 [1895].

Lockwood, David. *The Blackcoated Worker.* London: Unwin University Books, 1958.
Lopreato, Joseph. *Human Nature and Biocultural Evolution.* Boston: Allen and Unwin, 1984.
Lucas, Rex. "A Specification of the Weber Thesis: Plymouth Colony." *History and Theory* 10 (1971) 3: 318–346.
MacDonald, Kevin. *The People That Shall Dwell Alone: Judaism as a Group-Evolutionary Strategy.* Westport: Praeger, 1994.
Malthus, Thomas Robert. *Population: The First Essay.* Ann Arbor: University of Michigan Press, 1959 [1798].
MEW (Karl Marx, Friedrich Engels, *Werke*). Forty volumes, two supplementary volumes. Berlin: Dietz Verlag, 1957–1985. Vols. II and III of *Das Kapital* republished by Europäische Verlagsanstalt: Frankfurt, 1968.
Marx, Karl. *Grundrisse der Kritik der Politischen Ökonomie.* Moscow: Verlag für fremdsprachige Literatur, 1939–1941 [1857/1858].
Mazur, Allan. *Biosociology of Dominance and Deference.* Lanham: Rowman and Littlefield, 2005.
Merton, Robert K. *Social Theory and Social Structure.* Glencoe: Free Press, 1957.
Michels, Robert. *Political Parties.* Toronto: Collier-Macmillan Canada, 1962 [1915].
Mosca, Gaetano. *The Ruling Class.* New York: McGraw Hill, 1939.
Murray, Charles A. *The Underclass Revisited.* Washington DC: American Enterprise Institute Press, 1999.
Murray, Charles A. "Jewish Genius." *Commentary* 123 (2007) 4: 29–36.
Nietzsche, Friedrich. *Die fröhliche Wissenschaft.* München: Goldmann, 1950 [1882].
Nietzsche, Friedrich. *Zur Genealogie der Moral.* München: Goldmann, 1999 [1887].
Pareto, Vilfredo. *Vilfredo Pareto. Sociological Writings.* Edited by S.E. Finer. Totowa: Rowman and Littlefield, 1966.
Parsons, Talcott. "An Analytical Approach to the Theory of Social Stratification." In Talcott Parsons, *Essays in Sociological Theory*, 69–88. New York: Free Press, 1954a [1940].
Parsons, Talcott. "Social Classes and Class Conflict in Light of Recent Sociological Theory." In Talcott Parsons, *Essays in Sociological Theory*, 323–335. New York: Free Press, 1954b [1949].
Parsons, Talcott. "A Revised Analytical Approach to the Theory of Social Stratification." In Talcott Parsons, *Essays in Sociological Theory*, 386–439. New York: Free Press, 1954c [1953].
Parsons, Talcott. "Some Sociological Aspects of the Fascist Movement." In Talcott Parsons, *Essays in Sociological Theory*, 124–141. New York: Free Press, 1954d [1942].
Parsons, Talcott. *Structure and Process in Modern Societies.* New York: Free Press, 1960.
Parsons, Talcott. "On the Concept of Influence." *Public Opinion Quarterly* 27 (1963) 1: 37–62.
Parsons, Talcott. *The Social System.* New York: Free Press, 1964a [1951].
Parsons, Talcott. "Some Reflections on the Place of Force in Social Process." In Harry Eckstein (ed.) *Internal War, Problems and Approaches.* New York: Free Press, 1964b.
Parsons, Talcott. "Evolutionary Universals in Sociology." In Lewis A. Coser and Bernard Rosenberg (eds) *Social Evolution and Social Change*, 684–710. London: Collier-Macmillan, 1969 [1964].
Parsons, Talcott. "Equality and Inequality in Modern Society, or Social Stratification Revisited." *Sociological Inquiry* 40 (1970) 2: 13–72.

Peel, John D.Y. *Herbert Spencer On Social Evolution; Selected Writings.* Chicago: University of Chicago Press, 1972.
Pinker, Steven. *How the Mind Works.* New York: Norton, 1997.
Pollett, Thomas V. and Daniel Nettle. "Partner Wealth Predicts Self-reported Orgasm Frequency in a Sample of Chinese Women." *Evolution and Human Behavior* 30 (2009) 2: 146–151.
Rapport, Michael. *1848 – Year of Revolution.* New York: Basic Books, 2008.
Rushton, Philippe J. *Race, Evolution and Behavior.* New Brunswick: Transaction Publishers, 1997.
Schoeck, Helmut. *Envy. A Theory of Social Behavior.* New York: Harcourt, Brace & World, 1969.
Spencer, Herbert. *Social Statics.* London: Williams and Norgate, 1868 [1850].
Spencer, Herbert. *The Study of Sociology.* London: Kegan Paul, 1887 [1873].
Spencer, Herbert. *The Principles of Sociology.* Volume I-2, II-2. New York: D. Appleton and Company, 1897.
Spencer, Herbert. *Life and Letters of Herbert Spencer.* Edited by David Duncan. London: Methuen, 1908.
Stone, Lawrence. *The Family, Sex and Marriage in England 1500–1800.* Harmondsworth: Penguin, 1979.
Sumner. William Graham. *The Challenge of Facts and Other Essays.* New Haven: Yale University Press, 1914.
Sumner, William Graham. *Essays of William Graham Sumner.* Edited by Albert G. Keller and Maurice R. Davie. Two volumes. New Haven: Yale University Press, 1934.
Sumner, William Graham. *What Social Classes Owe to Each Other.* New York: Arno Press, 1972 [1883].
Sumner, William Graham. *Folkways and Mores.* Edited by Edward Sagarin. New York: Schocken Books, 1979 [1906].
Sumner, William Graham. "The Absurd Effort to Make the World Over." In Robert C. Bannister (ed.) *On Liberty, Society and Politics. The Essential Essays of William Graham Sumner,* 251–261. Indianapolis: Liberty Fund, 1992 [1894].
Veblen, Thorstein. "The Beginnings of Ownership." *American Journal of Sociology* 4 (1898) 3: 352–365.
Veblen, Thorstein. *The Theory of the Leisure Class.* New York: Mentor Books, 1953 [1899].
Weber, Max. *Grundrisse der Sozialökonomik III. Wirtschaft und Gesellschaft.* Tübingen: J.C.B. Mohr, 1922
Weber, Max. *Soziologie, weltgeschichtliche Analysen, Politik.* Edited by Eduard Baumgarten. Stuttgart: Alfred Kröner Verlag, 1968.
Weber, Max. *The Protestant Ethic and the Spirit of Capitalism.* New York: Charles Scribner's Sons, 1958 [1904–5].
Wilson, Edward O. *Sociobiology.* Cambridge: Harvard University Press, 1975.
Wilson, Edward O. *On Human Nature.* Cambridge MA: Harvard University Press, 1978.
Wright, Robert. *The Moral Animal.* New York: Vintage Books, 1995.

4 Inequality's Inner Secrets
The Cultural Evolution of Social Inequality

Past theories of social inequality ignored key features of the distribution of cooperative achievements: the role of contingent causes and conscious human choice in the origins and maintenance of inequality, the frequent persistence of sub-optimal or harmful distributive structures, and their discontinuous and conflict-prone historical pathways. Because these flaws derive from the basic logic of these theories they cannot simply be patched up. A new theoretical framework is needed. To get there requires two steps: a reconsideration of the role of contingency and of agency in social life, and the development of a theory which can explain their interaction in the evolution of structures of social inequality.

The Rediscovery of Contingency

Materials and circumstances are contingent if they contribute to the pursuit of human goals although their contribution is "accidental" or "blind" because they are not caused by the use which is made of them. All human actions incorporate preexisting materials and resources, fortuitous changes of environments, unexpected events and the work and ideas of others. Some of these are sought out while others appear as unforeseen risks or opportunities, part of a complex and unpredictable world where we often do not know what will happen next. Contingency can frustrate or support human plans and actions. Just as biological evolution always alters forms and structures which already exist, cultural evolution finds new meanings and new uses in what is already there.

Classical theorists of inequality knew that contingent causes could influence the history of inequality and entrench distributive structures which were disadvantageous and harmful to most of the participants. They suppressed such insights because they were incompatible with the rationalist and deterministic logic of their theories. Isaac Newton already struggled with the "endless and impossible (task) to bring every particular to direct and immediate observation." His compulsive reworking of his conclusions and his unwillingness to publish them reflected his failure to reconcile his mathematical schemes with an often disorderly reality. He concluded that nature itself was corrupted and that God could and would correct its imperfections. Natural processes followed deterministic laws. "Less elegant and important" facts which fell outside these laws could be neglected as trivial (Newton cited in Markley 1991: 135, 136).

Modern positivism and rationalism applied this view to the social world. Taking their cues from Newton's laws of motion, they assumed that social systems, like natural ones, tended towards normal states of equilibrium or constant motion. These states were altered only by external forces, and the resulting change was proportional to the force applied. Action and reaction, cause and effect were synchronic and independent of time and context and were therefore reversible and repeatable. The belief in equilibria, linear causality and predictability became a cornerstone of social science. Max Weber's warning that the "truly infinite variety" of social processes defied any deterministic explanation was ignored. Contingent causes with disproportional and unstable consequences, and the resulting historically unique, irreversible causal sequences disappeared from the sociological agenda (Smith 1993; Mattausch 2003). With the discovery of normal statistical distributions in the nineteenth century, probability was interpreted as a first step towards certainty whereas chance was treated as residual unexplained variance which would disappear with more research and better measurements. Sociologists preferred Durkheim's assurance that their subject matter consisted of discrete "social facts" which stood in orderly and measurable relations to each other. Chance was acknowledged only as a disturbing force, "the dark side of modernity" (Giddens 1991: 122), which caused environmental risk or distorted rational choice. The general view was that chance fell "outside of existing sociological theory" because it was incompatible with theoretical frameworks "specifically designed to account for an outcome" (Mahoney 2000: 513–514).

There is some irony in the fact that the rediscovery of chance began in the natural sciences from which the social sciences had borrowed their deterministic premises. Natural scientists, too, had worked primarily in the controlled environment of laboratories and had acknowledged irregularities in physical or chemical reactions only as experimental error. But as early as the second half of the nineteenth century, Maxwell and Boltzmann realized that random processes such as the movement of gas molecules were common in physical environments. Maxwell was an early critic of Newton's dogma that like causes had like effects. He argued that, whereas this was true for many physical phenomena,

> there are other cases in which a small initial variation may produce a very great change in the final state of the system, as when the displacement of the "points" causes a railway train to run into another instead of keeping its proper course.
>
> (Maxwell 1952: 13–14)

In the early twentieth century, Hadamard and Poincaré showed that minor changes in mathematical calculations could produce rapidly diverging results which made prediction impossible, whereas quantum mechanics and Heisenberg's discovery of the uncertainty principle questioned the determinism of classical physics. By the 1960s, chaotic behavior had been found in many natural processes such as weather patterns, the turbulence of fluids, the spread of epidemics, ecological population movements and the fibrillations signaling the onset of heart attacks. Such processes could change from irregular flows or rhythms to stable patterns around attractors, but their precise behavior could not be predicted.

Three measurement problems make non-linear causal sequences intractable. First, precipitating causes can be so small that they can no longer be measured with precision. Second, it is difficult and in complex social systems usually impossible to isolate specific causes from the potentially infinite web of other causes which affect an outcome. The third problem is computational. A few causal components – four chemical bases of DNA, eight notes of an octave, 26 letters of the alphabet – combined with some simple rules, can produce extremely complex results. For any of these reasons, social processes which began with identical causes can have divergent results, and identical results may have different causes.

In controlled environments and closed systems with few variables, such conditions are rare enough to be treated as negligible. But social systems are open, and our knowledge of them is always partial and approximate. Large actor networks, shifting perceptions and high rates of cognitive innovation constantly introduce novelty and uncertainty. In social systems the Newtonian paradigm is reversed. Rather than return to a state of rest or equilibrium they are unpredictably poised between order and instability. Cause and effect are typically not proportional: small and apparently trivial changes can have large, cascading consequences. Finally, contingency and complexity make causal sequences diachronic rather than synchronic: they become time- and context-sensitive, and therefore historically unique and irreversible. In complex social systems, contingent causation is pervasive. It can decide military victory or defeat, trigger stock market crashes, revolutions and inventions, and lead to the rise and fall of social structures. It imposes fundamental limits on causal analysis and prediction which cannot be avoided by improved measurement or the inclusion of more causal variables (Baldus 1990).

Among the few sociologists who recognized the role of chance in social processes was Niklas Luhmann (1927–1998). In his view all systems, whether individuals, organizations or societies, faced the fundamental problem of coping with contingent events which he defined as anything that was neither necessary nor impossible. Because contingency severely restricted advance planning and always confronted social actors with more options than they could use, societies could no longer be seen as rational-functional constructs. Their primary task was instead to achieve stability "in the face of a relentlessly variable environment that changes independent of the system and therefore makes a constant search for other possibilities unavoidable" (Luhmann 1970: 39). This could be done by reducing complexity and unpredictability, subjectively through the selective construction of "sense," and structurally through the establishment of procedures and rules which put an end to the interminable weighing of options. Sense imposed meaning on a contingent world by differentiating system from environment, inside from outside, what mattered from what did not. Rules, regulations and hierarchically organized decision-making terminated potentially endless procedural regress and legitimated systemic choices such as court judgments and election outcomes in the eyes of the participants. Unlike Parsons, Luhmann did not confuse sense with consensus and procedure with function. Complexity reduction was a necessary but purely formal process. Sense and procedure merely achieved a temporary stabilization of the relationship between system and environment, but that stability was not necessarily optimal or efficient but could be irrational, redundant or harmful.

Complexity reduction made contingent environments understandable and manageable, but Luhmann was neither interested in the actual construction of sense nor in its content or its structural consequences. To him, all systems were alike. They could communicate, become functionally interdependent and, in his later work, "self-referentially" organize around central themes through internal differentiation and external closure. But he studiously avoided the subject of social inequality, except to revert to the idea that societies traversed successive developmental phases, from early segmentary differentiation to the functional stratification of modern societies (Luhmann 1997: 489). Here the differentiation between rich and poor was merely another form of complexity reduction, "nothing more than the repetition within systems of the difference between system and environment" (Luhmann 1984: 7).

Acknowledging contingency does not reduce sociological research to a simple narrative. Some precipitating causes still appear with greater frequency, social actors still respond to them in similar ways, and selective external constraints and internal feedback still create continuity. But the resulting order differs fundamentally from deterministic or rationalist equilibria: it always remains in the realm of probability and never acquires the strength of laws or rational-functional perfection. Structural changes, including social inequality, can emerge as the non-linear, unanticipated outcome of seemingly trivial events. Their evolution over time depends on negative and positive feedback loops which weaken or amplify them, and their stability is measured by their resistance to disturbances, and by greater or lesser – but never entirely absent – degrees of freedom available to social actors. Actions and events can cluster and form regularities and structures but are in principle unique. We can trace them back to ancestral historical events and to selective dynamics which stabilize or change them, but not to universal causes and laws. Prediction is replaced by the projection of future possibility spaces (Allen 1992).

The Rediscovery of Agency and Cooperation

If the social sciences found it difficult to deal with contingency, the problems were even greater when it came to human agency, innovation and cooperation. The fear of what unbounded human action might do was a traumatic theme that ran through western culture, from the biblical story of the fall from paradise to the sixteenth century peasant rebellions, the French Revolution and the rise of working class power. The result was a profound ambiguity in the treatment of human agency. On one hand, the ability to invent and choose was seen as uniquely human. It, Marx argued, was what "distinguished the worst architect from the best of bees" (MEW 23: 193). But the foundational myth underlying this view, Adam and Eve's abuse of the freedom God had given to them, also suggested that human choice could foment individual sin and social unrest. Spencer therefore bound individual agency tightly into laws of competition. Durkheim dismissed it in favor of supra-individual "social facts" and diverted collective solidarity into the safe channels of the division of labor and a corporatist social structure. Parsons derived shared goals from a process that filtered out non-consensual individual motives. Luhmann, too, sidestepped the content and subjective meaning of sense-making. Constructivist sociology made values the proprietary right of individuals and groups, thereby putting them beyond analysis and critique. Much like the pre-scientific notion that nature abhorred a vacuum and filled it immediately with denser matter, social scientists assumed that inheritance, social laws or rational constraints would rush in to impose order on the apparent chaos of human thought. The few efforts to address the genesis of values (Joas 2000) followed Durkheim in treating them as exceptional rather than routine events. The neglect of creativity and innovation became "a persistent embarrassment to social theory in our century" (McGowan 1998: 297).

An exception to this trend was the work of pragmatists such as James, Dewey and Mead. James argued that thought variations arose spontaneously and continuously in the human mind, independent of their eventual use. They were then selectively rejected or accepted through trial and error comparisons with individuals' goals. These goals were not determined by rational choices between objects with given utilities, but were flexible, pragmatic "ends in view" based on what was deemed possible in changing environments. Pragmatism's major weakness was its neglect of the structural consequences of agency. This left key inequality-related questions unanswered: why did some people have to abandon their ends-in-view under the force of social circumstances while others were free to pursue theirs and reap the benefits?

Pragmatism found little recognition in modern positivist and functionalist theories. Sociology and economics reduced social behavior to rational actions by selfish agents who pursued given preferences and were in possession of all relevant information. After Pareto, sociologists lost interest in non-rational behavior and the ambiguity of values and goals. They looked instead for "latent" functions and hidden social benefits in dysfunctional traits. Ignorance, for example, helped to preserve social inequality and maintained smooth social relations "by preventing jealousy and internal dissension where differential rewards ... are not based upon uniformly known and accepted criteria" (Moore and Tumin 1949: 790).

Cooperation which seemed to involve at least some measure of consideration for others caused particular problems. Cooperative behavior is common among animals, both between genetic relatives and unrelated individuals, and can be culturally transmitted across generations (Sapolsky and Share 2004; Thornton et al. 2010). In human societies, trust and cooperation among genetic strangers is pervasive, from carefully calculated reciprocity to self-sacrificing altruism. Specialization and divisions of labor are possible only on the basis of trust. We leave our children with teachers and daycare workers, give our savings to banks and brokers, and exchange goods for intrinsically worthless paper. Trust was as essential to the economy of Renaissance Florence (McLean and Padgett 1997) as it is to modern markets (Uzzi 1996). Cooperation can lead to intense emotional satisfaction (Lawler and Yoon 1996). Its betrayal can cause feelings of guilt and shame and the desire to punish cheaters, even if that is costly and the benefits are reaped by others (Fehr and Gächter 2002). The obvious social advantages of cooperation and the high level of resource sharing in early societies led to suggestions that an "egalitarian revolution" marked the split of the human species from its non-human ancestors (Svensson 2009).

Darwin had already argued that early humans must soon have discovered that cooperation brought obvious advantages because "selfish and contentious people will not cohere, and without coherence nothing can be effected." Natural selection would therefore have favored cooperative over selfish social behavior (Darwin 1981: 165, 166). The crucial issue here was that cooperative behavior required some "cognitive sophistication" to think of the welfare of others and to maintain group identities (Sober and Wilson 1998: 140), a view which acknowledged human agents as intentional selectors whose choices were at least in some measure independent of genetic constraints. Such group-selection arguments remained controversial because they contradicted the fundamental Neo-Darwinist premise that cooperative or altruistic behavior would always be exploited by selfish actors and could therefore not evolve. Ideological factors were also at work. By the late nineteenth century, concepts like solidarity and cooperation had become associated with working class movements and were seen as threatening the established order (Dixon 2008). The argument that mutual help could create new resources and long-term benefits greater than those of short-term self-interest was made only by outsiders such as Kropotkin. The dominant paradigm assumed that self-interest was a universal adaptive strategy. Cooperation and altruism were "self-destructive behavior performed for the benefit of others" and reduced individual fitness "by definition" (Wilson 1975: 578; 3). What appeared to be altruistic or cooperative acts were in fact cultural constructs based on selfish interest: abnormal outgrowths of parental care (Williams 1966: IX), or hypocrisy designed to make self-interested motives more acceptable (Ghiselin 1974; Ridley 1996).[1] The real reason for altruistic acts was to gain status through conspicuous kindness, one more competitive strategy along the route to social inequality. The sole exception was altruism between close relatives because self-sacrifice preserved their shared genotype.

Interest in cooperation was revived by game theory, an extended version of rational choice theories where participants optimized not only individual preferences but also strategic interactions with others. These could stabilize selfish or cooperative interactions, although they led more often to equilibria between "hawks" and "doves," "expropriators" and "suckers," finely tuned by natural selection to balance the needs of the losers with the steady flow of wealth to the exploiters. Game scenarios typically involved closed systems with few players and constant environments, and presupposed an innate desire to mistrust other players and to engage in preemptive self-interested action. They bore little resemblance to real-life nuances of haggling and alliance-making, and to the ambiguities of dealing with friends or strangers. Nor did they account for the fact that, in the real world, actors varied their preferences in response to outcomes.

Nevertheless, game theories revealed important features of the evolution of inequality. Distributive dilemmas often had no rational solution. Cooperation thrived where participants were few, knew each other and interacted frequently, had equal status and valued objectives and returns in similar ways. Here, defectors were easily identified, and co-operators might punish cheaters even if that entailed costs to themselves. By contrast, short-term cooperation where one was not likely to face the threat of later retaliation, large interacting groups where participants remained anonymous, and long delays between giving and receiving made cooperation vulnerable to cheaters. Equilibria were therefore often temporary and volatile. Selfish behavior did not always carry the day, and co-operators did not always lose.

Two results are particularly relevant for the study of social inequality. First, the level of cooperation depends on the distribution of resources. If the returns of future cooperation are too small, or if participants have few means of punishing defectors, cooperative behavior is less likely to emerge. Incidental shifts of strategic resources can thus significantly skew the balance between exploitation and cooperation and make an accidental gain of resources self-reinforcing, a frequent occurrence in the evolution of inequality structures.

Second, people base their choices not on what others do, but on what they *appear* to be doing. Needs are always interpreted needs, and therefore subject to social influences. The vaguer common goals are, and the less accessible they are to scrutiny, the more they can be exploited to create the illusion of fairness. This is particularly likely in large social systems where the anonymity of powerful groups and the reach of mass media can influence public perceptions and values. As a result, the outcomes of interactions are neither always the most efficient nor, in terms of the actors' preferences, the best. In one of the earliest studies of negotiated interaction, cultural norms led North-American children to persist in competitive behavior when it clearly yielded fewer rewards than cooperative alternatives (Nelson and Kagan 1972). Socialization and ideology can entrench distributive structures even where their outcomes are disadvantageous to the majority of participants.

An Evolutionary Solution?

Darwin's theory of evolution would seem to provide a theoretical framework which contains what was missing in conventional theories of inequality: a contingent, blind variation which supplies the raw material for all selection, a selecting agent, and a branching pattern of results which has no inherent direction and includes both adapted and imperfect forms.

Unfortunately, changes in evolutionary perspectives over the twentieth century considerably narrowed the meaning of these components, and therefore also their usefulness for understanding the growth of structures of social inequality. Neo-Darwinism shifted the emphasis of evolutionary theory away from living individuals, and towards specific traits, their genetic origins and their distribution in populations. Selection became an entirely external process, driven by genetic mutation and the parsing power of environments. Organisms functioned as conduits for these two forces and had no independent role in selection. What they did while they were alive mattered only to the extent that it influenced birth, reproduction and death (Lenormand et al. 2008: 158). Natural selection retained only what contributed to reproductive success or to its cultural equivalent, "competence" or "viability" (Blute 2010: 145).

When this restrictive framework was used in the evolutionary study of human culture (Barkow, 2006; Mesoudi et al. 2006; Gintis, 2007; Blute, 2010; Hodgson and Knudsen, 2010) it revealed two significant shortcomings. First, it could not resolve the striking contrast between the genetic homogeneity of the human species and its extraordinary behavioral and cultural diversity. In order to account for the high rate of cultural variation and the frequent persistence of redundant or maladaptive traits it had to resort to evasive explanations. Cultural diversity was seen as variation around adaptive means and was dismissed as "plasticity" or as cultural "working around" inherited traits (Richerson and Boyd 1999; Barkow 2006: 37). In the end it always returned to fitness-enhancing pathways (Barkow 1989: 321) and was therefore of no theoretical interest (Wilson 2012: 236–240). The Neo-Darwinist version of evolutionary theory offered no tools for examining the complex causes of social inequality, its changing historical forms and its divisive consequences.

Second, Neo-Darwinist evolutionism could not account for the fact that cultural selection seemed to be largely internal and to rely on cognitive, imagined selection criteria which could be arbitrarily varied. It accepted that human culture could influence evolution through learning and dual inheritance, coevolution or niche construction, but maintained that such effects were unintentional and endured only if they were adaptive. Concepts such as "free will" were denied scientific credibility (Blute 2010: 138). Durham (1991) did acknowledge the role of "selection by preferences," both as individual choices and as imposition of preferences by powerful others, but gave them no significant role in cultural evolution. More commonly, consciousness was seen as a form of self-delusion (Barkow et al. 1992: 90) or "a system of poorly understood internal drives and rewards that direct the activity and choices of the individual ... towards maximization of self-satisfaction" (Cavalli-Sforza and Feldmann 1981: 363). Whatever these mysterious drives were, they had to increase either biological fitness or cultural "efficaciousness" (Hodgson and Knudsen 2010: 189).

Creativity, innovation and social change, the most volatile features of human culture, posed particular problems. Durham's (1991) magisterial study of gene-culture coevolution made just five short references to innovation. Adapted minds had no need to innovate because they were already in tune with their environments. Without external shocks or cultural copying- and transmission-errors, cultural variation tended towards equilibrium (Blute 2010: 52, 143), much like the Newtonian model in sociology assumed that social systems had a natural tendency to return to stable states. Inequalities of authority, power and wealth "notwithstanding challenges and rebellions ... evolved in order to ensure the chances of survival of both the individual and the group" (Hodgson and Knudsen

2010: 203). In the real social world, such challenges and rebellions, from the Renaissance and Reformation to the French and Industrial Revolutions, caused major cultural change, but they had no place in Neo-Darwinist thought.

The curious result was that the actual life span, the sole preoccupation of individual organisms – and also of course of anyone interested in the evolution of culture – disappeared from view. Darwin's belief in the cognitive abilities of animals was dismissed as a Lamarckian aberration and vanished from the agenda of evolutionists (Griffin 1984: 22; Mayr 1988: 143). Lifetime experiences were considered "banal" because they said nothing about cumulative, cross-generational replication (Pinker 2012).

Just as frustration with the variability of human culture led many sociologists to abandon the search for a general theory in favor of subjective constructivism or post-modern relativism, many evolutionists began to think of human culture as a uniquely purposive product governed by Lamarckian rather than Darwinian principles,[2] or toyed with non-evolutionary intelligent design, if not by a divine agent then by the purposeful guidance of exceptional conquerors, leaders and elites (Pinker 2012). Sociologists and evolutionists wrote about consciousness and intent as Victorians did about sex: as something that was known to exist but should not be mentioned in respectable company. Conspicuously absent was the thought that human cognition could play an independent role in cultural selection.

An Expanded Evolutionary Paradigm: Culture as Internal Selection

If we want to see the cultural evolution of social inequality as a natural process which is to a significant degree shaped by human choice, we must bring the lifetime experience of culture by human agents back into evolutionary analysis. Darwin's original ideas provide the tools for such a reorientation (Baldus 2015).[3] He argued, first, that biological and cultural change were products of a single process of natural selection. He wrote in 1871 that whereas the differences between the most stupid man and the most intelligent animal was still immense, they were the result of a long, gradual process which had shaped the physical as well as the intellectual and cultural traits of the human species.

Second, he gave organisms a limited but important independent role in selection while they were alive. Genetic variation and environments alone often determined the survival chances of life forms. But equally often they merely opened a range of options. In that case, they influenced selection only to the extent and in the way they were seen by organisms during their lifetime and were "seized" as relevant to their life situation. What was discovered was preserved through "use" and "habit," learned precursors of any eventual preservation through genetic inheritance. One example was the larger titmouse, a bird which expertly hammered seeds to get to the kernel. It was not difficult to imagine that natural selection preserved slight variations which better adapted the beak to break open the seeds "at the same time that habit, or compulsion, or spontaneous variations of taste, led the bird to become more and more a seed eater." The crucial point here was that natural selection occurred "subsequently to, but in accordance with slowly changing habits or taste." (Darwin 1958: 250).

By experimenting with their inherited abilities and by discovering opportunities and risks in their environments, organisms took an active part in the selection process. Adoption now preceded adaptation. Organisms had to find workable solutions to the problems of living before passing the results on to subsequent generations. This was their essential contribution to natural selection, and it required some cognitive judgment "even among animals low in the scale of nature" (Darwin 1958: 228). In the *Descent of Man* and *The Expression of Emotion* he showed that traces of many human intellectual faculties could already be found in animal behavior. In sexual selection, animals chose their partners based on a "preference for beauty in tone, color or form." If mental abilities helped in the choice of others, they could obviously play a similar role in exploring what use could be made of one's own faculties.

Third, Darwin was keenly aware that evolution did not always produce perfect adaptations. Many of its results were slipshod or useless. Human cultural evolution, in particular, seemed to create "highly complex sentiments" and "the strangest customs and superstitions" which, although "in complete opposition to the true welfare and happiness of mankind, have become all-powerful throughout the world" (Darwin, 1981: 99). Darwin had seen the central problem facing an evolutionary explanation of human culture: the extraordinary diversity of human behavior could not simply be explained in terms of its adaptive consequences.

These ideas suggest that evolution takes two connected but distinct forms, each with different properties. Genetic change happens across generations and responds to long-term changes in environments. Cultural change happens during people's lifetime. It is fast, innovative and highly unpredictable in what it preserves. Variation and selection are primarily cognitive and internal and help individuals to cope with a short-term, rapidly changing and often unpredictable social world. Selection employs creative and highly variable evaluation and choice criteria. Instead of forming uniform populations or discrete competing units, human societies have shifting and opaque social boundaries. This makes it difficult to assign functional or adaptive benefits and costs to cultural traits or specific individuals or groups. Only a small portion of observable cultural variety can be attributed to adaptive consequences, and while cultural evolution creates trans-generational traditions, only a few of them have long-term genetic effects. Culture is evolutionary not because it replicates the mechanics of genetic selection, but because both are distinct expressions of *the first principle of all evolution: that the production of blind variety, whether genetic or cultural, maximizes the chance of surviving and functioning in an uncertain world.*

Later research confirmed Darwin's hunch about two paths of selection. On one side, the preference of human infants for tonal harmonies (Zentner and Kagan 1996: 29), their recognition of sounds conveying negative emotions such as anger (Sauter et al. 2010), or their sense of fairness and sympathy for others (Smith et al. 2013; Kanakogi et al. 2013) are some of the inherited human behaviors which are shared across cultures. At the same time, research on animal behavior has shown that the shift towards cultural evolution began long before the appearance of the human species. Primates can recognize their own and others' facial images (Pokorny and de Waal 2009), anticipate others' wishes (Yamamoto et al. 2012), use symbols, gestures and pantomime (Russon and Andrews 2011), use culturally acquired knowledge to solve new problems (Gruber et al. 2009) and communicate it to others (Sapolsky and Share 2004; Luncz et al. 2012). They show abstract representational abilities by play-acting with objects (Kahlenberg and Wrangham 2010), and are capable of imagining the mind state of unseen others, demonstrating a capacity for a Theory of Mind which is still often held to be exclusively human (Bugnyar et al. 2016). Animals form and transmit cultural traditions (Aplin et al. 2015), even if they are arbitrary and do not lead to any reward (Bonnie et al. 2007). Primates form coalitions of subordinates to control dominant individuals, although the lack of language reduces their effectiveness where abusive dominance is not observed by the sanctioning coalition and cannot be described by the victim (de Waal 1982; Boehm 1999: 191, 192).

Such learned and culturally transmitted behaviors are crucial for the lifetime search for potential uses of inherited traits and changing environments. In mainstream evolutionism, however, entrenched demarcation lines between animals and humans worked against the idea that organisms could have an independent role in selection. Among social scientists and evolutionists, "whenever (animal) abilities are said to approach ours, reaction is often furious" (de Waal, 2001). The more proximate reason was that, unlike bones, eggs or feathers, cognition and behavior left few fossil traces. Traditionally, evolutionary trees were therefore based on morphological similarities or the genetic closeness of species. No transformational tree has been constructed for the evolution of behavior and culture. Campbell tried to remedy this omission by tracing the evolution of internal, discriminating choice to early forms such as the simple trial and error interaction of protozoa with their environment: lack of food initiated blind, random locomotion, ingestion was attempted at all sites, toxic locales were avoided, and movement stopped at nutritious locations. Problem solving was immediate and past experiences were not remembered. Nevertheless, "the animal has learned that there are some solvable problems. Already the machinery of knowing is focusing in a biased way upon the small segment of the world which is knowable" (Campbell 1970: 56).

Campbell's observation suggests that internal, cognitive selection evolved as a response to the lifetime experience of contingent, unpredictable environments. Its further evolution followed two lines. The exploration of environments gradually moved from simple random locomotion to more vicarious probing through vision or echolocation, the storage of information in memory, and the ability to share it with others through pheromones, gestures and sounds, and eventually through language. On the selection side, early stimulus-response mechanisms evolved into more virtual cognitive search criteria which made it possible to surround environments in advance with imagined use, reward and risk scenarios in order to extract from them as much utility as possible. The adaptive advantage of these developments came not from specific responses to fixed environments but from the *overall* efficiency in extracting utility from an uncertain world. Information could now be collected without direct exposure to environments, and advantages and risks could be simulated before actions were taken. In complex, variable social environments fixed responses could easily become maladaptive or fatal. Inherited behaviors did not disappear, but in the course of evolution they were overlaid by creative mental abilities which could modify them beyond recognition. Where action outcomes are uncertain, a probing, innovative brain is of much greater adaptive value than a brain consisting of specialized modules. That is why most of what we know about the world has never been directly experienced, and most of what we imagine is never put into practice.

What is it Like to Evolve? Evolution as a Lived Experience

In order to understand the role of internal selection in the evolution of inequality structures we must explore how we experience evolution while we are alive, how we come to our knowledge and how we act upon it. Knowledge has a broadly evolutionary structure: more of it is produced than can be used or retained, and some form of selection decides what is kept and what is discarded. Culture, including the distribution of the results of collective activities, is a product of such selective processes. The key to understanding its evolution lies not in searching for fitness effects in every cultural trait but in applying a variation-selective retention framework systematically to the ongoing cognitive interaction between individual and a contingent world.

Humans, like all evolved life, use trial and error to explore the relevance of perceived environments for imagined preferences and applications. Experience and imagination work in tandem: memory is constantly refreshed by new impressions and depleted by forgetting, whereas assimilated uses are revised by creative innovation. Internal selection therefore offers far more degrees of freedom than a purely external selection.

How much "blindness" and how much "intent" there is in cultural selection has caused much confusion. Neo-Darwinists argued that cultural variations differed from blind mutations because they were purpose-driven, acquired during the lifetime of individuals, and culturally transmitted. Because this seemed to contradict the basic biological principle that acquired traits could not be inherited, they either saw human culture as a Lamarckian, non-evolutionary product or assumed that what appeared to be intentional behavior followed in fact "genetically specified biases" (Mesoudi 2008). In the lifetime experience of evolution this problem disappears. Like all living organisms we face a world not made for our use and must find opportunities and risks which appear salient to our interests.

This search uses two blind resources. The first are external, contingent features discovered by exploring our environments or by searching our memory which, like un-activated DNA, serves as a random-access reservoir of past experiences that are retained for unknown future use. The second blind resource consists of James' "spontaneously generated thought variations," cognitively generated search criteria which examine contingent experience or stored memories for possible correspondence. Whether they lead to the experience of success or innovation can neither be predicted nor forced. Creative insights are the most elusive product of our minds. They can appear as the result of idle curiosity or methodical work, suddenly and unexpectedly or after years of frustrating efforts. They occur to dilettantes and specialists, arrive independently to different people or may be seen by one and missed by another working on the same project. They yield solutions for mundane everyday problems and major discoveries in technology, science and medicine. Evolution requires that creativity *must* be flexible and blind because in an uncertain world key parameters of choice are unknown, success becomes apparent only in hindsight, and there are always alternatives whose unknown consequences could be better or worse. As a result, human choices are fluid, fallible and reversible, they can be well defined or ambiguous and they can be pursued with vigor or hesitation. The more flexible they are, the higher the probability of extracting utility from known or uncertain environments. Animals already shift to randomizing, stochastic behavioral strategies when environments become complex and uncertain (Tervo et al. 2014). Here lies the adaptive benefit of all creativity.

Internal selection converts these blind resources into perceived advantages and risks. In human lifetimes, environments are rarely compelling or catastrophic. Their uses have to be discovered. "Forget that commodities are good for eating, clothing and shelter; forget their usefulness and try instead the idea that commodities are good for thinking; treat them as a nonverbal medium for the human creative faculty" (Douglas and Isherwood 1979: 62). The world we experience is made up of Dewey's "ends in view," pragmatic visions of what we consider possible or desirable. The fantasy world of young children's play is the first manifestation of the human ability to imagine virtually unlimited worlds, but it is not uniquely human. Studies of animal behavior show earlier evolutionary forms, such as when crows solve complex problems by testing multiple options (Taylor et al. 2010). Those aspects of an environment which are deemed useful – although often mistakenly – are selected, retained as habits and are gradually assembled into more permanent expectations, values and structures. Some of them turn into lasting cultural patterns, and a very small portion of these affects the long-term survival of the species. The cultural evolution of technical storage devices such as writing, printing and electronic communication has greatly extended the capacity to gather and retain information and simulate uses, but has also made social environments more complex and human choices more error-prone.

Internal selection seamlessly blends contingent and intentional elements of human choice. Because the discovery or creation of something new and useful is intensely rewarding, the essential contribution of blind environments and stored memories, and the unpredictable nature of discovery and innovation, are easily overlooked. As a result, humans are prone to celebrate the inventor as genius, to discount the value of pre-done work and to forget the contribution of subordinates. The routine creativity in everyday life is ignored whereas breakthroughs are exaggerated. The history of inventions looks cumulative and progressive because wasted trials and harmful consequences are quickly forgotten. Conflating blind and intentional elements is also made easier by the causal fog of complex environments: statistically improbable events occur with surprising frequency (Diakonis and Mosteller 1989), making it easy to see order where it does not exist, to claim credit for things one did not do, and to use fortuitous events for political or ideological advantage. In modern societies the increasing organization of scientific research and information storage further encourages the misconception that creative activity is an intentional, rational pursuit.

The Cultural Evolution of Social Inequality

In evolution, order and structure appear as improbable states in a contingent world. The central question for an evolutionary theory of inequality is how and why under such circumstances inequality structures begin, stabilize, and change or disappear. An internal selection perspective reveals four important characteristics of this process. First, inequality can begin with seemingly insignificant initial variations in material and social environments which have disproportionally large and unexpected structural results. Darwin already noted that "a grain in the balance may determine which individuals shall live and which shall die" (Darwin 1987: 375). New opportunities constantly arose, and natural selection worked "like a hundred thousand wedges" to pry them open (Darwin 1958: 433). The evolution of inequality is shaped by the change-inducing potential of contingency and innovation, and the order-inducing effects of selection.

In our lifetime-experience, uncertainty increases the further we move from the familiar and the longer the time span we contemplate. How we meet our partners or find our jobs, how our children turn out, whether we remain healthy or ill, whether adversity hurts us or has the proverbial silver lining is mostly beyond our control. At times, our environments seem to dictate our choice. At others, a minute change in our own behavior proves in hindsight to have been crucial for success or failure. What is true for individuals holds for societies. Human history frequently arrived at nodal points which offered multiple options: between clockwise or counter-clockwise arrangement of numerals on fourteenth century clock faces (Arthur 1990: 94), between a male or female god or hierarchical or participatory governance in the young Christian church of the third century (Pagels 1979), or between different models of industrial ownership and distribution at the beginning of industrialization (Sabel and Zeitlin 1985).

At first glance, this seems to move the analysis of inequality from the apparently safe ground of a "universal necessity which calls forth stratification in any social systems" (Davis and Moore 1966: 47) to the quicksand of countless precipitating causes. Fortunately, an evolutionary view distinguishes contingent variation from order-generating selection. Whereas there is no limit to contingent causes which can start the growth of social inequality, some categories of causes cluster in regions of opportunity, and typical self-reinforcing dynamics add order and structure to the process of selection. An evolutionary analysis can therefore reveal causal regularities in the growth and change of inequality, although they always remain in the realm of probability.

Second, internal selection throws light on the role of human agency in the growth of social inequality. Social actors are neither marionettes on the strings of fitness requirements or functional needs, nor are they the rational makers of their world. Instead they are imaginative, creative opportunists, superbly equipped to make the best (or the worst) of situations which they did not create and over which they often have little or no control. They respond to fluid environments with blind, creative variation and select from it what they consider useful for the management of their lives. An evolutionary study of inequality investigates how opportunities for social differentiation are first discovered, how winners acquire and maintain their gains, how the losers respond to their position, and how their respective views affect the endurance or change of inequality structures. This is particularly important because winners easily forget or deliberately obscure contingent contributions to their gains, such as accidental shifts in resources, the labor of workers and employees, the role of inherited wealth and privileged access to schools, support from social or ethnic networks, or government subsidies and bailouts.

Third, internal selection does not necessarily produce adaptive or viable matches between preferences and environments. In the world of sociological and economic rationalism, preferences were given, means were known, choices could be optimized, and results could be shared among the participants in proportion to their contribution. Self-correcting mechanisms eliminated dysfunctional, redundant or harmful structures. In the real world, distributive choices can endure in the face of better alternatives and where few benefit and many lose. Human history is replete with individual and collective error, from the use of lead-based make-up by Edo-period Samurai women which made their babies sick (Nakashima et al. 2011) to the incompetence that caused the financial collapse of 2008. Such consequences can be mitigated by learning from experience, but in an uncertain world there are no mechanisms which preserve only rational or competent practices, routinely purge sub-optimal traits and set cultural evolution on a progressive path. The "survival of the mediocre," not the optimal, is the hallmark of cultural selection (Hallpike 1986).

Internal selection produces high rates of redundancy and mistakes because creativity and trial and error probing require room for experimentation with non-lethal outcomes and the freedom to learn from mistakes. Human choices are forays into the unknown, pragmatic, chance-taking processes which produce utility and redundancy, success and failure, function and harm. Trial and error always creates excess, whether as unexpressed parts of genomes or as redundancy built into word-processing software, fashion markets, library collections, safety margins engineered into bridges and buildings, or product diversification designed to protect against changing markets. Excess serves as a hedge against unknown environments, unpredictable consumer tastes or uncertain risks. The price is redundancy and waste. Most new companies go bankrupt, most new products are commercial failures, most scientific articles are not cited, most patents are never used, and most innovations never leave the private sphere of the inventor. At the same time, waste does not routinely disappear. Much of it enters personal and cultural memories which serve as blind reservoirs for future use. A common diabetes drug proves helpful in treating breast cancer. Thalidomide, initially prescribed with disastrous consequences to help pregnant women sleep, is now used to treat bone marrow cancer, and the most recent medical use for aspirin, first marketed in 1899, is in the treatment of colon cancer.

A further cause of high rates of error and social harm is the virtually limitless human ability to imagine selection criteria. It greatly increases the chances to find utility in a contingent world, but also makes it easy to deceive oneself and others. Human imagination can impose a startling variety of meanings on the most adverse circumstances and is highly sensitive to persuasion and threat. People can inflict pain on themselves and others for what they consider perfectly ethical reasons. Ideologies can convince the poor that their fate is deserved and the wealthy that their privileges were fairly earned. This is particularly common where gains by one group inflict losses on others and therefore require legitimation and defense. When the stakes for winners are high, persuasion and threat can stabilize inequality for long periods of time.

Fourth, uncertain environments and highly variable selection criteria turn cultural evolution, like its genetic twin, into a process of descent with modification. The evolution of social inequality can therefore be traced back to ancestral, precipitating events but not to determining causes, and it follows no directed developmental pathway. Instead its origins and subsequent paths are located in fields of tension between disturbance- and order-creating social forces.

Variation

Contingent causes of inequality arise along two fault lines of social life, one structural and the other behavioral. Like their tectonic equivalent, they create contradictory structuring and destabilizing forces: shorter or longer periods of stability are disturbed by tremors and occasionally by profound structural realignments. Along the structural fault line, instability is created by potentially unlimited number of fortuitous variations in natural and social environments which can start the evolution of inequality. Ordering dynamics, on the other hand, come from the fact that these accidents recur with greater probability in regions of opportunity and can have compounding self-reinforcing consequences which stabilize their subsequent growth. Along the second, behavioral, fault line disturbances derive from the tension between trust and cooperation, and the opportunities for deception and self-interested defection which they create. Order-producing dynamics arise because each of these behaviors has opportunity costs which affect its strength. The inner secrets of the evolution of inequality structures lie in these destabilizing and ordering forces.

Structural Fault Lines: Contingency and Self-Reinforcement

Variations that start the evolution of inequality structures are subject to the double contingency of external chance and cognitive discovery. It is therefore uncertain what causes will precipitate inequality, when they will do so, and what their actual consequences will be. An evolutionary analysis can, however, identify areas of social life where such processes are particularly likely to start.

Mosca, Michels and Weber identified administrative and bureaucratic structures as incubators of inequality. Sumner warned of the potential of competitive markets to come under plutocratic control. Marx saw the seedbed of structural change in the gap between what class interests permitted, and what social and technological knowledge made possible. An accidental gain of strategic resources, being the first to settle on fertile land or to bring a new technology to market, fortuitous access to strategic knowledge, the ambiguity surrounding trust and cooperation or weaknesses in sharing arrangements in early societies are areas of social behavior where inequality particularly frequently begins. The causal potential of such regions of opportunity remains, however, probabilistic. They do not allow us to predict the emergence of inequality, nor are they the only areas of social life where it can arise. They merely narrow the search for causal antecedents of inequality structures.

Contingent causes are subject to a second ordering force: they are likely to have self-reinforcing consequences which favor the consolidation of inequality. Initial re-allocations of strategic resources, whether coincidental or intentional, can yield compounding economic or political returns (Sorensen 1996; Gilens 2012). They also give beneficiaries the means to legitimate and defend their newly-gained advantages and to blunt demands for change. Such self-reinforcing effects facilitated the rise of numerous ruling classes. Around AD 1040 the first priority of a marauding knight such as Richard of Aversa was to use his booty to increase his war band: "What he could carry off he gave and did not keep ... in this way the whole land around about was plundered and his knights multiplied ... he had had sixty horsemen and now he had a hundred" (cited in Bartlett 1993: 44). Two centuries later his kind had leveraged such early gains into the accoutrements of aristocratic exclusiveness: sumptuous castles, a "noble" descent line, and a status chasm that separated them from lesser beings.

More generally, self-reinforcing dynamics appear where large initial commitments of material resources or effort lead to high returns or lock participants into a position of dependence from which they can withdraw only at considerable cost, where one or more participants receive large opportunity windfalls or chance gains which are not available to others, where learning effects lead to cumulative concentrations of expertise, where coordination and network effects favor the growth of intellectual, political or economic coalitions or technical synergies, or where halo effects create self-fulfilling status or power expectations (Arthur 1994: 94).

Behavioral Fault Lines: Trust and Deception

Luhmann summed up the fundamental social importance of trust:

> Trust in the broadest sense, as confidence in one's own expectations, is an elementary fact of social life. In many situations the individual has a choice whether he will place his trust in certain circumstances or not. But without any trust at all he could not leave his bed in the morning. He would be overcome by boundless anxiety and paralyzing fear. He could not even entertain

a certain mistrust and make it grounds for defensive arrangements; this after all would imply that he trusts in other respects. Everything would be possible. No human being could stand such an unmitigated confrontation with the external complexity of the world.

(Luhmann 1973: 1)

The systemic role of trust was seen by Durkheim, Weber and Parsons. It allowed members of a society to delegate tasks to other individuals or institutions in order to give them autonomy and time to assemble resources needed to achieve collective goals. Without trust, social relations could not extend beyond the immediate present. For Durkheim and Parsons, trust supported divisions of labor and systems of values. For Luhmann, it reduced the complexity of uncertain social environments. Social actors could either trust past experience as a source of tried and true clues for navigating through a contingent present because the past no longer offered possibilities. It was already reduced complexity. Alternatively, actors could use trust to reduce the complexity of future interactions with others who had their personal interpretation of the world and could make one's own situation fundamentally unpredictable. Here, trust relied on the presumption of certainty in their behavior and on one's ability to distinguish trustworthy from unreliable partners.

Trust is a personal relationship, a plea for a joint future with others, an attempt to reduce the unknown in one's relations with them. It does not simply look for advantages in other people's behavior but grants them freedom to act, hoping for reliable and dependable conduct but knowing that they have the possibility or the motivation to disappoint the trust placed in them. By bridging the time between commitment and fulfillment, trust greatly extends the range of social interaction from a few collaborators working on one project to networks of individuals cooperating in different places on multiple projects over long periods.

Trust is always initiated in one direction: the trusting person takes the first step, and the trusted person responds. Recipients are expected to honor the advance, to set contrary interests aside and use their freedom of action in trustworthy ways. Trust cannot be imposed but must be voluntary. It relies on signals of mutual consent and binds people together. It gets stronger with repeated use and is weakened by neglect (Gambetta 1988: 234). It can be instrumental, based on perceived cost of leaving, or affective. Once established, it can be reinforced through emotions of fairness and obligation, or through sanctions which correct breaches of trust and assign responsibility. Unlike relations of reciprocal self-interest, trust can become a preference in its own right. It can turn into a powerful source of solidarity, form the basis for enduring collective action and serve as the functional equivalent of hierarchical organization in long-term task performance.

Durkheim, Parsons and Luhmann understood the social functions of trust but underestimated its vulnerability. Just as Durkheim dismissed deviations from solidarity as residual *anomie,* Parsons neglected the subtleties of the negotiation and betrayal of trust and considered only its extreme deflationary or inflationary abuses. Neither of them noticed that the systematic exploitation of trust could become a structuring, system-defining force. The weakness of trust is that its first step is always an act of faith. Trust suspends close and continuous scrutiny of partners' actions, tolerates small deviations or reinterprets them to bring them in line with original expectations. Only by adopting such a deliberate blindness can one find out whether trust will be reciprocated. The trusting person therefore faces a dilemma: trust is inherently risky because it creates opportunities for betrayal and deception, but any effort to reduce this risk by monitoring or controlling one's partner reduces the effectiveness of trust. Hobbes understood this well: the threat of a war of all against all was not created by an innate human greed or lust for power but by the *opportunity* offered by social life to include in one's own rights the right to exploit others. Because it was impossible to predict when this would happen, even those who wished to live in peace were forced to be suspicious and to protect themselves. "For though the wicked were fewer than the righteous, yet because we cannot distinguish them, there is a necessity of suspecting, heeding, anticipating, subjugating, self-defending, ever incident to the most honest and fairest conditioned" (Hobbes 1983: 33). The harm done by trust betrayed can thus outweigh the gain from trust confirmed.

Trust has a second weakness: it requires constant confirmation and care and is therefore costly to build and maintain. One must convince others of one's own trustworthiness while accepting theirs on good faith. Trust must be protected against error and misunderstanding. Even where it has become formal and routine, it requires regulatory rules, supervisory institutions and periodic audits. The cumbersome process of monitoring trust makes it relatively ponderous and inflexible and requires high levels of emotional commitment and alertness.

Compared to trust, selfishness is more nimble because it assumes the worst, namely that others will act in the same way as oneself. Unlike trust, it makes no advance commitment. In the worst case it succumbs to the superior self-interest of others. In the second-best scenario it is the victor in competition, although competition always involves costs. In the best case, it deceives and takes advantage of the trust of others in order to gain something for nothing. This is made easier because relations of trust tend to be cooperative and transparent. By contrast, deception thrives in secrecy and is easily practiced by individuals. The strength of selfishness lies in its solitary character. It needs no allies, entails no commitment or obligation to others, is under the actor's sole control and is therefore easily terminated, revived or concealed, or combined with cooperation (Uzzi 1996). To these characteristics it owes its flexibility, the speed with which it can subvert trust and cooperation, and its quintessentially entrepreneurial character.

Behavioral Fault Lines: Cooperation and Defection

Trust is the motivational prerequisite for cooperation. Cooperation has three advantages over individual action. First, it expands the range of productive interaction. A cooperator makes an advance offer of effort but extends the time frame for reciprocation beyond the tit for tat of immediate exchange. Partners in a shared project are expected to make a corresponding contribution sometime in the future. Second, it yields significant economies of scale. Cooperating with other people multiplies what one can achieve by working alone. This leveraging power was recognized by early human communities which relied on cooperation and trust as much as modern organizations today (Tjosvold et al. 2004). Third, cooperation facilitates the management of risk. In an unpredictable world, isolated individual action is vulnerable to catastrophic failure. Cooperation increases the number of eyes which notice danger and it distributes the impact of risks. Like trust, cooperation can become a rewarding motivation of its own.

Like trust, however, it also has an inherent weakness. Cooperation encourages one side to act without knowing whether the other will do its part. Strict equivalence must therefore be relaxed or postponed, and reciprocation is assumed but not guaranteed. The temptation for defection is created by the value which cooperation adds to individual effort, and by the co-operator's diminished control over the outcome of a collective action. Both create opportunities for a free ride. Defectors can walk away with their partners' contribution or reduce their own effort below what was expected. Disasters such as the 2004 tsunami or the 2010 Haiti earthquake caused a flood of international help, but also gave rise to fraudulent charitable websites, the commercial sale of donated food and materials, trade in orphans, public relations gestures by unpopular governments and false damage claims. Rather than human "selfishness," it is the *opportunity* for abuse created by trust and cooperation that is the root of such behaviors. It may be seen or missed, found after intense search or by blind luck, and may be exploited for a wide range of motives.

Like trust and cooperation, deception and defection have characteristic weaknesses. In order to thrive and make gains at others' expense, they must maintain what they exploit lest they kill the goose that lays the golden eggs. Deception is costly because it must preserve the fiction of trust and avoid detection which might lead to ostracism, retaliation or the termination of interaction. Maintaining the appearance of trust is the basic theme of all ideological efforts to justify social inequality, just as attempts to reduce inequality invoke claims of fairness violated and trust betrayed. Marx already noted that the first priority of newly established ruling classes was to make their interest look like the common good. Historically, social control systems designed to legitimate, persuade and coerce closely follow the first appearance of social inequality, *prima facie* evidence of its unstable nature.

Just as deception must maintain trust, defection requires continued cooperation. Acts of complete expropriation are self-defeating. Rulers must have people to rule over; looted and empty houses pay no taxes. Even in highly coercive inequality systems, such as Sparta's reign of terror over its Helots or the periodic raids of neighboring territories by the Aztecs, exploitation was calculated not to eliminate the subject populations. Defectors must consider the welfare of the deprived in order to ensure their cooperation and prevent their resistance. By doing so, however, they not only incur the costs of manipulation and social control, but also keep alive the potential for demands by the deprived for a more equitable distribution of cooperative achievements.

It is important to see the volatile, unstable nature of these configurations. The line between trust and deception, cooperation and defection is blurred by the ambiguities of giving and taking, asking and extorting. Distributive structures can be accepted as fair exchange or resisted as ostentatious injustice. In Indian caste relations

> Different landowning masters and other high-caste people treat Muli (a low caste member) quite differently from one another, and he responds differently to each of them. In some circumstances, he works as a faithful and subservient employee; at other times he seeks indirect ways to escape his plight; sometimes he cheats his employer; and sometimes he openly revolts against what he considers unfair and excessive oppression. Moreover, the same employer treats Muli differently at different times, and conversely, Muli's ambivalent responses reflect respect for, affection for, resentment of, and rebellion against the same person.
> (Freeman 1979: 54)

The distribution of collective achievements always involves varying proportions of trust and deception, cooperation and defection. Pure cooperative or exploitative social structures do not exist. The former always produce opportunities for defection which will sooner or later be discovered. The latter cannot exist without a measure of trust and cooperation, no matter how artificial and skewed.

Selective Retention

The Consolidation of Distributive Choices

In classical sociological and biological theories the causes of social inequality also explained its recurrence and persistence. From an evolutionary point of view, the causation and stabilization of inequality are different processes – one belonging to the sphere of variation, the other to that of selective retention. Inequality frequently begins with accidental precipitating events, but they cannot be dismissed as noise because they do not necessarily cancel each other out. Some become subject to selective dynamics which make initial causes cumulative and self-reinforcing. In modern societies, early gains can facilitate social closure to maintain income inequalities (Weeden 2002), increase political influence (Gilens 2012), or strengthen reputational advantages which secure better-paying jobs, access to strategic networks or advantageous marriages (Bowles and Gintis 2001; Burris 2004; Soares 2007; Mullen 2010). Inequality structures may grow more resistant to change the farther they evolve, and may become locked in even if they are less efficient than known alternatives. By the same token, they deprive the losers of resources they could use to oppose or reverse their losses.

Initial gains can also give beneficiaries added means to change the perception of inequality among the losers through social control. Bourdieu (1980: 210) noted the concurrence of exploitation and legitimation: as the former increased, so did symbolic testimonies of gratitude, homage, respect and moral debts.

Social control takes two forms: direct intervention or the use of complementary opportunities. Interventive control involves intentional efforts by beneficiaries of resource gains to use persuasion and coercion to increase the acceptance of inequality by the deprived and to prevent or suppress resistance. Its main advantage is that it can target specific legitimation needs and specific groups. Its disadvantage is that legitimation and coercion are visible, intrusive and costly.

Taking advantage of complementary opportunities is a far less noticeable but equally important strategy. Here, initial gains allow the more efficient use of fortuitous opportunities such as the demise of a competitor or disunity among opponents, which beneficiaries did not create but which strengthen their position and favor their interests. Observing the conflict between two warring adversaries of Rome, the historian Tacitus commented: "When fate knocks at the gates of the empire, the greatest gift it can offer us is discord among our enemies" (Tacitus 1956: 30). Complementary opportunities can arise from singular events or long-term conditions: feudal peasants, low castes and slaves developed enduring autonomous beliefs which inadvertently supported their inequality structures. Although the use of complementary opportunities is an elementary strategy of all lived evolution, the control of strategic resources increases its compounding, inequality-reinforcing returns. This effect is enhanced by low costs because complementary conditions can be used in their existing form with little or no modification.

All structures of inequality depend for their maintenance on a mix of intervention and complementarity. Proportions vary from high intervention systems such as European feudalism which relied largely on persuasion and coercion, to slave societies such as the *Machube* which rested primarily on legitimating myths created by the slaves themselves, and on internal divisions between them. At the same time, social control never establishes complete compliance. There have been few periods in history "when subjects have not groaned under the political and economic burdens of social class (and) expressed the view, in the quiet security among trusted friends, that the system itself was not a fair exchange" (Goode 1978: 150).

The Stabilization of Excess, Redundancy and Harm

Functional sociological theories argued that inequality increased efficiency by regulating access to scarce resources, by reducing friction and distribution costs, or by creating incentives which matched the most talented people with the most important societal tasks. By contrast, an evolutionary perspective assumes that internal selection in social environments with high levels of uncertainty leaves behind a continuous flow of the visibly irrelevant. The pursuit of status and prestige, such as the conspicuous competition between lineages on Easter Island, can lead to the catastrophic destruction of the environment (Wright 2004; Hunt 2006), whereas deception and defection can generate wide-spread support for structures which create costs for many and benefits for few. The history of culture, just like the history of technology, is a history of the superfluous, not the necessary (Basalla 1988: 13, 208). The duration and frequency of inequality in human societies is neither an indicator of its social utility nor of the superior qualities of its elites.

A seminal article by Alchian (1950) pointed out that in contingent environments rational planning or optimization are impossible. At the same time, even purely random actions can produce differential rates of individual or group "success," as well as structures and action sequences of extremely long duration. In economic processes, uncertain environments are on one hand necessary conditions for the emergence of profits and the differentiation of successful from unsuccessful firms. On the other, they make the calculation of future costs and returns highly uncertain. Each choice yields no longer a unique outcome but a distribution of possible ones. Once it is made, its success becomes evident only in hindsight (Alchian 1950: 212). For the same reason there is no way to ensure cumulative progress towards optimal practices and structures because it is not known what would have happened if different choices had been made.

> Realized positive profits, not *maximum* profits, are the mark of success and viability. It does not matter through what process of reasoning or motivation such success was achieved.... The crucial element is one's aggregate position relative to actual competitors, not some hypothetically perfect competitors. As in a race, the award goes to the relatively fastest, even if all the competitors loaf. Even in a world of stupid men there would still be profits. Also, the greater the uncertainties of the world, the greater is the possibility that profits would go to the venturesome and lucky rather than to logical, careful, fact-gathering individuals.
>
> (Alchian 1950: 213)

If enough people buy lottery tickets, one will eventually pick the right numbers. If enough players act in a random manner, one of their strategies will in retrospect turn out to have been optimal. If enough investors buy and sell stocks, there will be one who buys just when stock prices are lowest, and sells just on the day when they peak.

> In the early 1950s you might have invested in a risk class of firms that included Xerox. In 1950 all of these firms would have looked alike and all would have had an equal expected rate of return. *Ex post*, some would have gone broke and disappeared, most would have earned the market rate of return, some would have earned more than the market rate of return, and a few, perhaps one, would have been an investment such as Xerox. Those who owned shares in it became wealthy.
>
> (Thurow 1975: 151)

There are four reasons why contingent elements in the evolution of social structures like inequality are frequently overlooked. First, in a complex world there are usually many causes which have a roughly equal chance of being associated with an outcome. In ancient Rome no major decision was taken without propitious signs or omens such as the flight of birds or an eagle alighting on a public building. These "were fully incorporated into the governmental apparatus ... the pontiffs, the augurs and the others entitled to perform sacrifices, organize cult activities and interpret the divine signs were men who also sat in the Senate and held magistracies" (Finley 1983: 93). Augurs were accorded the status and privileges of high officials, and their predictions gave them de facto veto power over public decisions. The Athenian democracy between the sixth and fourth century BC relied extensively on the opinions of itinerant soothsayers and the oracle at Delphi. In addition, it allowed many of its public functions to be performed by officials who had been drawn by lot. Finley (1983: 95) notes that there is no evidence that the selection process was manipulated by wealthy citizens. In modern societies, stock traders in India base their choices on sacrifices to incur divine favor, their Chinese colleagues follow *feng shui* or auspicious numbers, and European or North American investors place their faith in the forecasts of financial experts and economists, the augurs of modern economies. All obtain broadly similar results. Personnel and salary decisions in organizations are routinely based on extra-functional criteria such as the candidate's weight (Swami et al. 2008), height (Judge and Cable 2004), facial appearance (Rennenkampff 2005), attractiveness (Todorov et al. 2005; Hamermesh 2011; Sierminska 2015), race (Brezina and Winder 2003), perceived social background (Baldus and Tribe 1978) or voice pitch (Klofstadt et al. 2012). Advantages gained from physical attractiveness can follow individuals throughout their life (Jaeger 2011). Gossip compensates for incomplete information in establishing social ties (Sommerfeld et al. 2007). Medically unnecessary or harmful procedures are common in hospitals (Palmieri et al. 2005). Payer (1996) documents major cultural variations in modern medical diagnoses and treatments in the US, England, Germany and France which have broadly similar results. Sociologists and economists often assume that such non-rational choices are episodic and will be corrected by market forces. In reality, they reflect the fundamental inability to manage a potentially unlimited amount of often ambiguous information, although this is usually hidden behind rules of confidentiality and procedural secrecy. In a complex and often rapidly changing world, what appear to be rational and non-rational choices bring broadly similar returns and are accompanied by similar rates of unanticipated consequences. The randomization of choice can therefore, as in the case of Athens and Rome, become a successful strategy, just as choosing investments by throwing darts at stock market pages often wins out over the advice of investment experts. No major financial firms or individuals consistently outperform market averages without the aid of luck, market control or illegal insider information (Augustin et al. 2015). Historical returns on equity in portfolios are shaped by random events rather than foresight, and no process for accurate macro-economic or budget forecasting has been devised (Ormerod 1997; Ormerod and Maunfield 2000; Penner 2002). Between 1980 and 2012, factors supposed to "predict" future stock market returns proliferated. Most of them were irrelevant or represented false positives generated by "overfitting" multiple investment strategies to historical stock market data (Harvey et al. 2013; Bailey et al. 2014). Formulas claiming to provide "a perfect hedge against market uncertainty"[4] have been no more successful than "zero intelligence" (random trading) models (Farmer et al. 2005). Boulding, noting the rapid growth of lawyers' fees, suggested that if a social experiment allowed no-one with an IQ above 100 to enter the legal profession, the overall outcome would still be the same: people would still look for the best lawyer, and differential results would still be obtained in court (1966: 110).[5]

The second reason which makes it easy to ignore the role of chance is that establishing arbitrary causal links between fortuitous events also makes it easy to attribute them to personal effort. Like Alchian's "realized profits," claims of functional importance, organizational efficiency or personal ability belong to the *post facto* reconstruction of success and failure but are easily attributed to personal foresight and converted into political or financial gain. Concepts of personal merit have undergone significant historical variations (Carson 2007). Order of appearance and timing at high-level international competitions, although randomly assigned, significantly influences the final ranking of competitors and their subsequent economic success (Ginsburgh and van Ours 2009). Repeated blind product evaluations by "experts" produce rankings and awards which are largely the result of chance (Hodgson 2009: 1). This is made easier because alternatives remain unexplored, and because in a complex world even highly unlikely coincidences are not unusual (Diakonis and Mosteller 1989). Winners tend to take personal credit for their success no matter how fortuitous or how much it owes to the work of others. Losers will tend to leave the scene quietly regardless how superior their efforts and how unfortunate their loss.

> Income ... depends on luck: chance acquaintances who steer you to one line of work rather than to another, the range of jobs that happen to be available in a particular community when you are job hunting, the amount of overtime work in your particular plant, whether bad weather destroys your strawberry crop, whether the new superhighway has an exit near your restaurant, and a hundred other unpredictable accidents. Those who are lucky tend, of course, to impute their success to skill, while those who are inept believe that they are merely unlucky. If one man makes money speculating in real estate while another loses it, the former will credit his success to good judgment while the latter will blame his failure on bad luck ... luck has far more influence on income than successful people admit.
> (Jencks 1972: 227)

The third factor which conceals random elements in the distribution of wealth is that fortuitous gains are not likely to be lost in the same way. As Alchian noted, random walks can generate highly unequal distributions of wealth regardless whether they start from conditions of equality or inequality, and regardless of the ability of the participants. But once concentrations of wealth are achieved, there is no corresponding randomization of loss as long as beneficiaries engage in routine risk diversification, earn normal market rates of return, and do not deliberately squander their gains. Such asymmetrical compounding dynamics, rather than efficient management or inherited talent, explain the survival patterns of feudal aristocracies, family dynasties or capitalist firms (Ormerod et al. 2001).

Fourth, random, redundant and harmful outcomes of human decisions tend to be made invisible by termination strategies which prevent their further investigation. Luhmann argued that the fundamental reason for formal rules and institutional routines was not to increase efficiency but to reduce the unmanageable number of options confronting social actors in a contingent world. The act of deciding becomes more significant than its consequences and is justified by typical termination routines. *Sampling problems*, the recruitment of "suitable" individuals to social positions, are solved by devices such as succession rules, aptitude tests, credentials, entrance barriers, and extra-functional selection criteria. *Assessment problems* such as the potentially infinite regress into evidence relevant to hiring, promotion and dismissal, performance evaluations or judicial decisions, are solved by hierarchically organized decision power or judicial appeal processes. *Allocation problems*, the distribution of the proceeds of cooperative actions, are solved by property rights, professional monopolies, wage or salary conventions, or negotiating power. *Justification problems*, the protection of sampling, assessment and allocation decisions against questioning and third party review, are solved by devices such as confidentiality and secrecy, contempt of court rules which prevent the critique of legal decisions, self-regulation which protects professional groups from competition and external scrutiny, and more generally through social control. Such "legitimation by procedure" (Luhmann 1972: 264) imposes far less stringent criteria on cultural selection than those demanded by rational-functional theories. Termination strategies are prone to be influenced by social inequality and can ensure the persistence of outcomes which are inferior to possible alternatives and have costly or detrimental consequences.

That does not mean that social behavior is devoid of foresight and planning, that social structures arise at random and have no instrumental value, and that human ability cannot devise surprising solutions for complex problems. Rational action in uncertain environments is subject to severe limitations, but social actors are not helpless. Imitating practices which worked for others, learning from mistakes and collecting as much information as possible about risks and opportunities are some of the strategies that can help individuals to navigate through an unpredictable world. But in uncertain environments, such efforts can alleviate but not eliminate the effect of contingency on human choice. Human actors are prone to confuse being lucky with being better, and to mistake self-serving structures as the common good. As a result, their actions frequently have sub-optimal but enduring consequences. Resistance to suggestions from subordinates can prevent the acceptance of good ideas in organizations (Burt 2004). Enforced competitiveness can lower industrial innovation (Carmichael and MacLeod 2000). Incompetence can be absorbed by the operational complexity of large organizations. Internal competition, the defense of rank and the assignment of blame can prevent organizational learning from mistakes (Tjosvold et al. 2004). The promise of ongoing medical research is routinely exaggerated (*Nature Neuroscience* 2010: 651). Corporate leaders turn ordinary and mundane performances into extraordinary achievements (Alverson and Svenigsson 2003) and use performance-based incentive plans to further their own rather than their shareholders' interests (Buck et al. 2003). Organizational *hubris* can encourage a loss of vigilance and the assumption of irrational risk (Stein 2003). Group pressures can impair judgment (Baron 2005). Mistrust and close supervision can reduce the productivity of work (Falk and Kosfeld 2006). Large pay differentials may choke off rather than improve performance whereas work motivation, satisfaction and creativity may thrive when pay and income differences are reduced (Ariely et al. 2008). The flaws of hierarchy are usually embellished after the fact.

> Most professions resemble a rich snob whose family fortune was founded many generations before by a horse-thieving or bootlegging ancestor. The road to respectability – from journeyman practitioners to cosmopolitan professionals – was likely to be littered with episodes of greed, prejudice, intellectual foolishness, and political manipulation that today's professionals would just as soon forget. For any profession, the first item on the agenda is to gain jurisdiction over a chosen field. There is no second item on the agenda.
>
> (Sutton 2001: 275)

The Long-Term Evolution of Inequality Structures: Path-Dependence and Indeterminate Outcomes

Uncertain environments and volatile choices turn the long-term evolution of inequality into a path-dependent process: innovation and external shocks constantly introduce variety whereas compounding effects, structural inertia or social control narrow the range of possible outcomes. The probability of changes in path direction is stochastic: it depends largely on specific events occurring close to or immediately prior to each change and allows therefore no reliable long-term prediction.

Research on path-dependence (Thelen 1999; Mahoney 2000; Pierson 2000; Streek and Thelen 2005; Vergne and Durand 2010) has focused on critical junctures where historical event sequences became locked into a particular course which participants eventually saw as a new logic of the system. Skocpol (1992), for instance, suggested that in the US the early fragmentation of state power favored the growth of shop unions and prevented the emergence of a unified labor movement and a comprehensive social insurance scheme. In countries like Germany, by contrast, the creation of a state-run social security system and the organization of unions by entire industrial sectors forced industry to accept both (Streek 1992). Other work (Arthur 1990, 1994; North 1990) has shown how the fortuitous adoption and subsequent lock-in of technologies and institutions led to prolonged market dominance in spite of later, better solutions. Basalla (1988) documents the cultural selection of widely divergent uses of similar technologies in Japan, China and Europe between AD 800 and 1600.

The critical junctures perspective showed the unpredictability of path-dependent processes, but treated narrowing options and lock-in, once begun, as a mechanical process from which there was no escape. Little was said about the contributions of actors to path-creation: what role they had in initiating change, and what made them stay in, or escape from, lock-in situations (Garud et al.

2010). To understand such decisions we must realize that what is now the past was once the future, a time when individuals faced multiple opportunities for action. Only then can history be treated not simply as what was or what had to be, but as actual choices by participants based on their understanding of obstacles, opportunities and alternative courses of actions. An evolutionary analysis of social inequality must therefore not only address the historically observable, but examine the counterfactual "objectively 'possible' or 'probable' response of individuals to actual or imagined potential actions of others" (Weber 1968: 114).

In path-dependent processes, past events can increase or lower the probability of subsequent change. An event path is absorbing if it diminishes the degrees of freedom for social actors and increases the likelihood of particular outcomes. In the evolution of inequality, absorbing pathways are usually caused by feedback and social control. Path segments can also be more of less independent of each other, producing a random walk which follows an irregular long-term pattern, and where the probability of a variety of outcomes is roughly equal. Finally, paths can be expanding and show an increasing probability to change direction or to branch. Such is the case in times of political and social revolutions, or when key inventions, such as nineteenth century mechanized production or late twentieth century information technology, open new social or technological possibilities.

The theoretical advantage of path-dependence analysis lies in making social causation time and context sensitive. It is important not only to know what caused an event, but when it occurred. Path-dependent processes always retain contingent, random elements and are never immune to change. Small events can therefore never be dismissed as insignificant, and alternatives never completely disappear. Just as a process may become self-reinforcing, it may carry the seeds of change. Dominant institutions may, as Marx and Pareto recognized, succumb to their own rigidity, monopolies may encourage the growth of niche competitors and religious dogmatism may open sectarian fissures. No social consensus, norms or rules are ever free of ambiguity, loopholes and deviance (Streek and Thelen 2005: 15). Pathways to inequality are often particularly unstable in their early stages. At the beginning of feudal rule, alliances were erratic and confused: today's friend was tomorrow's target for a raid. Only a few succeeded, and of the many who failed few traces remained. But for the winners the path became absorbing as they benefited from compounding positive and negative feedback. "The more land (they) had, the more knights (they) could enfeoff, and the more knights (they) had, the easier it was to conquer new land," to coerce peasants, and to suppress revolts (Bartlett 1993: 47). Feudalism's own demise, and the onset of an expanding path leading to the French Revolution, began equally imperceptibly. Over the long term, irregularly cyclical patterns of growth, stability and decline are typical of early inequality structures (Mann 1986: 38–40; Flannery and Marcus 2012), early modern European state-elite complexes (Lachmann 2009) and modern family fortunes, dynasties, or capitalist corporations (Fligstein 1990; Ormerod et al. 2001). Stability derives from periodic shocks of luck which replenish the fortunes of elites (Becker and Tomes 1979; Mookherjee and Debraj 2002), and from the compounding effects of social control. Decline occurs as dynasties die out, initial returns diminish, or competing groups succeed, and it too can become self-reinforcing. Tainter (1988) distinguished three periods in the evolution of historical inequality systems. The "runaway train" phase was characterized by a growing concentration of wealth and power, an accelerating exploitation of natural and technological resources, a growing population and deteriorating environments. In the second phase, powerful vested interests prevented appropriate responses to these problems and pursued a policy of self-destructive inertia which entrenched their own objectives at the expense of common concerns. The third phase, the "house of cards," saw the often rapid collapse of the entire inequality structure.

Genetic and Cultural Aspects of Social Inequality

Conventional Neo-Darwinist theory has told only half of the story of evolution. Just as genes do not dictate traits, organisms do not automatically fit into niches. What can be done with a trait has to be explored, and niches have to be discovered. This is the crucial evolutionary role of internal selection. Social inequality is, for the most part, a product of lifetime, internal choices rather than of inherited traits. The centuries of selective marriage and procreation by Europe's feudal aristocracy did not produce a superior class of people but a normal distribution of talent, with a few enlightened rulers, much average, and arguably more than the normal share of incompetents and wastrels. Differences in wealth have no long-term effect on natural selection and do not enhance differential biological or social fitness (Courtiol et al. 2012). Lived selection and genetic selection nevertheless remain linked. Inequality can have a devastating impact on the survival chances and the reproductive success of human groups, just as it can lead to genetic adaptations such as differential ratios of male and female births in response to socially induced stress, including inequality-related poverty (Catalano and Bruckner 2006).

There is no evidence that past environments consistently favored inequality-inducing traits. The Malthusian scenario of competition for scarce resources often invoked by evolutionary views of human culture is at odds with the sharing, cooperative economies of hunter-gatherer societies. Darwin already noted the survival value of cooperation in the small bands of early humans. This trend would have been strengthened by the familiarity of partners and the inability to leave the group. Prolonged human collaboration in subsistence activities should have created social pressure to share the results and to observe norms of fairness and distributive justice (Hamann et al. 2011).

Aggression and self-interest were neither the only nor the most productive solutions to early survival problems. Conditions of early human evolution were more likely to favor on one hand a variety-generating, creative brain able to explore as many uses of environments as possible, and on the other a genetic polymorphism which preferred cooperative over self-interested strategies, first in sexual (Gavrilets 2012) and then in more general social relations. Young children are far ahead of primates in the ability to cooperate, and this may have given humans a crucial advantage in exchanging knowledge and acquiring social skills (Dean et al. 2012). Pre-verbal infants prefer helping over obstructive social behavior (Hamlin et al. 2007), toddlers help each other spontaneously at 18 months (Warneken and Tomasello 2006). Prosocial behavior appears in children as young as two years (Warneken 2013). Three-year-old children avoid helping adults who appear to cause harm to others (Vaish et al. 2010) and show an increasing aversion to inequality as they get older (Fehr et al. 2008; Steinbeis et al. 2012). The desire to be seen as cooperative and to avoid exploitation by selfish group members makes people accept costs for actions that benefit the group (Alford and Hibbing 2004; Hibbing and Alford 2004). Cross-cultural research shows uniform cooperative responses to typical game scenarios (Henrich et al. 2005), although they are subject to cultural influences. Also, cooperation seems to be intrinsically satisfying, encouraging people to stay in cooperative relationships even if there are higher-return alternatives, and to prefer new joint ventures based on a normative promise to desist from defection (Lawler and Yoon 1996). Third party punishment of violators of collective norms, even if this brings no direct benefit, is similar across cultures, and its evolution may have been favored by the close ties and low mobility of early human communities (Roos et al. 2014; Fehr and Fischbacher 2004). The evolutionary origins of aggression may lie as much in its use to punish cheaters as in the self-interested competition for scarce resources because the pressures of group living made it important to distinguish helpful others from those one could not trust.

Sharing and distributive reciprocity in early human societies became the basic blueprint for modern divisions of labor, systems of social security, car or health insurance, and redistributive taxation. Formal inequality structures appeared relatively late in human cultural evolution, most likely as the result of more favorable environments for deception and defection, among them the larger size of human communities, greater anonymity and social distance between individuals, and increasing opportunities for incidental resource appropriation and accumulation caused by advances in economic productivity.

Contingency, Merit and Inequality Revisited

In Jonathan Swift's 1726 novel, *Gulliver's Travels*, the emperor of Lilliput selected his court officials by letting them jump over a tightrope. The empire's highest honors, silken threads in blue, red or green, were awarded in a competition of "leap and creep" which required the contestants to jump over or crawl under a stick held by the emperor or his ministers. In one of Gulliver's next stops, scientists spent their time trying to extract sunbeams from cucumbers, build houses from the roof down, and discover painless taxes. Gulliver's strange adventures were thinly disguised parodies of the appointment policies of the English court, the criteria for awarding distinctions such as the Order of the Bath, and the staying power of perfectly useless enterprises. One hundred and fifty years later, Gilbert and Sullivan's *HMS Pinafore* lampooned the miraculous rise of Sir Joseph Porter, KCB, from an office boy who polished door handles to the lofty position of First Lord of the Admiralty. His junior partnership in a law firm may have been "the only ship he had ever seen," but it taught him some timeless lessons for social advancement: hang around the front door to be noticed by your peers, don't think independently, wear a clean collar and a new suit, and "stick to your desk and never go to sea, and you may be ruler of the Queen's navee."[6]

Parody puts common occurrences into sharper relief. Most sociological explanations of social inequality succumbed to three fallacies. They misread distributive structures as the work of providential causal laws or rational constraints, assumed that their historical longevity was proof of their utility and efficiency, and argued that, except for episodic friction, people accepted inequality as inevitable or because it reflected differences in fitness, ability or functional contribution. This chapter has shown a more complex picture: inequality has multiple contingent causes which make its onset unpredictable. Compounding and social control give it structure and endurance. These can give to a few the means to justify their privileges no matter how they were acquired, to portray the fate of the losers as divine punishment or the impersonal justice of the market, and to take advantage of the fact that those who bear the costs of inequality lack the means to resist.

This seems to remove a cornerstone of both theoretical and ideological views of social inequality: the link between personal merit and social position. In past theories, that link produced either a functional hierarchy based on differential contributions to shared goals, or a fitness-based hierarchy of unequally endowed competitors for scarce goods. The obvious advantages of inequality, "present in every human society," then reconciled the losers to their lot and made them "take for granted even those distributive arrangements which work to their disadvantage and are not essential" (Lenski 1966: 32).

Such views continue to reflect a long-standing ambiguity towards individual agency in evolutionary and social sciences. They celebrated intentional choice as the defining feature of human life but feared its potential to destabilize established social structures. As a result, social scientists simultaneously overstated and understated the role of individual effort. On one hand, they tended to see in individual achievement, ability, or just being the first to lay claim to a resource (which seemed to imply superior qualities) the true causes of social inequality. On the other, they made sure that these abilities were only exercised in the confines of distributive laws, or functional or biological necessity, and not for the purpose of challenging existing inequality structures and striving for greater equality.

From an evolutionary perspective, two processes weaken the link between individual effort and structural inequality. On one side, individual contributions to collective action cannot be isolated from contingent preconditions and the cooperation of others. This is why concepts such as "ability" and "intelligence" have undergone such major historical changes in their cultural meaning (Gould 1981; Carson 2007) and remain highly ambiguous. On the other side, the blending of agency and contingency also makes it easier to exaggerate and embellish the role of victors in distributive disputes and to blame the victims for their fate.

Explaining culture as lived evolution does not deny the importance of personal ambition and ability, but reduces its weight. People are not shunted into social positions by inherited talent or meritocratic recruitment. The route is more circuitous. The Big Man at the top of Melanesian inequality structures seemed

> so thoroughly bourgeois, so reminiscent of the free enterprising rugged individual of our own heritage. He combines with an ostensible interest in the general welfare a more profound measure of self-interested cunning and economic calculation. His gaze, as Veblen might have put it, is fixed unswervingly to the main chance. His every public action is designed to make a competitive and invidious comparison with others, to show a standing above the masses that is the product of his own manufacture.
>
> (Sahlins 1963: 289)

But the Big Man also faced the constant risk of collapse of trust among his followers and suffered frequent ridicule and failure. Similarly, when in the early years of Athenian democracy after 561 BC, Peisistratos used charm, initiative and opportunism to trick the Athenian assembly into making him tyrant three times in a row,[7] he was just one of a long line of individuals who combined ambition and luck to advance their fortunes, no different from modern charismatic politicians and knights of the stock market.

Individual effort is merely one part of a very complex causal story (Jencks and Bartlett 1979). For every person whose achievement is celebrated in history books there are others whose crucial contributions go unnoticed. For every one who rises through personal ability there are more whose talents and abilities are blunted by social constraints. And for every competent performance in a high position there is incompetence protected by glass floors, professional immunity and golden handshakes. The reason is that it is neither possible to clearly distinguish contingent from personal contributions to past individual and collective achievements, nor to predict accurately what individuals will contribute to future results. Shifting environments can quickly turn "functional" choices into their opposites, and human imagination can easily construct causal connections between spurious events, claim credit for unearned gains or blame innocent victims for their misfortune. Lived evolution offers ample opportunity for incompetence to be rewarded and for inefficient and wasteful institutions to thrive because institutionalized secrecy, incumbency and the work of capable subordinates obscures bungling at the top. The resulting inequality creates strong incentives for beneficiaries to make such conditions last. Rather than reflecting differences in ability, inequality is likely to hinder their expression (Adkins and Vasey 2009). We would not hesitate to accept this as typical of feudal societies. Seeing it in our own inequality structures is made difficult by our closeness to them.

The same argument applies to the functions of institutions and structures. Marx already observed that inequality structures brought at least initially also some advantages to groups other than their immediate beneficiaries. The large military storage depots created by the Incas also protected local populations against harvest failures. Colonial rulers from ancient Rome to Victorian England spread new skills, roads or railways through the areas they controlled. Hierarchical management does sometimes increase the efficiency of organized action. But this neither tells us that "hierarchical institutions, which we recognize as the hallmarks of civilization, were *invented* as problem-solving tools during times of cultural strife" (Schele and Freidel 1990: 97), nor that high status is a reward for abstaining from free riding and for contributing to collective purposes (Willer 2009), nor that social differences emerge with quasi-natural force (Ridgeway et al. 2009). Even in an ideal environment of transparency, trust and cooperation where people collectively and freely choose divisions of labor which serve the common good, the resulting functional differentiation always involves an element of exclusion which can quickly and imperceptibly turn into discrimination or exploitation. Personal initiative and functional benefits are two of many causes and consequences of social inequality, but they are neither its necessary prerequisite nor its inevitable result.

Whereas an evolutionary theory of inequality puts a more modest face on the effects of individual ability, it broadens the role of individuals in choosing the social structures in which they want to live. In light of the reputation for genetic determinism acquired by Neo-Darwinist theory this may seem to be a surprising conclusion. But if we use an evolutionary paradigm which includes both the inherited and the lived part of evolution we see that our individual fate and our long-term success as a species depend to a significant degree on choices we make during our lifetime. Among these, the question how we distribute what we collectively produce is of pivotal importance.

Just as the causes that started the growth of inequality clustered in regions of opportunity, distributive choices have typical structural consequences which arise from the dilemmas inherent in trust and cooperation. Trust is the emotional essence of all sociality. It allows us to let our guard down and have confidence in others, to reach out to them in friendship, love and cooperation, and let them act on our behalf. Cooperation is equally indispensable for social life. It permits us to combine our efforts with those of others in order to do things which we could never achieve by ourselves, and it protects us from risks which could be fatal if we faced them alone. Trust and cooperation underpin a wide range of social relations, from pure altruism to fair market exchanges. Without them social life would degenerate into the corrosive mistrust of Hobbes' war of all against all.

Such benefits, however, also create the conditions for deception and defection. Trust offers others freedom from scrutiny whereas cooperation makes an advance contribution to a joint project. Both open opportunities for abuse and free rides. Recipients, knowing that their behavior is no longer closely monitored, can act contrary to our expectations or walk away with our contribution. At the same time, deception and defection, if they want to achieve more than a one-time advantage, must maintain at least the appearance of trust and preserve the value-adding effect of cooperation.

These countervailing forces place historical distributive structures on a gradient from participatory and equal to undemocratic and unequal (Douglas 2001). Trust with its back and forth of commitments engenders social relations which are participatory and democratic. Cooperation with its willingness to contribute to joint projects favors distributive structures tending towards equality. By contrast, violations of trust favor exclusion, secrecy and manipulative consensus, whereas defection aims at achieving an advantage for one side at the expense of another and encourages further self-interested behavior (Piff et al. 2012). The level of inequality in a society therefore broadly reflects the presence of trust and cooperation. The more they prevail, the more equal a society tends to be. As trust and cooperation diminish, inequality is likely to increase, and deception and defection will tend to masquerade as trust and cooperation. The consensus envisioned by Durkheim and Parsons presupposed a community of informed, free and equal partners. Only then could one assume that societies built on lies and deception would not last long. Marx, Pareto and Mosca had a more realistic view of the manipulative potential of trust-soliciting symbols and slogans.

Priorities for an Evolutionary Study of Inequality

An evolutionary view of inequality suggests three areas for further research: why and how actual inequality structures begin, what strengthens or weakens their subsequent growth, and whether there are ethical principles and practical options for alternative, more egalitarian distributions of collective achievements. The first of these requires an examination of the fine grain of distributive choices, the micro-processes where subjective preferences transform contingent physical and social environments into opportunities and risks. Because both preferences and environments are highly variable and blind, we should expect to find heterogeneous rather than universal causes at the beginning of pathways to inequality, and actual outcomes to diverge frequently from intended results. Pathways to inequality are examined in Chapter 5.

Second, the initial causes of inequality structures do not predict their subsequent course. Their long-term evolution is a historically specific, stochastic process which is continually affected by external change and subjective novelty. Processes which consolidate and maintain unequal distributions of collective achievements must therefore be examined separately from the causes with which pathways to inequality begin. The longer the path, the weaker is the link between initial causes and later consequences and between anticipated and actual outcomes. Chapter 6 examines self-reinforcing feedback and social control which can stabilize or increase inequality over time and reduce chances for alternative distributions of collective achievements.

Third, evolution is a branching, not a converging process. An evolutionary theory does not assume that past or present inequality structures are the best or the only possible ones, nor that they routinely bring the fittest or most capable individuals to the fore. Inequality can persist even if it emerged for fortuitous reasons and channels the results of collective action disproportionally to a small group of unremarkable individuals. Pharaonic rule in Egypt lasted for some 3000 years not because it made more efficient use of resources or because its ruling class had superior talent, nor because it was a necessary phase in the development of human societies. Its survival was due to conquest, ideology, and the efficient diversion of surplus to a small elite. At any point in its history Egyptian society, within its environmental and technological limits, could have organized its distributive system along different lines. Its surplus would not have been spent on pyramids, palaces and tombs, but like other societies of its time it would have developed its economy, increased its knowledge and the benefits may have gone to more of its members. Only the concentration of power and wealth prevented Egypt from taking an alternative historical path. Similarly, in today's societies such as the US, there is no compelling reason why 99 percent of American households made do with 58 cents of every dollar of income growth between 1976 and 2007, whereas the top one percent enjoyed the remaining 42 cents (Rajan 2010).

Once under way, evolving inequality structures generate powerful self-reinforcing dynamics which make them frequent and often long-lasting phenomena in human history. But reversals also occur. Just as small initial events can place societies on pathways to inequality, they can precipitate moves toward greater equality. Athenian democracy arose surrounded by autocratic societies. Christianity moved in less than a century from a persecuted belief to a state religion. Three Swiss Cantons chose rule by their citizens in the midst of feudal Europe. Luther succeeded against all odds in defying the Catholic church. Toussaint L'Ouverture's rebellion in Haiti created the first black government in the Americas, and the American and French Revolutions ushered in modern political systems.

If we assume that the division of collective achievements is determined by the fitness, ability or functional contribution of the participants, and that market mechanisms reconcile individual and collective interests, social choices are, as Spencer said, limited to adding oil to the movement of a world which can only be the way it is. If, on the other hand, we accept that lived evolution gives individuals the choice to explore and pursue alternatives to existing distributive structures, then additional questions arise. Is one person's choice not as good as another's? Why should we care how much inequality there is in a society? Why should wealth not stay in the hands of those who have it, especially if those receiving less seem to be content with their lot? Can evolutionary theory provide guidelines for a just distribution of collective achievements? These issues are explored in Chapter 7.

Notes

1 Segerstrale (2000) gives an overview of the evolutionary discussion of altruism. Wilson and Dugatkin (1992: 29, 30) cite a number of concepts in the evolutionary literature, such as "pseudo-altruism," "by-product mutualism," "quasi-altruistic selfishness" or "self-interested refusal to be spiteful" which imply that altruism is ultimately always selfish.
2 Gould 1990: 20; Basalla 1988: 3; Luhmann 1997: 436; Mokyr 2002: 218, 219; Mesoudi 2008: 250, to name just a few.
3 The following sections contain material from this article.
4 Robert Merton in his 1997 Nobel Prize lecture. The spectacular insolvency of Long Term Capital Management, the company which he and fellow winner Myron Scholes founded, began in 1998. The US Federal Reserve eventually assumed LTCM's liabilities.
5 Boulding did see one advantage in such an arrangement: "a valuable intellectual resource would be economized."

6 The real Sir Joseph was W.H. Smith, a bookseller of humble origins who had been appointed First Lord of the Admiralty by Disraeli although he did not have the requisite upper class naval background. He turned out to be one of the better tenants of the office.
7 A popular general who had gained trust through calculated generosity and promises, Peisistratos appeared before the assembly in Athens displaying (possibly self-inflicted) wounds, accused his enemies of trying to kill him, and convinced his audience to give him a bodyguard of 50 men. With their help he seized the Acropolis and installed himself as tyrant. Deposed a short time later he seized power again, this time by sending heralds announcing that the patron goddess of the city, Athena, had asked him to return. He and his supporters entered the city behind a young woman dressed as Athena, alluding to the myth of Heracles who was led to the home of the gods by Athena. The trick worked. Citizens bowed before the "goddess," and Peisistratos became tyrant of Athens again. Deposed once more he recruited a private army, defeated a small Athenian force and installed himself as tyrant for almost 20 years until his death in 528 BC. Herodotus considered the gullibility of citizens a particularly shameful chapter in Athens' history.

Bibliography

Adkins, Daniel and Stephen Vaisey. "Toward a Unified Stratification Theory: Structure, Genome, and Status across Human Societies." *Sociological Theory* 27 (2009) 2: 99–121.
Alchian, Armen A. "Uncertainty, Evolution and Economic Theory." *Journal of Political Economy* 58 (1950): 211–221.
Alford, John R. and John R. Hibbing. "The Origin of Politics: An Evolutionary Theory of Political Behavior." *Perspectives on Politics* 2 (2004) 4: 707–723.
Allen, Peter M. "Modelling Evolution and Creativity in Complex Systems." *World Futures* 34 (1992): 105–123.
Alverson, Mats and Stefan Svenigsson. "Managers Doing Leadership: The Extraordinarization of the Mundane." *Human Relations* 56 (2003) 12: 1435–1459.
Aplin, Lucy, Damien Farine, Julie Morand-Ferron, Andrew Cockburn and Alex Thornton. "Experimentally Induced Innovations Lead to Persistent Culture via Conformity in Wild Birds." *Nature* 518 (2015): 538–541.
Ariely, Daniel, Uri Gneezy, George Loewenstein and Nina Mazar, "Large Stakes and Big Mistakes." Rotman School of Management, University of Toronto. 2008. Available online at: www.rotman.utoronto.ca/newthinking/largestakes.pdf
Arthur, W. Brian. "Positive Feedbacks in the Economy." *Scientific American* February (1990): 92–99.
Arthur, W. Brian. *Increasing Returns and Path Dependence in the Economy*. Ann Arbor: University of Michigan Press, 1994.
Augustin, Patrick, Menachem Brenner and Marti G. Subrahmanyam. "Informed Options Trading Prior to M&A Announcements: Insider Trading?" May 2015. DOI: http://dx.doi.org/10.2139/ssrn.2441606
Bailey, David H., Jonathan M. Borwein, Marcos López de Prado and Qiji Jim Zhu "Pseudo-Mathematics and Financial Charlatanism: The Effects of Backtest Overfitting on Out-of-Sample Performance." *Notices of the American Mathematical Society* 61 (2014) 5: 458–471.
Baldus, Bernd. "Positivism's Twilight?" *Canadian Journal of Sociology* 15 (1990) 2: 149–163.
Baldus, Bernd. "Contingency, Novelty and Choice. Cultural Evolution as Internal Selection." *Journal for the Theory of Social Behaviour* 45 (2015) 2: 214–237.

Baldus, Bernd and Verna Tribe. "The Development of Perceptions and Evaluations of Social Inequality among Public School Children." *Canadian Review of Sociology and Anthropology* 15 (1978) 1: 50–60.

Barkow, Jerome. *Darwin, Sex, and Status*. Toronto: University of Toronto Press, 1989.

Barkow, Jerome. *Missing the Revolution. Darwinism for Social Scientists*. New York: Oxford University Press, 2006.

Barkow, Jerome, Leda Cosmides and John Tooby. *The Adapted Mind*. New York: Oxford University Press, 1992.

Baron, Robert S. "So Rights it's Wrong: Groupthink and the Ubiquitous Nature of Polarized Group Decisions." *Advances in Experimental Social Psychology* 37 (2005): 219–253.

Bartlett, Robert C. *The Making of Europe: Conquest. Colonization and Cultural Change*. Princeton: Princeton University Press, 1993.

Basalla, George. *The Evolution of Technology*. Cambridge: Cambridge University Press, 1988.

Becker, Gary and Nigel Tomes. "An Equilibrium Theory of the Distribution of Income and Intergenerational Mobility." *Journal of Political Economy* 87 (1979) 6: 1153–1189.

Blute, Marion. *Darwinian Sociocultural Evolution*. Cambridge: Cambridge University Press, 2010.

Boehm, Christopher. *Hierarchy in the Forest*. Cambridge: Harvard University Press, 1999.

Bonnie, Kristin E., Victoria Horner, Andrew Whiten and Frans de Waal. "Spread of Arbitrary Conventions among Chimpanzees: A Controlled Experiment." *Proceedings of the Royal Society B*, 27 (2007) 1608: 367–372.

Boulding, Kenneth E. *The Impact of the Social Sciences*. New Brunswick, NJ: Rutgers University Press, 1966.

Bourdieu, Pierre. *Le sens pratique*. Paris: Les Éditions de Minuit, 1980.

Bowles, Samuel and Herbert Gintis. "The Inheritance of Economic Status: Education, Class and Status." In Neil J. Smelser and Paul B. Baltes (eds) *International Encyclopedia of the Social and Behavioural Sciences*, 4132–4141. Oxford: Elsevier, 2001.

Brezina, Timothy and Kenisha Winder. "Economic Disadvantage, Status Generalization, and Negative Racial Stereotyping by White Americans." *Social Psychology Quarterly* 66 (2003) 4: 402–418.

Buck, Trevor, Alistair Bruce, Brian Main and Henry Udueni. "Long Term Incentive Plans, Executive Pay and UK Company Performance." *Journal of Management Studies* 40 (2003) 7: 1709–1727.

Bugnyar, Thomas, Stephan A. Reber and Cameron Buckner. "Ravens Attribute Visual Access to Unseen Competitors." *Nature Communications* 7 (2016): 10506. DOI: 10.1038/ncomms10506

Burris, Val. "The Academic Caste System: Prestige Hierarchies in PhD Exchange Networks." *American Sociological Review* 69 (2004) 2: 239–264.

Burt, Ronald. "Structural Holes and Good Ideas." *American Journal of Sociology* 110 (2004) 2: 349–400.

Campbell, Donald T. "Natural Selection as an Epistemological Model." In Raoul Naroll and Ronald Cohen (eds) *A Handbook of Method in Cultural Anthropology*, 51–85. Garden City: Natural History Press, 1970.

Carmichael, Lorne and W. Bentley MacLeod. "Worker Cooperation and the Ratchet Effect." *Journal of Labor Economics* 18 (2000) 1: 1–19.

Carson, John. *The Measure of Merit: Talents, Intelligence, and Inequality in the French and American Republics, 1750–1940*. Princeton: Princeton University Press, 2007.

Catalano, Ralph and Tim Bruckner. "Secondary Sex Ratios and Male Lifespan: Damaged or Culled Cohorts?" *Proceedings of the National Academy of Science* 103 (2006) 5: 1639–1643.
Cavalli-Sforza, Luigi L. and Marcus W. Feldman. *Cultural Transmission and Evolution: A Quantitative Approach*. Princeton: Princeton University Press, 1981.
Courtiol, Alexandre, Jenni E. Pettay, Markus Jokela, Anna Rotkirch and Virpi Lummaa. "Natural and Sexual Selection in a Monogamous Historical Human Population." *Proceedings of the National Academy of Sciences* 109 (2012) 21: 8044–8049.
Darwin, Charles. *Charles Darwin's Notebooks, 1826–1844*. Transcribed and edited by Paul H. Barrett, Peter J. Gautrey, Sandra Herbert, David Kohn and Sidney Smith. London and Ithaca: British Museum (Natural History) and Cornell University Press, 1987. Notebook D 135e.
Darwin, Charles. *The Origin of Species*, 6th edition. New York: New American Library, 1958 [1872].
Darwin, Charles. *The Descent of Man*. Princeton: Princeton University Press, 1981 [1871].
Davis, Kingsley and Wilbert Moore. "Some Principles of Stratification." In Reinhard Bendix and Seymour M. Lipset (eds) *Class, Status, and Power*, 47–53. New York: Free Press, 1966 [1945].
de Waal, Frans. *Chimpanzee Politics: Power and Sex among Apes*. London: Cape, 1982.
de Waal, Frans. *The Ape and the Sushi Master*. New York: Basic Books, 2001.
Dean, Lewis G., Rachel L. Kendal, Steven J. Schapiro, Bernard Thierry and Kevin N. Laland. "Identification of the Social and Cognitive Processes Underlying Human Cumulative Culture." *Science* 335 (2012) 6072: 1114–1118.
Diakonis, Persi and Frederick Mosteller. "Methods for Studying Coincidences." *Journal of the American Statistical Association* 84 (1989) 408: 853–861.
Dixon, Thomas. *The Invention of Altruism. Making Moral Meanings in Victorian Britain*. Oxford: Oxford University Press, 2008.
Douglas, Kate. "Playing Fair." *New Scientist* 169 (2001) 2281: 38–42.
Douglas, Mary and Baron Isherwood. *The World of Goods*. New York: Basic Books, 1979.
Durham, William H. *Coevolution. Genes, Culture, and Human Diversity*. Stanford: Stanford University Press, 1991.
Falk, Armin and Michael Kosfeld. "Distrust – The Hidden Cost of Control." *American Economic Review* 96 (2006) 5: 1611–1630.
Farmer, J. Doyne, Paolo Patelli and Ilija Zovko. "The Predictive Power of Zero Intelligence in Financial Markets." *Proceedings of the National Academy of Sciences* 102 (2005) 6: 2254–2259.
Fehr, Ernst and Simon Gächter. "Altruistic Punishment in Humans." *Nature* 415 (2002): 137–140.
Fehr, Ernst and Urs Fischbacher. "Third-Party Punishment and Social Norms." *Evolution and Human Behaviour* 25 (2004) 2: 63–87.
Fehr, Ernst, Helen Bernhard and Bettina Rockenbach. "Egalitarianism in Young Children." *Nature* 454 (2008) 7208: 1079–1083.
Finley, Moses. *Politics in the Ancient World*. Cambridge: Cambridge University Press, 1983.
Flannery, Kent and Joyce Marcus. *The Creation of Inequality*. Cambridge: Harvard University Press, 2012.
Fligstein, Neil. *The Transformation of Corporate Control*. Cambridge: Harvard University Press, 1990.

Freeman, James M. *Untouchable. An Indian Life History*. Stanford: Stanford University Press, 1979.
Gambetta, Diego. *Trust. Making and Breaking Cooperative Relations*. New York: Blackwell, 1988.
Garud, Raghu, Arun Kumaraswamy and Peter Karnøe. 2010. "Path Dependence or Path Creation?" *Journal of Management Studies* 47 (2010) 4: 760–774.
Gavrilets, Sergey. "On the Evolutionary Origins of the Egalitarian Syndrome." *Proceedings of the National Academy of Science* 109 (2012) 35: 14069–14074.
Ghiselin, Michael. *The Economy of Nature and the Evolution of Sex*. Berkeley: University of California Press, 1974.
Giddens, Anthony. *Modernity and Self-Identity. Self and Society in the Late Modern Age*. Stanford: Stanford University Press, 1991.
Gilens, Martin. *Affluence and Influence. Economic Inequality and Political Power in America*. Princeton: Princeton University Press, 2012.
Gintis, Herbert. "A Framework for the Unification of the Behavioral Sciences." *Behavioral and Brain Sciences* 30 (2007): 1–61.
Ginsburgh, Victor A. and Jan C. van Ours. "Expert Opinion and Compensation: Evidence from a Musical Competition." *American Economic Review* 93 (2003) 1: 289–296.
Goode, William J. *The Celebration of Heroes*. Berkeley: University of California Press, 1978.
Gould, Stephen J. *The Mismeasure of Man*. New York: W. W. Norton, 1981.
Gould, Stephen J. "Shoemaker and Morningstar." *Natural History* 99 (1990) 12: 14–20.
Griffin, Donald R. *Animal Thinking*. Cambridge, MA: Harvard University Press, 1984.
Gruber, Thibaud, Martin N. Muller, Pontus Strimling, Richard Wrangham and Klaus Zuberbühler. "Wild Chimpanzees Rely on Cultural Knowledge to Solve an Experimental Honey Acquisition Task." *Current Biology* 19 (2009) 21: 1806–1810.
Hallpike, Christopher R. *The Principles of Social Evolution*. Oxford: Clarendon Press, 1986.
Hamann, Katharina, Felix Warneken, Julia R. Greenberg and Michael Tomasello. "Collaboration Encourages Equal Sharing in Children but Not in Chimpanzees." *Nature* 476 (2011) 7360: 328–331.
Hamermesh, Daniel. *Beauty Pays*. Princeton: Princeton University Press, 2011.
Hamlin, Kiley J., Karen Wynn and Paul Bloom. "Social Evaluation by Preverbal Infants." *Nature* 450 (2007) 7169: 557–559.
Harvey, Campbell R., Yan Liu and Heqing Zhu. "…and the Cross-Section of Expected Returns." *Social Science Research Network*, February 3, 2015. Available online at: http://ssrn.com/abstract'2249314 or DOI: http://dx.doi.org/10.2139/ssrn.2249314
Henrich, Joseph, Robert Boyd, Samuel Bowles, Colin Camerer, Ernst Fehr, Herbert Gintis, Richard McElreath, Michael Alvard, Abigail Barr, Jean Ensminger, Natalie Smith Henrich, Kim Hill, Francisco Gil-White, Michael Gurven, Frank W. Marlowe, John Q. Patton and David Tracer. "'Economic Man' in Cross-Cultural Perspective: Behavioral Experiments in 15 Small-Scale Societies." *Behavioral and Brain Sciences* 28 (2005): 795–855.
Hibbing, John R. and John R. Alford. "Accepting Authoritative Decisions: Humans as Wary Cooperators." *American Journal of Political Science* 48 (2004) 1: 62–76.
Hobbes, Thomas. *De Cive*. Edited by Howard Warrender. Oxford: Clarendon Press, 1983 [1651].
Hodgson, Geoffrey M. and Thorbjørn Knudsen. *Darwin's Conjecture. The Search for General Principles of Social and Economic Evolution*. Chicago: University of Chicago Press, 2010.

Hodgson, Robert T. "An Analysis of the Concordance among 13 Wine Competitions." *Journal of Wine Economics* 4 (2009) 1: 1–9.
Hunt, Terry L. "Rethinking the Fall of Easter Island." *American Scientist* 94 (2006) 5: 412–419.
Jaeger, Mads Meier. "A Thing of Beauty is a Joy Forever? Returns to Physical Attractiveness over the Life Course." *Social Forces* 89 (2011) 3: 983–1003.
Jencks, Christopher. *Inequality: A Reassessment of the Effect of Family and School in America*. New York: Basic Books, 1972.
Jencks, Christopher and Susan Bartlett. *Who Gets Ahead? The Determinants of Economic Success in America*. New York: Basic Books, 1979.
Joas, Hans. *The Genesis of Values*. Chicago: University of Chicago Press, 2000.
Judge, Timothy A. and Daniel M. Cable. "The Effect of Physical Height on Workplace Success and Income: Preliminary Test of a Theoretical Model." *Journal of Applied Psychology* 89 (2004) 3: 428–441.
Kahlenberg, Sonya. M. and Richard W. Wrangham. "Sex Differences in Chimpanzees' Use of Sticks as Play Objects Resemble those of Children." *Current Biology* 20 (2010) 24, R1067-R1068.
Kanakogi, Yasukiro, Yuko Okumura, Yasuyuki Inoue, Michiteru Kitazaki and Shoji Itakura. "Rudimentary Sympathy in Preverbal Infants: Preference for Others in Distress." *Public Library of Science* One 8 (2013) 6: e65292.
Klofstadt, Casey A., Rindy C. Anderson and Susan Peters. "Sounds Like a Winner: Voice Pitch Influences Perception of Leadership Capacity in Both Men and Women." *Proceedings of the Royal Society* B . 279 (2012) 1738: 2698–2709.
Lachmann, Richard. "Greed and Contingency: State Fiscal Crises and Imperial Failure in Early Modern Europe." *American Journal of Sociology* 115 (2009) 1: 39–73.
Lawler, Edward J. and Jeongko Yoon. "Commitment in Exchange Relations: Test of a Theory of Relational Cohesion." *American Sociological Review* 61 (1996) 1: 89–109.
Lenormand, Thomas, Denis Roze and Francois Rousset 2008. "Stochasticity in Evolution." *Trends in Ecology and Evolution* 24 (2008) 3: 157–165.
Lenski, Gerhard E. *Power and Privilege*. New York: McGraw-Hill, 1966.
Luhmann, Niklas. *Soziologische Aufklärung. Aufsätze zur Theorie sozialer Systeme*. Opladen: Westdeutscher Verlag, 1970.
Luhmann, Niklas. *Rechtssoziologie*. Hamburg: Rowohlt, 1972.
Luhmann, Niklas. *Vertrauen*. Stuttgart: Ferdinand Enke, 1973.
Luhmann, Niklas. *Soziale Systeme: Grundriss einer allgemeinen Theorie*. Frankfurt: Suhrkamp, 1984.
Luhmann, Niklas. *Die Gesellschaft der Gesellschaft*. Frankfurt: Suhrkamp, 1997.
Luncz, Lydia V., Roger Mundry and Christophe Boesch. "Evidence for Cultural Differences between Neighboring Chimpanzee Communities." *Current Biology* 22 (2012) 10: 922–926.
Mahoney, James. "Path Dependence in Historical Sociology." *Theory and Society* 29 (2000) 4: 507–548.
MEW (Karl Marx, Friedrich Engels, *Werke*). Forty volumes, two supplementary volumes. Berlin: Dietz Verlag, 1957–1985. Vols. II and III of *Das Kapital* republished by Europäische Verlagsanstalt: Frankfurt, 1968.
Mann, Michael. *The Sources of Social Power*. Cambridge: Cambridge University Press, 1986.
Markley, Robert. "Representing Order: Natural Philosophy, Mathematics, and Theology in the Newtonian Revolution." In Katherine N. Hayles (ed.) *Chaos and Order*, 125–148. Chicago: University of Chicago Press, 1991.

Mattausch, John. "Chance and Societal Change." *The Sociological Review* 51 (2003) 4: 506–527.
Maxwell, James Clerk. *Matter and Motion*. New York: Dover, 1952 [1876].
Mayr, Ernst. *Toward a New Philosophy of Biology*. Cambridge: Harvard University Press, 1988.
McGowan, John. "Toward a Pragmatist Theory of Action." *Sociological Theory* 16 (1998) 3, 292–297.
McLean, Paul D. and John F. Padgett. "Was Florence a Perfectly Competitive Market? Transactional Evidence from the Renaissance." *Theory and Society* 26 (1997) 2/3: 209–244.
Mesoudi, Alex. "Foresight in Evolution." *Biology and Philosophy* 23 (2008) 2: 243–255.
Mesoudi, Alex, Andrew Whiten and Kevin N. Laland. "Towards a Unified Science of Cultural Evolution." *Behavioral and Brain Sciences* 29 (2006): 329–383.
Mokyr, Joel. *The Gifts of Athena*. Princeton: Princeton University Press, 2002.
Mookherjee, Dilip and Ray Debraj. "Is Equality Stable?" *American Economic Review* 92 (2002) 2: 252–259.
Moore, Wilbert E. and Melvin M. Tumin. "Some Social Functions of Ignorance." *American Sociological Review* 14 (1949) 6: 787–795.
Mullen, Ann L. *Degrees of Inequality*. Baltimore: Johns Hopkins University Press, 2010.
Nakashima, Tamiji, Koji Matsono, Masami Matsushita and Takayuki Matsushita. "Severe Lead Contamination among Children of Samurai Families in Edo Period Japan." *Journal of Archeological Science* 38 (2011) January: 23–28.
Nature Neuroscience. "A Case for Cautious Optimism." (Editorial) 13 (2010) 6: 651.
Nelson, Linden L. and Robert Kagan. "The Star-spangled Scramble." *Psychology Today* (1972) September: 53–54, 56, 90–91.
North, Douglass C. *Institutions, Institutional Change, and Economic Performance*. Cambridge: Cambridge University Press, 1990.
Ormerod, Paul. "The Impossibility of Accurate Macro-Economic Forecasting." *Economic Affairs* 17 (1997) 1: 44–49.
Ormerod, Paul and Craig Maunfield. "Localized Structure in the Temporal Evolution of Asset Prices." Paper presented to the New Approaches to Financial Economy Conference, Santa Fe, 2000.
Ormerod, Paul, Helen Johns and Laurence Smith. "Marshall's 'Trees' and the 'Global Forest': the Extinction Patterns of Capitalism's Largest Firms." *Volterra Consulting* 2001: 1–12. Available online at: www.volterra.co.uk
Pagels, Elaine H. *The Gnostic Gospels*. New York: Vintage Books, 1979.
Palmieri, Rachel, Kathleen N. Lohr, Gerald Gartlehner, Meer Viswanathan and Katherine Hartmann. "Outcome of Routine Episiotomy." *Journal of the American Medical Association* 293 (2005) 17: 2141–2148.
Payer, Lynn. *Medicine and Culture*. New York: Holt, 1996.
Penner, Rudolph G. "Dealing with Uncertain Budget Forecasts." *Public Budgeting and Finance* 22 (2002) 1: 1–18.
Pierson, Paul. "Increasing Returns, Path Dependence, and the Study of Politics." *American Political Science Review* 94 (2000) 2: 251–267.
Piff, Paul K, Daniel M. Stancato, Stéphane Côté, Rodolfo Mendoza-Denton and Dacher Keltner. "Higher Social Class Predicts Increased Unethical Behavior." *Proceedings of the National Academy of Science* 109 (2012) 11: 4086–4091.
Pinker, Steven. "The False Allure of Group Selection." *Edge* 2012. Available online at: http://edge.org/conversation/the-false-allure-of-group-selection

Pokorny, Jennifer J. and Frans B.M. de Waal. "Monkeys Recognize the Faces of Group Mates in Photographs." *Proceedings of the National Academy of Science* 106 (2009) 51: 21539–21543.
Rajan, Raghuram G. *Fault Lines: How Hidden Fractures Still Threaten the World Economy.* Princeton: Princeton University Press, 2010.
Rennenkampff, Anke. *Aktivierung und Auswirkungen geschlechtsstereotyper Wahrnehmung von Führungskompetenz im Bewerbungskontext.* Doctoral Dissertation, University of Mannheim, Germany, 2005.
Richerson, Peter J. and Robert Boyd. "Complex Societies: the Evolutionary Origins of a Crude Superorganism." *Human Nature* 10 (1999) 3: 253–289.
Ridgeway, Cecilia L., Yan E. Li, Kristan G. Erickson, Kristen Backor and Justine E. Tinkler. "How Easily Does a Social Difference Become a Status Distinction? Gender Matters." *American Sociological Review* 74 (2009) 1: 44–62.
Ridley, Matt. *The Origins of Virtue.* Harmondsworth: Penguin, 1996.
Roos, Patrick, Michele Gelfand, Dana Nau and Ryan Carr. "High Strength-of-Ties and Low Mobility Enable the Evolution of Third-party Punishment." *Proceedings of the Royal Society B.* 281 (2014) 1776: 20132661.
Russon, Anne and Kristin Andrews. "Orangutan Pantomime: Elaborating the Message." *Biology Letters* 7 (2011) 4: 627–630.
Sabel, Charles and Jonathan Zeitlin. "Historical Alternatives to Mass Production: Politics, Markets and Technology in Nineteenth Century Industrialization." *Past and Present* 108 (1985) August: 133–176.
Sahlins, Marshall D. 1963. "Poor Man, Rich Man, Big Man, Chief: Political Types in Melanesia and Polynesia." *Comparative Studies in Society and History* 5 (1963) 3: 285–303.
Sapolsky, Robert and Lisa J. Share. "A Pacific Culture Among Wild Baboons: Its Emergence and Transmission." *Public Library of Science Biology* 2 (2004) 4: 0534–0541.
Sauter, Disa A., Frank Eisner, Paul Ekman and Sophie Scott. "Cross-cultural Recognition of Basic Emotions through Nonverbal Emotional Vocalizations." *Proceedings of the National Academy of Science* 107 (2010) 6: 2408–2412.
Schele, Linda and David Freidel. *A Forest of Kings.* New York: William Morrow, 1990.
Segerstrale, Ullica. *Defenders of the Truth.* Oxford: Oxford University Press, 2000.
Sierminska, Eva. "Does it Pay to be Beautiful?" *IZA World of Labor* 2015: 161. DOI: 10.15185/izawol.161.
Skocpol, Theda. *Protecting Soldiers and Mothers: The Political Origins of Social Policy in the United States.* Cambridge, MA: Belknap Press, 1992.
Skocpol, Theda. *Diminished Democracy.* Norman: University of Oklahoma Press, 2003.
Smith, Craig E., Peter R. Blake and Paul L. Harris. "I Should but I Won't: Why Young Children Endorse Norms of Fair Sharing but Do Not Follow Them." *Public Library of Science One* 8 (2013) 3: e59510.
Smith, Mike. "Changing Sociological Perspectives on Chance." *Sociology* 27 (1993) 3: 513–531.
Soares, Joseph A. *The Power of Privilege: Yale and America's Elite Colleges.* Palo Alto: Stanford University Press, 2007.
Sober, Elliott and David S. Wilson. *Unto Others. The Evolution and Psychology of Unselfish Behaviour.* Cambridge: Harvard University Press, 1998.
Sommerfeld, Ralf D., Hans-Jürgen Krambeck, Dirk Semmann and Manfred Milinski. "Gossip as an Alternative for Direct Observation in Games of Indirect Reciprocity." *Proceedings of the National Academy of Science* 104 (2007) 44: 17435–17440.
Sorensen, Aage B. "The Structural Basis of Stratification." *American Journal of Sociology* 101 (1996) 5: 1333–1365.

Stein, Mark. "Unbounded Irrationality: Risk and Organizational Narcissism at Long Term Capital Management." *Human Relations* 56 (2003) 5: 523–540.

Steinbeis, Nikolaus, Boris C. Bernhardt and Tania Singer. "Impulse Control and Underlying Functions of the Left DLPFC Mediate Age-Related and Age-Independent Individual Differences in Strategic Social Behavior." *Neuron* 73 (2012) 5: 1040–1051.

Streek, Wolfgang. *Social Institutions and Economic Performance*. Newbury Park: Sage, 1992.

Streek, Wolfgang and Kathleen Thelen (eds). *Beyond Continuity: Institutional Change in Advanced Political Economies*. Cary: Oxford University Press, 2005.

Sutton, John R. *Law and Society. Origins, Interactions and Change*. Thousand Oaks: Pine Forge Press, 2001.

Svensson, Eric I. "Understanding the Egalitarian Revolution in Human Social Evolution." *Trends in Ecology and Evolution* 24 (2009) 5: 233–235.

Swami, Viren, Flora Chan, Vivien Wong, Adrian Furnham and Martin Tovée. "Weight-based Discrimination in Occupational Hiring and Helping Behavior." *Journal of Applied Social Psychology* 38 (2008) 4: 968–981.

Tacitus, Publius Cornelius. *Germania*. Stuttgart: Reclam Verlag, 1956 [approximately AD 98].

Tainter, Joseph A. *The Collapse of Complex Societies*. Cambridge: Cambridge University Press, 1988.

Taylor, Alex H., Gavin R. Hunt and Russell D. Gray. "Complex Cognition and Behavioural Innovation in New Caledonian Crows." *Proceedings of the Royal Society B*. 277 (2010) 1649: 2637–2643.

Tervo, Dougal G.R., Mikhail Proskurin, Maxim Manakov, Mayank Kabra, Allison Vollmer, Kristin Branson and Alla Y. Karpova. "Behavioral Variability through Stochastic Choice and Its Gating by Anterior Cingulate Cortex." *Cell* 159 (2014) 1: 21–32.

Thelen, Kathleen. "Historical Institutionalism in Comparative Politics." *American Review of Political Science* 93 (1999) 2: 369–404.

Thornton, Alex, Jamie Samson and Tim Clutton-Brock. "Multi-Generational Persistence of Traditions in Neighboring Meerkat Groups." *Proceedings of the Royal Society B* 277 (2010) 1700: 3623–3629.

Thurow, Lester. *Generating Inequality*. New York: Basic Books, 1975.

Tjosvold, Dean, Yu Zi-you and Hui Chun. "Team Learning from Mistakes: The Contribution of Cooperative Goals and Problem-Solving." *Journal of Management Studies* 41 (2004) 7: 1223–1245.

Todorov, Alexander, Anesu Mandisodza, Amir Goren, and Crystal Hall. "Inferences of Competence from Faces Predict Election Outcomes." *Science* 308 (2005) 5728: 1623–1626.

Uzzi, Brian. "The Sources and Consequences of Embeddedness for the Economic Performance of Organizations: The Network Effect." *American Sociological Review* 61 (1996) 4: 674–699.

Vaish, Amrisha, Malinda Carpenter and Michael Tomasello. "Young Children Selectively Avoid Helping People with Harmful Intentions." *Child Development* 81 (2010) 6: 1661–1669.

Vergne, Jean-Philippe and Rodolphe Durand. "The Missing Link between the Theory and Empirics of Path Dependence: Conceptual Clarification, Testability Issue, and Methodological Implications." *Journal of Management Studies* 47 (2010) 4: 736–759.

Warneken, Felix and Michael Tomasello. "Altruistic Helping in Human Infants and Young Chimpanzees." *Science* 311 (2006) 5765: 1301–1303.

Warneken, Felix. "Young Children Proactively Remedy Unnoticed Accidents." *Cognition* 126 (2013) 1: 101–108.
Weber, Max. *Soziologie, weltgeschichtliche Analysen, Politik.* Edited by Eduard Baumgarten. Stuttgart: Alfred Kröner Verlag, 1968.
Weeden, Kim A. "Why Some Occupations Pay More than Others? Social Closure and Earnings Inequality in the United States." *American Journal of Sociology* 108 (2002) 1: 55–102.
Willer, Robb. "Groups Reward Individual Sacrifice: The Status Solution to the Collective Action Problem." *American Sociological Review* 74 (2009) 1: 23–43.
Williams, George C. *Adaptation and Selection.* Princeton: Princeton University Press, 1966.
Wilson, David and Lee Dugatkin. "Altruism: Contemporary Debates." In Evelyn Fox Keller and Elisabeth A. Lloyd (eds) *Keywords in Evolutionary Biology*, 29–33. Cambridge: Harvard University Press, 1992.
Wilson, Edward O. *Sociobiology.* Cambridge: Harvard University Press, 1975.
Wilson, Edward O. *The Conquest of the Earth.* New York: Liveright Publishers, 2012.
Wright, Ronald. *A Short History of Progress.* Toronto: Anansi, 2004.
Yamamoto, Shinya, Tatyana Humle and Masayuki Tanaka. "Chimpanzees' Flexible Targeted Helping Based on an Understanding of Conspecifics' Goals." *Proceedings of the National Academy of Science* 109 (2012) 9: 3588–3592.
Zentner, Marcel R. and Jerome Kagan. "Perception of Music by Infants." *Nature* 383 (1996) 6595: 29.

5 Variation
Pathways to Inequality

Most theories of inequality assumed that some form of equality was a common feature of the earliest human "state of nature." Agreement ended there. For authors like Hobbes, equality was part of a primitive existence when "the life of man (was) solitary, poor, nasty, brutish and short." Inequality, whether as "a common Power to keep (members of a society) in awe" (Hobbes 1991: 89, 88) or as a set of differential rewards which spurred self-interest, was the tool by which humanity dug itself out of this hole.

By contrast, for Rousseau, Marx, Engels or Herder, early societies lived a life of "childlike simplicity" without coercion or poverty where "all are equal and free – the women included" (Engels 1972: 159). They shared the proceeds of their work and lived in balance with nature. It was all downhill from there. The creation of private property ushered in the decline of equality and freedom, and modern capitalist markets finished them off. The lost paradise was not easily recovered. Rousseau, like Thomas Jefferson, dreamt of a return to a happy, harmonious and equal state in small communities of agrarian producers where everyone received the same necessities of life, and where popular assemblies prevented the usurpation of power by a central government. For Marx and Engels, equality could only be regained after societies went through the purgatory of successive class struggles.

The ideological divisions continue,[1] but it is now widely accepted that hunting and foraging was the common way of life of human social groups for perhaps three million years prior to the advent of agriculture some 10,000 years ago. Hunter-gatherers were not simple and homogeneous. They formed culturally and socially complex societies, built large ceremonial centers (Curry 2008), lived in widely differing habitats and adapted to them with sophisticated resource-gathering techniques. They were neither "harmless people" nor the "original affluent society" (Sahlins 1972). Differences in rank and possessions, conflict, violence and slavery were not unknown to hunter-gatherers (Suttles 1968; Ames 1995; Kelly 1995). And whereas those who lived in areas with diverse year-round resources could obtain the necessities of life with little effort, others frequently experienced hunger and starvation (Burch and Ellana 1994). Such cultural variations occurred around common traits. In most hunter-gatherer societies economic production was cooperative, and their distribution systems were based on various forms of sharing. Their political and social structures were decentralized and relatively egalitarian. Individual authority tended to be weak, and long-term accumulations of wealth were rare. Distributive and political egalitarianism characterized the arctic Innu and the Kung of Botswana, the North American Iroquois and African "tribes without rulers."

Cooperation occurred in tasks such as hunting large game, driving animals into nets or traps, gathering edible plants, constructing shelters and sharing information. An observer who witnessed such a project in the Kalahari Desert in 1851 described the scale such cooperation could reach:

> We passed a magnificent set of pitfalls which the Bushmen who live about these hills had made. The whole breadth of the valley was staked and bushed across. At intervals the fence was broken, and (here) deep pitfalls were made. The strength and size of timber that was used gave me a great idea of the Bushman industry, for every tree had to be burnt down and carried away from the hills, and yet the scale of the undertaking would have excited astonishment in far more advanced nations. When a herd of animals was seen among the hills, the Bushmen drove them through the valley up to the fence; this was too high for them to jump, so that they were obliged to make for the gaps, and there tumbled into the pitfalls.
> (Cited in Jordaan 1975: 154)

Cooperation took different forms. Generalized reciprocity distributed the results of hunting and foraging among members of a community regardless of whether they participated in food-producing activities or not. Balanced reciprocity involved a more careful calculation of equivalence: for each contribution a commensurate or "fair" return was expected within a set time (Sahlins 1972: 194, 195). Sahlins distinguished such cooperative interactions from negative reciprocity, "the attempt to get something for nothing with impunity" (Sahlins 1972: 195), or at least to receive returns which were greater than one's own contribution. Here, the predominant motive was the desire to maximize one's own utility at another's expense.

Generalized reciprocity could consist of immediate distribution after foraging or hunting expeditions. No appreciable surplus was generated. The results of foraging were consumed as they came in. The roles of producer and consumer were interchangeable. Work parties could be organized or sporadic, have the same or different members, involve few or many people, and give men and women the same or different tasks. Alternatively, food could be centrally stored to be redistributed in times of need or on special occasions such as the potlatches of the American and Canadian northwest coasts or the *cargo* system of Meso-America. Storage often used sophisticated technology to preserve seasonal food such as acorns or salmon, or the herding and fattening of animals such as pigs. Whether immediately shared or stored, food was considered a common resource although those who hunted or gathered, as well as their families, often had first access.

> Not only do families pool the day's production, but the entire camp – residents and visitors alike – shares equally in the total quantity of food available. The evening meal of any one family is made up of portions of

144 *Variation*

> food from the supplies of each of the other families resident. Foodstuffs are distributed raw or are prepared by the collector and then distributed. There is a constant flow of nuts, berries, roots, and melons from one family fireplace to another until each person has an equitable portion. The following morning a different combination of foragers moves out of the camp and, when they return later in the day, the distribution is repeated.
>
> (Lee 1969: 58, 59)

Cooperative production and reciprocal distribution were accompanied by weak authority structures. Decisions tended to be made collectively, and social control processes curtailed self-interested behavior such as concealing the fruits of hunting or gathering for one's own benefit. Turnbull's description of the *Mbuti* gives a picture of life in a resource-rich rainforest environment:

> There was a confusing, seductive informality about everything they did. Whether it was a birth, a wedding, or a funeral ... there was always an unexpectedly casual, almost carefree attitude.... Between men and women there was ... a certain degree of specialization, but little that could be called exclusive. There were no chiefs. Nor formal councils. In each aspect of life there might be one or two men or women who were more prominent than others, but usually for good practical reasons. This showed up most clearly of all in the settling of disputes. There was no judge, no jury, no court.... Each dispute was settled as it arose, according to its nature.
>
> (Turnbull 1962: 110)

Positions of authority, such as that of headman or chief, could be filled by rotation, reputation or inheritance, but carried only limited power, were easily challenged, and offered few opportunities for gaining permanent control of power or resources. Chiefs were essentially spokespersons and coordinators. They consulted but did not give orders or impose their will. Tacitus observed the often irritating informality of decision-making in Roman Germany: tribesmen came to their monthly meetings as they pleased. On the set night, only a few might show up. As a result, a second or even third day passed without decision. When all were assembled, carrying their arms, chiefs were allowed to speak, but more to suggest than to command. "If they disliked a proposal, the assembly rejected it by grumbling; but if it found approval they banged their spears together" (Tacitus 1956: 12, 13). Similarly, North American Iroquois

> rejected all ... forms of domination as a basis for their social organization. Violence and public exhibitions of authoritarian behavior were regarded as illegitimate and disruptive of the social fabric. Leaders had to win public approval by exhibiting self-restraint, wisdom, and generosity. The latter requirement linked political authority to redistribution.
>
> (Trigger 1990: 135)

Chiefs often administered staple goods and goods acquired through trade or gifts, but social control curtailed the potential for abuse of trust. Ungenerous individuals quickly lost their status, and stingy chiefs became the target of gossip and were accused of endangering the health of the community. "While chiefs and their lineages could cultivate influence by means of their generosity, public opinion ... effectively curbed the abuse of power and defended the sharing ethic that was fundamental to Iroquoian culture" (Trigger 1990: 136, 139).

Although recent research has provided a more accurate picture of the productive, distributive and political structures of early societies, it stopped short of reexamining the causes and consequences of such structures. Here older, more simplistic assumptions still prevailed. First, early social structures, whether egalitarian or hierarchical, were almost universally attributed to uniform causes, ranging from single "prime movers" such as population growth (Binford 1968; Harris 1968), resource depletion (Harris 1977) or innovations such as herding, agriculture or irrigation, to as many as seven "critical factors" (Chang 1983: 107). Hunter-gatherer egalitarianism was seen as a specialized survival strategy in marginal environments (Lee and DeVore 1968; Harris 1979; Winterhalder 1986). Finely tuned optimal foraging strategies limited wants and reduced demands on the environment (Bettinger 1991: 83–111), long lactation controlled population numbers, potlatches maintained the resource-population balance (Piddocke 1965), and meat sharing limited sporadic fluctuations in protein intake (Kelly 1995). Alternatively, hunter-gatherer egalitarianism merely expressed "reverse dominance," a variant of a more "universal drive to dominance" which suppressed leaders' drift into despotism (Hayden 1995: 24; Boehm 1999).

Second, these highly specialized adaptations were assumed to trap hunter-gatherers in a life of stagnation and low productivity. Their mobile lifestyle, their discontinuous and sporadic work and their primitive technology limited opportunities for accumulating wealth (Woodburn 1982; Lenski and Lenski 1982: 122). Their egalitarian structures survived only by suppressing "significant genetic limits to humans' ability to sacrifice personal interest for the common good" because "whenever personal acquisitiveness is not effectively controlled by public opinion it prevails over cultural conventions" (Trigger 2003: 680). Cooperative, egalitarian societies were a terminal social type, unable to overcome their inherent limits. When they reached thresholds of environmental or population change they had to adopt hierarchical forms of organization.

> The Egyptians appear to have responded in precisely similar terms as did their Sumerian contemporaries when faced with the social pressure arising from sudden population growth. They seem to have devised an exactly similar solution, the development of elites and hierarchies which came to personify, as it were, the stability of society. Only in detail did they differ; in Sumer the priesthood was first of all the repository of power to be eventually replaced by Kings.... In Egypt they adopted the far more inspired concept of the divine King.
>
> (Rice 1990: 83, 84)

Once established, inequality developed along a directed, step-wise path. Egalitarian societies adopted more efficient rank-based and eventually fully stratified structures which could better manage complex collective efforts such as irrigation, agriculture and defense. The process culminated in state societies which formalized "basic principles of organization" such as hierarchy and private property (Fried 1967).[2]

Widely different reasons were given for the universal need for hierarchies. They encouraged "intensification by conspicuously rewarding those who work harder than others" (Harris 1977: 103). Elites were needed to manage population pressure (Keeley 1988), material (Hayden 1995) or symbolic resources (Cohen 1981). They administered agriculture and irrigation, invested wealth on behalf of their community, distributed basic staples and trade goods (Trigger 2003: 666) and served as military leaders who solved internal conflict by imposing a "queuing system" (Carneiro 1970, 1977) or by providing protection against outsiders (Webster 1975). They built palaces and pyramids to strengthen social solidarity or to waste resources in order to retard population growth (Dunnel cited in Wenke 1999: 368). Elites were even credited with helping people through the psychological trauma of losing their egalitarian institutions. Maya elites responded to this crisis "by adapting an ideology to fit actual social experience. They asserted through myth and symbol that differential social ranking and a ruling elite are the natural order of existence ordained by the gods" (Schele and Miller 1986: 106, 107). Elites were rewarded for their services with greater shares of resources (Van den Berghe 1974; Hayden 1995) or more mating opportunities (Betzig 1986) than ordinary people.

Third, the emergence of hierarchies was not a matter of choice. Just as "political-economic egalitarianism is (a) theoretically predictable structural consequence of the hunter-gatherer infrastructure" (Harris 1979: 81), inequality simply could not be avoided. So obvious were its benefits that rank, stratified and state societies rose "in the same quiet way and were institutionally fully present before anyone fumbled for a word by which to designate them" (Fried 1967: 226, 183). Function begot hierarchy:

> The ubiquity of patterns of elite art, monumental architecture, and refined, upper class lifestyles suggest that they fulfilled significant functions that were necessary for the operation of early civilizations, providing symbols that structured identity, promoted social stability, and gave meaning to life. From a vast range of possibilities, they created coherent cultural patterns, goals, and aspirations for people to follow ... (and) provided meaning to what people did in what would otherwise have been a chaotic situation.
> (Trigger 2003: 658, 659)

The possibility that hierarchies invented functions to legitimate their privileges was dismissed as "particularities" (Steward 1955) or as "stylistic" cultural noise (Dunnell 1978). Neither the interests of elites nor subordinates could alter the inevitable evolution of hierarchies.

Early Societies Revisited

These theoretical simplifications contrast with the empirical complexity of egalitarian societies. They foraged, farmed and herded animals, lived in resource-rich temperate coasts and tropical forests or in the hostile surroundings of the circumpolar regions or the deserts of Africa, Australia, Asia and the Americas. They were peaceful and war-loving (Kelly 1995), sedentary and nomadic, formed small communities and large "tribal republics" which created networks of cooperating non-relatives across wide areas (Moore 1992; Flannery and Marcus 2012: 27). Similarly, hierarchical structures emerged at widely different levels of productive technology (Earle 1997: 29), group size and population density (Feinman 1995: 260; Earle 1997: 33, 45, 93).

Nor did egalitarian structures invariably make way for inequality. Mixed types were common. Chiefs on the American Northwest coast could command slave labor but had to "cajole, manipulate, and wheedle their household into doing what they ... wanted them to do" (Ames 1995: 180). Pueblo societies in the American southwest allowed talented individuals to rise to positions of respect but also maintained safeguards that prevented permanent inequality. Such balanced social structures endured for long periods of time (Flannery and Marcus 2012: 160, 183). Some societies oscillated between equality and inequality, periodically overthrowing inequality and returning to more egalitarian ways of life (Flannery and Marcus 2012: 159, 191–197). Egalitarian structures proved remarkably adaptable and robust, able to manage successfully major ecological challenges. Following mortuary remains of two lineages identified by genetic markers over 20 successive generations on a site in Thailand occupied between 2000 and 500 BC, Higham and Thosarat (1994) showed that egalitarian social structures endured through periods of significant change such as the shift from fishing to the cultivation of rice. Over a period of 500 years individual grave goods did not vary significantly. Fortunes rose and fell over two or three successive generations, suggesting that status differences were due to personal reputation rather than inherited right (Higham and Thosarat 1994: 64). This pattern of fluctuating, minor social differences gave way to hierarchical organization only around 500 BC with the introduction of iron ore smelting. Then, elites emerged not as inventors or functional managers, but because they gained control of a new technology which consolidated their power.

The need for hierarchical management of complex tasks has been routinely overestimated. Sophisticated collective undertakings, from the construction of iron-age causeways (Coles 1989) to the administration of large irrigation systems or the construction of megalithic monuments, were well within the purview of cooperative work (Earle 1997: 78, 166; Demarest 2000: 286). The large carved stone structures of Göbleki Tepe in Turkey dating back to at least 9000 BC were erected by hunter-gatherers whose religious practices and later permanent settlements predated the invention of agriculture (Schmidt 2006). Nor did people readily seize opportunities for inequality. The Iroquois retained an egalitarian structure almost a thousand years after the adoption of agriculture, and 600 years after beginning a sedentary way of life (Trigger 1990: 124). In northern Europe, farming techniques were known as early as 4500 BC, but were not adopted until about 3000 BC, and in parts of Eastern Europe even later. Instead, food supplies were increased through improved hunting and gathering technologies (Zvelebil 1986). When hierarchy did emerge it tended to follow rather than to initiate productive improvements (Gunawardana 1981). Instead of acting as "munificent squires and managers of the common wealth," elites exploited the wealth of others (Gilman 1995: 237). Where they were involved in production or trade it was for the purpose of constructing legitimating monuments or acquiring prestige goods. Their use for conspicuous display and status competition brought not only no direct local economic benefits (Demarest 2000: 291) but could cause severe social and ecological harm (Diamond 2005).

Finally, there is abundant evidence that both egalitarian and unequal social structures involved careful deliberation and active participation.

> Inequality is not something that appears spontaneously once population has increased, or agriculture has produced a surplus, or people have accumulated lots of shells and pigs. Inequality is orchestrated. At the same time, it is not enough for one segment of society to demand privileges for itself and its heirs. Would-be nobles need leverage, an advantage of some kind, or their privileges will be taken back by the rest of society.
>
> (Flannery and Marcus 2012: 206)

Just as people defended their egalitarian structures,

> political elites consciously and strategically employ specialization and exchange to create and maintain social inequity, strengthen political coalitions, and fund new institutions of control, often in the face of substantial opposition from those whose well-being is reduced by such actions.
>
> (Brumfiel and Earle 1987: 3)

Structure and Opportunity: The Micro-Sociology of Distributive Change

An evolutionary approach expects that "cultural and environmental contexts are so variable, and the combinations of forces and circumstances so multifarious and uncertain as to render the search for (single or ultimate causes) not only futile but unnecessarily constraining" (Lewis 1981: 204). Egalitarian and hierarchical structures are not types but processes. Instead of the wholesale replacement of one by the other and the unequivocal acceptance of the result by the participants, we would expect them to evolve, change and disappear, be accepted or contested, and take an irregular historical course.

Evolutionary processes always combine external and impersonal factors with human innovation and selection. Considering only external causes would

> deny any possibility of developing a truly evolutionary theory of *cultural process* in which *ideas and the motives of individuals* – the most distinctive

part of the thing we call culture – have any active part, or in which selection can play a definable role akin to that which it has in the natural sciences.

(Bettinger 1991: 219)

Understanding the evolution of inequality must begin with the micro-processes which transform social and physical environments into individual perceptions and choices. Instead of assuming that elites inevitably drift into power the question is "what allows aspiring leaders to be successful in one situation but fail utterly in another?" (Earle 1997: 2).

Egalitarian structures gain their support from two widely understood advantages of reciprocal sharing. One is the efficiency-multiplying effect of cooperation which is the basis of all divisions of labor. Second, pooling and mutual aid create an insurance against hard times. Injury can debilitate an individual, bad luck in hunting and foraging can threaten the survival of a family, a crop failure can lead to collective famine. Generalized reciprocity reduces that risk for the individual. Central storage and delayed redistribution reduce it for the group. Both forms of reciprocity can also even out natural differences of gender and age in the use of resources (Dallos 2010: 220).

Members of early egalitarian societies knew their vulnerability to uncertain environments and appreciated the advantages of cooperation (Boehm 1999: 192). Willingness to share one's own resources with others and to oppose bossiness and aggression were important norms of all egalitarian societies and were actively defended. The attitude of East African pastoralists

> towards any authority that would coerce them is one of touchiness, pride, and reckless disobedience. Each determines to go his own way as much as possible, has a hatred of submission, and is ready to defend himself and his property from the inroads of others.
>
> (Butt cited in Boehm 1999: 105)

Whereas elders or chiefs had to avoid carefully any appearance of self-aggrandizement, leadership also offered opportunities for deception and defection. Sharing and reciprocity had many nuances and interpretations. Turnbull observed that when the hunt returned to a *Mbuti* camp, men and women would sometimes use the general confusion to conceal more than their share of meat. Cheating in favor of one's family overcame loyalty to band rules (Turnbull 1965: 120). Norms of distribution were thus always subject to ambiguity.

Gregor's (1977) study of Mehinaku, a small village on a tributary of the Amazon, provides an intimate picture of the tension between collective and self-interest. Built along a wide central path with houses and porches oriented towards a public space, and surrounded by high rain forest, the village formed "a theatre in the round" with "splendid acoustics and few obstructed seats" (Gregor 1977: 64, 33). In this visible area people acted out the rituals which observed the village's norms. Here the results of slash and burn agriculture, hunting and fishing were demonstratively shared in accordance with standards of generalized reciprocity. Polite greetings and amiable conversation were exchanged, decorum in appearance was maintained, matrimonial harmony was put on display and conspicuous generosity was shown by lending valuable possessions such as body pigments or necklaces to less prosperous neighbors. But the village was also surrounded by networks of forest paths and a patchwork of gardens. On this backstage a more complex, informal social life took place which often violated official rules of conduct. Trails were used to take produce or fish surreptitiously to one's house without sharing. The relaxed attitude of the Mehinaku community to property facilitated theft from gardens or houses, often under the cover of darkness. Extramarital affairs were also conducted in this area. The same sanctions and rules which insured the stability of Mehinaku society also offered opportunities for innovative and potentially deviant cultural interpretations.

In stable egalitarian systems, social control measures – mediation, criticism and ridicule, expulsion, deposition or desertion of leaders, and in more extreme cases violence or assassination – prevent such challenges from endangering the normative or structural status quo. Turnbull (1962) describes some examples of unsuccessful deviance among the *Mbuti*. A cheater who set up nets in front of the communal ones was humiliated and forced to surrender the illegal catch. An incestuous affair with a cousin led to the culprit being chased into the surrounding forest while his hut was burned. A thief was beaten and ostracized by his family. In all cases the offenders returned to the village after a few days and the offense was forgotten.

No social norm and no distributive convention is so well defined or so carefully enforced that it will not sooner or later be questioned or opposed, whether by intent, error or a novel interpretation. Innovation and deviance are close cousins, and it is impossible to predict when they occur, how many adherents they acquire, and what their consequences will be. We can, however, look for sensitive or weak areas in the social fabric of societies where inequality is particularly likely to take root, and identify exploitative strategies which are particularly likely to succeed.

Starting Processes: Dynamics of Change

Parasitism is common in nature. It is an efficient way of acquiring resources: instead of investing time and energy in producing food, organisms can find others who have made such investments and can exploit them at lower cost (Machalek 1995, 1996). Human cultural selection offers much greater potential for deception and defection. Early egalitarian societies show typical regions of opportunity where inequality recurrently enters cooperative social networks. Whether and where it does, however, remains a matter of probability. How probability can be converted into inequality is shown by a study of human sacrifice and inequality in 93 traditional Austronesian societies (Watts et al. 2016). On its own, human sacrifice in egalitarian societies did not lead to inequality. But it created opportunities for priests and chiefs to display their power and instil fear of opposing their authority. Once these were discovered, inequality and human sacrifice coevolved. Instigators were now typically people of high status, while victims came from lower classes. Ritual human sacrifice became a tool of social control which stabilized social inequality and protected it against reversals.

Cryptic and Deceptive Processes

Game theory suggests that anonymity creates opportunities for defection from cooperative relations. Resources can be diverted from cooperators to exploiters by stealth or by deliberate concealment. Prehistoric houses sometimes reveal efforts to conceal grain in cells or storage pits, allowing extended families to live on the ground floor confident that their neighbors did not know what was stored below (Flannery and Marcus 2012: 137, 155). Feudal rulers hid the reduced silver content of newly minted coins by burying them in manure to make them look old and authentic. Secrecy remains essential to modern financial fraud, internet scams, white collar crime, insider trading or tax evasion. Confidence-abusing crimes often involve a systematically planned string of deceptions. Perpetrators may pose as legitimate and trustworthy figures who request an advance and promise high returns. Once victims have lost their investment, the con crime may be terminated through additional deceptions designed to "cool the mark out" and discourage them from informing the police (Goffman 1952). Protective, retaliatory or counter-exploitative reactions are thus avoided. Goebbels, the mastermind of Nazi propaganda, used the same principle in political deception.

> That is the secret of propaganda: to permeate the person it aims to grasp, without his even knowing that he is being permeated. *Of course* propaganda has a purpose, but the purpose must be concealed with such cleverness and virtuosity that the person on whom this purpose is to be carried out doesn't notice it at all.
>
> (Cited in Evans 2005: 127)

The recipe has remained a staple of modern political manipulation: preambles and principles accompanying legislation often invoke common-good values as a means to encourage public acceptance of laws whose actual consequences contradict their declared intent (Edelman 1971, 2001).

Caging and Coercion

Coercion and caging succeed where exploiters gain access to resources which allow them to change or revoke the terms of cooperation unilaterally, or where social, economic or geographical boundaries prevent cooperators from evading exploitation. Warfare, perhaps the oldest historical form of coercion, was the root of the "great discovery (that) men as well as animals can be domesticated. Instead of killing a defeated enemy, he might be enslaved; in return for his life he could be made to work" (Childe 1936: 134). Offensive or protective military power, initially voluntarily bestowed upon existing kinship or redistributive offices in order to protect people, land or herds against enemies, offered ready opportunities for the centralization of coercive power. Communities were particularly likely to surrender collective power to military leaders in times of crisis and external threat (Earle 1997: 49). Although coercion could lead to quick returns, it was also risky and vulnerable to competition. Hawaiian chiefs

> rarely died in bed; they were killed in battles of rebellion and conquest or were assassinated by their close affiliates.... Rebellion, betrayal, and intrigue fill the Icelandic sagas, the narratives of the Hawaiian lineages, and the accounts of Andean lords. While leaders depend on their warriors to extend political power, they must always be on the lookout for treachery. Ultimately warrior might is a destabilizing and divisive power in institutions of leadership; it is only effective as long as it can be reined in and directed strategically.
>
> (Earle 1997: 8)

Caging (Carneiro 1970, 1977) intensifies the effects of coercion. Environmental or social circumscription by deserts, mountains or hostile powers blocks escape routes for victims. Gilman (1981) suggests that inequality in bronze-age Europe arose first in areas of capital-intensive production such as irrigation, plough agriculture or offshore fishery, not because such technologies required hierarchical management but because long-term capital investment in irrigation canals, forest clearance, slow-growing vines or olive trees and large boats created attractive targets for coercive takeovers or protection rackets. These could be avoided only at the cost of abandoning the result of years of hard work. Submission to extortion in exchange for a guarantee of "security" was therefore the likely outcome. Mair (1977) describes a similar process among East African cattle herders: as herds and surplus animals increased, herders became increasingly vulnerable to outside raiders who offered protection in return for payments.

Inversion

Inversion redefines existing cooperative practices in a way which turns their original function into its opposite. It is usually gradual and at least initially imperceptible. Its early stages may be unintentional, and inverted structures can maintain the appearance of serving common interests long after they have become exploitative. Max Weber suggested that, historically, property rights arose from the appropriation of centrally administered common goods (Weber 1968: 66). Initially common and public positions such as priestly or judicial offices or the administration of common land or food stored by family heads or chiefs can become vulnerable to the incumbents' pursuit of material and political advantage. The career of the Melanesian Big Man usually began with excessive generosity which impoverished the giver but also built up a reservoir of trust and obligations which, under favorable conditions such as weak social control, inverted existing cultural norms of reciprocity in order to accumulate personal prestige and attract followers tied to the giver by loyalty and obligation. Factions were fragile and had to be continuously cultivated and renewed, lest followers shifted their allegiances to someone else (Sahlins 1963: 256). But some Melanesian Big Men were able to take a crucial next step. "Eating the big-man's renown" by belonging to his faction was now considered sufficient reward, freeing the Big Man from actual payments to his followers. The benefits the Big Man provided for his faction now became immaterial and symbolic, a major step towards greater exploitation and increased social distance between Big Man and faction. In Polynesia, this evolutionary path culminated in the emergence of the hereditary Hawaiian chief whose large court and standing army required large payments from commoners who, in return, were allowed to watch

> lavish rituals meant to impress; transcendent ecstatic initiations meant to emotionally bond members to a group ... sumptuous displays of wealth and economic power involving boastful consumption; the creation of labor-intensive art and jewelry; construction of impressive buildings or commemorative monuments; and the conspicuous use of food and costly materials in important marriages, alliances, burials, and assumptions of office.
> (Hayden 1994: 235)

Flannery (1972) describes the inversion of two traditional cooperative institutions: the rotation of financial sponsorship of local governmental offices (*cargo*) and of the major village fiestas (*mayordomia*) among the "responsible" townspeople in a Mexican village. Both gave sponsors access to status, but also leveled inequality by imposing the costs of offices and fiesta on wealthier members of the community. At the end of the nineteenth century these institutions were used by a villager to take over his neighbors' land. With the help of the church he made sure that sponsorship was rotated among all villagers regardless of their wealth. Flannery does not tell us whether he did so with the motivation to deprive or out of genuine democratic pathos at a time just prior to the Mexican revolution. When the hard-to-refuse honor put poorer villagers into debt, he lent them money, taking land as collateral. By 1915, he and his relatives had acquired 92 percent of the arable land, including virtually all irrigated land. These gains were reversed by the land reform that followed the Mexican revolution.

Redistributive offices also provide common routes for inversion. The high level of trust which usually surrounds incumbents gives them latitude to define the limits of their office. Greek tyrants of the seventh and sixth centuries BC gained power by using public offices such as that of *polemarch* who administered criminal cases and was entitled to a share of fines imposed. "The job, like a tax collector's, must have been highly prized: the honest *polemarch* could not help but make money, and the corrupt *polemarch* might become very rich" (McGlew 1993: 72). In many early societies, initially communal divine symbols or astronomical rituals designed to assure good harvests and propitiate supernatural forces were taken over by elites to claim privileged access to gods and were turned into tools for extracting surplus and for cementing alliances and consolidating power (Earle 1997: 170, 174; Demarest 2000: 287; Haviland and Moholy-Nagy 2000). Monumental construction often increased rapidly during periods of status competition, and subsided once power structures stabilized (Earle 1997: 178, 179). The right of chiefs and priests to allot common land or to mobilize labor for communal purposes provided similar opportunities.

Cowgill (1975) and Hayden (1994) argue that prosperity also facilitated inversion. When resources were scarce their distribution tended to be closely scrutinized. Abundant supplies weakened collective watchfulness and increased the possibility that communal supplies were used for competitive generosity such as the *potlatch* or the *moka* of New Guinea. Societies which stored seasonally abundant foods were particularly vulnerable to inversion because individuals who were charged with the redistribution of food had many opportunities to divert communal stores for their own use and legitimate such actions by reference to their social status (Testart 1982: 527, 528). Stored goods, now in the hands of elites, could then be exchanged for rare feathers or jade used as status symbols, for obsidian and metal used for weapons, or for locally unavailable foods such as salt, cocoa beans or specialty meat (Schele and Freidel 1990: 93; Hayden 1994: 237). Such status goods also facilitated coalitions and marriages which further strengthened inequality.

Opportunity Intensification

Opportunity intensification includes initially random or fortuitous allocations of material or symbolic resources which directly increase the likelihood of further resource gains. The abandonment of children by the *Batomba* provided nomadic *Fulbe* with a windfall supply of slave labor. Warring feudal factions in Japan rapidly adopted Portuguese firearms and used them to centralize political power. Hawaiian chiefs took advantage of the fortuitous arrival of Western arms to conquer neighboring islands and create a unified chiefdom (Earle 1997: 44). Initial settlement along rivers in fertile Central American valleys turned generations later into strategic locations which controlled access to water and land, providing the economic foundation of Maya aristocracy just as North American urban sprawl brought wealth to immigrants who had bought land well beyond the city limits to continue their rural life. Many cultures, from the Hopi of the American southwest to the Bembe in southern Africa, used claims of being "first to be here" to establish privileged "founder" status (Flannery and Marcus 2012: 166, 167). Throughout human history the control and monopolization of technologies created opportunities for consolidating economic and political power, just as in modern societies the material wealth of parents opens education, employment and social opportunities to their children which become self-reinforcing and extend across generations.

Proximity and Distance: Kinship, Coalitions, Networks and Marginalization

Kinship relations are particularly rich in trust and therefore particularly vulnerable to invasion by inequality. On one hand the equality and shared interests typical of kinship counteract hierarchical status distinctions, but strong relations of trust can also lead to a relaxation of supervision. Close relatives are more willing to overlook each other's violations of trust and to tolerate more inequity, a response already present among primates (Brosnan et al. 2004). Kinship can therefore open opportunities for the unchecked accumulation of possessions and power. Inability to meet bride wealth or reciprocity obligations can be converted into permanent debts of loyalty, work or slavery (Klein 2002: 116; Flannery and Marcus 2012: 79). Myths of descent from an older or first-born brother can grow into distinctions between senior and junior tribe or clan and drive the latter onto poor land or into inferior crafts (Arnold 1995; Flannery and Marcus 2012: 106). In a recent study of the conversion of an egalitarian into an unequal society, Dallos (2010: 213) shows how, by using age and kinship categories, "self-aggrandizers and their supporters openly manipulated social structures and mechanisms commonly associated with the 'egalitarian' ethic to promote inequality" successfully and without being challenged. In many early societies, kinship ties created opportunities for the gradual transformation of communal land into heritable but still unalienable family ownership, and eventually into private property and the growth of a land-owning class.

Kinship categories can be extended to create relations of social proximity and distance with non-kin ethnic or religious groups and marginalize and discriminate against those considered inferior (Buchan et al. 2002). Sahlins (1961) shows the mobilization of such distinctions by the Central African Tiv during predatory warfare to intensify internal solidarity and to stress the inferiority of target populations. Coalitions for the purpose of external trade or military alliance can be imbued with surrogate kinship solidarity, and social distance can be reinforced by sumptuary laws or by the exclusive knowledge of writing or a prestigious language by Chinese or Maya elites (Chang 1983: 90; McAnany 2001: 140). Such distinctions can be reinforced by using generalized, balanced and negative reciprocity to discriminate between different kinship categories.

Starting Processes: Dynamics of Continuity

The evolution of inequality structures does not erase cooperative and egalitarian social relations. Elites have a twofold interest in maintaining cooperation by subordinates. Economically, it is needed to produce the surplus on which elites depend. Ideologically, it maintains the appearance of continued mutuality, legitimates elite positions and reduces social tensions. In fifteenth century feudal societies,

> the peasant was imagined simultaneously as useless and as the provider of wealth; as bestial and as a human exemplar; as an object of derisive or fearful contempt and as sanctified. For most of the Middle Ages ... higher orders ... agreed, in large measure, that rustic labor fed and supported the leisure of the rest of society. Peasants' subordination might be explained by positing an intrinsic character that rendered them apt for work. More often, some moral credit attached to his labor, although this was not to be paid off in any worldly context.
>
> (Freedman 1999: 38)

However, such ambiguity also keeps alive lower class questions about the fairness of the inequality structure in which they live. Assertive egalitarianism and resistance to the accumulation of unilateral power was widespread in early egalitarian societies (Woodburn 1982; Erdal and Whiten 1996; Boehm 1999) and often continued long after hierarchical structures had taken root. Among the Iroquois, sharing and consensual leadership survived well after the disturbance of traditional life by European settlement, disease, enforced relocation and incorporation into modern trade (Trigger 1990: 144). Europeans, on the other hand, sometimes adopted native communal culture to escape hierarchical discipline. The reversion of French Canadian fur traders "to the Indian mode of life ... the indifference about amassing property, and the pleasure of living free of all restraint" and the resulting "licentiousness of manners" gave much grief to late eighteenth century fur company agents and missionaries (Mackenzie 1927: 9, 10).

Anthropologists like Malinowski and historians like Polanyi recognized that early forms of cooperation and redistribution were functional precursors of more complex modern equivalents. For Malinowski, the chief was a tribal banker, accumulating wealth for use in tribal enterprise, warfare and public ceremonies, thus becoming a prototype for modern public finance and taxation (Malinowski 1921, 1935). Polanyi suggested that cooperative forms of social life were common throughout human history until they were destroyed by the advent of capitalist markets (Polanyi 1957: 3). Although both authors recognized the evolutionary potential of cooperation, their views remained incomplete. Malinowski saw solidarity-based institutions as the basic functional morphology of social organization. This forced him, just like Durkheim and Parsons, to downplay the likelihood that they could be subverted by special interests for their own purposes. Polanyi's polarization of cooperation and capitalist markets implied that cooperative social organization could be recovered only by eliminating the market nexus. If Malinowski's functionalism blinded him to the potential of deception and defection, Polanyi underestimated the potential for the survival of cooperation even under capitalism.

Both authors were, however, correct in noting the ability of cooperative and egalitarian systems to adapt, change and produce major political, social and technological innovations which were essential for subsequent social evolution. Early forms of cooperation and redistribution evolved into sophisticated, large-scale divisions of labor, and into redistribution systems such as the large storage facilities across the Inca Empire, the huge clay vessels in Minoan Knossos and the construction of large "warehouses" in Harappan cities after 2600 BC. These societies maintained and strengthened their cooperative organization. Harappan cities showed few signs of social differentiation and no monumental buildings, but had a highly developed municipal infrastructure of grid-like streets, sewers and water supplies, suggesting that "in the Indus Valley, a technologically advanced, urban, literate culture was achieved without the usually associated social organization based on hereditary elites, centralized governments (states, empires), and warfare" (Wenke 1999: 504). In Çatal Hüyük, a large, organized Neolithic settlement endured for some 1500 years, combining hunting and gathering with agriculture and domestic livestock and developing a complex culture without archeological evidence of inequality. Even where cooperative relations were eventually superseded by inequality, they assumed new functional roles. Past archaeological research has focused on palaces and defensive walls which were taken as evidence of a strict hierarchical separation of elites and the rest of the population. In societies such as Mycenaean Greece (1400–1200 BC), actual interaction was far more complex and decentralized (Nakassis 2013). The ruling elite interacted with semi-autonomous crafts and farmers and rewarded them in turn with centralized redistribution. Dominant classes in ancient Egypt, Central and South America, China and feudal Europe lived off the wealth created by an enduring cooperative agricultural economy, but in doing so also maintained the potential for a future reassertion of equality.

A Shifting Balance: Equality and Inequality in Early Societies

Mesopotamia

Permanent agricultural villages existed in the northern Mesopotamian plain as early as the seventh millennium BC. Cities evolved through a gradual merging of decentralized settlements, not through centralized planning and state intervention (Adams and Niessen 1972; Ur et al. 2007). By 3000 BC, there were some 40 of them, each with their own territory, temple and principal deity, but sharing a sense of common cultural and political identity. Individualism and a strong resistance to central political control were predominant characteristics of the Sumerian city-state (Oates 1986: 24). Leadership was short-lived and no city achieved long-term dominance. Prior to 3000 BC, cemeteries and residential areas reveal no major differentiations of wealth, and words for "king" and "palace" occur in written records only later. Although Flannery and Marcus rightly remain open to the possibility that early Mesopotamia had forms of rank that were hard to detect, their survey of archaeological research finds no, or at most ambiguous, evidence for inequality in Southern Mesopotamia prior to 2500 BC (Flannery and Marcus 2012: 288–294). Dynastic control and inequality increased rapidly after that time, leading to cycles of centralization, political breakdown and resurgence of regions, and to a brief unification of the area under Hammurabi (1792–1750 BC).

Communal social and political structures survived and evolved far beyond a hunting and gathering economy. Intensive irrigation farming made it possible to produce and store food for large, concentrated settlements. Land and irrigation systems remained under local control and management (Adams 1965). Quarrels over water rights were common (Oates 1986: 14), but the basic need "to control scarce water supplies amicably and distribute them equitably must have been a strong cohesive force within early village communities" which encouraged the cooperative collection and distribution of agricultural and manufactured surpluses (Oates 1986: 14). By 4000 BC, standardized pottery ration bowls were produced in enormous quantities. Cities organized extensive trade, aided by a landscape with few obstacles to movement. The evolution of cooperative structures was accompanied by technological advances. By 3500 BC, Mesopotamian cities managed large-scale storage and redistribution, had a sexagesimal system of numbers, wheeled transport, boats, copper tools, ploughs and axes, musical instruments, craft specialization, standardized seals for marking goods and long-distance trade. Pictographic writing appeared after 3200, and cuneiform syllabic writing impressed on clay tablets around 2800 BC. The earliest texts are lists of livestock and agricultural tools (Oates 1986: 15).

Temples were the organized centers of cooperation. They were administered by the community and were "one element in an intricate, and in our terms essentially secular, community structure" (Oates 1986: 24, 25). They functioned as religious and economic institutions, collecting and redistributing agricultural produce, administering irrigation and sponsoring specialized crafts and industries. They stored grain in different localities to provide seed loans to people on favorable conditions (Postgate 1992: 170) and to reduce the risk of prolonged drought or the loss of water caused by silting and shifting river beds. Temples may also have had a role in administering trade and imported goods. In keeping with the Mesopotamian belief that cities and land were linked to local deities since the day of creation (Oates 1986: 25), temples and communities held land as communal property and distributed harvests.

As late as 2500 BC, temple lands still comprised between 25 and 50 percent of the total area of city states (Diakonoff 1969: 176). These lands were farmed directly for the benefit of the temple (and possible redistribution), assigned to temple staff as subsistence fields or were rented to sharecroppers. Land allotted to temple staff or sharecroppers could not be sold. Land not under temple control was the communal property of extended families. Its sale, often at nominal prices, required the consent of elected representatives of the kinship group and often of the popular assembly (Diakonoff 1969: 177). Communal ownership allowed substantial economies of scale. The use of plows and seeder funnels "must have been an initiative of the temples, improving their efficiency and enhancing their advantage over private enterprise" (Postgate 1992: 189, 226). Large communal fields facilitated irrigation and allowed more economical ploughing with oxen.

Participatory political processes accompanied economic cooperation. Communities were run by assemblies of free citizens made up of an upper house of elders and a lower house of men (Jacobsen 1976: 26). Both were elected (Diakonoff 1969: 186), and retained various communal functions over a period of some 4000 years, a testimony to their viability and adaptability. During this extraordinarily long time, small communities grew into the world's first large urban centers, large-scale irrigation and major technological advances intensified production and trade, variations in food supply were mediated by centrally organized redistribution, and cultivated areas were periodically relocated in response to the salination of land and silting of canals. These achievements were not linked to the emergence of inequality structures.

Inequality entered these societies through the inversion of communal offices, the intensification of opportunities offered by the broad powers of temple priests and staff and the diffuse role of deities in the Mesopotamian religious universe, and through the weakening of accountability resulting from the growing size of communal institutions. Power gradually accumulated in the hands of the overseers of temple and canal construction, and of secular kinship positions such as "master" of a house, slave or field. Temple staff became a cohesive bureaucracy whose strategic role in land and water allocation created opportunities for leasing formerly common temple land to clients, and for turning voluntary sacrifices to temples into regular taxes. Criticism of abuse of office could be interpreted as disrespect of the deity itself, and the increasing size of temple operations reduced the public scrutiny of temple officials. Temple courts were divided into public areas for worshippers and closed areas for priests (Diakonoff 1969: 186, 188). Large-scale popular protest appeared only late in the second millennium when the despotic nature of these changes was plain to see.

The role of elected and temporary secular leaders underwent a similar transformation. The traditional functions of Mesopotamian gods as providers and protectors against floods and thunderstorms were assumed by secular powers, surrounding formerly communal offices with a sense of awe. After 2500 BC there were increasing signs of corruption and embezzlement. Temple overseers began to transfer their office to their eldest son and heir, and their wives claimed part of temple estate previously dedicated to wives of gods (Flannery and Marcus 2012: 489ff.). Secular rulers eventually annexed temple estates, sometimes with the help of small standing armies, sometimes by appointing their wives as priestesses or by assuming priestly functions (Diakonoff 1969: 189). By 1500 BC, temple estates had become royal property. Traditional elections and votes disappeared or became empty formalities (Diakonoff 1969: 191), but secular rulers carefully exploited the legitimating power of existing traditions. They claimed to have been elected to office by an assembly of city gods. Hammurabi's stela dating to 1754 BC or later shows him receiving his law code directly from the sun god Shamash. From around 2000 BC to the 650 BC stela of Assurbanibal, kings are frequently depicted carrying baskets of building materials, an image designed to portray them both a hands-on cooperators and to exploit pre-dynastic symbolism associated with the founding of temples. Kings acted as representatives of the city in seeking the favor of gods and took credit for fortuitous or imagined benefits (Oates 1986: 28; Diakonoff 1969: 183). Assertions to have advanced the prosperity of the country and claims of divine descent became common in inscriptions of Sumerian kings. Kingship was symbolized by hat, stick and stool, the origin of all later royal crowns, scepters and thrones.

Cooperative institutions were also transformed into tools of dynastic revenue collection and judicial and political administration (Postgate 1992: 290, 300). Temples became part of a state economy and were run by state accountants. Redistribution was formally retained, but now as highly visible populist acts such as arbitrary debt remissions or price controls. Kings claimed to protect widows and orphans, and Hammurabi boasted that his legal code protected the weak against the strong, a tacit acknowledgment of continuing resistance to economic exploitation. In the second millennium, well after the consolidation of despotism, epics still described communal forms of political participation, although they were now ideological tools of royal control (Postgate 1992: 301; Oates 1986: 26; Diakonoff 1969: 184).

The transformation of cooperative into hierarchical practices occurred over a long period of experimentation. Whereas it created new, innovative forms of administration and social control, it also preserved the potential for reversing the balance of common and hierarchical interests. Under Hammurabi's sons, central power disintegrated and egalitarian institutions reasserted themselves. Cities regained considerable autonomy and self-government, making them, in the first millennium BC, forerunners of the Greek *polis* and the cities of medieval Europe (Diakonoff 1969: 201). The dissolution of hierarchy reached all sectors of life: significant towns like Mashkan-Shapir developed a diverse craft economy without central rulers or residential segregation between elites and commoners (Stone and Zimansky 1995).

Central and South America: Maya, Aztecs and Inca

Homogeneous settlements, undifferentiated burials and simple pottery suggest that lowland Maya lived prior to 300 BC in egalitarian communities of smallholders who cooperatively farmed highly productive dry land, riverine and irrigated fields. Opportunity intensification allowed early settlers to use their fortuitous occupation of the best land to transform themselves into "founding families." These claims were strengthened by the Maya practice of sub-floor burials which allowed "founders" to use Maya cosmology to connect their homes to privileged genealogies, thereby bolstering land claims and resource privileges (McAnany 2001: 147). Shamans, belonging to or colluding with founder kin, acquired increasingly secular power under the guise of communicating with gods and ancestors through bloodletting and vision quests. Institutionalized inequality and kingship appeared rapidly after 100 BC. Temples and plazas at Cerros were built in the space of two generations (Schele and Freidel 1990: 103). At the same time there was also a rapid differentiation of house types, indicating clear differentials of wealth. Between 200 and 50 BC, massive construction projects were built by communal labor. Early elites still remained anonymous and self-effacing. Their names and actions did not appear on public monuments (Schele and Miller 1986: 109). Friezes and stelae portrayed them as public-interest mediators between human and supernatural world (Schele and Freidel 1990: 91), using blood-letting rituals to open access to supernatural power on behalf of the community, the image standing in for the – probably increasingly rare – actual performance. Soon, however, these structures became stages for elite rituals in "theatre states" (Demarest 2004). By the first century BC in Tikal, a large nobility had appeared whose members were about 10 cm taller than the poorer population, enjoyed better food, had more surviving children and were engaged in incessant warfare with competing neighboring kingdoms (Schele and Freidel 1990: 380; Haviland and Moholy-Nagy 2000).

Increasing population density also allowed "founders" to use their control of prime farmland and water to extort one-sided tribute and sharecropping obligations, justified as "sustaining the lives of those who sustain the prosperity of the community" (Schele and Freidel 1990: 93). Elites had no functional managerial role in the economy (Demarest 2004: 284, 285) but used labor, captives and long-distance trade to display their power through architecture and art. Stelae now recorded personal triumphs and conquests. Faces carved in stone were no longer stylized but became recognizable portraits of rulers who took the title of "divine king." Ceremonial centers and performances were used "to make inequality enchant" (Geertz 1980: 123). The calculation of propitious dates legitimated recurrent wars between rulers of Mayan cities. Nevertheless, Maya inequality remained unstable and went through multiple crises before the exhaustion of land, mass impoverishment and popular uprisings caused its rapid collapse between AD 800 and 900. The ideological use of communal symbolism continued right to the end: kings were depicted as warriors but also as listening to petitioners (McAnany 2001: 138).

A similar co-optation of communal structures occurred in Aztec society. After a series of battles between 1429 and 1433, the Aztec alliance of three cities quickly extended its domination over the central valley of Mexico and beyond. Early Aztec social organization centered on communal institutions, the *calpulli*, which could comprise a village or a section of a city. Their members owned land jointly and could neither sell nor lease it. Elected leaders acted as judges, assigned common land to individuals and redistributed it if it was not worked for two years. Houses were built by communal labor, as were larger public works. A council of *calpulli* heads elected a Chief Speaker, an office which first appeared in 1376. *Calpulli* provided land and labor for the chief speaker but his powers were limited. He could declare war only with the consent of a war council and was obliged to store food for redistribution during the frequent famines which hit the central valley of Mexico.

Inequality was not unknown to Aztec society. A small class of state officials and warriors who had proven their bravery was relieved of agricultural work when their state functions required it. The *calpulli* themselves may have been ranked to some extent. Some were wealthier; others carried out specialized crafts and represented merchant and craft guilds. But these unequal characteristics were balanced by strong collective elements. Conquest itself was a communal achievement, relying on periodic levies of able-bodied men who were equipped with arms from state stockpiles. So was the construction of public projects such as aqueducts and drainage that created a highly productive agriculture.

The records of Aztec history compiled by the Spanish give a detailed example of the intensification of military opportunity and the resulting growth of a military aristocracy. Diego Duran's *History of the Indies of New Spain* reports a stormy disagreement between commoners, warriors and leaders during the early conquest. Warriors supported the campaign which the majority of *calpulli* members opposed. Aztec mythology claimed that this conflict was resolved through a pact: in case of defeat the leaders and warriors promised to place themselves at the disposal and vengeance of ordinary people. The latter, in turn, answered:

> We undertake, if you are successful, to serve you, to pay tribute money to you, to be your bondsmen, to build your houses and to serve you as

veritable lords and to place at your disposal our sons, brothers and nieces and while you are waging war, to bear your loads and your arms and to serve you everywhere, wherever you may go and finally to sell to you our possessions and persons for your service for ever.

(Duran in Katz 1972: 146)

This rather uneven bargain, almost certainly embellished after the fact, says as much about the reluctance of commoners to join a military gamble they considered contrary to their interests, as it does about the willingness of a warrior caste to exploit opportunities for conquest and pillage. The latter wasted no time in taking advantage of their victory, helping themselves to large portions of conquered land while "to the common people who had shown themselves in this battle to be cowardly and fearful and had sworn to serve the lords and victors ... no land at all was given" (Duran in Katz 1972: 147). This result was reinforced by an elaborate falsification of history: the Aztec elite ordered all images and records of their own obscure origins and of their communal traditions destroyed (Sahagun 1965: 128).

The roughly 100 years from the beginning of Aztec power to the Spanish conquest between 1519 and 1521 saw a rapid growth of social inequality. Warriors became a hereditary aristocracy, distinguished from commoners by dress and ornaments, by two-story houses concentrated near religious structures, by privileged access to tribute and land and by a variety of special legal rights including that of polygamy. They were permanently freed from agricultural work and received the largest part of the massive flow of tribute from surrounding conquered lands. By the end of the fifteenth century the Chief Speaker had become a divine incarnation and his decisions a manifestation of the gods' will. Initially, commoners who distinguished themselves in war could still enter the nobility, but Moctezuma, the last pre-conquest Aztec Chief Speaker, cleansed the aristocracy of people with common background, reserved state offices for nobles, and intensified the social distance between his own office and the rest of society. Cortés, familiar with Spanish court ritual, observed that "the customs at the Mexican court are more varied, splendid and ceremonious than at the court of an oriental potentate" (cited in Katz 1972: 241). Ironically, the pall of obedience this system imposed on Aztec society became a major contributor to its defeat by the Spanish.

At the same time, early communal institutions remained crucial to this now highly centralized society. The *calpulli* system was incorporated into the Aztec state bureaucracy. Periodic conspicuous redistribution maintained the formal appearance of sharing, although it now followed a strict order of rank. State stores were opened to commoners on the occasion of religious feasts or when food supplies were scarce. *Calpulli* provided compulsory labor and food to nobles, collected taxes and replaced local deities with state-supported ones. Moctezuma expertly used ideology and force by engaging in populist measures such as the abolition of debt slavery after the 1505 famine, and in unpredictable but highly public punishment of pride and presumptuousness of wealthier commoners such as merchants.

Like the Aztecs, the Inca conquered a huge Andean territory between 1438 and their defeat in November 1532 when Pizarro, in command of some 150 Spanish soldiers, snatched the Inca ruler Atahualpa in a daring *coup de main* from the midst of his large army. Like the Aztecs, the Inca integrated traditional cooperative structures into a rapidly evolving system of social inequality. Inca society began as a small tribe of cooperative clan units (*ayllu*) which still exist in many Andean areas and are organized around collective landownership and mutual help. Formerly elected tribal chiefs had already made their position heritable prior to the Inca expansion, but their rapid growth into an aristocratic elite relied on the skillful exploitation of existing cooperative traditions.

The *ayllu* system allowed the Inca elite to act out a piece of political theatre by inverting the traditional role of the village elders who looked after the well-being of their people. The reallocation of common land through the *ayllu* was now used to distribute conquered territory among Inca rulers, priests, and local peasants. The tradition of mobilizing voluntary labor (*mita*) for collective projects now served to recruit forced labor to build roads, palaces, and irrigated terraces. The ancient custom of storing and redistributing food (*aymi*) was inverted to redirect a large surplus of local products to the court at Cuzco and to Inca armies. In exchange, local communities received small donations for local feasts or for alleviating occasional famines.

This system disguised the diversion of surplus to the aristocracy as a mutually beneficial exchange. On the surface little appeared to have changed. Peasants were still allotted subsistence land, received "gifts" in exchange for labor services and paid into a "common" store administered by their Inca superiors. Inca officials, including members of royal families, still performed traditional rituals such as asking the gods each year whether crops should be planted (the answer was always affirmative), and organized state-sponsored feasts to mark the start of forced labor tasks (Murra 1960: 399; Katz 1972: 291). The appearance of shared interest was also enhanced by maintaining local authority structures while tying them closely to the empire. Local religious idols were brought to Cuzco, sons of local chieftains were educated there, and young women were taken to the capital as Virgins of the Sun to weave the cloth reserved for the aristocracy, serve as concubines, or to be returned with great ceremony to their homes in order to be sacrificed on mountaintops across the empire (Silverblatt 1988).

Behind this veil of continuity, a wide gap separated the central elite residing in monumental buildings in Cuzco from commoners. Sumptuary laws allowed only the nobility to wear golden earplugs, jewelry or fine woolen cloth. They were freed from manual work, had large retinues of servants and ate high-status food such as corn instead of the low-status staple of potatoes (Murra 1960). The Inca Empire created one of the largest pre-industrial states without money and writing, and with rudimentary transportation, accounting and communication systems. Its ingenuity lay in recognizing the potential of harnessing cooperative structures to the interests of a ruling class. In this sense, the Inca Empire was thoroughly modern. It concealed its exploitative nature so well that modern historians such as Katz (1972: 288) saw it as a highly centralized but also benign redistributive state, a form of early communism in pursuit of the common good.

164 *Variation*

The Roman Republic

The history of Rome from its legendary founding in 753 BC to the end of the Republic in 31 BC illustrates particularly well the see-saw between the growth of inequality and the resurgence of equality. Archaic Italian communities were family- and clan-centered. Family heads or elders administered communal and family-owned land and performed religious duties such as the interpretation of omens, an Etruscan heritage which became an important part of Roman political culture. The secular and religious power of individual clan leaders and elected "kings" was curtailed by local communities (*curiae*), a senate of clan elders or "fathers" who would become the patricians, and a popular assembly (*comitia curiata*) which made or ratified important decisions. All Roman sources confirm that social divisions between patricians and plebeians grew during this period. Clan heads used their right to assign land as a means to build strategic client networks and to increase the social standing of their clan. A parallel expansion of priestly and military power by Rome's "kings" ended with the overthrow of the last of them, Tarquinius Superbus ("the Arrogant") and the declaration of a republic in 510 BC.

The republic reestablished participatory principles: a collegial government by two consuls whose term was limited to one year and who received their *imperium* or power from the Roman people through senate and curiate assemblies. Plebeians also had access to political offices. The senate quickly began to roll back these concessions. Patricians supplied most of its 300 members, and an inner circle claiming descent from Rome's original "founding" clans raised their status to that of *nobiles* who provided the majority of consuls, state officials and colonial governors. Only rarely could a "new man" make his way into this group. The fact that the senate was governed by custom, not law, facilitated the concentration of legal, procedural and ritual expertise in the hands of the senatorial nobility. This group also controlled appointments in conquered territories which provided access to enormous booty and slave labor. Administrative monopoly and wealth made it possible to reward clients with access to offices and land, and to bribe urban voters. Patronage became an essential part of senatorial – and after the fall of the republic – imperial power.

Land ownership was the second source of inequality in the Roman republic. The institution of public land (*ager publicus*) probably had its roots in early communal clan ownership of pasture and farmland. More public land was added as Rome expanded and was made available to colonists and retired soldiers. In theory it had to be returned to the state when its recipient ceased to work it, but members of senatorial clans used their role as administrators of public land to keep as much of it as possible in their hands and lease it either to clients or turn it into large *latifundia* worked by slaves. As Rome's power expanded beyond Italy, privileged access to colonial offices also opened the way to foreign *ager publicus* and to slaves whose numbers soon vastly exceeded the indigenous Roman debt-slavery. The influx of external wealth into Rome also no longer required the payment of taxes, freeing wealthy Romans from an onerous but also equalizing burden.

The fact that plebeians made up the bulk of the citizen levies in military campaigns, and the power of these legions once they were in the field, gave them the leverage to strike back. Their refusal to fight in 494 BC, the first of a series of "secessions of the people" or general strikes, gained them the right to elect tribunes of the people who could veto decisions of the consuls and provide protection for the plebs. In 451 BC, they established a body of ten elected judges to create written and publicly posted laws designed to end arbitrary interpretations of customary laws and affirm the principle of public control of all land. The senate countered with laws which abolished the tribunes and forbade marriage between patricians and plebeians. These were soon rescinded under plebeian pressure. During a series of wars in the fourth and third centuries BC, plebeian power reached its highest point. Creditors could only dispose of debtors' property and not enslave their persons. The two consular offices and those of augur and pontiff were opened to plebeian candidates, decisions taken by plebeian assemblies had the force of law, property qualifications were abolished and plebeians gained the right to elect the majority of military tribunes. Community control of public lands was reaffirmed and limits were placed on the amount of land which individuals could occupy.

Such efforts were staunchly contested by a patriciate whose wealth from plundering Rome's conquered provinces allowed them to bribe the Roman electorate and to surround themselves with bodyguards of slaves and clients which intimidated voters and extorted land from smallholders. Tiberius Gracchus, and after his assassination in 133 BC his brother Gaius, attempted and partially succeeded in strengthening community ownership of land, limiting the amount of land which individuals and families could hold and giving Roman settlers and veterans access to *ager publicus* in conquered territories. These reforms were countermanded and, in 111 BC, the limits on land-holdings were removed. Rome began its long slide into sometimes benign, often disastrous, imperial rule.

The tensions between patricians and plebeians reveal the opposing forces of inequality and cooperation. Patricians could maintain their position only by securing the indispensable military and labor services of plebeians, and by pretending their support of Rome's traditional common-interest values, the *mos majorum*, although these served now as an ideological cover for the enrichment of the Roman elite. Plebeians found in these same values the confirmation of the basic equality of citizens and a justification for opposing senatorial power. Even when in imperial Rome virtually all land was in the hands of private owners, cooperation of the plebs had to be bought. In 123 BC, Gaius Gracchus had introduced bulk-buying and storage of corn to be sold at below-market rates to stabilize prices and prevent profiteering after bad harvests. Under the reign of Augustus (27 BC to AD 14), this system grew from temporary relief into a centralized state-run redistribution on a scale unparalleled until the modern welfare state. It gave an estimated 320,000 citizens free rations of about 45 kg of grain per month. Towards the end of the empire, oil, wine and pork had been added. Rome's enormous revenues from its conquered provinces still enriched first and foremost patrician families, but the ration system swallowed up as much as one-fifth of the state's total revenue. Patricians were well aware that bread and circuses were the price for their own prosperity. Throughout this period unrest flared up whenever dole payments were reduced; the emperor Tiberius feared in AD 22 that, should they fail, "the utter ruin of the state will follow" (Reader 2005: 58).

Pathways to Inequality: Transitions and Continuities

The evidence examined in this chapter suggests, first, that early cooperative structures were no evolutionary dead ends. Their leveraging and risk-reducing effects were adapted, modernized and produced significant technological innovation and change. Nor did they disappear with the emergence of inequality. The pyramids of Egypt were made possible by a communal agricultural and labor system that was already ancient when they were built. Many Linear B tablets of Mycenaean culture in Bronze-age Greece contain accounts used in the centralized distribution of goods like wool and grain (Nakassis 2013). Bread and circuses were the redistributive pillars which propped up Rome's emperors. Cooperative village structures formed the backbone of European feudalism. Early storage and redistribution systems became prototypes for modern taxation, social security and public and private insurance systems. Inequality structures offered no inherent advantages of efficiency or economies of scale which dictated their preferential cultural selection over more egalitarian alternatives. Historically, productive improvements tended to precede rather than follow the emergence of inequality. Inequality structures exploited the accomplishments of existing cooperative arrangements more often than they generated new technological and social change.

Second, shifts towards more (or less) inequality were initiated by a wide variety of circumstances. These tended to cluster in regions of opportunity where contingent changes or weaknesses of trust and cooperation were particularly likely to trigger the emergence of inequality, although the result was never predictable. Initial settlement on good land facilitated the rise of the Maya aristocracy, but early communities did not always choose advantageous locations, and if they did, inequality did not always result (McAnany 1995: 155). Big Men evolved as often into chiefs as they suffered ignominious failure, and chiefdoms reverted to Big Man status rivalries. Kinship offered numerous opportunities for the centralization of power but also showed a "remarkable capacity ... to resist divisions of labor leading to class formation, to resist the lifelong exploitation of one class by another, and to foment rebellions that may threaten or even destroy archaic states" (Bender 1990: 255).

Third, whether the opportunity was actually recognized depended on the imagination of the participants. Because human foresight and planning were severely limited, the long-term evolution of distributive structures followed an irregular course of consolidation, fragmentation and devolution. In the island-hopping expansion of Melanesian and Polynesian populations, gradual increases in inequality were interspersed by egalitarian reversals (Currie et al. 2010), whereas in other parts of the world cycles of equality and inequality were more abrupt (Mann 1986: 39; Earle 1997: 98; Abrutyn and Lawrence 2010). Cooperative structures dominated social life in Western Europe until well after the collapse of the Roman Empire while elsewhere, such as the Balkans (Mann 1986: 63), they succumbed much more swiftly. Inequality can be extremely tenacious, but also, as in the case of the Maya, experience a catastrophic decline.

If cooperation is vulnerable to inequality, inequality is weakened by its need for cooperation. Alone one cannot be unequal. Inequality needs labor to produce a surplus and a populace which accepts its unequal distribution. But this is also its Achilles heel. Cooperation, even where it is placed in the service of inequality, maintains the potential for demands for greater equality. These may be suppressed, but they invariably resurface. A short but significant renaissance of urban liberty followed the demise of Babylonian dynasties. Greek democracy evolved in a sea of despotism. Popular assemblies made economic and political decisions in Switzerland, Iceland and in North American native societies hundreds of years before 1776. Structures of social inequality are a common feature of human history, but in the broad scheme of things equality has fared just as well. Its waves, to use Michels' image, may not have washed upon the shore as often, but when they did, they did so with great force.

Notes

1 From Thomas' *Harmless People* (1959) to Eibl-Eibesfeldt's "Myth of the Aggression-free Hunter-gatherer Society" (1974), from Brody's *The Other Side of Eden* (2001) to LeBlanc's *Constant Battles: The Myth of the Peaceful, Noble Savage* (2003).
2 The nineteenth century preference for developmental models of history persisted in later literature (Service 1962; Lenski 1966; Redman 1978; Hayden 1995; Luhmann 1997; Diakonoff 1999; Fukuyama 2002). With the exception of Hayden, these studies offered few details of the process by which social inequality enters previously unstratified societies.

Bibliography

Abrutyn, Seth and Kirk Lawrence. "From Chiefdoms to States: Toward an Integrative Theory of the Evolution of Polity." *Sociological Perspectives* 53 (2010) 2: 419–442.

Adams, Robert McC. *Land Behind Baghdad*. Chicago: University of Chicago Press, 1965.

Adams, Robert McC. and Hans J. Niessen, *The Uruk Countryside: The Natural Setting of Urban Societies*. Chicago: University of Chicago Press, 1972.

Ames, Kenneth M. "Chiefly Power and Household Production on the Northwest Coast." In T. Douglas Price and Gary M. Feinman (eds) *Foundations of Social Inequality*, 155–187. New York: Plenum Press, 1995.

Arnold, Jeanne E. "Social Inequality, Marginalization, and Economic Process." In T. Douglas Price and Gary M. Feinman (eds) *Foundations of Social Inequality*, 87–103. New York: Plenum Press, 1995.

Bender, Barbara. "The Dynamics of Non-hierarchical Societies." In Steadman Upham (ed.) *The Evolution of Political Systems*, 247–263. Cambridge: Cambridge University Press, 1990.

Bettinger, Robert L. *Hunter-Gatherers. Archeological and Evolutionary Theory*. New York: Plenum Press, 1991.

Betzig, Laura L. *Despotism and Differential Reproduction: A Darwinian View of History*. Hawthorne: Aldine, 1986.

Binford, Lewis. "Some Comments on Historical versus Processual Anthropology." *Southwestern Journal of Anthropology* 24 (1968): 267–275.
Boehm, Christopher. *Hierarchy in the Forest*. Cambridge: Harvard University Press, 1999.
Brody, Hugh. *The Other Side of Eden: Hunters, Farmers, and the Shaping of the World*. New York: North Point Press, 2001.
Brosnan, Sarah F., Hillary C. Schiff, Hillary and Frans B.M. de Waal. "Tolerance for Inequity May Increase with Social Closeness for Chimpanzees." *Proceedings of the Royal Society, Biology* (2004) 2947: 1–6.
Brumfiel, Elizabeth and Timothy K. Earle. *Specialization, Exchange, and Complex Societies*. Cambridge: Cambridge University Press, 1987.
Buchan, Nancy R., Rachel T.A. Croson and Robyn Dawes, Robyn. "Swift Neighbours and Persistent Strangers: A Cross-Cultural Investigation of Trust and Reciprocity in Social Exchange." *American Journal of Sociology* 108 (2002) 1: 168–206.
Burch, Ernest S. and Liona J. Ellana. *Key Issues in Hunter-Gatherer Research*. Providence: Berg, 1994.
Carneiro, Robert L. "A Theory of the Origin of the State." *Science* 169 (1970): 733–738.
Carneiro, Robert L. "Political Expansion as an Expression of the Principle of Competitive Exclusion." In Ronald Cohen and Elman R. Service (eds) *Origins of the State: The Anthropology of Political Evolution*, 205–223. Philadelphia: Institute for the Study of Human Issues, 1977.
Chang, Kwang-chih. *Art, Myth and Ritual: The Path to Political Authority in Ancient China*. Cambridge: Harvard University Press, 1983.
Childe, V. Gordon. *Man Makes Himself*. London: Watts, 1936.
Cohen, Abner. *The Politics of Elite Culture: Explorations in the Dramaturgy of Power in a Modern African Society*. Berkeley: University of California Press, 1981.
Coles, John E. "History's Longest Road." *Scientific American* 261 (1989) 5: 100–106.
Cowgill, George L. "On Causes and Consequences of Ancient and Modern Population Changes." *American Anthropologist* 77 (1975) 3: 505–525.
Currie, Thomas, Simon Greenhill, Russell Gray, Toshikazu Hasegawa and Ruth Mace. "Rise and Fall of Political Complexity in Island South-East Asia and the Pacific." *Nature* 467 (2010) October 14: 801–804.
Curry, Andrew. "Seeking the Roots of Ritual." *Science* 319 (2008) 5861: 278–280.
Dallos, Csilla. *From Equality to Inequality. Social Change among Newly Sedentary Lanoh Hunter-Gatherer Traders of Peninsular Malaysia*. Toronto: University of Toronto Press, 2010.
Demarest, Arthur. "Ideology in Ancient Maya Cultural Evolution." In Michael Smith and Marilyn Masson (eds) *The Ancient Civilizations of Mesoamerica*, 279–299. Malden: Blackwell, 2000.
Demarest, Arthur. *Ancient Maya: The Rise and Fall of a Rainforest Civilization*. Cambridge: Cambridge University Press, 2004.
Diakonoff, Igor M. "The Rise of the Despotic State in Ancient Mesopotamia." In Igor M. Diakonoff (ed.) *Ancient Mesopotamia*, 173–202. Moscow: Nauka Publishing House, 1969 (1956).
Diakonoff, Igor M. *The Paths of History*. Cambridge: Cambridge University Press, 1999.
Diamond, Jared. *Collapse: How Societies Choose to Fall or Succeed*. New York: Viking, 2005.
Dunnell, Robert C. "Style and Function: A Fundamental Dichotomy." *American Antiquity* 43 (1978) 2: 192–202.
Earle, Timothy. *How Chiefs Come to Power*. Stanford: Stanford University Press, 1997.

Edelman, Murray J. *Politics as Symbolic Action: Mass Arousal and Quiescence*. Chicago: Markham Publishing, 1971.
Edelman, Murray J. *The Politics of Misinformation*. Cambridge: Cambridge University Press, 2001.
Eibl-Eibesfeldt, Irenäus. "The Myth of the Aggression-Free Hunter-Gatherer Society." In Ralph L. Holloway (ed.) *Primate Aggression, Territoriality, and Xenophobia: A Comparative Perspective*, 435–457. New York: Academic Press, 1974.
Engels, Friedrich. *The Origin of the Family, Private Property and the State*. New York: International Publishers, 1972 [1884].
Erdal, David and Andrew Whiten. "Egalitarianism and Machiavellian Intelligence in Human Evolution." In Paul Mellars and Kathleen Gibson (eds) *Modelling the Early Human Mind*, 139–150. Cambridge: MacDonald Institute for Archeological Research, 1996.
Evans, Richard J. *The Third Reich in Power, 1933–1939*. London: Allen Lane, 2005.
Feinman, Gary M. "The Emergence of Inequality." In Douglas T. Price and Gary Feinman (eds) *Foundations of Social Inequality*, 255–279. New York: Plenum Press, 1995.
Flannery, Kent. "The Cultural Evolution of Civilizations." *Annual Review of Ecology and Systematics* 3 (1972) 1: 399–426.
Flannery, Kent and Joyce Marcus. *The Creation of Inequality*. Cambridge: Harvard University Press, 2012.
Freedman, Paul. *Images of the Medieval Peasant*. Stanford: Stanford University Press, 1999.
Fried, Morton. *The Evolution of Political Society*. New York/Toronto: Random House, 1967.
Fukuyama, Francis. *The End of History and the Last Man*. New York: Harper Collins, 2002 [1992].
Geertz, Clifford. *Negara: The Theatre State in Nineteenth-Century Bali*. Princeton: Princeton University Press, 1980.
Gilman, Antonio. "The Development of Social Stratification in Bronze Age Europe." *Current Anthropology* 22 (1981) 1: 1–23.
Gilman, Antonio. "Prehistoric European Chiefdoms." In Douglas T. Price and Gary M. Feinman (eds) *Foundations of Social Inequality*, 235–251. New York: Plenum Press, 1995.
Goffman, Erving. "On Cooling the Mark Out." *Psychiatry* 15 (1952) 4: 451–463.
Gregor, Thomas. *Mehinaku: The Drama of Daily Life in a Brazilian Indian Village*. Chicago: University of Chicago Press, 1977.
Gunawardana, R.A.L.H. "Social Function and Political Power: A Case Study of State Formation in Irrigation Society." In Henri J.M. Claessen and Peter Skalnik (eds) *The Study of the State*, 133–154. The Hague: Mouton Publishers, 1981.
Harris, Marvin. *The Rise of Anthropological Theory: A History of Theories of Culture*. New York: Crowell, 1968.
Harris, Marvin. *Cannibals and Kings: The Origins of Cultures*. New York: Random House, 1977.
Harris, Marvin. *Cultural Materialism*. New York: Random House, 1979.
Haviland, William A. and Hattula Moholy-Nagy. "Distinguishing the High and Mighty from the Hoi Polloi at Tikal, Guatemala." In Michael Smith and Marilyn Masson (eds) *The Ancient Civilizations of Mesoamerica*, 39–48. Malden: Blackwell, 2000.
Hayden, Brian. "Competition, Labor, and Complex Hunter-Gatherers." In Ernest Burch and Linda J. Ellana (eds) *Key Issues in Hunter-Gatherer Research*, 223–239. Providence: Berg, 1994.

Hayden, Brian. "Pathways to Power. Principles for Creating Socioeconomic Inequalities." In Douglas T. Price and Gary M. Feinman (eds) *Foundations of Social Inequality*, 15–86. New York: Plenum Press, 1995.

Higham, Charles and Rachanie Thosarat. "Thailand's Good Mount." *Natural History* 103 (1994) 12: 60–66.

Hobbes, Thomas. *Leviathan.* Edited by Richard Tuck. Cambridge: Cambridge University Press, 1991 [1651].

Jacobsen, Thorkild. *The Treasures of Darkness. A History of Mesopotamian Religion.* New Haven: Yale University Press, 1976.

Jordaan, Ken. "The Bushmen of Southern Africa: Anthropology and Historical Materialism." *Race and Class* 17 (1975) 2: 141–160.

Katz, Friedrich. *The Ancient American Civilizations.* New York: Praeger, 1972.

Keeley, Lawrence H. "Hunter-Gatherer Economic Complexity and "Population Pressure": A Cross-Cultural Analysis." *Journal of Anthropological Archeology* 7 (1988) 4: 373–411.

Kelly, Robert L. *The Foraging Spectrum: Diversity of Hunter-Gatherer Lifeways.* Washington, DC: Smithsonian Institution Press, 1995.

Klein, Martin. *The A to Z of Slavery and Abolition.* Lanham: Scarecrow Press, 2002.

LeBlanc, Steven A. *Constant Battles: The Myth of the Peaceful, Noble Savage.* New York: St. Martin's Press, 2003.

Lee, Richard B. "!Kung Bushmen Subsistence: An Input-Output Analysis." In Andrew P. Vayda (ed.) *Environment and Cultural Behaviour*, 47–79. New York: Natural History Press, 1969.

Lee, Richard B. and Irven DeVore. *Man the Hunter.* Chicago: Aldine, 1968.

Lenski, Gerhard E. *Power and Privilege.* New York: McGraw-Hill, 1966.

Lenski, Gerhard E. and Jean Lenski. *Human Societies: An Introduction to Macrosociology.* New York: McGraw-Hill, 1982.

Lewis, Herbert S. "Warfare and the Origin of the State: Another Formulation." In Henri J.M. Claessen and Peter Skalnik (eds) *The Study of the State*, 201–221. The Hague: Mouton Publishers, 1981.

Luhmann, Niklas. *Die Gesellschaft der Gesellschaft.* Frankfurt a.M.: Suhrkamp, 1997.

Machalek, Richard. "Basic Dimensions and Forms of Social Exploitation: A Comparative Analysis." *Advances in Human Ecology* 4 (1995): 1–30.

Machalek, Richard. "The Evolution of Social Exploitation." *Advances in Human Ecology* 5 (1996): 1–32.

Mackenzie, Alexander. *Voyages from Montreal.* Edited by John W. Garvin. Toronto: Radisson Society, 1927 [1801].

Mair, Lucy. *Primitive Government.* London: Scholar Press, 1977.

Malinowski, Bronislaw. "The Primitive Economics of the Trobriand Islanders." *The Economic Journal* 31 (1921) 121: 1–16.

Malinowski, Bronislaw. *Coral Gardens and their Magic: A Study of Tilling the Soil and of Agricultural Rites in the Trobriand Islands.* Two volumes. London: Allen & Unwin, 1935.

Mann, Michael. *The Sources of Social Power.* Cambridge: Cambridge University Press, 1986.

McAnany, Patricia A. *Living with the Ancestors: Kinship and Kingship in Ancient Maya Society.* Austin: University of Texas Press, 1995.

McAnany, Patricia A. "Cosmology and the Institutionalization of Hierarchy in the Maya Region." In Jonathan Haas (ed.) *From Leaders to Rulers*, 125–148. New York: Kluwer Academic, 2001.

McGlew, James F. *Tyranny and Political Culture in Ancient Greece.* Ithaca: Cornell University Press, 1993.
Moore, Alexander. *Cultural Anthropology: The Field Study of Human Beings.* San Diego: Collegiate Press, 1992.
Murra, John. "Rite and Crop in the Inca State." In Stanley Diamond (ed.) *Culture in History, Essays in Honour of Paul Radin,* 393–407. New York: Columbia University Press, 1960.
Nakassis, Dimitri. *Individual and Society in Mycenaean Pylos.* Leiden: Brill, 2013.
Oates, Joan. *Babylon.* London: Thames and Hudson, 1986.
Piddocke, Stuart. "The Potlatch System of the Southern Kwakiutl: A New Perspective." *Southwestern Journal of Anthropology* 21 (1965) 3: 244–264.
Polanyi, Karl. *The Great Transformation.* Boston: Beacon Press, 1957 [1944].
Postgate, J. Nicholas. *Ancient Mesopotamia.* London: Routledge, 1992.
Reader, John. *Cities.* London: Vintage, 2005.
Redman, Charles L. *The Rise of Civilization.* San Francisco: Freeman, 1978.
Rice, Michael. *Egypt's Making. The Origins of Ancient Egypt 5000–2000 BC.* London: Routledge, 1990.
Sahagun, Bernardino de. *Die Rückkehr der Götter.* München: Deutscher Taschenbuch Verlag, 1965 [1585].
Sahlins, Marshall D. "The Segmentary Lineage. An Organization of Predatory Expansion." *American Anthropologist* 63 (1961) 2: 322–343.
Sahlins, Marshall D. "Poor Man, Rich Man, Big Man, Chief: Political Types in Melanesia and Polynesia."*Comparative Studies in Society and History* 5 (1963) 3: 285–303.
Sahlins, Marshall D. *Stone Age Economics.* Chicago: Aldine, 1972.
Schele, Linda and Mary Ellen Miller. *The Blood of Kings. Dynasty and Ritual in Maya Art.* New York: Kimbell Art Museum, 1986.
Schele, Linda and David Freidel. *A Forest of Kings.* New York: William Morrow, 1990.
Schmidt, Klaus. *Sie bauten den ersten Tempel. Das rätselhafte Heiligtum der Steinzeitjäger. Die archäologische Entdeckung am Göbekli Tepe.* München: C.H. Beck, 2006
Service, Elman R. *Primitive Social Organization: An Evolutionary Perspective.* New York: Random House, 1962.
Silverblatt, Irene. "Imperial Dilemmas, the Politics of Kinship, and Inca Reconstruction of History." *Comparative Studies in Society and History* 30 (1988) 1: 83–102.
Steward, Julian H. *Theory of Culture Change: The Methodology of Multilinear Evolution.* Urbana: University of Illinois Press, 1955.
Stone, Elizabeth C. and Paul Zimansky. "The Tapestry of Power in a Mesopotamian City." *Scientific American* (1995) April: 118–123.
Suttles, Wayne. "Coping with Abundance: Subsistence on the Northwest Coast." In Richard Lee and Irven Devore (eds) *Man the Hunter,* 56–68. Chicago: Aldine Publishing, 1968.
Tacitus, Publius Cornelius. *Germania.* Stuttgart: Reclam Verlag, 1956 [approximately AD 98].
Testart, Alain. "The Significance of Food Storage among Hunter-Gatherers: Residence Patterns, Populations Densities, and Social Inequalities." *Current Anthropology* 23 (1982) 5: 523–537.
Thomas, Elizabeth Marshall. *The Harmless People.* New York: Vintage Press, 1959.
Trigger, Bruce. "Maintaining Economic Equality in Opposition to Complexity: An Iroquoian Case Study." In Steadman Upham (ed.) *The Evolution of Political Systems: Sociopolitics in Small-scale Sedentary Societies,* 119–145. Cambridge: Cambridge University Press, 1990.

Trigger, Bruce. *Understanding Early Civilizations*. Cambridge: Cambridge University Press, 2003.
Turnbull, Colin M. *The Forest People*. New York: Touchstone, 1962.
Turnbull, Colin M. *Wayward Servants*. Garden City: Natural History Press, 1965.
Ur, Jason A., Philip Karsgaard and Joan Oates. "Early Urban Development in the Near East." *Science* 317 (2007) 5842: 1188.
Van den Berghe, Pierre L. "Bringing Beasts Back In: Toward a Biosocial Theory of Aggression." *American Sociological Review*. 39 (1974) 6: 777–788.
Watts, Joseph, Oliver Sheehan, Quentin D. Atkinson, Joseph Bulbulia and Russell D. Gray. "Ritual Human Sacrifice Promoted and Sustained the Evolution of Stratified Societies." *Nature* (2016). DOI: 10.1038/nature17159
Weber, Max. *Soziologie, weltgeschichtliche Analysen, Politik*. Edited by Eduard Baumgarten. Stuttgart: Alfred Kröner Verlag, 1968.
Webster, David. "Warfare and the Evolution of the State." *American Antiquity*, 40 (1975) 4: 464–470.
Wenke, Robert J. *Patterns in Prehistory*. New York: Oxford University Press, 1999.
Winterhalder, Bruce. "Diet Choice, Risk, and Food Sharing in a Stochastic Environment." *Journal of Anthropological Archeology* 5 (1986) 4: 369–392.
Woodburn, James. "Egalitarian Societies." *Man* 17 (1982) 3: 431–451.
Zvelebil, Marek. "Postglacial Foraging in the Forests of Europe." *Scientific American* 254 (1986) 5: 104–115.

6 Selection
Self-Reinforcement and Social Control

As long as it was assumed that social inequality was a natural, rational or historical necessity, there was, as Fried saw it, no point in asking "why ... people permitted themselves to be seduced, bilked, murphied, or otherwise conned into relinquishing a condition of egalitarianism for one of inequality" (Fried 1967: 183). Both Durkheim and Marx believed that people could only be temporarily deceived about the nature of the social structure in which they lived. Before long they would recognize their true interests and take corrective action. Social scientists therefore paid little attention to how ceremonial centers became palaces of rulers, public offices acquired absolute power and cooperative institutions were transformed into lasting structures of exploitation.

In the real world, the public perception of their positions was very much on the minds of economic and social elites. They may have craved naked power, but they preferred to be seen as selfless servants of the public good. Throughout the history of inequality, fear was the twin of privilege: from the biblical observation that "the full stomach of the rich man will not let him sleep" (Eccl. 5:10) to Henry I who, in the same night, woke up to three nightmares during which nobility, clergy and peasantry rose up against him,[1] and to the nineteenth century employer who felt that he lived "in his factory like the colonial planters in the midst of their slaves, one against a hundred," except that "the barbarians who menace society are (now) in the suburbs of our industrial cities" (cited in Hobsbawm 1962: 70). After a tour of the manufacturing districts of Lancashire in 1842, a clerical observer reported back to his bishop:

> As a stranger passes through the masses of human beings which have accumulated round the mills and print-works ... he cannot contemplate these "crowded hives" of humanity without feelings of anxiety and apprehension almost amounting to dismay. The population, like the system to which it belongs, is *new*; but it is hourly increasing in breadth and strength.
> (Cited in Kuczynski 1967: 77)

What made things worse was that industrial workers were no longer uneducated, god-fearing feudal peasants but an increasingly literate and organized population aware of its strength. The French Revolution showed disenfranchised groups that they could topple long-established social structures, whereas the Industrial

174 *Selection*

Revolution raised the prospect of a cooperative society as a practical alternative to capitalism (Hobsbawm 1962: 248) and gave the laboring classes the means to educate themselves, organize and agitate for a greater share of industrial wealth. Dr. Ure, the propagandist of nineteenth century capitalism in England, saw the resulting threat. Industries

> naturally condense a vast population (of laborers) within a narrow circuit; they afford every facility for secret cabal ... they communicate intelligence and energy to the vulgar mind; they supply in their liberal wages the pecuniary sinews of contention.
>
> (Cited in Thompson 1980: 397)

Owners of industrial capital had no intention of waiting for the inevitable. Baron von Bibra's chamberlain recommended Engels' *Conditions of the Working Classes in England* to his master "in order to profit by the experiences of that great nation and to render the proletariat harmless in its infancy, before it grows (as it has there) into a giant, and threatens the social *status quo*" (Kuczynski 1967: 83). Ure made similar recommendations to his English patrons:

> It is ... excessively in the interest of every mill-owner *to organize his moral machinery on equally sound principles with his mechanical*, for otherwise he will never command the steady hands, watchful eyes, and prompt cooperation, essential to excellence of product.
>
> (Cited in Thompson 1980: 397)

Concern that demands for greater equality and freedom could mislead the masses quickly spread to Britain's colonial backwaters. Across the Atlantic, school reformer Edgerton Ryerson convinced the burghers of Upper Canada to pay taxes for a public school system by arguing that education was "the poor man's elevation and the rich man's security," and that "an army of schoolmasters was ... better than an army of soldiers" (Baldus and Kassam 1996: 335).

Contingency and Continuity

Historically, the emergence of inequality structures has always been followed by the growth of systems of legitimation and social control. Distributive structures are unstable because they remain vulnerable to the small and heterogeneous causes which affect all social structures, and because they are located on normative divides which raise inevitable questions about their equity and justice. At first glance these factors should work in both directions: equality and inequality should wax and wane through human history in roughly equal measure. In fact, given the obvious benefits of trust and cooperation and the evidence that early societies actively defended their egalitarian ways, inequality should be a relatively rare historical phenomenon. That is clearly not the case. Social inequality frequently took root in human societies and, once established, proved often highly resistant to change, but its arrival was neither inevitable nor unopposed. Gains made at other people's expense do not provide sound foundations for their subsequent enjoyment. Losers rarely voluntarily surrender resources or transfer loyalty from family and community to a new and often distant authority. The causes of inequality structures tell us little or nothing about why they persist. As in all evolution, variation (the blind material for selection) and selection itself are separate processes. In order to understand how resistance is overcome and "how elites acquire and maintain their power in spite of the fact that, much of the time, their actions are against the interests of the mass of the population" (Gilman 1981: 4) we must examine how social control transforms the relationship between participants once inequality structures have begun to evolve.

Strategies of Social Control

Conceding that one's fortune was obtained by chance, stealth, or deceit is neither likely to enhance one's self-confidence nor to elicit admiration from others. At the same time, an increase in wealth, no matter how achieved, creates both incentives and resources for making it last. The basic goal of social control is to modify subjective perceptions of inequality. It transforms trust into acquiescence in order to maintain the perception that an unequal distribution of joint results is fair and just, and converts cooperation into cooptation in order to secure the continued contribution of the deprived without which no added value can be produced.

These changes can be achieved by two strategies: *interventive control* and the use of *complementary conditions*. Interventive control allows beneficiaries of inequality to justify and strengthen their social position through the intentional creation of legitimating beliefs and through threats and coercion, knowing that "what quality soever maketh a man beloved, or feared of many; or the representation of such quality, is Power; because it is the means to have the assistance, and service of many" (Hobbes 1991: 62). Plato's *Republic* had already suggested that an elite of philosopher-rulers should use religious myths to restrain the "appetitive instincts" and irrational conduct of common people. Rulers were justified in using any means to maintain social harmony, including deception which was as essential for the well-being of society as was a bitter medicine prescribed by a doctor. Comte recommended the creation of a "religion of humanity," complete with priests, sacraments, hymns and prayers, which could generate uncritical acceptance by lower classes of the edicts of their betters and maintain the stability of society. Such ideological constructs could give inequality the appearance of fairness, habituate lower-ranked groups to their social position, and discourage them from demanding distributive change.

Interventive control through persuasion or fear can be fine-tuned to fit specific circumstances and can achieve long-lasting results. Its downside is that it is often visibly linked to dominant interests, is costly to create and disseminate and may be difficult to undo when circumstances change. It therefore remains vulnerable to unanticipated consequences and may cause resentment rather than compliance, envy rather than awe and conflict rather than acquiescence. Even in modern organizations the cost of interventive control increases when it generates mistrust and is seen as imposed (Falk and Kosfeld 2006).

Interventive control usually requires deliberate, purposeful design. Often, however, conditions capable of stabilizing an inequality structure do not have to be created because they already exist. The use of such complementary windfalls represents a second, less visible but highly effective form of social control. Goffman's (1961) study of "total institutions" such as mental hospitals illustrates the interplay of interventive and complementary control strategies. Interventive control was used to familiarize patients with the institution's declared objectives (protection of society, therapy or cure), and with the rules, prohibitions and penalties deemed necessary to realize these goals. Such interventive strategies required investments in communication, supervisory staff and physical facilities such as locked wards and fences.

By contrast, complementary behavior originated in the "underlife" of such institutions, the complex reactions of inmates to their new environment. Commitment to a mental hospital was often traumatic and involved severe restrictions of movement, the removal of possessions and the intrusive authority of staff. In response, inmates invented a complex compensatory culture. Towels were used as rugs on cold floors, rolled-up newspapers served as pillows and laundry was washed in bathroom sinks and dried on radiators. Patients discovered illicit access to food, tobacco and reading materials. Privacy was obtained by laying claim to personal spaces or by finding places that were free of surveillance. New prestige hierarchies formed among inmates. Ingratiation with staff provided a chance of patronage or an opportunity to "pass for normal." Opposition to staff was expressed in ways which minimized the risk of retaliation.

Unlike interventive indoctrination and sanctions, these behaviors were the patients' own creative adaptations to their new life, and their success often depended on remaining unknown to the administration. Subjectively, they eased the deprivation, loss of control and boredom of institutional life and helped patients to retain a semblance of self-worth. At the same time they also made an unintentional complementary contribution to the maintenance of the institutional inequality structure. Inmates were generally unaware of this effect, just as the administration's knowledge of patient subculture did not amount to much more than a general assessment of the potential for trouble, and the corresponding calculation of persuasive and coercive measures required for the smooth functioning of the institution: the more stable the appearance of the patient population, the lower the investment in interventive control.

The use of complementary conditions as a control strategy has three advantages. The first is its low cost. Interventive control requires outlays for persuasion and coercion. By contrast, complementary conditions offer cost-free opportunities which dominant groups can often use without any change. Where costs do arise they are usually minor expenses of finding and stabilizing complementary circumstances.

Second, the motivations behind complementary behaviors are generally of no concern to its beneficiary. Whereas persuasion and coercion often target specific beliefs among subordinates, complementary conditions are first and foremost judged by their utility, not by the intentions or causes that produced them. As a result, the range of behaviors that can be used in complementary control strategies is greatly increased.

Third, complementarity changes the appearance of social control. It permits the maintenance of inequality while tolerating a high degree of autonomy in subordinate populations. Complementary strategies take advantage of behavior in its existing form and therefore make social control less intrusive. Dominant groups can realize their objectives by letting dependent groups pursue their own goals. Complementarity does not even require direct contact or interaction. Secrecy, inaction or ignorance among subordinates can become powerful contributors to the maintenance of social control. Inequality structures which rely primarily on complementary conditions are less likely to be seen as domination and make it easier to portray relations between dominant and subordinate groups as voluntary cooperation. Complementary conditions are therefore particularly suitable for eliciting acquiescence and cooptation. Their disadvantage is that they are not directly under the beneficiary's control, and are therefore less predictable and less reliable.

Dynamics of Self-Reinforcement

Interventive and complementary strategies are elementary tools of the trial and error exploration of environments. All social actors, not just the powerful and wealthy, use persuasion and coercion to modify the behavior of others and to scan natural and social environments for opportunities and risks. Social inequality adds material and psychological self-reinforcing effects to these strategies and skews their returns. Material gains usually have compounding effects for winners and losers. They can create powerful winner-take-all dynamics (Hacker and Pierson 2010) by facilitating the accumulation of more wealth and increasing the chances of benefitting from complementary windfalls. They provide added means to influence the behavior of subordinates through direct rewards or punishment, by inspiring admiration and imitation through conspicuous displays and by constructing symbolic images of the advantages of conformity and the dangers of opposition. By the same token they reduce the ability of losers to resist the erosion of their position and to take advantage of complementary conditions. Material gains can also have important psychological consequences. Regardless how they were obtained, they can make people feel more self-important, experience a greater sense of entitlement, and be less sensitive to the suffering of others and more likely to engage in unethical behavior (Piff 2014). On the other side, a lack of resources, greater dependence and lower rank can reduce the ability to plan for the future, force one to constantly juggle local and temporary problems, and lead people into a scarcity trap from which it is difficult to escape (Mullainathan and Shafir 2013). It encourages a view of the world as beyond one's control and reduces the chance to see and take advantage of complementary opportunities (Kraus et al. 2009).

Their wealth allowed Sumerian kings and Maya rulers to depict their lineages and the defeat of their rivals on monumental buildings, medieval aristocrats to sponsor sculptures and church windows which linked the bliss of heaven and the fires of hell to the acceptance or rejection of the feudal order, and Hawaiian chiefs to employ specialists who kept their genealogies but made it *tabu* for commoners to compile their own (Earle 1997: 36). In modern societies, increased wealth provides added means to shape political decisions through lobbying and political donations (Gilens 2012), and public opinion through the control of media (Neckerman and Torche 2007; McCall and Percheski 2010; Carruthers and Kim 2011). Barthes describes the social control effects of such "political language":

> Myth does not deny things, on the contrary, its function is to talk about them ... it gives them a natural and eternal justification, it gives them a clarity which is not that of an explanation but that of a statement of fact.... In passing from history to nature, myth acts economically: it abolishes the complexity of human acts, it gives them the simplicity of essences.
> (Barthes 1972: 143)

Political myths and symbols trickle down to lower classes through observation and imitation. In Europe from the thirteenth century onward, aristocratic values, mannerisms and fashions were imitated by clergy, bourgeoisie and common people, even though they may have objected to feudal rule (Heer 1962: 32). In modern societies, "cultural capital" derived from social status such as the prestige rankings of "elite" universities create self-reinforcing effects for the PhD and grant market (Burris 2004). Such consequences are not always intended and can have unanticipated results: imitation from below can dilute the exclusiveness of symbols, forcing upper classes to maintain the desired social distance by inventing ever new social barriers, conspicuous consumption or exclusionary language (Brown 1965: 51–68). But self-reinforcement can also gather enough strength to survive the publication of nonsense (Sokal and Bricmont 1998), to hide prolonged incompetence and avoid criticism and accountability.[2]

Interventive Control

From Cooperation to Cooptation: The Reconstruction of Dominant Interests as the Common Good

In all inequality structures, interventive control focuses on four basic themes: to emphasize common purposes and benefits of inequality; to portray classes and their relationship; to describe mutual obligations and aspirations; and to erect boundaries which define behavior that endangers the prevailing distributive order. Beneficiaries of inequality structures appeal to common objectives or to the interests of the deprived because the continued cooperation of losers is needed if winners wish to enjoy more than a one-time gain. In Rousseau's view this was done initially through the clever fraud in which the rich, not yet secure in their hold over their possessions, pretended to use their wealth to guarantee order and security, thus luring the poor into accepting legal property rights which in fact cemented their inferiority. With the beginning of industrialization the priority became to prevent

> the lower orders, that valuable portion of the community whose labor (is) so essential to the social system under which we live, (from being) tempted by the delusive and wicked principles instilled into their minds, to direct their strength to the destruction of the government, and to the overthrow of every civil and religious establishment.
> (William Wilberforce 1817, cited in Hammond and Hammond 1968: 210)

The dilemma was how to profess adherence to the "rights of man" while making the practical application of these rights compatible with the new industrial inequality. The most common solution was to pare down more radical interpretations of the democratic, egalitarian and cooperative principles of the American and French Revolutions. In the course of the nineteenth century in the US these principles were gradually

> drained of their old significance; a new content was injected; and it was generally supposed that nothing had happened, because the labels remained unchanged. The conservative exponent of a basically undemocratic ethos could now bolster up his argument with the language of democracy itself.
> (McCloskey 1951: 16)

Equality was purged of connections to wealth and was reduced to the universal right to vote and to equality before the law. Liberty came to mean the unrestricted use of private property and the protection of markets from state intervention. Fraternity and cooperation were reduced to integrating employees into a functional division of labor. Academics like Sumner and industrialists like Carnegie claimed that private wealth would trickle down through society because the rich were "trustees of their fellow men" (Smucker 1977: 271), custodians of the public good and munificent contributors to charitable causes. Workers and employers had the same interests; the worker should "throw his hat up in the air and cheer for (employers') success, for their success is his success" (cited in Bliss 1974: 89). Demands for higher wages risked workers' prosperity while unions threatened their freedom to sell their labor. Workers were "happily secure" when working from sunrise to sunset. Shorter work hours would expose them to temptation, vice and crime (Smucker 1977). Modern political processes continue to invoke common interests to create public acceptance of political and economic actions which further the interest of wealthy and politically influential groups. Anti-trust laws, pollution controls or tax cuts frequently have preambles which emphasize values such as fairness, equity, environmental sustainability, or describe profits as incentives for job creation (Edelman 1988, 2001).

The Reconstruction of Success and Failure

Medieval guilds were the first to break with the aristocratic ideology of inherited rank by linking social status to personal effort. They also invented the first modern forms of legitimating this link by using secrecy and rituals to exaggerate their expertise, monopolize skills and reduce competition by closing access to their ranks (White 1972: 275). Like the principles of liberty and equality, however, the nexus between effort and success was plagued by ambiguity where large fortunes were visibly gained through chance or unethical practices, and where poverty persisted in spite of hard work and frugal living. The ideological solution was to dilute the meaning of success and failure by attributing it on one hand to individual motivation and effort, and on the other to the often severe but always impartial power of competitive markets.

For the rich, these new notions of success offered a convenient hindsight justification of their wealth, while they directed the poor to the intimate sphere of personal scrutiny and self-doubt. Wealth was not the result of greed; the "pursuit of mammon" was universally condemned in business publications, church sermons and schoolbooks (Baldus and Kassam 1996). It was "pretty sure to end in disappointment" (cited in Bliss 1974: 17). Profit was the compensation the business owner received for laboring long and hard to create work for others while his employees enjoyed fixed hours and limited responsibility. Nineteenth century Ontario schoolbooks told children that the wealthy obtained their fortune through personal sacrifice, and warned the poor that pleasure "was ever bought with pain" (Baldus and Kassam 1996: 346). "Don't shoot the millionaire" was a recurrent theme in stories of success of cult figures such as Edison and Carnegie (Cawelti 1965). Wealth was not only a source of charity but a school of character: it strengthened the self-denial, intelligence and energy which made civilization and progress possible. As the size of companies grew and the late nineteenth century merger movement created large corporate units, stories of personal success gave way to impersonal images of capitalist firms as the source of employment and economic prosperity. By the early twentieth century, corporations had turned into quasi-human entities, "corporate citizens" responsible for the "corporate family" of their employees (Bakan 2004: 26, 27).

The portrayal of the poor underwent similar changes. In early eighteenth century English landscape painting, poverty did not appear. Rural laborers were shown as distant figures or as allegorical representatives of the landed gentry. After the mid-eighteenth century they appeared more frequently as industrious and sober inhabitants of Merry England, part of a harmonious and contented rural society unaffected by the radical transformation of agriculture wrought by enclosures and the migration of rural labor to the cities. Rural poverty became an object of aesthetic interest, a world where the poor lived simple, self-sufficient lives and did not question their social condition (Barrell 1980: 16). After the French Revolution, depictions of rural labor increased sharply and took a more nationalistic tone to prove that English peasants were immune to political temptation. With the advent of industrialization, idyllic rural settings also offered a pleasing contrast to the grime and social ills of industrial cities. Generally, painters used light to reflect social differences; sunshine fell on the rich while the poor and their houses remained on "the dark side of the landscape" (Barrell 1980: 22).

Popular literature, widely read by the mid-nineteenth century, focused more on living conditions in the cities. The two most common types of urban poor in Victorian fiction were the good poor who were unskilled, often illiterate and impoverished through no fault of their own. They had upright moral characters and were eager to improve themselves. Authors such as Dickens often used their suffering to stir the conscience of the reader and allowed them to be rescued by an initially mysterious patron. The second most frequent type were the debased poor whose fate was caused by drunkenness, crime, brutality and vice (Keating 1971).

Both images reflected the prevailing ideological view that poverty had personal, not structural causes. The self-help movement which blossomed after 1850 placed the onus for poverty and success on proper motivation, walking a tightrope between encouraging a desire for improvement and dampening hopes for unrealistic ambition and structural change. True happiness could be found in the acceptance of the limitations of one's position. Misery could be a "school for life," an idea that revived older images of pain and misfortune as a condition of salvation. Striving for success should not "aim too high." Nineteenth century Ontario schoolbooks mixed stories with titles such as "do not grasp at too much, or you will lose all," "a humble condition brings safety" or "a good name is better than great riches" with poems which praised the dignity of poverty (Baldus and Kassam 1996: 342). Church sermons told people that bitterness and envy could best be reduced by "contrasting one's own condition with that of those who were worse off" (Wise 1991: 174). Begrudging the good fortune of the wealthy did not help; they had acquired it at the price of much hardship and risk. Advocates of more equality were only out "to make a wreck of the social order for the sake of dividing among themselves the spoils of the rich, which would not support the community for a month" (Channing 1838 cited in Cawelti 1965: 84). Between 1846 and 1910, only one of the hundreds of stories in Ontario schoolbooks suggested that political measures could relieve poverty. These morality tales were fleshed out by the ideological set pieces in popular fiction by authors such as Horatio Alger[3] whose heroes, usually boys between 12 and 18 and orphaned or forced into poverty by a drunken father, achieved modest success by dint of honesty, hard work, punctuality and deference toward employers. Their true aim was respectability and happiness; Alger reminded his readers frequently that large fortunes led to unhappiness and greed. An element of luck, such as the discovery by a patron, served as a literary device to explain why striving for self-improvement alone did not guarantee a better life.

Relations between Classes

Late eighteenth and early nineteenth century ideologies still portrayed class relations as part of a providential design. The "turbulent advocates of equality" failed to see the mutual benefits of this arrangement.

> The *artificial* wants of the rich are a constant supply to the *real* wants of the poor.... It is in the order of God's Providence that the poor should derive their support from the rich; and, if you cut off the rich, the poor must necessarily wither and decay. The poor can no more live without the rich, than the rich without the poor; they are mutually dependent upon, and mutually useful to, each other.
>
> (1793 sermon cited in Wahrman 1995: 84, 85)

During the nineteenth century, markets and technologies dissolved pre-industrial ties of loyalty and obedience and created new definitions of the relations between employer and worker. Industrial labor markets demanded an increasing variety of skills. Workers could contract with different employers, and changing economic conditions could rapidly increase or reduce the demand for labor. These structural changes found their ideological reflection in a more flexible work ethic, generic concepts of authority and compliance, and in the discovery of the worker as a consumer.

Ideological notions of individual achievement and mobility, anathema to static pre-industrial societies, were now extended to the worker. Self-improvement was integrated into labor markets portrayed as hierarchical occupational structures waiting for workers with commensurate ambition and skill. Individuals were encouraged to envision and train for a career and aim for a rise in social position, however modest. With the rise of modern corporations the image of failure also changed. Poverty and unemployment retained their stigma, but were increasingly seen as resulting from market mechanisms which allowed only a few to rise to the top and confronted the rest with a modern normality of limited careers, monotonous work and modest incomes.

Relations of authority and compliance also became more generic. Pre-industrial ties of personal loyalty were replaced by impersonal concepts of authority and compliance which could be called upon by different employers for variable tasks. Milgram's classic 1974 study illustrates this compliance with technical-functional hierarchies and faceless authority.

The last change in the ideology of class relations, beginning in the early twentieth century, was the discovery that workers were not only producers but consumers. Economic crises in pre-industrial societies were crises of underproduction (or, from the aristocratic vantage point, over-consumption by peasants). Famines or food shortages were dealt with by forcing peasants to produce more or eat less. Industry owners initially failed to understand that the increased output of factory-produced goods and the limited purchasing power of labor caused an entirely new type of economic crisis characterized by overproduction which swamped markets with unsold goods. Well into the twentieth century the standard response to economic downturns was therefore to lay off workers and reduce wages, a policy which lowered spending and reduced consumption. Not until the New Deal was the role of consumers and mass markets fully understood.[4] Ideology now moved into the sphere of consumption, not just production. Where early advertising simply praised a product, goods were now increasingly linked with private desires and anxieties. By the mid-1920s advertising began to assume modern forms. *Middletown*, an early sociological study of a mid-western American town, observed that advertising aimed

> to make the reader emotionally uneasy, to bludgeon him with the fact that decent people don't live the way he does.... (Advertising) points an accusing finger at the stenographer as she reads her motion picture magazine and makes her acutely conscious of her unpolished fingernails ... and sends the housewife peering anxiously into the mirror to see if her wrinkles look like those that made Mrs. X in the advertisement "old at thirty-five" because she did not have a Leisure Hour electric washer.
>
> (Lynd and Lynd 1929: 82)

The discovery of the consumer by modern advertising suggested new channels for personal creativity, self-fulfillment and social advancement, and redirected expectations for social change. Poverty could now be disguised and personal fulfillment could be gained through the consumption of goods which offered real or imagined access to status, youth and beauty. Advertising simultaneously displayed, concealed and overcame social differences. A mind thus primed was not likely to give much thought to distributive change.

The Construction of Boundaries

Boundaries are demarcations of the forbidden, warnings of futility, sin and disorder, symbolic barriers against critiques of distributive structures and demands for alternatives. In their simplest form, they merely prohibit behavior considered dangerous to the established order. But boundaries can also redirect dissatisfaction with inequality at scapegoats or create controlled and safe channels for the release of discontent. Sin and damnation served as all-purpose boundary devices in feudal societies, linked the fate of the peasantry to biblical vice and encouraged the poor to atone for their sins which were the cause of famines, wars and epidemics (Cohn 1970: 128). Carnivals, turn-around days, jester figures and witch-hunts allowed the managed expression of dissent. The French Revolution required new boundary images. As Charles Inglis, Anglican bishop of Nova Scotia saw it in 1794,

> The history of mankind ... furnishes no instance ... of so general a phrenzy seizing a populous and polished nation; a phrenzy that is not confined to any particular description, but diffused through all ranks and orders of people. The high and the low, the peer and peasant, the learned and the ignorant, are equally stimulated to the perpetration of the most atrocious crimes; delighting in slaughter and unbridled cruelty; sporting with the lives and property of mankind; destroying all religion and subordination; openly avowing atheism; and sinking into a total depravation of principles and manners.
>
> (Cited in Wise 1991: 164)

Through the nineteenth century a variety of groups were singled out as threats to civilization and public order, from the Jacobins to Reform and Chartist movements. Later in the century, fears were redirected at associations and unions of industrial workers who, instead of blaming themselves and improving their character, held owners of industries and governments responsible for the conditions in which they lived and asked for shorter hours and higher wages.

Their demands went to the heart of the distributive dilemma: the question of who should control production and how the proceeds should be shared between owners and workers. After bitter struggles, the right of labor to organize was recognized by 1870 in most industrial countries, but employers remained overwhelmingly hostile to unions (Bliss 1974: 74, 76). The fear was that unionization would reduce employers' control over industrial property and profits. For most industrialists the laws of the market determined profits and wages, and these laws could not be changed. In their view, unions were generally run by "vultures of the labor world" that lived off union dues while exempting themselves from industrial work. As early as 1825 when journeymen went on strike in Boston for a shorter work day, "labor trouble' was also traced – probably for the first but not the last time – to "foreign agitators" (Kuczynski 1967: 98).

By 1870, schoolbooks in Canada and the US drew a clear line between acceptable and unacceptable social change. American schoolbooks carefully distinguished between legitimate rebellion against tyranny such as the American Revolution, and unjustified opposition against present-day order. The former was necessary to sustain natural rights which had been perverted by British rule. By contrast, labor protests against American authorities, such as the Haymarket riot in Chicago in 1886, were "criminal" and inspired by "turbulent leaders."

> There is no doubt that the nineteenth century child who was influenced by his school books would identify labor organization with violence and probably with doctrines subversive of American institutions. He would know nothing of the background of the growth of labor unions, and he would probably assume collective bargaining to be a device designed by unscrupulous men in search of personal gain. The laborer who accepted American labor conditions and worked hard would get ahead. To question American labor conditions was un-American.
>
> (Elson 1964: 251)

The schoolbooks also made the first references to socialism and communism, boundary labels whose use increased precipitously after the Russian Revolution. By the time of Hess and Torney's (1967) study of American children's political values, boundary concepts projected a polarized view of the world. Legitimate symbols like the flag contrasted with terms such as "revolutionary," "subversive," "trouble-maker" and "communist" which defined the limits of political tolerance. Their use intensified in times of perceived crises: the "red scare" of the Depression years, the cold war, or episodic fears of terrorism fostered intensely hostile reactions to political "enemies" (Stouffer 1963). Modern boundaries create "stopping points" which separate what are judged realistic and sensible reforms from unreasonable and unacceptable alternatives (Benson and Kirsch 2010). These channel fears toward ever-changing and highly selective targets and distinguish political friends from enemies.

Complementarity and Social Control

In contrast to the often deliberately planned and carefully targeted forms of interventive control, complementary conditions can hold widely different appeals for different participants. Roman gladiatorial games which originated in Etruscan funeral rites were used by Roman aristocrats to display their wealth and advance their political careers through sponsorship. Roman emperors staged them as political theatre to show their largesse and power, and to claim commitment to long-abandoned republican traditions by occasionally deferring to the spectators' wishes for the fate of victims. For Roman plebeians the games offered a surrogate experience of violence and triumph of Rome's military conquests, whereas the anonymity of the amphitheater gave them a rare chance to express opposition to imperial rule. Surviving gladiators made careers, became celebrities and sex symbols, made money by fixing the outcome of combats and bought their freedom with the proceeds. However, there can be little doubt that the complementary benefits of the games were far greater for emperors and Roman elites than for other groups (Hopkins 1983).

Because complementary conditions require little or no further modification they lead to substantial savings compared to interventive control. Occasionally, history permits a direct comparison of the costs of the two strategies. The Spanish conquest of the Aztec Empire between 1519 and 1521 relied on Cortés' skillful exploitation of two complementary circumstances. Populations subjected by the Aztecs supplied him with guides and an auxiliary army. More important, the Aztec ruler Moctezuma fatally misinterpreted the arrival of the Spanish as the return of Quetzalcoatl, a legendary religious reformer whose second coming was predicted in Aztec mythology.

Cortés' campaign shows the typical features of complementarity. First, his advantage was entirely fortuitous. The conquered unwittingly furthered their own demise; they were neither persuaded nor coerced by the Spaniards. Second, the complementary circumstances allowed Cortés to enter Mexico with a spectacularly small force and with minimal loss in life and material, a cost which became evident when after a senseless massacre the Aztecs finally rose against their occupiers. The Spanish were forced to retreat, suffered heavy casualties and lost their looted gold. The second conquest took a year to prepare, required Spanish reinforcements from Cuba, some 80,000 native soldiers and the construction of 13 ships to blockade and attack the Aztec capital from the lake. Even then it was only after 80 days of fighting and heavy losses that Cortés was able to enter the capital for the second time.[5] Similarly dramatic cost differentials can be found in the conversion of English and Japanese workers to the time-discipline of industrial production. English workers, used to seasonal and relatively autonomous agricultural work, strenuously resisted the long unbroken hours of factory labor. Factory owners had to enforce discipline with a multitude of costly fines and penalties (Thompson 1967; Hammond and Hammond 1968: Chapter 2). In Japan, intensive agriculture had long required detailed time planning by peasants. Japanese capitalists enjoyed the complementary advantage of a disciplined workforce and paternalistic family traditions whose ties of mutual obligation, loyalty and obedience were easily transferred to new managerial hierarchies in the factory (Smith 1986).

Adjustment and Accommodation

Not all complementary conditions provide a perfect, cost-free fit with dominant group objectives. Beneficiaries may have to modify them to reap their full complementary advantages. The Inca incorporated indigenous chiefs into fictitious kinship lines headed by Inca god-rulers (Silverblatt 1988). Roman governments appeased conquered populations by transferring their deities to Rome and incorporating them into the Roman panoply of gods. British colonial administrations in Africa and India relied on indirect rule which used indigenous local governments to control subject populations.

Complementary opportunities can also be improved by the inadvertent adjustment by subordinate groups to the constraints which inequality imposes on their lives, from boring work and material deprivation to the stigma of poverty or the perceived gap between one's own life and ideological images of success. Slowing down production in order to avoid cuts in piece rates or inventing games and practical jokes help to relieve the monotony of work (Roy 1958). Assembly line workers "double up" by doing each other's job or let their work pile up so they can race to catch up with the line, creating "a few minutes of seemingly purposeful exertion ... hills and troughs, minor goals and fulfillments while you're waiting for the day to end or the line to break down" (Rinehart 2001: 143). Low caste villagers may assume high caste surnames when they work at government office in order to disguise their background (Parish 1996: 113, 115). Laid-off professionals may go to great length to preserve the appearance of a continued middle-class life style (Ehrenreich 2005: 203, 204).

The gap between social position and social expectations can be bridged by imitating higher status groups, but also by reducing the attractiveness of higher social positions. Factory workers may believe that the rich worry more about losing their money and are as a result less healthy and less happy (Lane 1962: 260). Indian untouchables with steady employment refuse to associate with other untouchables who do the typical casual labor (Freeman 1979: 53). Carefully measured hostility can offer a way of getting back at high-status others. In pre-revolutionary France apprentices mocked their master by engaging in a richly symbolic massacre of his wife's cats (Darnton 1984a). Low caste people manipulate or make fun of higher caste in such a way that there is little danger of retaliation (Freeman 1979: 153). Petty theft of tools and merchandise by employees reduces dissatisfaction with low pay or close supervision (Zeitlin 1971). Such behaviors relieve stress for the individual, but they also unintentionally reduce social tension and consolidate the position of superior groups.

The Growth of Cultures of Dependence

The subjective relief from tension, anxiety and conflict can make adjustive behavior self-reinforcing. Chronic lack of opportunity dulls hope and encourages resignation (Newman 1988: 93–94). The longer the gates to greater equality remain shut or the smaller the opening, the thinner the crowds waiting to get in. Habituation and resignation can spread from wealth differences to other forms of inequality such as racial and gender discrimination, crime or political authoritarianism and lead to their long-term acceptance as a just world (Tepperman and Gheihman 2013).

Kaplow (1972) described the dense web of psychological adjustments among the poor in pre-revolutionary eighteenth century Paris which combined the cult of saints, loyalty to the king, escapes into drink, domestic violence, sexual license disguised as religious fervor, and petty crime. Jahoda, Lazarsfeld and Zeisel (1971) traced the long-term adjustment of the people of Marienthal, an Austrian town which lost its only major industry during the Depression in 1929. Initial adjustment by buying cheaper foods or mending worn clothing led eventually to a more permanent acceptance of unemployment as a regular way of life. Chinoy's (1955) study of the life-course adjustment of young automobile workers showed how early hopes to leave the factory to open a small business gave way to more modest ambitions centering around security and seniority, union careers and hopes for the future of their children. Long-term welfare recipients, mostly mothers with dependent children, resort to claims of chronic illness and poor health to legitimate their situation and avoid the stigma of personal failure (Cole and Lejeune 1972). Sennett (1998) records the gradual adjustment of computer scientists and engineers to downsizing, first by blaming their company and managers, then shifting to more permanent self-blame for failing to see the change in the computer market, and sometimes to inward-directed, born-again religion. Nash (1972) and Grätz (2003) describe the sacrifices, magic and diviners used by South-American and African miners to control the chance of finding ore, to relieve the danger of work and to cope with poverty. Such cultures of dependence can have lasting complementary consequences:

> Both self-blame and the defensive rationalizations against self-blame ... contribute to the maintenance of ... existing institutions and the tradition of opportunity itself. To the extent that workers focus blame for their failure to rise above the level of wage labor upon themselves rather than upon the institutions that govern the pursuit of wealth or upon the persons who control those institutions, American society escapes the consequences of its own contradictions.
>
> (Chinoy 1955: 129)

At the same time, adjustive responses always coexist with layers of contradictory feelings which can disable or reverse their complementary effects. Even in the extreme conditions of the eighteenth century slave trade, officers, crew and slaves were bound together by a complex balance of adjustment, coercion and insurrection (Rediker 2007: Chapter 9).

Strategies of Social Control: Long-Term Trends[6]

Inequality structures always employ interventive and complementary control strategies. How much of each is present in a particular society shapes its political appearance. Interventive control tends to be typical of centralized political systems. In the high-inequality societies of Tonga and Hawaii "chiefly families utilized the entire playbook: sacred authority, genealogical seniority, military force, and political and economic expertise" (Flannery and Marcus 2012: 209). Such strategies can create high levels of conformity between rulers and ruled, rich and poor. By contrast, complementary strategies allow subordinate groups to pursue their own goals as long as the results serve the interests of their superiors. This creates decentralized inequality structures which tolerate, within broad boundary limits, relatively high levels of autonomy among subordinates.

Feudal inequality relied primarily on interventive social control. Throughout the medieval period the lord's right to interfere directly in the behavior of his subordinates was an essential tool of exploitation, but it also involved much effort and cost. It worked best on the feudal manor with its personal ties and close supervision. When peasants and an urban bourgeoisie claimed a larger measure of independence, feudal aristocracies responded by intensifying and centralizing interventive control, culminating in the appearance of absolute monarchies. The cost of maintaining persuasion and coercion grew apace. Erikson's (1966) study of a Puritan community in seventeenth-century Massachusetts sheds some light on what happens when the logistic limits of interventive strategies are reached. Here social control was maintained by a small church elite which enforced rigid beliefs and imposed strict penalties for deviance. Control in Puritan communities was probably more intense than in feudal systems. Even at the height of the religious crazes and persecutions which periodically swept medieval Europe, some segments of feudal societies – the poor, the disreputable, and even the peasantry – enjoyed that strange measure of freedom that sometimes comes from being considered utterly irrelevant. But the basic principles of social control were the same in both societies. With the appearance of mass deviance in the form of three waves of heresy, Puritan interventive control quickly reached the point where it could not handle any more offenders, and conviction rates leveled off. Interventive control strategies thus seem to encounter typical limits in dealing with complexity, and that capacity can only be slightly expanded.[7] As early as the sixteenth century there were clear indications that aristocratic rule had also reached such limits. It tried to cope with epidemics of deviance with ever more frequent and cruel punishment such as branding, flogging and executions, but interventive control was in fact falling apart. In the end, the death penalty was invoked for minor offenses not so much for deterrence but to cut the logistic costs of trials and punishment, leading to rates of executions which seemed to threaten the supply of rural labor (Harrison cited in George 1971: 398). In pre-revolutionary France, police inspectors made valiant but hopeless attempts to stay ahead of the flood of subversive ideas of the *philosophes* and of the *libellistes* who published them (Darnton 1984b). It was a futile effort. By the eighteenth century, aristocratic governments faced so many centrifugal forces that it became impossible to maintain more than a semblance of centralized power. The diversity of ideas and the complexity of industrial production rendered the centuries-old feudal tools of control ineffective.

Feudal inequality collapsed for many reasons, but the failure of its social control system was surely one of the most important. From that angle the theoretical "problem of order" which preoccupied social philosophers and sociologists from the eighteenth century onward is really the question why feudalism failed to respond to the challenge to order whereas industrial capitalism succeeded. The answer lies in the new and creative ways with which capitalism reduced the costs of social control. The feudal aristocracy had bent its underclass to its own wishes by ideology and force. The bourgeoisie realized not only that this was no longer possible, but that it was not necessary. It was the historic discovery of the individual capitalist that he could let others work for himself while allowing them to pursue their own personal goals. It was the historic discovery of capitalists as a class that this could be done on a large scale, and that many of their needs could be met by complementary features in the laboring population with the added advantage of giving their relationship the appearance of mutual autonomy and consent. Seen from this perspective, the liberal freedoms which the bourgeoisie had proclaimed as its proudest achievements were simply a shift to a more cost-effective mix of social control strategies.

Nothing exemplifies the nature of this change better than the development of self-regulating markets where industry owners and workers contracted as legally independent partners, a relationship so different from the personal obligations which linked the feudal peasant to the lord. The freedom to contract was of course curtailed by an essential *fait accompli* – the concentration of industrial capital in the hands of a new class of owners. But at the same time markets also granted the industrial working class an unprecedented degree of autonomy, and capitalists learned to live with and ultimately profit from it. Their tolerance of independence and diversity in the laboring population did not come overnight. The first decades of industrialization are characterized by a tenacious survival of pre-industrial ways of thinking, visible in the rigid enforcement of a quasi-feudal discipline in many factories. But such views were soon replaced by the realization that workers sought factory employment out of a *variety* of personal motives which could be integrated unchanged into the capitalist process of production.

The growth of industrial capitalism thus altered the mix of social control strategies. Reliance on interventive control diminished while the systematic use of complementary features in the behavior of subordinate groups increased. Interventive strategies such as corporate lobbying and financing of political campaigns in support of existing inequalities of income and wealth did not disappear. At the same time, however, wealthy groups increasingly employed techniques first used by working-class movements in order to oppose progressive taxation, public healthcare or redistributive social policies, and disguised their true goals behind populist claims (Frank 2004; Martin 2013). Interventive strategies also became more residual and reactive and were used only when complementary behavior could not meet capitalist goals. An interventive view of poverty as a personal flaw whose correction required workhouses, low wages as a cure for "laziness" and the physical punishment of "vagrants" persisted well into the nineteenth century. As early as the seventeenth century, however, welfare payments also began to track the rise and fall of social unrest (Piven and Cloward 1971). Reducing conflict by buying off protesters became more cost-effective than using coercion or correcting the suspected moral and motivational deficiencies of the poor.

This reactive approach became the predominant form of managing social conflict in modern welfare systems (Peel 2003: 98ff.). The shift toward a systematic use of complementary conditions is reflected in the growth of institutions which identify, assess and reinforce complementary behavior. Market research and polling in contemporary industrial societies systematically search for complementary consumer and political preferences which can increase sales or make political measures palatable. Democracy begins to erode: voting becomes a routine but inconsequential outlet for collective discontent, and formal political processes create the appearance of public consent for political decisions which favor dominant interests. With the growing use of complementary conditions, lower classes assume a greater role in the reproduction of inequality, whereas dominant groups are less often required to intervene directly to create the conditions they need to pursue their interests. As a result they become progressively less visible: from the pervasive presence of aristocracies in economic, political, religious and cultural affairs to the still extensive social role of the factory owner in early paternalistic capitalism, and finally to the low visibility of the modern capitalist. By the early twentieth century, popular media had replaced the "heroes of production" with "heroes of consumption," the high-spending celebrities of sports or film (Loewenthal 1961). These changes indicate a shift in social control, not in power: popular complementary sentiments from below assume an ever greater role in reinforcing the inequality structure of modern societies.

The focus of the remaining interventive control moves from the control of the motivational antecedents of behavior to the control of its results. The often rapid and unpredictable political, technological and economic change in modern societies can make indoctrination quickly obsolete and require high costs of resocialization. Interventive control becomes more pragmatic and less prescriptive. "Shared" values and political symbols become vague in content but high in emotional appeal, turning them into flexible tools for mobilizing desired behavior in a variety of changing and unforeseen situations.

Elson observed this shift towards affectively loaded, content-free and therefore highly elastic ideological concepts, noting that nineteenth century American schoolbooks presented values such as "liberty" as "a desirable but undefined and almost mystical entity" (Elson 1964: 258, 289). Sutton, Harris, Kaysen and Tobin (1962) attributed the generality of business concepts such as "free enterprise" to the need to sustain the legitimacy of capitalist industry in diverse and changeable circumstances. Hess and Torney (1967) found similarly general characteristics in political and social values taught in American elementary schools. Easton and Dennis (1969) observed the creation of "diffuse support" for basic capitalist institutions in schools which increased its usefulness for the flexible, transferable legitimation of social institutions. The behavioral consequences are exemplified by the willingness of children to judge people on the basis of superficial information about their social position (Baldus and Tribe 1978). The same vagueness and flexibility can be found in boundary labels, in corporate brand loyalties which remain unaffected by variations in products, and in a fluid "audit culture" of flexible and transferable standards for product safety and product risks (Benson and Kirsch 2010).

Modern media with highly concentrated ownership act as agents of reinforcement by ranking the priority of political issues, and by "priming" people's evaluation of political alternatives through channeling new events into familiar ideological categories (Kinder 2003). Simple, repetitive symbols and uniform messages facilitate the construction of populist political values and the denial of social harm. As a result, modern inequality structures appear less as systems of domination and more as mutual opportunity structures. Dominant groups scan subordinates for conditions that support their own objectives and intervene generally only where these conditions are insufficient. Subordinate groups, in turn, discover opportunities for the realization of their own goals in the inequality that surrounds them. Employees may use petty theft at their workplace to relieve work stress, to retaliate for what they see as unfair treatment or miserly wages, or for the excitement of "getting away with it." Companies, knowing that the amounts are usually small and that prevention through close supervision would not be cost-effective, may tacitly tolerate an acceptable level of "controlled larceny" and add it to their cost accounting. The resulting increase in worker satisfaction avoids more costly problems such as high turnover, low productivity, or strikes. From the company's point of view, employee theft, if kept within acceptable limits, becomes a managerial tool to maintain employee morale and reduce labor costs (Zeitlin 1971). Relative gains are unequal: companies draw greater profit from labor peace than employees derive from pilfering company property, but such mutual opportunity structures easily acquire the semblance of a fair exchange.

In modern inequality structures adjustive responses to inequality have themselves become major markets which offer complementary opportunities for commercial exploitation. Social media have become easy venues for the release of anger and frustration which remain largely inconsequential but are highly profitable. Advertising shows a world of happy, young and prosperous people which bears no resemblance to demographic or any other typical characteristics of society. Marketing popular culture from gambling to music to sports has become a major part of modern economies. Information technology has increased the tools for surveillance and for probing individual behavior for commercial opportunities. Such forms of social control have made capitalism itself more secure. Its main beneficiaries no longer need to remain in the background: their demonstrative display of oversized yachts and 50-room mansions show that Veblen's conspicuous leisure and conspicuous consumption have not lost their allure.

Control, Continuity and Change

All distributive structures must rely on complex systems of social control if they want to be stable. Egalitarian, cooperative systems must protect themselves against free riders. Inequality must ensure the continued cooperation of the deprived. There are, however, typical differences in their control strategies. Cooperative systems must maintain a strong basis of solidarity and trust among their members and must validate specific action choices and demands on members by referring to common values. In addition, they must protect trust against deception and defection, informally through ostracism, shame or altruistic punishment, and formally through audits and sanctions. This requirement is particularly onerous where trust is impersonal and requires complex formal-legal safeguards against malfeasance (Shapiro 1987). Motivating solidarity and protecting cooperation from abuse requires high levels of interventive control. Interventive control is costly, potentially intrusive and relatively inflexible. Cooperators cannot easily tap into the rich social control potential of complementary opportunities offered by the actions and motivations of others.

By contrast, beneficiaries of inequality systems have greater access to complementary control strategies. They can turn losers into unwitting accomplices, and can co-opt their labor without their formal consent or knowledge. They can therefore meet their social control needs flexibly and with lower costs. This is made easier because inequality always also redistributes resources for social control, creating self-reinforcing effects which account for much of its strength and resilience to change.

Nonetheless, social control is not seamlessly efficient. Nineteenth century business leaders, like their feudal predecessors, were at times woefully inaccurate in their assessment of the world in which they lived (Baldus and Kassam 1996), and their ideas and actions ran counter to their own interests. Nor were they always of one mind. Andrew Carnegie's ringing defense of the survival of the fittest was plagued by private concern over the corrosive effect of his business activities on his moral convictions. In the mind of school reformers like Edgerton Ryerson, the cold calculation of the potential of public education to protect the class structure stood next to a genuine interest in improving the literacy of children.

Social control therefore remains vulnerable to continuing trial-and-error exploration. The ingenious co-optation of subjected populations by the Inca also preserved the memory of an egalitarian past. As a result, Inca domination was interrupted by cycles of "defiance in consent, subversion in rule" (Silverblatt 1988: 99). In 1789, the same Parisian poor who seemed to be so god-fearing, had a saint for every physical and social ailment and appeared to be capable of little more than pub brawls, moved within weeks from an insurrection of journeymen and artisans in a wallpaper factory to storming the Bastille in the name of liberty, equality and fraternity. A century later, strong working class parties had changed the political and social landscape beyond early industrialists' worst nightmares. Social control can stabilize inequality structures but cannot eliminate the potential for distributive change.

Notes

1. Depicted in the twelfth century Chronicle of John of Worcester.
2. Starr (1982, Chapter 3) charts the cumulative consolidation of the power of the medical profession in the United States through a variety of interventive measures and complementary circumstances, including the development of an exclusive jargon, control over medical education, licensing laws and malpractice protection, as well as the adoption of a corporate business identity in the late nineteenth and early twentieth century.
3. Alger wrote numerous books between 1867 and his death in 1899. The genre persisted until the 1930s.
4. Keynes' famous recommendation that governments should pay people for burying and digging up empty bottles to increase purchasing power without producing more goods inspired the economic recovery of the New Deal. Older views that wage cuts and private charity could solve economic crises and poverty resurfaced in neo-conservative economic policies in the 1980s.
5. The conquest of Mexico and Peru was also helped by the silent complementarity of the smallpox virus spread by the Spanish. It killed 50 to 75 percent of the native population which had no immunity.
6. Some of the material in this section was previously published in Baldus 1977.
7. Puritan communities which did successfully control deviation did so at price of economic and social stagnation (Lucas 1971). Diamond (1964) describes the staggering administrative costs involved in maintaining the minute regulations governing forms of address, manner of dressing, order of precedence when entering church or the types of weapons assigned to different ranks in the seventeenth-century feudal experiment of New France along the St. Lawrence River.

Bibliography

Bakan, Joel. *The Corporation*. Toronto: Penguin, 2004.

Baldus, Bernd. "Social Control in Capitalist Societies: An Examination of the "Problem of Order" in Liberal Democracies." *Canadian Journal of Sociology* 2 (1977) 3: 247–262.

Baldus, Bernd and Meenaz Kassam. "Make Me Truthful, Good and Mild: Values in Nineteenth Century Ontario Schoolbooks." *Canadian Journal of Sociology* 21 (1996) 3: 327–358.

Baldus, Bernd and Verna Tribe. "The Development of Perceptions and Evaluations of Social Inequality among Public School Children." *Canadian Review of Sociology and Anthropology* 15 (1978) 1: 50–60.

Barrell, John. *The Dark Side of the Landscape*. Cambridge: Cambridge University Press, 1980.

Barthes, Roland. *Mythologies*. New York: Hill and Wang, 1972.

Benson, Peter and Stuart Kirsch. "Capitalism and the Politics of Resignation." *Current Anthropology* 51 (2010) 4: 459–486.

Bliss, Michael. *A Living Profit*. Toronto: McClelland and Stewart, 1974.

Brown, Roger. *Social Psychology*. New York: Free Press, 1965.

Burris, Val. "The Academic Caste System: Prestige Hierarchies in PhD Exchange Networks." *American Sociological Review* 69 (2004) 2: 239–264.

Carruthers, Bruce G. and Jeong-Chul Kim. "The Sociology of Finance." *Annual Review of Sociology* 37 (2011): 239–259.

Cawelti, John G. *Apostles of the Self-made Man*. Chicago: University of Chicago Press, 1965.

Chinoy, Ely. *Automobile Workers and the American Dream*. Boston: Beacon Press, 1955.

Selection

Cohn, Norman. *The Pursuit of the Millennium*. New York: Oxford University Press, 1970.

Cole, Stephen and Robert Lejeune. "Illness and the Legitimation of Failure." *American Sociological Review* 37 (1972) 3: 347–356.

Darnton, Robert. *The Great Cat Massacre*. New York: Basic Books, 1984a.

Darnton, Robert. "A Police Inspector Sorts His Files: The Anatomy of the Republic of Letters." In Robert Darnton (ed.) *The Great Cat Massacre*, 145–189. New York: Basic Books, 1984b.

Diamond, Sigmund. "Old Patterns and New Societies: Virginia and French Canada in the Seventeenth Century." In Werner J. Cahnman and Alvin Boskoff (eds) *Sociology and History*, 170–190. New York: Free Press, 1964.

Earle, Timothy. *How Chiefs Come to Power*. Stanford: Stanford University Press, 1997.

Easton, David and Jack Dennis. *Children in the Political System*. New York: McGraw Hill, 1969.

Edelman, Murray J. *Constructing the Political Spectacle*. Chicago: University of Chicago Press, 1988.

Edelman, Murray J. *The Politics of Misinformation*. Cambridge: Cambridge University, 2001.

Ehrenreich, Barbara. *Bait and Switch*. New York: Owl Books, 2005.

Elson, Ruth Miller. *Guardians of Tradition. American Schoolbooks of the Nineteenth Century*. Lincoln: University of Nebraska Press, 1964.

Erikson, Kai T. *Wayward Puritans*. New York: Wiley, 1966.

Falk, Armin and Michael Kosfeld. "Distrust – The Hidden Cost of Control." *American Economic Review* 96 (2006) 5: 1611–1630.

Flannery, Kent, and Joyce Marcus. *The Creation of Inequality*. Cambridge: Harvard University Press, 2012.

Frank, Thomas. *What's the Matter with Kansas?* New York: Holt, 2004.

Freeman, James M. *Untouchable. An Indian Life History*. Stanford: Stanford University Press, 1979.

Fried, Morton. *The Evolution of Political Society*. New York/Toronto: Random House, 1967.

George, C.H. "The Making of the English Bourgeoisie 1500–1750." *Science and Society* 35 (1971) 4: 385–414.

Gilens, Martin. *Affluence and Influence. Economic Inequality and Political Power in America*. Princeton: Princeton University Press, 2012.

Gilman, Antonio. "The Development of Social Stratification in Bronze Age Europe." *Current Anthropology* 22 (1981) 1: 1–23.

Goffman, Erving. *Asylums. Essays of the Social Situation of Mental Patients and Other Inmates*. Garden City: Doubleday, 1961.

Grätz, Tilo. "Gold-Mining and Risk Management: A Case Study from Northern Benin." *Ethnos* 68 (2003) 2: 192–208.

Hacker, Jacob S. and Paul Pierson. "Winner-Take-All Politics: Public Policy, Political Organization, and the Precipitous Rise of Top Incomes in the United States." *Politics & Society* 38 (2010) 2: 152–204.

Hammond, John L., and Barbara Hammond. *The Town Labourer*. Garden City: Doubleday, 1968.

Heer, Friedrich. *The Medieval World. Europe 1100–1350*. New York: New American Library, 1962.

Hess, Robert D. and Judith V. Torney. *The Development of Political Attitudes in Children*. Chicago: Aldine, 1967.

Hobbes, Thomas. *Leviathan.* Edited by Richard Tuck. Cambridge: Cambridge University Press, 1991 [1651].
Hobsbawm, Eric J. *The Age of Revolution, 1789–1848.* New York: New American Library, 1962.
Hopkins, Keith. *Death and Renewal. Sociological Studies in Roman History.* Cambridge: Cambridge University Press, 1983.
Jahoda, Marie, Paul F. Lazarsfeld and Hans Zeisel. *Marienthal: The Sociography of an Unemployed Community.* Chicago: Aldine, 1971 [1933].
Kaplow, Jeffrey. *The Names of Kings. The Parisian Poor in the Eighteenth Century.* New York: Basic Books, 1972.
Keating, P.J. *The Working Classes in Victorian Fiction.* London: Routledge, 1971.
Kinder, Donald R. "Communication and Politics in the Age of Information." In David O. Sears, Leonie Huddy and Robert Jervis (eds) *Oxford Handbook of Political Psychology*, 357–393. Oxford: Oxford University Press, 2003.
Kraus, Michael W., Paul K. Piff and Dacher Keltner. "Social Class, Sense of Control, and Social Explanation." *Journal of Personality and Social Psychology* 97 (2009) 6: 992–1004.
Kuczynski, Jürgen. *The Rise of the Working Class.* New York: McGraw Hill, 1967.
Lane, Robert E. *Political Ideology.* New York: Free Press, 1962.
Loewenthal, Leo. *Literature, Popular Culture, and Society.* Englewood Cliffs: Prentice Hall, 1961.
Lucas, Rex. "A Specification of the Weber Thesis: Plymouth Colony." *History and Theory* 10 (1971) 3: 318–346.
Lynd, Robert S. and Helen M. Lynd. *Middletown.* New York: Harcourt, 1929.
Martin, Isaac. *Rich People's Movements.* New York: Oxford University Press, 2013.
McCall, Leslie and Christine Percheski. "Income Inequality: New Trends and Research Directions." *Annual Review of Sociology* 36 (2010): 329–347.
McCloskey, Robert G. *American Conservatism in the Age of Enterprise 1865–1910.* New York: Harper, 1951.
Mullainathan, Sendhil and Eldar Shafir. *Scarcity. Why Having Too Little Means So Much.* New York: Times Books, 2013.
Nash, June. "The Devil in Bolivia's Nationalized Tin Mines." *Science and Society* 36 (1972) 2: 221–233.
Neckerman, Kathryn M. and Florencia Torche. "Inequality: Causes and Consequences." *Annual Review of Sociology* 33 (2007): 335–357.
Newman, Katherine. *Falling From Grace: The Experience of Downward Mobility in the American Middle Class.* New York: Free Press, 1988.
Parish, Steven M. *Hierarchy and its Discontents. Culture and the Politics of Consciousness in Caste Society.* Philadelphia: University of Pennsylvania Press, 1996.
Peel, Mark. *The Lowest Rung. Voices of Australian Poverty.* Cambridge: Cambridge University Press, 2003.
Piff, Paul K. "Wealth and the Inflated Self. Class, Entitlement, and Narcissism." *Personality and Social Psychology Bulletin* 40 (2014) 1: 34–43
Piven, Frances F. and Richard A. Cloward. *Regulating the Poor: The Functions of Public Welfare.* New York: Pantheon, 1971.
Rediker, Marcus. *The Slave Ship.* London: John Murray, 2007.
Rinehart, James. *The Tyranny of Work.* Toronto: Harcourt, 2001.
Roy, Donald F. "Banana Time." Job Satisfaction and Informal Interaction." *Human Organization* 18 (1958) 4: 158–168.

196 Selection

Sennett, Richard. *The Corrosion of Character: The Personal Consequences of Work in the New Capitalism*. London: W.W. Norton, 1998.

Shapiro, Susan P. "The Social Control of Impersonal Trust." *American Journal of Sociology* 93 (1987) 3: 623–658.

Silverblatt, Irene. "Imperial Dilemmas, the Politics of Kinship, and Inca Reconstruction of History." *Comparative Studies in Society and History* 30 (1988) 1: 83–102.

Smith, Thomas C. "Peasant Time and Factory Time in Japan." *Past and Present* 111 (1986) May: 165–197.

Smucker, Joseph. "Ideology and Authority." *Canadian Journal of Sociology* 2 (1977) 3: 263–282.

Sokal, Alan and Jean Bricmont. *Fashionable Nonsense. Postmodern Intellectual's Abuse of Science*. New York: Picador, 1998.

Starr, Paul. *The Social Transformation of American Medicine*. New York: Basic Books, 1982.

Stouffer, Samuel A. *Communism, Conformity and Civil Liberties*. Gloucester: Smith, 1963.

Sutton, Francis X., Seymour E. Harris, Karl K. Kaysen and James Tobin. 1962. *The American Business Creed*. New York: Schocken, 1962.

Tepperman, Lorne, and Nina Gheihman. *Habits of Inequality*. Don Mills: Oxford University Press, 2013.

Thompson, Edward P. *The Making of the English Working Class*. London: Penguin, 1980 [1963].

Thompson, Edward P. "Time, Work Discipline and Industrial Capitalism." *Past and Present* 38 (1967) December: 56–97.

Wahrman, Dror. *Imagining the Middle Class*. Cambridge: Cambridge University Press, 1995.

White, Lynn Jr. "The Act of Invention: Causes, Contexts, Continuities, and Consequences." In Melvin Kranzberg and William H. Davenport (eds) *Technology and Culture*, 275–291. New York: Schocken Books, 1972.

Wise, Sydney F. "Sermon Literature and Canadian Intellectual History." In Arthur Silver (ed.) *An Introduction to Canadian History*, 160–175. Toronto: Canadian Scholars' Press, 1991.

Zeitlin, Lawrence R. "A Little Larceny can do a Lot for Employee Morale." *Psychology Today* (1971) June: 22–26, 64.

7 Possible Worlds
Pathways to Equality

Since the eighteenth century, social philosophy identified the conflict between self and collective interest as the central issue of social justice and saw its resolution as an essential prerequisite for social life. Darwin, too, thought that evolution would favor cooperative over selfish human behavior although he noted that this did not seem to prevent many cultural traits which harmed human welfare and that moral norms "were liable to be disobeyed" even if they contributed to the vigor and health of the group.

The major problem preventing the further exploration of alternatives to existing inequality structures was the unsettled feelings among social and evolutionary scientists toward human choice. The social sciences preferred fixed human preferences which operated within the boundaries of rational or functional necessity. Evolutionists were equally weary of the possibility that "the long-term consequences of inequity will always be visibly dangerous." Thinking about major change might waken a slumbering beast. Altruism and the search for distributive justice could therefore never be more than selfishness in disguise, "circuitous technique(s) by which genetic material has been and will be kept intact. Morality has no other demonstrable ultimate function" (Wilson 1978: 199, 167).

For people facing the reality of inequality, the search for alternatives had a more immediate salience. Depending on their situation it either posed a threat to their wealth or offered hope for a better existence. The first known images of an ideal life of plenty for all appeared in Egyptian murals some 4000 years ago. Biblical prophets warned of divine punishment for people "who defraud a man of his home, a fellow man of his inheritance." Plato thought that conflict between rich and poor could be prevented only by a governing elite which had renounced selfishness, lived in communal houses without family or private property, and was immune to the temptations of material gain. Such exemplary virtues would inspire their fellow citizens to emulate their leaders, accept a five-fold limit on increases in wealth during their lifetime and reduce social strife. Aristotle argued that one could not be rich and good at the same time. He envisioned an ideal society of landowners whose moderate property assured economic independence and who were equal enough to avoid the hubris which so often surrounded wealth. Plutarch praised Lycurgus and Solon, the early lawgivers of Sparta and Athens, for recognizing that limits placed on property and wealth were essential to ensure social harmony.

The ideal of a selfless and virtuous life was revived by the medieval church, although mostly by turning it on its head: the onus of living simply was placed on the peasants who were told that poverty and suffering atoned for their sins and assured their salvation. That did not discourage popular beliefs that kings who once ruled with justice and kindness would reappear from their mountain lairs to punish oppressors and tyrants, dreams of utopian worlds where food was abundant and required no toil, or visions of paradise where people, lions and lambs lived in harmony. Renunciation of worldly desires inspired Cathars, mendicants and other movements of monastic reform. Demands for greater equality drove the European peasant rebellions between the fourteenth and sixteenth century. In 1516, Thomas More described an imaginary egalitarian island, Utopia, where cities were built to standard design, inhabitants switched houses and rotated work periodically to eliminate differences in wealth and skills, worked six-hour days and met their needs from central storehouses. There were no markets or money, and doors remained unlocked because without inequality there was no crime. Between 1649 and 1651, the English Diggers occupied common land and tried to establish egalitarian rural communes. Around the same time the Levelers asked for an end to corruption, for religious tolerance and an expanded suffrage.[1] Most of these efforts foundered on the inexperience of their proponents or the power of their adversaries, but their recurrence shows that both sides were aware of contingent, undeserved causes of their social position. Lasting prosperity for the winners could be bought only through material or ideological accommodation of the losers. Without it, social conflict choked off the flow of privilege. But any accommodation also encouraged demands for a more equitable sharing of jointly achieved wealth. This was the basic political dilemma facing all inequality structures.

Modern conceptions of distributive justice arose with the emergence of markets. Where earlier views were based on a providential order, Adam Smith recognized that justice had its roots in the social nature of human existence. If someone grew up in solitude without communication with others

> he could no more think of his own character, of the propriety or demerit of his own sentiments and conduct, of the beauty and deformity of his own mind, than of the beauty or deformity of his own face. Bring him into society and he is immediately provided with the mirror which he (lacked) before ... and it is here that he first views the propriety and impropriety of his own passions.
>
> (Smith 1774: 198, 199)

Smith realized that, like the picture of Dorian Gray, the mirror might reveal the ugly image of unscrupulous exploitation. His and Hume's elegant solution was to divide distributive justice into two strands. The private pursuit of "baubles and trinkets" brought little good beyond the admiring gaze of others. True personal happiness could only come from compassion towards family, friends, and those who suffered undeserved misery because it gratified both giver and recipient. In markets, however, the pursuit of wealth ultimately enriched the society as a whole. This unintended consequence absolved individuals from the stigma of greed: even the tawdriest personal motivations could have social benefits. Smith softened the distinction somewhat by arguing that both inner and market virtue encouraged laudable motives, the former by creating sympathy for others, the latter by inspiring prudence, self-control and contractual rather than violent settlement of disputes. Nevertheless, the separation of private motives from public consequences allowed self-interest to operate unburdened by moral considerations. These were taken care of by the impersonal power of the market.

This set the stage for modern views of distributive justice. In the first half of the nineteenth century, evangelical political economists still interpreted Smith's "invisible hand" as a divine allocation of poverty and wealth and as earthly proof of sinfulness and virtue, but moral elements soon disappeared from economic theory. In 1871, Jevons declared the "laws of exchange" to be akin to the laws of physics. Rational, equal and independent individuals attached value to goods and services they wished to buy or sell. Markets then acted like auctions, determining an exchange price based on the utility and rarity of the goods tendered. For Jevons and his contemporary Walras, that also applied to the price of labor. Wages were determined by the marginal utility of labor, i.e. the last unit of work that the capitalist could justify buying in the market and still achieve a profit. This "natural" wage created equilibrium between workers who wanted to maximize their wages and employers who wanted to reduce their costs, yielding an optimal and therefore also just distribution. Market participants could increase their share of wealth only through economic growth. Any arbitrary redistribution of market results by the state would make production less efficient.

The work of Walras and Jevons marked a paradigm shift from earlier labor theories of value which saw the causes of inequality in historical power differences between market participants which the state could change. In the new neoclassical view, state intervention was acceptable only where people were excluded from the market altogether. Locke and Kant had already argued that full individual rights required a material basis for market participation. Where people had neither labor nor goods to sell, supporting them by taxing others was justified because it restored basic civic rights. For Kant this obligation was ultimately rooted in "good will," a moral *a priori* that enabled one to value others as more than a means to an end. It was the ethical duty of wealthy individuals to help those unable to help themselves and to enjoy in return personal satisfaction and public respect. This duty extended to the state as the legal representative of citizens. Kant's view of justice did not, however, envision fundamental structural change. The purpose of redistribution was to prepare the individual for re-entry into the market. Social inequality remained the normal outcome of economic life.

The theories that follow propose principles for a just distribution of collective achievements. They also address issues which must be solved by an evolutionary argument for greater equality.[2] Nozick, Rawls and Sidgwick agreed that discovery and invention justified some claim to personal ownership of the result, a view also shared by Locke, Rousseau and Marx. All of them also saw that unearned and fortuitous advantages placed some limits on such claims. All realized that this created an obligation to correct the unrestricted growth of social inequality in order to restore some measure of distributive justice, although they disagreed widely why and how this should be done. Finally, all of them were in some form aware of the adverse effect which an unjust distribution could have on social cohesion.

Four Theories of Distributive Justice

The Argument from Possession: Libertarian Views

Libertarian theories of justice followed Locke's argument that individual labor transformed previously unowned objects into property. As long as this left "enough and as good" for others it did not harm their rights. What made Locke's argument attractive to libertarians was the possibility of turning the act of taking possession into an act of labor, both because it required an effort by the appropriator and because it created wage employment for those without possessions. Private property thus acquired a normative value which could be used to reject other distributive options such as communal ownership or an equitable sharing of returns among all participants.

Pursuing this argument, libertarians like Hayek (1899–1992) and Nozick (1938–2002) located distributive justice in the sphere of the acquisition of goods, not their distribution. Where objects were initially unowned, taking possession established the right to own, enjoy and use them. Most goods, however, were obtained in markets which could only work if their participants were free, independent and consenting. The first task of distributive justice was to ensure such conditions. If this was done, markets not only yielded just returns for individuals but increased the prosperity of all. Inequality resulted from natural differences in individual ability and effort. To consider them unjust made as little sense as questioning the justice of lightning strikes. No participant had a right to more goods than the market provided. To demand justice from markets was "obviously absurd, and … it is evidently unjust to separate out specific people by giving them a legal right to particular shares" (Hayek 1981: 95). Demands for a redistribution of wealth were either moral posturing or attempts to use false pretenses to gain an undeserved share of market returns. Individual self-interest and free economic exchange ensured that property was put to profitable use instead of being hoarded, and that it created work for property-less individuals. Any effort to redistribute market returns imposed a penalty on those who got their share through "just acquisition."

Just acquisition took three forms: taking possession of previously unowned objects or by inventing an entirely novel use of a thing, acquiring objects from consenting others through gifts, inheritance or market transactions, and the restitution for injustice, i.e. where the first two principles were violated through fraud, violence, conquest, enslavement or undue market domination. Correcting such injustices required an assessment of the historical circumstances under which property was obtained. If individuals acquired their property justly, the overall distribution – the result of numerous individual market transactions – was also just. The fact that markets allowed some to gain control over capital merely redefined workers' economic environment and created new incentives to seek employment. The accumulation of private capital restructured, but did not abrogate, workers' freedom to choose.

The only principle of distributive justice was therefore "from each as he chooses, and to each what others are willing to transfer or do for him, or what he deserves by way of compensation for past injustice" (Nozick 1974: 33). The state had neither right nor obligation to withhold or redistribute resources, and could not force individuals to surrender property for a common good. Its only legitimate role was to protect market exchanges from violence, theft and breach of contract. Redistribution was justified only where it restored property to those who were wrongfully deprived, or who for reasons of illness or misfortune had no marketable assets they could exchange. Because not every historical instance of unjust acquisition could be examined, Nozick offered a rule of thumb: since the worst-off in any society were also the most likely victims of past injustice, the best way to rectify injustice was to "organize society so as to maximize the position of whatever group ends up the least well-off in the society" (Nozick 1974: 231). Hayek (2001–2003: 361) added a further reason: public help for the needy was "in the interest of those who require protection against desperate acts of the poor."

Historically, markets and private property were first protected by private groups for a fee. Markets eventually encouraged a consolidation of this service; this was the origin of the state. In view of this history, the state's power to tax should be limited to what individuals would have to pay to protect their justly acquired property. Taxation for any other purpose, in particular to create greater equality, would be

> on par with forced labor ... it is like forcing the person to work (additional) hours for another's purpose.... This process whereby they take the decision from you makes them a part-owner of you; it gives them a property right in you.
> (Nozick 1974: 169)

The Argument from Prudence: John Rawls

Rawls (1921–2002) also approached the problem of justice from the point of view of rational maximizers of self-interest, but with two important provisos: people lived in a contingent world of unpredictable risks and opportunities, and individual achievements always involved contributions of others and therefore had to ensure their willingness to cooperate. Rawls asked what rules of justice a group of free, equal and rational people would likely agree to in a hypothetical "original position" where they did not yet know what their future social standing would be, and where they could therefore not bargain in advance for personal advantage. Under such a "veil of ignorance" the participants would probably act with prudence and caution and accept three basic rules of justice.[3] First, they would agree that some all-purpose "primary goods" such as basic rights and freedoms, including the right to own property, should be available to all and should not be reduced for the sake of gains in power or economic growth.

Second, they would place restrictions on inequalities of power and wealth. They would not oppose inequality as such, but because they did not know what the future held, they would hedge against the possibility that they themselves ended up among the worst-off, or that others in such situations would become disaffected, cause social conflict, and withdraw their cooperation. They would therefore agree that the greater good of many should not be gained at the price of greater hardship for some. An increase in inequality was acceptable only if it also improved the situation of the worst-off. This principle overrode the requirements of efficient production and economic growth. A just society should be as unequal as necessary but as equal as possible. Among alternative distributive policies, those should be chosen which gave the worst-off the greatest advantage.

Third, justice had to take into account not only future but past contingencies. Personal effort and ability could not establish an exclusive right to the results of one's actions because inherited traits, family background, luck and help from others created a "natural lottery" of circumstances for which no individual could claim credit. Justice therefore required treating them as "common assets" whose benefits should be shared. Distinctions in ability should not be ignored but they should be used "so that these contingencies work for the good of the least fortunate" (Rawls 1971: 101, 102). More generally, common asset obligation arose from the fact that wealth was a social, cooperative product. Where the contribution of others irretrievably blended with one's own, the results were no longer a matter of individual but collective rights. To guarantee equality of opportunity was not enough. Salary differences between doctors and nurses were justified only to the extent that they led to better care for the sickest patients. Income differences between owners and workers were just only if they made production more efficient and allowed the resulting material benefits to spread through society to the least advantaged.

Considering the needs of others was not just "one desire among the rest" (Rawls 1971: 674) but increased collective solidarity and reduced social conflict. A just society was stable because public acceptance of justice principles legitimated distributive decisions, made people agree to limitations of their private wants and discouraged free riders by subjecting them to closer scrutiny. In a just society the "rational" – the desire to maximize utility – was tempered by the "reasonable," the recognition of the need for "reciprocity and mutuality: all who cooperate must benefit, or share a common burden, in some appropriate fashion as judged by a suitable benchmark of comparison" (Rawls 1980: 528). This included future generations. Those living now could not indiscriminately exploit their resources but had to retain "just savings" by imagining "the life of a people ... as a scheme of cooperation spread out in historical time." This meant conserving capital, natural resources and knowledge "to improve the standard of life for later generations of the least advantaged, thereby abstaining from the immediate gains available" (Rawls 1971: 289, 293).

Implementing these principles needed government intervention to maintain competition and full employment, and to redistribute wealth through progressive taxation and compensatory payments. Rawls acknowledged that all this was "terribly imprecise." The point was not to agree on a particular distribution of wealth but on a "range of justice" which identified "with greater sharpness the graver wrongs a society should avoid" and convinced people "that something of this kind must be argued if ... inequalities are to be just" (Rawls 1971: 201, 78). Nor was the pursuit of justice tied to a particular political system. It could be achieved by capitalist or socialist societies, as long as they aimed to create a social order where the distribution of wealth was widely accepted. Maintaining justice was an ongoing effort, requiring constant weighing of efficiency against fairness, of taxation and redistribution to the poorest against reduced economic growth which would worsen their lot even more, and of the needs of current and future generations, but "consenting to one of these procedures is surely preferable to no agreement at all" (Rawls 1971: 354).

The Argument from Expediency: Henry Sidgwick

Utilitarians such as Bentham (1748–1832), James Mill (1773–1836) and John Stuart Mill (1806–1873) based their principles of justice not on the acquisition of goods or on considerations of prudence, but on the distribution of subjective satisfaction. In the same way as the actions of individuals were guided by their experience of happiness or pain, the acts of public institutions should be judged by the degree to which they furthered the greatest happiness of the greatest number.

This view faced empirical and ethical problems. Happiness was fleeting and malleable. Bentham already noted that no two individuals would ever feel the same way about the same object. If interpersonal comparisons of satisfaction were not possible, then it seemed also impossible to guarantee its fair distribution. Nor could one construct an index of collective happiness: utility did not come in measurable units, and if it was defined as an average quantity, large gains in happiness by a few could outweigh a decline in happiness for many and conceal major inequities. On the ethical side, the pursuit of happiness had its obvious limits where it took pleasure in harming others, or where unscrupulous governments or powerful groups lulled public opinion into a false sense of well-being. Similar issues arose where unethical actions had unanticipated but beneficial collective consequences.

Measuring individual satisfaction and collective welfare remained the central difficulty of utilitarian views of justice. Welfare economics tried to avoid the problem by moving to marginal utility, the increase or loss of satisfaction caused by purchasing or forgoing an additional unit of a good. Because empirical observation suggested that the utility of a good declined the more of it one had, and because wealthy people derived less pleasure from additional goods than people with lower income, the overall welfare of the society could be increased by transferring income from richer to poorer populations until an optimum of collective satisfaction was reached. Pareto distinguished between "efficient" improvements in income distribution which increased the welfare of at least one person and left all others at least as well off as before, and potential improvements where the gains of some could be used to improve the lot of others or to compensate them for losses. Most welfare economists considered the latter a normative decision which fell outside the purview of their field. Efforts to define economic welfare optima required restrictive assumptions such as stable personal preferences, constant income distributions and market transparency, and the use of money to measure utility. In view of this, Arrow's (1951) "impossibility theorem" concluded that no unambiguous rule for the summation of individual preferences and their optimal satisfaction across a population could be found.

James and John Stuart Mill proposed a different and more ingenious solution to the problem of maximizing collective utility. In order to avoid comparisons of subjective preferences they suggested equalizing the conditions which gave individuals the best opportunity to realize whatever preferences they had. Politically, this could be achieved by a participatory democracy where frequent elections forced governments to act in the interest of voters. Discussions of scientific, moral and justice issues were most productive when exposed to criticism, the flow of new ideas and the heat of debate. Openness and free expression were the best defense against dogmatism and intolerance. Since people were spontaneously inclined to consider the welfare of others and could distinguish between "higher and lower pleasures," governments should find it easy to develop common-sense guidelines of "generalized benevolence" which ensured that no person's satisfaction came at the expense of another's.

It was Henry Sidgwick's (1838–1900) self-professed interest in applying theoretical ideas to practical problems which made him see that political equality could serve as a "rough and approximate" justice principle which could solve the problem of unmeasurable preferences and unpredictable desires. His work stood in the context of debates over electoral property qualifications (abolished in England only in 1918; the right to vote was extended to women in 1928). The predominant fear of the time was that allowing the laboring poor to vote would create an oppressive and irresponsible political majority. Sidgwick dismissed three main arguments supporting this view: that propertied electors contributed more to the economy, were on average better educated, and were therefore more responsible voters than the poor. In reality, he argued, there was no assurance that private wealth would not lead to fraud, corruption and economic harm. Education provided no guarantee for sound political judgment, and "it is impossible to divide society into classes which remain identical and equally distinct for all legislative purposes: as we pass from one proposed law to another, we find that the important lines of division are continually changing" (Sidgwick 1891: Chapter 20, 5).

Sidgwick argued that, in view of such uncertainty, electoral equality was the pragmatic, expedient way to distribute utility fairly across all members of society. Although it was obvious that not everyone was equally informed or interested in public affairs, everyone should have an equal right to run for political office or vote for candidates. This would occasionally lead to wrong decisions or the choice of incompetent or corrupt politicians, but on balance the risk of error was smaller than if one tried to assess each person's public-spiritedness and match it with political tasks. Locke's 1689 *Letter on Toleration* had made a similar argument for religious equality: because we had no way of finding out in this life which religion was true, freedom of conscience and tolerance of different faiths was most likely to increase our chance of salvation. Rousseau concurred: the best way to respond to the many differences in strength, ability or political preferences was to grant equal political rights to everyone.

Sidgwick was a reformer, not a radical. He hedged his support for electoral equality by suggesting that parliamentary representatives for the poor should be paid by donations from their voters, and he did not extend his argument to the distribution of wealth because he thought that equal incomes would remove the incentive to work and diminish efficiency and productivity. His arguments were eventually used in Pigou's *Wealth and Welfare* (1912) to justify economic equality: because the marginal utility of goods was inversely related to the quantity one possessed, an egalitarian income distribution was most likely to maximize happiness in a society. Pigou was also the first economist who pointed out that market prices often failed to include the social and environmental costs of production and consumption, and that these should be part of the search for just distribution. Sidgwick's lasting contribution was to have seen that an equal allocation of resources was a pragmatic solution to the problem of measuring and comparing subjective satisfaction. By extension, it could also be applied to Rawls' conundrum about how to account for common asset components when distributing the results of collective achievements. His and Pigou's ideas gave rise to a number of later proposals for one-time "stakeholder grants," starting capital, or guaranteed annual base incomes to achieve equal starting or living conditions for all citizens (Dworkin 2000; Ackerman et al. 2006).

The Argument from Participation: Habermas' Discourse Ethic

Habermas (1929–) criticized the justice principles proposed by Libertarians and Rawls for ignoring the real history of bargaining and communication which led to distributive decisions. Any investigation of how people arrived at concepts of social justice had to examine conditions which facilitated or restricted the ability of participants to discuss issues such as distributive fairness, to resolve differences of opinion and to reach a consensus. For Habermas, the justice of norms, including those governing distribution, ultimately derived from the way in which they had been argued and decided. Prior to the eighteenth century, communication was shaped by feudal rulers and was non-participatory and one-sided. Capitalism created for the first time a public sphere where social dialogue was not subject to central control, but it also created new, restrictive communication environments. Ideas became commodities which were marketed, and mass media began to shape public opinion. Communication split into separate spheres. One was the "life world" of informal cultural knowledge and everyday meanings which enabled people to achieve agreement with others and served as a source of social integration. This life world "stored" the communicative possibilities of a society (Habermas 1981: Vol. II, 164). The other sphere was the "system world" of rationalized legal, economic and political structures which subjected public debate to "system imperatives" of modernization, innovation and the efficient use of resources. Powerful, unaccountable media steered communication away from common objectives and from Max Weber's "ethic of brotherliness." Capitalism "re-feudalized" and colonized the public sphere by replacing critical debate with a fragmentation of interests, the commercialization and impoverishment of choices and the loss of personal autonomy (Habermas 1984: 565).

The critique of historical changes in communication led Habermas to search for conditions which allowed participants with different interests to come to a "reasoned agreement" on social and political issues such as distributive justice. Agreements always grew out of an exchange between someone who advanced a claim to validity and tried to prove it, and a respondent who was convinced by the claim. Claims could mobilize supporting evidence or trust, but it was ultimately the practical communicative interaction between individuals that established the strength of a norm. Norms were valid if people agreed that convincing reasons for their acceptance had been given, and if they preferred the consequences to known alternatives. Such agreements created deeper emotional ties than justice principles which rested on prudence or expediency. They established a "public morality" which strengthened social solidarity and harmonized individual action plans (Habermas 1981: Vol. I, 385).

A "discourse ethic" specified criteria by which actual agreements could be evaluated: their truth, defined as their potential of finding consensus among all participants; their acceptability, that is their social appropriateness and fit with the preferences of those involved; their sincerity, the degree to which they were considered authentic and non-deceptive; and the extent to which they were intelligible and could be understood. Strong, persuasive communications met all four criteria. More commonly, statements were accepted as valid if only some of these criteria were met. What really mattered was to create conditions of communication which encouraged participants to take the views of others into account, to submit their own claims to general criticism, and to accept vindication by better arguments instead of irrationally defending their own views. This presupposed a basic equality of participation. Discourse on matters such as distribution had to be public and allow everyone who was competent to speak freely in debates, to introduce or question claims and to gather information about their consequences. All participants should be able to bring their interests into the formulation of norms, and nothing should be excluded in advance through coercion or "subtle or covert" ideological manipulation. Only then could one assume that participants were not just "talked into" a consensus. Such "argued agreement" required neither complete congruence of individual interests nor an unqualified endorsement by all participants. Religious tolerance did not entail joining a particular religion, and democratic decisions did not have to be uncritically accepted. Nor did all consequences of a norm have to be known. What mattered was that

> participants, themes and contributions are not limited, except where they do not contribute to the examination of problematic validity claims; that there

is no coercion other than that of the better argument: that therefore all motives other than the cooperative search for the truth are excluded. If under these conditions a consensus is reached on the recommendation to accept a norm through argumentative, i.e. hypothetically proposed richly alternative justifications, then this consensus expresses a "rational will."

(Habermas 1973: 148)

Theories of Distributive Justice: Central Problems

These four theories address key issues of distributive justice, namely the link between individual effort and the right to its result and the effect of contingent contributions on such rights, but they also have significant problems. First, they offer widely different views of the relative importance of contingency and personal effort in collective achievements. Libertarians came down on the side of effort, a view rooted in the biblical edict that God granted humans dominion over plants and animals, including the right, as Thomas Aquinas put it, to make "use of them without hindrance." Contingent contributions disappeared from view. For Locke it was the act of labor which removed an object from its state of nature and turned it into property. The resulting value was "wholly owing to labor and industry ... without which (they) would scarcely be worth anything.... Nature and the earth furnished only the most worthless materials (by) themselves" (Locke 1947: sections 27 and 43). Locke's argument eliminated in one stroke the contribution of contingent environments and of the cooperation of others, and therefore also the possibility that the result of labor and industry could be distributed in any form other than private appropriation. This view carried over into modern theories of justice: to give contingent causes a role in the evolution of inequality was a denial of merit which turned people into

> passive objects of ontological accidents and causal constraints.... Personal existence and moral subject-being rest essentially on the contingency-defying self-appropriation and sense-making of the given world; only through such processes of appropriation and meaning-giving can contingency be disarmed, can we fend off the oppressiveness of chance and create instead an internal, content-rich and contingency-free perspective by means of which we then design and live our life, from which we can gain a basis for self-challenge and self-responsibility.
>
> (Kersting 2000: 66)

Marx, although far more critical of unconditional property claims, also dismissed the role of contingency. Having separated the instinctive behavior of animals from the creative imagination of humans, he argued that the latter allowed them to subordinate the powers of nature to their own purposes. Nature did not build machines, railways or telegraphs. It merely supplied inert materials which were transformed into materialized knowledge by the human brain (Marx 1939–1941: 594). Where for Locke and Nozick the act of appropriation established the right to self-ownership from the start, for Marx self-ownership was fully realized only at the historical end point of a communist society where advances of production, technology and science created a society of unlimited material means and made the question of ownership irrelevant.

Rawls' great achievement was to have seen the role of contingency more clearly, both as an unknown future which counseled precaution, and as an unearned past which placed encumbrances on one's accomplishments. But he was not willing to accept that unearned and cooperative contributions added common asset obligations to *all* achievements. Instead, he divided society into two parts: a normal, primary market system where inequality resulted from individual differences in ability, and a compensatory system where past and future contingencies required the transfer of some of the wealth produced by the first sector to the worst-off. That was Rawls' only, albeit significant, departure from the classical liberal model. He did not address the question of how much should be transferred to the worst-off, ignoring the possibility that justice principles were met where the bulk of market returns went to the rich while the lives of the worst-off were "improved" by a few crumbs from their tables.

Sidgwick also realized that

> a man does not create matter by his labor, but only modifies it: and the fact that he has spent his labor on material to which he had no right could at most give him a right to an equivalent for the additional utility that it has thereby acquired.
>
> (Sidgwick 1891: Chapter 5, 2)

Like Rawls, however, he stopped short of concluding that human action always contained unearned components which invalidated claims to exclusive self-ownership. Instead, he opted for a case by case examination how such claims encroached upon the rights of others, and sought a resolution in "a careful balance of conflicting inconveniences" (Sidgwick 1891: Chapter 5, 1). The full contribution of contingent components to human action and any resulting debts to the physical and social environments remained unexamined.

The second problem of these theories was the anemic and one-dimensional depiction of human agency. Individuals acted for the most part out of simple self-interest and had no past.[4] Neither Nozick nor Rawls explained how the worst-off ended up in their position and how the better off had gained theirs. The veil of ignorance covered not only the interests of the participants but the history of their relationship. Society appeared as

> a fluctuating, constantly changing social association which solely follows the tides of self-interest, without any comprehensive or stabilizing structure, without a normative framework and without a binding constitution.... The market becomes the model for all social formations.
>
> (Kersting 2000: 319)

The real world of inequality, market power and manipulated wants differed from these scenarios.

> The proprietors of the modern world are not the legitimate heirs of Lockean individuals who performed ... acts of original appropriation; they are the inheritors of those who, for example, stole, and used violence to steal the common lands of England from the common people, vast tracts of North America from the American Indian, much of Ireland from the Irish, and Prussia from the original non-German Prussians. This is the historical reality which is ideologically concealed behind any Lockean thesis.
>
> (MacIntyre 1984: 234)

In his later work, Habermas, too, moved from a historical to a more technical view of life- and system worlds. After his debate with Luhmann (Habermas and Luhmann 1971) he began to see markets, governments and laws as "non-linguistic media" which relieved individuals of the impossible task of constantly renewing their communications. Modern societies were governed by systemic imperatives whose pathological consequences appeared almost inevitable.

Third, the restricted view of agency led theories of justice to underestimate both the leveraging power of cooperation and its vulnerability to defection and deception, and therefore to unequal distributions of benefits and costs. Cooperation based on self-interest and prudence produced a thin solidarity which precluded "any conception of human community in which the concept of ... contributions to collective duties towards a community which is striving for common goods could become the basis for judgments about virtue and justice" (MacIntyre 1984: 335). Even Habermas, who initially defended modernity as the pursuit of universal Enlightenment values, later reduced the scope of justice in modern societies to the resolution of tensions between conflicting interests (Habermas 1990: 97).

Because such thin solidarity rested on rational decisions by informed, self-interested partners, these theories assumed that deception, defection and free riding would soon be discovered and were of little or no importance. They ignored the possibility that surface consent could hide power relations which reduced

> non-owners to resources, to tools and means. Even when formally and legally correct contractual agreements exist between them, even when the criterion of free consent is not deliberately violated, a person without property, faced with a lack of meaningful self-determination, an absence of options and decision alternatives, and a complete lack of possessions, has no other choice but to offer his menial services and to commit himself into dependence.
>
> (Kersting 2000: 343)

Nozick assumed that basic rules for contracts and compensation for occasional violations sufficed to deal with the problem. Rawls (1971: 570) thought that free riders would soon lose the cooperation of others. Moreover, their actions would quickly lead to a visible deterioration of the situation of the worst-off and therefore call for correction. He failed to see the many ways in which social control could use token measures to buy the acquiescence of the poor, create the illusion of equality by inflating the value of what they got, and give an appearance of fairness to exchanges which consolidated the position of the rich.

Habermas was also convinced that a well-reasoned discourse alone made communication and consensus immune to deception and defection because it led to solutions for which there was "no alternative." For him, free riders chose to remain outside the realm of rational discourse and merely feigned participation (Rehg 1994: 175). But in social control, feigning is the norm rather than the exception. Ideologies typically neutralize or denigrate the rationality of others, render one's own opinion impervious to their arguments, and disguise self-interest as common goals.

An Evolutionary Argument for Greater Equality

Distributive structures are products of evaluation and choice. Choice and human agency are also the core of any theory of distributive justice. If we believe that culture is a natural product of evolution we must seek an understanding of the ontological nature and role of choice. How values arose and what role choice played during the lived phase of evolution was "not adequately answered ... either in moral philosophy or political science or by the social scientific diagnoses of contemporary society" (Joas 2000: XI). That was also true for the extensive post-Darwinian debate over the possibility of evolutionary ethics. The search for fitness effects of specific human values soon encountered the familiar Neo-Darwinist inability to account for the complexity and situation-dependence of ethical principles and moral norms. Authors such as Mayr (1976) and Wilson (1978) tried to circumvent this problem by suggesting that actual morality varied around inherited "open" or "deep" moral programs. Others saw moral choices as disguises for selfishness or as an evolutionary extension of kin altruism to a calculating reciprocal altruism. Still others dismissed the search for evolutionary ethics altogether as a "naturalistic fallacy" which tried to derive ought from is.

An evolutionary understanding of internal, cultural selection sheds more light on the interplay between contingency, choices and consequences. In a contingent world values and choice become indispensable cognitive tools for the management of complexity. They allow human actors to give meaning to uncertain environments, to compensate for imperfect foresight, and to make decisions and undertake actions. Without choice, contingency and uncertainty would make life unlivable. Without contingency, life would have nothing to choose from.

Among sociologists, Max Weber and Niklas Luhmann recognized the unavoidably value-bound nature of human life. Internal selection confirms this view but seems to lead to an ethical relativism which precludes any effort to develop evolutionary principles of distributive justice. Choices made in uncertain environments and using creative selection criteria require constant adjustment and frequently produce unforeseen results. In such conditions any effort to base justice criteria on categorical normative imperatives, rational economic welfare optima or adaptive or functional needs is bound to fail. Internal selection can use past experiences to devise pragmatic responses to recurrent problems and to construct ends in view as guides for the future, but these always remain preliminary and fallible. Even if we assume that evolution expanded kin altruism into a more general human inclination to help others and work for the good of a community, its actual realization is subject to a myriad of shifting considerations of possible recipients of help and of possible forms it should take.

The solution to this problem is to recognize that in an unstable world principles of distributive justice cannot be found by specifying preferred results of cultural selection, but by understanding the effects which distribution has on the *process* of internal selection. Different distributive choices create typical environments of selection. These broaden or narrow options for cultural evolution. Equality and inequality respectively increase or restrict access to three essential resources of this process: material and social contingencies which supply opportunities for human choice, creative novelty which generates cognitive choice criteria, and cooperation which magnifies the power of individual action and without which, as Darwin noted, little could be accomplished. An evolutionary view of distributive justice assumes that greater equality facilitates the process of cultural evolution.

Equality and Contingency

In cultural evolution, "new kinds of made things are never pure creations of theory, ingenuity or fancy" (Basalla 1988: viii). Human actions always combine fortuitous circumstances, pre-existing material resources and knowledge, and collaborative contributions by others with their own creative exploration. The theoretical problem is whether such common assets can be separated from individual effort in order to arrive at a just distribution of collective achievements. Past authors tried to distinguish "justified" inequality based on individual ability or effort from the apparent moral arbitrariness of contingency which unfairly favored some over others. Rawls accepted individual market-based differences as long as they recognized contingent contributions by paying off the least fortunate and leaving behind just savings for future generations. Dworkin (2000) and Ackerman et al. (2006) proposed the creation of equal starting conditions which then justified life-time inequalities in income and wealth resulting from personal ability and effort. Flannery and Marcus (2012) separated ability- and achievement-based "natural" inequalities from artificial, "socially inherited" inequality based on pretense and power. Sorensen (2000), Wright (2000) and Stiglitz (2012) drew the line between inequalities arising in properly functioning markets, and "rents" derived from market imperfections or abuse.

An evolutionary view shows that contingent contributions penetrate human agency far more deeply than these proposals acknowledge. In lived evolution, contingent and personal components of collective efforts become indistinguishable and can therefore not be used to justify distributive claims. But Rawls and Sidgwick's logic remains valid: where this is the case, an equal distribution is most likely to recognize the common asset components in joint achievements. This can be done by diverting joint achievements to common purposes, by more equitable distributions of income and wealth, by ensuring participatory decision-making, or by the conservation and sustainable use of common resources.

Inequality negates these obligations because it privatizes common assets and socializes contingent risks. The more contingent contributions are obscured, the greater the likelihood of unjustified claims, self-aggrandizement, and the abuse or destruction of resources for short-term gain. The more they are recognized, the greater the incentive for distributive equality.

Equality and Creativity

In lived evolution, creativity is the source of criteria for internal selection. It transforms blind cognitive novelty into practical use and innovation. The more open this process is, and the less it is subject to ideological, political or economic constraints, the more options it creates and the more it is able to correct error and misjudgment. The more restricted it is, the slower the rate of change and the fewer the opportunities we find in our natural and social environment. Equality of creativity requires freedom of inquiry and unrestricted access to its results. Where this is not the case, the flow of innovation diminishes and its results remain inconsequential. Equality encourages discovery and innovation. Inequality tends to monopolize ideas and to divert research and innovations to partial rather than common purposes.

Equality and Solidarity

Cooperation multiplies the potential of individual actions. Solidarity, if we use Durkheim's term, is cooperation writ large. It can create bonds of social cohesion which transform individual interests into broader collective goals and mobilize the required resources. It can create new forms of institutional trust which counteract deception and defection in large organized activities. Cooperation and solidarity engender social equality; equality favors cooperation and solidarity. Inequality tends to turn cooperation into co-optation, and solidarity into the manufactured consensus of social control. The weaker the ties of solidarity, the less transparent and participatory a society becomes, and the more easily vested interests can masquerade as the common good.

Historically, the fear of what solidarity of the lower classes could do to the fabric of privilege had haunted pre-industrial elites and was heightened by the French Revolution. Individually the poor were no threat, but acting together they had a power many times greater than their number. *Fraternité* was therefore the first of the demands of the French Revolution which disappeared from the vocabulary of nineteenth century politics and philosophy, surviving only in the language of comradeship in working class movements. Cleansed of its dangerous volatility, solidarity resurfaced in the social sciences as Comte's "rational submission to the preponderance of the laws of nature," Durkheim's acceptance of one's social role, Parsons' carefully distilled shared values, or Luhmann's complexity-reducing "sense."

Communitarian critics such as Putnam (2003) who found such universal concepts of solidarity meaningless and deplored at the same time the apparent disintegration of solidarity in modern societies looked for new, de-centralized forms of cohesion. They argued that common goods could be successfully administered only by local organizations, a view also voiced in neo-liberal arguments for a "massive disassembling of the public bureaucracy" and the devolution of power to "parishes, computer networks, clubs, teams, self-help groups, small businesses – everything small and local" (Ridley 1996: 264). Self-interest remained the dominant motivation, and social capital was treated not as a common but a negotiable asset in the hands of local interest groups. There were as many solidarities as there were communities seeking recognition. The search for social justice shifted from distributive inequality to the recognition of ethnic diversity and minority rights. One of the few dissenting voices was MacIntyre (1984) who argued that the decentralized, fractured value structure of contemporary societies was not a harbinger of a new post-industrial culture but a symptom of a long-term weakening of social integration which began when liberal markets replaced traditional cooperative practices and unifying narratives with individualism, competition and contracts. In such fissured societies, segmentary and corporate interests could flourish (Michaels 2006).

For a more comprehensive view of the link between solidarity and the "fatal accident" of inequality we must turn to Rousseau. His "general will" linked liberty with equality. Liberty could not be achieved where the wealthy "flaunted the meanest interest brazenly as the public good." Real liberty demanded material and psychological restraint:

> with regard to wealth, no citizen should be rich enough to be able to buy another, and none poor enough to be forced to sell himself, which presupposes moderation in wealth and influence on the part of the upper classes, and moderation in avarice and covetousness on the part of the lower classes.
> (Rousseau 1988: 116)

The stability of the state depended on leveling social differences as much as possible. The larger they were, the more likely they led to tyranny and ideological seduction. Excessive wealth could be reduced by allowing each person enough property to assure "the common necessities of life" and by taxing away any "superfluities," suggestions which were influenced by Rousseau's romantic view of the frugal life of Swiss peasants. Moderation required that individuals subordinated their wants to the needs of larger communities. These were formidable tasks. People might have to be re-educated or even "forced to be free" (Rousseau 1988: 92, 95). These comments have often been portrayed as advocating a totalitarian society, a communal dictatorship which infringed on individual rights. In fact Rousseau's point was that the distortion of liberty by inequality required proportional measures if it was to be undone. The solidarity of the general will had to be built and protected because it was vulnerable to deception. Inequality was the enemy of the common good.

Solidarity can transform personal trust into support for impersonal institutions. Personal trust rests on direct ties to others and often involves strong emotional attachment. Individuals and organizations prefer cooperating with partners they know because personal trust reduces the chance of abuse and malfeasance

(Granovetter 1985: 440, 491). It creates strong incentives for compliance and is relatively immune to abuse. It does, however, make trust less flexible. In complex social systems it is not possible to establish personal trust with every participant, nor to become a jack of all trades who needs no help. Enlisting the skills of others in areas where one lacks expertise is the basis of all divisions of labor.

Any large-scale joint effort must therefore rely on impersonal trust: formal transfers of power and authority to distant institutions. Weber, Parsons and Luhmann saw the systemic function of bureaucracies in acting as buffers between political process and public demands. Because political decisions usually closed other options, an ever-growing list of unrealized choices could become increasingly divisive. Political and bureaucratic institutions maintained impersonal trust in the face of a bewildering range of alternatives.

Whereas greater distance between individual and trustee expands the range of joint actions, it also increases the risk of deception and the cost of prevention. Where trustees can set the terms of contracts, have an advantage of expertise, power or information, or operate under a cloak of secrecy, it is difficult to monitor their performance. Where inexperienced individuals place assets into the hands of experienced trustees, where assets cannot easily be withdrawn or where formal barriers prevent an evaluation of a trustee's performance, opportunities for self-serving increase (Shapiro 1987: 635). Regulatory arrangements such as licensing, audits or codes of ethics can reduce this danger but can also lead to costly spirals of control and supervision which destroy the chief advantage of impersonal trust: to bridge temporal and spacial gaps between individual input and collective returns. Solidarity can link personal and impersonal trust, giving direction to the first while infusing the second with personal, emotional commitment, a sense of closeness to others, a partial abandonment of self-interest to collective causes. Without this attachment, impersonal trust remains empty. Without impersonal trust, personal trust remains ineffective.

Solidarity thus establishes a bridge between individual and the wider society. Organizations become more productive if employee autonomy and impersonal trust is high (Deckopp et al. 1999; Falk and Kosfeld 2006; Grund and Harbring 2009). Prosocial reputation increases with the scale of cooperative behavior (Macfarlan et al. 2013). Solidarity can forge nations out of disjointed local cultures and traditions, blend conflicting interests into collective goals (Weber 1976) and enhance economic growth (Knack and Keefer 1997). The more it is present, the more likely it is that individuals experience a "horizontal comradeship," and public institutions command the emotional legitimacy of "imagined communities" (Anderson 2006). As with all cultural evolution, the results are not certain. Historically, solidarity has created major social and cultural benefits, but in the hands of charlatans and demagogues it has also rallied large numbers of people behind disastrous adventures. Inequality is most likely to favor the misuse of trust. Equality encourages participation in collective choices and makes solidarity resistant to abuse.

Internal Selection and Distributive Equality

Internal selection both frees and limits human agency. It gives participants considerable latitude for making choices and for imagining alternatives, but how they choose to allocate strategic resources imposes structural limits on subsequent selection. These limits are broadly proportional to the degree of inequality in a society. The more inequality there is in a society the more probable it is that some of its members will make undeserved claims for wealth and power, that creativity will serve partial rather than common interests, and that private goals will be disguised as common goods. An evolutionary view of distributive justice argues that greater equality reduces these consequences and places fewer restrictions on the overall process of cultural selection. It does not compel us to favor more equality, nor does the inherent contingency of internal selection allow us to specify permanent criteria for what constitutes a just society. It merely suggests something like this: as human beings our culture is part of the natural process of evolution. Understanding our role in this process should make us choose among known distributive options those that are most equal because that is best able to acknowledge the role of Rawls' common assets, the contingent contributions of physical and social environments, in our achievements. Opting for greater distributive equality also increases the likelihood that we can freely create and access information and use it to innovate, and that we can count on the solidarity of others in pursuing goals we share and in protecting ourselves against risk, including that of defection and deception. How we distribute the results of collective activities remains our choice, and complex social environments and our own imagination will frequently change the options which face us. But we are responsible for the consequences of what we choose. That implies that we can criticize distributive decisions and imagine and work for alternatives. All the while, internal selection remains part of the long-term process of natural selection. Whereas only a minute number of lifetime cultural choices will have adaptive consequences, social inequality with its tendency to favor short-term over long-term uses of strategic resources and to prefer private over common purposes, is among the most likely cultural choices to affect the long-term survival of our species.

Pathways to Equality

Internal selection, like all evolution, works like Darwin's "one hundred thousand wedges" to find opportunities and risks in material and social environments. If we accept that greater equality facilitates the lived process of evolution, making it a reality requires a practical, ongoing search for better ways to acknowledge contingent contributions, to increase the flow of creativity and innovation and to strengthen cooperation and solidarity. The following examples show a range of policies and institutions in contemporary industrial societies which move towards these goals. They are mere starting points. For an evolutionary analysis all options remain on the table. Many authors have proposed more far-reaching policies for greater distributive equality, ranging from the strategic (Daly 1991,

1996; Wright 2010) to the practical (McDermott 2010; Fuentes-Nieves and Galasso 2014; Piketty 2014).

Equality and Contingency: Recognizing the Contribution of Workers and Employees

During the past century, policies for distributing returns from economic activity have fluctuated greatly. High levels on inequality around 1920 were followed by periods of greater equality, public ownership and state economic planning in the wake of the Great Depression and the Second World War. Neo-liberal policies reversed this trend after 1980. Deregulated financial markets, lower corporate and marginal tax rates (Piketty and Saez 2006) and a reduced economic role of governments led to very high concentrations of personal wealth (Hacker and Pierson 2010). Instead of manufacturing and production, wealth was increasingly derived from market dominance, tax reductions that favored high incomes, tax evasion and international tax avoidance, and from the use of large pools of liquidity to create favorable conditions for speculation in financial, commodity and stock markets (Krippner 2011). In the US, the financial industry's share of GDP began to exceed that of manufacturing in the early 1990s (Johnson and Kwak 2010: 59). These changes were "gradually pushed and shoved up the legislative ladder by a conjunction of business lobbying, the contingent and situational initiatives of judges, and ... emerging balances of power" (Plesch and Blankenburg 2007: 15).

These changes created revenue shortfalls for governments which became a justification for austerity and reduced social benefits. Stagnating or slowly growing lower incomes could be improved only by longer working hours, the entry of women into the labor market to increase family incomes and a growing reliance on credit to cover the gap between income and expenditures. At the same time, costs for corporate failures were socialized, culminating during the 2008/2009 recession in the largest use of public funds in the history of capitalism to bail out corporations and financial institutions.

These general trends hide considerable cross-national differences in the division of corporate profits among its producers. Median CEO salaries in the US are substantially larger than in the UK and continental Europe (Conyon et al. 2009). Since 2005, ratios of executive to average wages have increased faster in the US than in most other industrialized countries. Similar discrepancies exist in policies regarding hours of work, health insurance, pensions and other worker benefits, both within and between countries. Today there are widely differing corporate practices in dividing profits between management, shareowners and workers, ranging from part-time "associates" with little job- and social security to employees receiving extended benefits, profit-sharing, employee share-ownership plans (ESOPS) or stock options. In 2010, 47 percent of employees in the US had some form of share in the companies they worked for (Blasi et al. 2013: 164), including some of the largest American corporations. Industrial countries also differ widely in paid vacations and holidays given to employees (Ray and Schmitt 2007). The US is the only industrial country that does not require employers to provide paid leave. One in four American workers, mostly low-wage and part-time employees, receives neither paid leave nor paid holidays, compared to the statutory 30 or more days in most European countries.

The advantages of more equitable sharing for companies lie in higher worker productivity, less turnover, more employee suggestions for innovations and lower costs for supervision (Blasi et al. 2013: 177–188). Profit sharing has tended to increase rather than diminish productivity, innovation and economic growth. There are also more general economic and social consequences. Social mobility rates are inversely related to inequality (OECD 2008). Economic growth is higher in countries with more equality, and sustained redistribution enhances efficiency and well-being (Helliwell 2006; Helliwell and Huang 2008; Olsen 2002, 2011). Many international corporations operate profitably in different countries under widely different national regulations.

Employee share-ownership is usually too small to influence management decisions and remains vulnerable to management changes, economic uncertainty and stock manipulation. Some companies such as Lincoln Electric, an American manufacturer of welding equipment (Koller 2010) have gone further and offered employees non-hierarchical organizational structures, elected employee advisory boards, worker ownership and employment guarantees. A more permanent division of collective achievements exists at Bosch, a German company with some 280,000 employees worldwide which manufactures auto parts, appliances, tools and building technology. Descendants of the company founder still hold eight percent of shares and seven percent of voting rights. The rest is divided between a trust company which manages the corporation and holds the balance of voting rights but owns no shares, and a charitable foundation which owns the balance of shares but has no voting rights. This structure protects Bosch against buy-outs and take-overs, permits a high reinvestment of profits in research and facilitates long-term planning and generous employee benefits. The charitable foundation is obliged to use its dividend income to support community projects in health, international relations and education, art and volunteer work.

Cooperatives represent an additional step towards a democratic organization of work and an equitable distribution of the proceeds of collective production. Producer-, banking- and consumer cooperatives evolved in the late eighteenth century as alternatives to hierarchical, non-participatory capitalist production. Many early cooperatives such as the Rochdale Pioneers (England), Raiffeisen (Germany) or the Desjardins Group (Canada) have grown into large cooperative organizations, and cooperatives today have more than one billion members and employ more than 100 million people worldwide in fields like banking and insurance, health and social services, and in agricultural, consumer and industrial cooperatives. Their organizing principles are always similar: democratic control by members rather than by shareholders, use of retained earnings and member dues for investment capital, an egalitarian working environment and the distribution of a share of profits to members and community. Worker-managed, employee-owned and cooperative industries have combined efficient production with low wage and salary differentials and with worker participation in management (Pencavel 2001; Logue and Yates 2001), even though they often operate in hostile political environments which favor capitalist ventures. The Mondragon cooperatives, founded in Spain in 1956 and today a large, diversified company with more than 80,000 employees, divide profits between member dividends, a social fund for community services and a reserve fund for capital investments. The cooperative also runs health and social services, a technical university and banking and retail services. Pay differentials between lowest and highest salaries are limited to a ratio of 1:6. Economic and social policies are set by elected employee councils, and management is recruited from employees. These policies have ensured high levels of worker participation and work motivation. By eliminating the need for supervision they have increased productivity and reduced conflicts between employees and management. For more than 50 years, Mondragon cooperatives have shown that an equitable distribution of profits and worker participation in management furthers efficient, large-scale industrial production.

On a statutory level, worker contribution in industrial production is recognized in German legislation allowing worker participation in industrial governance. Created after WW I and later replaced by the Nazis with party-controlled labor organizations, these laws were revived after WW II, together with a provision in the German constitution which limited private property rights. The German co-management and company organization laws define employment as a relationship of trust and cooperation for the mutual benefit of companies and employees. They provide for the election of work councils in private companies with more than five employees. Members must be allowed to meet during regular working hours, and in larger companies there are paid, full-time employee representatives. Once in every quarter there must be a general employee meeting. Worker councils have access to information about the economic condition and future plans of their company for hiring, layoffs, work reclassifications or plant closures. Mid-size companies must appoint an economic committee which has access to financial and production data and to organization and investment plans, and has graduated rights ranging from advice to a veto on company decisions. In larger publicly traded companies, employees make up one-third to one-half of the supervisory board. Board chairs are always shareholders and can use their vote to break ties. The supervisory board appoints and dismisses managers; a two-thirds majority is needed for appointments. It also approves major investments or mergers. Steel and mining industries must have a labor director (or labor vice-president) on the board of directors. Labor representatives also make up half of government boards which regulate public pension, compulsory health insurance and worker safety. Advisory councils with equal numbers of employer and labor representatives sit on labor courts that adjudicate work and social insurance disputes. In addition, the law requires labor representation in a variety of public hearings, trade organizations and political advisory bodies.

These arrangements go a long way toward recognizing the cooperative contribution of workers and employees. Fears that union influence or bureaucratic costs could reduce corporate efficiency have proven unfounded. The German co-management law survived a constitutional challenge by German employers who claimed that it contravened property rights. Worker participation has created an important "original synthesis" between capitalism and socialism (Lampert 2007: 219, 220). It is generally credited with increasing worker satisfaction and high-quality manufacturing, and with the low level of industrial conflict that contributed to the post-war growth of the German economy.

Equality and Contingency: Recognizing the Contribution of Environments

Until recently, the significance of natural environments as contingent resources was rarely recognized. In reality, climate, environment and human history have been closely linked for at least the last 2500 years (Büntgen et al. 2011). Evidence of early environmental disasters such as the collapse of the society of Easter Island or the deforestation and erosion of much of the Mediterranean coast invalidates the traditional view that nature is a free resource with no monetary value and a zero-cost receptacle for polluted air and toxic waste. Today, there is a growing public awareness of the finite amount of natural resources, the importance of natural environments for health and quality of life, the threats to biodiversity posed by resource exploitation and pollution, and the need to put a price on social and environmental costs of economic activity.

The idea of preserving natural resources for public rather than private use had its modern origins in the creation of recreational parks, beginning with the opening of the Tuileries gardens during the French Revolution and the creation of the first public parks in the industrial cities of the nineteenth century. In 1864, Abraham Lincoln reserved part of what would become Yosemite Park for "public use, resort and education." Yellowstone followed in 1872 as a "public park or pleasuring ground for the benefit and enjoyment of the people." Often created against considerable resistance from private interests, more recent examples include Oregon's protection of its beaches as "a birthright of the people," Ontario's protection of the Niagara Escarpment, and "right to roam" laws in many countries which guarantee public access to private lands and national seashores. Climate change and its potentially catastrophic consequences have led to successful international actions such as the reduction of hydrofluorocarbons. They show that a combination of scientific research, public activism and government action can strengthen the protection of environments and recognize its importance for human and ecological wellbeing.

Equality and Creativity

Creativity is the paradigmatic example of a common asset. It always builds on already existing knowledge, has often long-term and unforeseen benefits, and unlike material resources it is not depleted by repeated use. From an evolutionary point of view, the less restricted creativity is and the more widely its results are shared, the larger the fund of contingent novelty available for cultural innovation, and the more widely its benefits will be distributed.

Prior to the sixteenth century, withholding or controlling ideas for private profit was rare. Early universities were founded on the principle of unrestricted inquiry and public access to new ideas. Resistance came mainly from rulers and church fearing for their established power, from guilds and early banking networks which sought to limit competition, and from commercial interests such as the Dutch tulip breeders who tried without success to hide new varieties under a cloak of secrecy. In the fourteenth and fifteenth century, letters patent began to protect particular trades against foreign competition and were soon also used to gain trade monopolies. Early copyrights in England and France were given to printing trades, in part to control the influx of subversive political ideas and in part to secure monopolies for guilds of printers and stationers. Historically, the driving force behind copyright and patents were not inventors but trade interests which sought to commercialize and monopolize creativity.

Today, patents, copyrights, and intellectual property rights are key issues which decide whether knowledge is a private or a public good. Corporations and governments have prolonged patent protection to prevent transfer into the public domain, curtailed the right to fair use of published work, restricted inventors' rights to publish findings and withheld profits derived from inventors' work. Privatization of knowledge also blurred the traditional distinction between discovery and invention, especially in efforts to patent DNA sequences, animal and plant genes and naturally occurring biological compounds.

The increasing penetration of public research institutions by corporate funding has diverted basic scientific work to applied fields and has neglected research that offers no commercial payoff or faces impoverished markets. Only one percent of new pharmaceutical drugs marketed between 1975 and 1997 were related to tropical diseases (Drahos and Braithwaite 2002: 80). Re-patenting or minor variations of existing drugs with few or no clinical advantages for patients are estimated to make up 85 to 90 percent of the new drugs licensed each year (Light and Lexchin 2012). The commercialization of medical and pharmaceutical research is major cause of increased drug and health costs and of the transformation of normal behavior into medicated illness (Lane 2007). The rapid growth of patent litigation has actually slowed the rate of innovation (Cowen 2011).

Material rewards are only one of many reasons why people create. There is little evidence that strong patent law and patent protection spur innovation (Lerner 2002; Jaffe and Lerner 2004) or that longer copyrights increase literary productivity (Breyer 1970; Lessig 2004). Historically, human cultural evolution has been directly related to increases in information exchange. In eighteenth and nineteenth century Europe, inventions increased and spread much faster in areas where patent protection and copyright were ineffective (Höffner 2010). The exponential growth of innovation following new communication technologies from Gutenberg to the World Wide Web resulted from open, not proprietary inventions. The founders of the Web decided in 1993 that no royalties should be charged for its use. Scientific and literary material is now widely available on public domain websites such as the Public Library of Science. Creative Commons movements and major universities have allowed free access to scientific research and created non-restrictive licensing and open-source courses. Fair

Use projects have fought for reduced copyright periods. Internet leaks have shed light on secret government and international tax avoidance, and have counteracted efforts to use internet tools to collect personal information for political and commercial purposes. In many countries, publicly owned television and radio stations are important sources of unbiased information. Public access can keep the collection and dispersal of information transparent and accountable and turn it into a contingent resource for further creative discovery and invention.

Governments already have a major role in supporting creativity and innovation because much of the research in areas such as communication technology or pharmaceuticals originated in publicly funded universities, research institutions and military research. Governments can counteract the tendency to socialize the risks associated with innovation and to privatize its rewards. Instead of limiting themselves to "de-risking" private industry, they can set research priorities which are in the public interest and can become active participants in furthering creativity in these areas through direct funding and by creating public companies or acquiring equity stakes in private corporations in order to keep costs of public interest goods such as pharmaceuticals low and divert profits to public funds (Mazzucato 2013).

Equality and Solidarity

Modern views of solidarity were shaped by two traditions. The first originated in the struggle by aristocracy and gentry in England to limit the power of the monarchy. The aim was to achieve individual freedom from central authority, and it influenced Spencer's opposition to the church-state complex as much as modern neo-liberal hostility toward the state. The second tradition grew from demands by nineteenth century working class movements in continental Europe for greater distributive equality, political power and for state intervention to pursue common goals, if necessary by correcting market results. This view also influenced Durkheim's and Parsons' recognition of the vital role of solidarity and shared values as an integrative counterforce to the divisive power of social inequality. These divergent traditions continue to be reflected in current public opinion. Americans are more likely to see economic success as the result of individual ability and effort and to attribute poverty to personal rather than social-structural causes. Europeans, by contrast, link wealth to a greater extent to luck and connections and see a greater role for the state in establishing economic fairness (Alesina et al. 2001; Alesina and Angeletos 2003).

Solidarity works on an emotional and an institutional level. On the first, it builds a sense of shared identity and of being allied with others in the pursuit of common goals. On the second, it legitimates collective projects and the mobilization of the necessary resources. In recent decades, both areas have undergone significant changes: emotional attachment to common causes has declined, and the role of states in realizing them has been weakened. Many authors (Putnam 2000, Paxton 2002, Costa and Kahn 2003) have deplored the decline of civic participation and democratic opportunities in Western societies. The privatization of the public sphere has allowed business to define public goals (Fraser

1990, Reich 2008), to mobilize grassroots participation for corporate objectives (Walker 2009), and to dispense selective charity as part of corporate branding and advertising policies. The result is a "captured democracy" where democratic procedures are used to favor elites (Acemoglu and Robinson 2008), and where common goals are replaced by claims of special interest groups (Michaels 2006).

Rising inequality is a major contributor to this fragmentation of the public sphere. Trust and civic participation weaken where income disparities grow (Costa and Kahn 2003). Voter participation and membership in political parties and unions have declined in most countries, but did so earlier and more significantly in high-inequality societies such as the UK and the US (Putnam 2002: 413). Income inequality lowers trust among poorer segments of societies (Alesina and La Ferrara 2002) and is accompanied by increased social costs (Wilkinson 2005; Roth 2009). Solidarity is replaced by a sense of collective vulnerability, fear and intolerance (Furedi 2005). People "hunker down" (Putnam 2007), mistrust politicians and "intellectual elites" and become receptive to populist ideologies purporting to speak for "ordinary people" (Frank 2004). Neo-liberal policies of tax reduction have shifted civic participation from the arena of politics to the market where people are unwilling to contribute to causes which do not bring them immediate benefits. Communitarian theorists hoped that limited notions of the common good would eventually coalesce into a larger participatory democracy, but solidarity is as unlikely to recover from below as the benefits of neo-liberal economics are to trickle down from above.

White (2003) distinguished three levels of solidarity. The first is the limited and often local private sphere of family, friendship, ethnic or neighborhood ties. The second, more extended sphere of charitable gifts, mutual help or collective advocacy targets particular causes and tends to reflect the idiosyncratic values of the donor which "often fragment whole, complex societies more than (they) unify them" (White 2003: 67). The third is the solidarity of civic nationalism. Here citizens identify collective goals and risks and agree to pay taxes to respond. The significance of such organized solidarity lies in the social cohesion derived from shared social rights and institutions which make "citizens feel like they belong to a country with which they are proud to identify" (White 2003: 67). This kind of solidarity cannot grow without the help of the state.

Rather than appearing in late stages of human history as "a unified functional response" to maintain order and strengthen stratification (Fried 1960: 37) or, as Marx suggested, as the organizing committee of capital, modern states are the descendants of early cooperative institutions charged with centralized storage and distribution. Even where their function to serve collective goals was taken over by autocratic rulers or elites, their ability to advance common goals and to counteract deception and defection did not disappear. The portrayal of modern states as threats to individual rights or as chronically inefficient bureaucracies originates not from its citizens, but from ideological efforts by powerful groups to weaken its power to regulate private and pursue common interests.

States have two crucial roles as defenders of the public good. As symbolic states they create a sense of shared goals, public welfare and social fairness. As redistributive and regulatory states they transform citizen interests into social policies, manage and equalize risk through public insurance programs, counteract organized defection and fraud, and reallocate collectively earned revenue through progressive taxation, market intervention and regulation. Modern states differ widely in how they perform these roles, but they always institutionalize some level of equality.

On the symbolic level,

> highly developed and comprehensive welfare states like Sweden's go beyond simply redistributing income and compensating people for market failure. Universal health care, childcare, and other social services and benefits decommodify and insulate human needs from commercialization. Equally important, they help to foster a greater sense of solidarity and social justice. And the encompassing and comprehensive nature of social policy in Sweden continues to generate a great deal of popular support for the welfare state.... The Swedish example is important because it shows that a downward convergence (to the level of low-support states such as the US and Canada) is not inevitable and can be resisted.
>
> (Olsen 2002: 196)

Public trust and subjective happiness depend on whether differences in income and wealth are perceived as fair or not (Layard 2005). High tax rates in many European countries are accepted because they even out income and wealth differentials, and because states provide services such as parental leaves, childcare and early childhood education, and prolonged protection against income loss through unemployment or illness. Such public services have greater positive effects on life satisfaction than per capita income, and strengthen the sense that government decisions can be influenced by citizens and are accountable and free of corruption.

As regulatory and redistributive organizations, states are custodians of three types of common assets. They protect natural commons such as clean air, water and biological and ecological resources. They protect working commons such as industrially used natural resources by making sure that they benefit all members of society and are preserved for future generation. They protect social commons through regulations which ensure fairness and transparency of economic and social policies. Contrasting approaches to the protection of working commons are illustrated by the Alberta Heritage Fund and the Alaska Permanent Fund, both created in 1976, and the Norwegian Petroleum Fund established in 1990 to use oil wealth to create a "qualitatively better society." The initial goal of these funds was to save some oil and gas revenue for a time when these resources were exhausted. Alaska's government distributed fund revenue as annual dividends (on average between US$1000–1500) to each Alaska resident. Profits from Alberta's fund were diverted to general revenue, the elimination of sales taxes and a one-time disbursement in 2008 of CA$400 to every resident of Alberta. Low royalties and generous concessions to resource companies kept fund income low. Of the total oil and gas revenue Alberta collected since 1976, 92 percent was spent and only eight percent was saved. In Norway, oil and gas industries are mostly state-owned and must contribute to a fund which is managed by the central bank. Net earnings of the fund are reinvested, and only four percent of annual deposits is available for regular government expenditures. The Norwegian fund defined clear public goals, did not invest in companies which violated ethical guidelines, and created a special environmental investment portfolio. In 2014 the value of the Alberta Heritage Fund was CA$17 billion and Alaska's fund was US$59 billion. Norway's fund had reached US$828.6 billion, about US$163,000 for each Norwegian citizen. England which began to produce North Sea oil at about the same time as Norway, used most of the resulting royalties for tax reductions which disproportionally benefited recipients of high incomes. No reserves were retained.

Protecting social commons involves the state in policies which ensure that public investments do not disproportionally favor privileged groups, that political processes are not influenced by powerful lobbies, that the cooperative nature of economic production is recognized through labor- and social legislation and that regulations prevent insider trading, tax avoidance, or market and media monopolies. Acemoglu and Robinson (2006, 2008) argue that the historical growth of western industrial societies was not due to favorable natural or religious environments but to a contest between citizens and elites for an open economy, unrestricted innovation and a parliamentary democracy which balanced conflicting interests. State institutions played a crucial role in preventing interest groups from using their power to reduce competition, consolidate gains and influence policies through lobbying and financial contributions. By contrast, states such as fourteenth century Venice whose economy was dominated by a small trading elite eventually experienced economic failure and social decline. The authors suggest that the rapid rise of inequality in recent decades may signal a return of such "extractive processes."

Where states act as trustees of the public good they can realize economies of scale which are not available to private business, balance short-term market interests with the consideration of long-term social needs and assign value to goods which markets treat as cost-free externalities. Public health insurance in Europe and Canada has been more accessible to patients and more efficient than private insurance in such key areas as preventable deaths (Nolte and McKee 2008) and administrative costs (Law et al. 2014). Public automobile insurance in four Canadian provinces costs significantly less than private insurance in the rest of the country. Public administration is not always efficient, immune to corruption, or free of secrecy, but it is subject to far greater public scrutiny and electoral controls than corporate practices. Where states act as protectors of common goods, people tend to return the favor (Putnam 2002: 414). When they are weakened or dismantled, their functions are taken over by well-organized special interests, and trust and civic participation declines.

State-Organized Redistribution

The redistribution of income and wealth is a central part of distributing the results of collective achievements more equally. Prior to the nineteenth century, redistribution was limited to episodic assistance to the poor and was used to quell periodic social disorder in cities. English poor laws from 1834 onward continued to rely mostly on workhouses (abolished in England only in 1929) and local relief for the poor which discriminated between the deserving poor and those deemed to use government help to avoid gainful work. The first graduated income tax established in England in 1798 was not meant to reduce inequality but to pay for the wars against Napoleon, a modern version of earlier war-levies imposed on gentry and aristocracy which was then passed on to retainers and peasants.

The redistribution of income and wealth as compensation for contingent advantages and risks emerged only in response to the growth of a strong organized working class, and against tenacious resistance from propertied classes who argued that long working hours kept workers away from sloth and vice, and that low wages reinforced the motivation to work. The first comprehensive social insurance system in industrial economies was introduced by Bismarck in Germany between 1884 and 1889 to cover illness, industrial accidents, long-term disability and old age. It was an explicit effort to blunt the increasing power of German working class parties by combining "serious efforts for an improvement of the fate of workers" with the repressive 1889 *Law Against the Common Danger Posed by the Ambitions of Social Democracy*. Although materially insufficient and a tool of authoritarian policy, Bismarck's reforms required employers to fund part or all of these services. They became the model for subsequent social legislation in other countries. Continental European countries with strong working class parties implemented redistributive schemes relatively early. Even here, social legislation followed the see-saw of political events. In Germany, progress after WW I was reversed when Hitler gained power 1933. In England, Canada and the US, the Depression and WW II became the real catalysts for modern social security programs. Neo-liberal policies weakened or dismantled social services after 1980, lowered corporate taxes and reduced the progressivity of tax systems, measures which favored recipients of high incomes.

Today, redistributive fiscal policies vary widely between comparable industrial countries. Social spending as percentage of GDP ranges from lows of 6.8 percent (Mexico) to 16–18 percent in the US, Canada, Ireland or Portugal, and to 28–31 percent in countries like Germany, France and Sweden (OECD 2008). Whereas inequality in market income has risen in many industrial countries, inequality in disposable, post-redistribution inequality has risen much less in Nordic and central European countries compared to the US, the UK and Canada (Brandolini and Smeeding 2007). Many European countries offer not only more generous protection against risks involving health, old age or unemployment, but also free university tuition, extended maternity and paternity leaves, paid retraining and education leaves and amenities such as pedestrian zones, urban parks and public transportation which increase work satisfaction, productivity and quality of life. People in countries where redistribution leads to greater income equality live longer, have lower rates of illness, delinquency, depression and teenage pregnancies than their more unequal counterparts (Wilkinson and Pickett 2009).

Outlook

Inequality structures tend to depict the future only as an extension of the present, and dismiss alternatives as the work of false prophets whose demands are unrealistic, whose predictions are stillborn, and whose ideals are utopian. This chapter has made an evolutionary argument for greater equality and has shown that a more equal distribution of collectively achieved economic value can increase both efficiency and well-being of the contributors.

Equality can be achieved through the slow modification of distributive policies or through radical structural change. In 594 BC, competing factions of Athenian nobles commissioned Solon to find a solution to the problem that "the many were enslaved to the rich." Against their expectations Solon began a revolutionary experiment in *eunomia*, a just and equitable order where "rough edges would be smoothed out, appetites tamed, and presumption curbed." He annulled mortgages, freed indebted peasants, replaced the monopoly of aristocratic power by a people's council and established a public judicial code to limit arbitrary interpretations of Athenian law by powerful elites. Interrupted by the populist dictatorship of Peisistratos, the resurgence of democratic sentiment led Cleisthenes in 507 to propose a more radical *isonomia*, a rule of equality which made Athenian democracy flourish for almost 200 years. Its defining moment came in the fight against an overwhelming Persian invasion force, won as much by its hoplite infantry as by the intangible strength of solidarity which extended to the very lowest and poorest strata of Athenian society. If the battle of Marathon had still been fought mainly by land-owning farmers who could pay for their helmet, shield and spear, the final victory at Salamis belonged to the "sea folk," the Athenian rabble who could not afford to buy weapons and served as rowers on the triremes. After Salamis their political fortunes soared. The result was an experiment in radical political equality: regular popular assemblies of all eligible citizens, per diem stipends to allow everyone to attend, elected court juries, a governing council and a bureaucracy chosen not by qualification but by lot (except for military leaders), one-year term limits for council members and administrators, public accounting, and severe penalties for abuses of power, including a ten-year exile from the city. It was a system which, with its bold disregard for qualifications and hierarchies, should never have worked.[5] It was also no egalitarian paradise: women could not vote or hold office, Athens' economy depended on slaves, and the city colonized a large part of the Mediterranean coast. It was plagued by corruption, demagogues and smear campaigns. But the Athenian experiment also created a period of unprecedented political freedom and an extraordinary flowering of science, philosophy, art, architecture and literature. When it succumbed in 338 BC, it was not to internal weakness but to the superior military force of Macedonian invaders. Its democratic ideals were never extinguished.

If Athenian democracy created a radically new political system, Marx's *Communist Manifesto* was a grand design for distributive change which, at first glance, miserably failed. This was the book which warned that the specter of communism was haunting Europe, that workers had nothing to lose but their chains and had a world to win, and that the fall of the bourgeoisie was as inevitable as the victory of the proletariat. The pathos of these passages and the hostility they still evoke obscure the fact that the *Manifesto* and the *Demands of the Communist Party in Germany*, both published in 1848, also asked for a progressive income tax, inheritance taxes, the creation of a central bank with control over credit and currency, nationalized transportation and postal systems, the abolition of child labor, free public education and the inclusion of vocational training in the curriculum of schools. It called for universal franchise at age 21 (except for people with criminal records), for parliamentary stipends so that workers could stand for election, for the separation of church and state, free legal services, state-guaranteed mortgages, and for national workshops which could provide income "for those who are incapacitated for work."

These, too, were revolutionary demands, although Marx may have added them to increase the *Manifesto*'s appeal to more moderate factions of the working class. None of them had been realized in 1848, and to many contemporaries they must have sounded as threatening as Marx's call for the abolition of capitalism. If he returned today he would realize that he had woefully underestimated the strength of capitalism, but he would also have much to be pleased about. All of his practical demands became reality, although they remain contested and are sometimes weakened or reversed. They did not overthrow capitalism, but they brought relief from insecurity and want which early industrialization had inflicted on working people and achieved a more equitable distribution of collective gains.

Any attempt to reduce inequality in contemporary societies faces formidable obstacles. The concentration of wealth in a few hands has reached almost incomprehensible levels; the 85 richest people in the world, easily fitted into a double-decker bus, own as much as the bottom half of the world's population (Fuentes-Nieves and Galasso 2014). Governments which try to protect common goods face the dilemma between cooperation and defection on a global scale. As successive attempts to reach an international agreement to reduce CO_2 emissions have shown, it becomes difficult to implement environmental regulations if partners defect to obtain an economic advantage.

At the same time, this book has shown that social inequality in human societies is the result of historical choices which were neither necessary nor irreversible. The distribution of collaborative wealth has varied substantially over recent decades. Citizens and governments have developed imaginative policies to protect public interests and have found forms of production which acknowledge the contribution of all contributors. Contrary to the conventional argument that such policies face an inevitable trade-off between equality and efficiency (Okun 1975), international comparisons show that greater equality enhances economic growth (Berg and Ostry 2011).

Evolution opens futures but does not prescribe them. New forms of communication can make cooperation more efficient, create a more active social citizenship, and show routes to a more equitable distribution of collective achievements. They can also create a dumbed-down public manipulated by a veneer of democratic theatre which camouflages private power. There have never been so many environmental treaties as today, but we also see a decline in ecosystems, soil and water degradation, loss of land and marine habitats, and increasing pollution and waste (United Nations Global Environment Outlook, Annual Report 2012). But governments also have powers which they refuse to use only because their political survival has become interwoven with wealthy interests. They can, like the two Roosevelt governments did in the US, dismantle monopolies. They can force industries receiving public contracts to pay living wages. They can weaken the influence of financial and corporate lobbies. They can reduce the attractiveness of international heavens for tax avoidance, as EU countries have done with Switzerland and Luxemburg. Just as many governments passed access to information laws, they can legislate more transparency for corporations and protect whistle blowers. They can pursue international agreements requiring corporations to pay taxes where they sell their products, not where they report their profits. They can use redistributive taxes to maximize the benefits of economic growth for all citizens, and reduce speculative gains by taxing financial and foreign currencies transactions at rates which amount to a fraction of a percent but can raise very large sums which could then be invested in public causes. An evolutionary view tells us that options for greater equality lie in our hands.

Notes

1 Zeitlin (1997) gives a concise outline of classical visions of just rule. Cohn (1970), Hill (1978) and Kendrick (2004) survey early utopian movements.
2 Walzer (1983), Cohen (1995), Kersting (2000) and Nussbaum (2006) are among the many contributors to debates about social and distributive justice.
3 Versions of these principles can be found in Rawls 1971: 303 and 1982: 5. In Rawls' later work, cooperation becomes a more important motivating factor than self-interested prudence.
4 Theories of justice have eliminated historical complexity for the sake of analytical simplicity since the earliest reconstructions of "states of nature." Rawls' actors lived in a featureless "original position." Nozick had Robinson Crusoe explain to his man Friday his proprietary right to a shell he found on a beach. Dworkin (1981) placed shipwrecked strangers on an island to arrange an auction of needed resources. Ackerman (1980, 1991) put them on a spaceship where they had to decide on rules of distribution on a planet they were about to settle, and Roemer's (1986) theory of exploitation began on a credit market island and a labor market island.
5 A study by Pluchino, Rapisarda and Garofalo (2010) shows why it may have succeeded. Assuming that all modern hierarchies are affected to some degree by the Peter Principle which states that employees tend to be promoted past their maximum level of competence, the efficiency of organizations would actually be increased by random promotions. The study was ridiculed by the Harvard-based Ig-noble committee, perhaps because it threatened the institutional self-esteem of its members. In fact it explains why organizations work even though recruitment and promotion always involve elements of uncertainty and randomness.

Bibliography

Acemoglu, Daron and James A. Robinson. *Economic Origins of Dictatorship and Democracy*. Cambridge: Cambridge University Press, 2006.
Acemoglu, Daron and James A. Robinson. "Persistence of Power, Elites, and Institutions." *American Economic Review* 98 (2008) 1: 267–93.

Ackerman, Bruce. *Social Justice in the Liberal System*. New Haven: Yale University Press, 1980.
Ackerman, Bruce. *We the People*. Cambridge: Belknap Press, 1991.
Ackerman, Bruce, Ann Alstott and Philippe van Parijs. *Redesigning Distribution: Basic Income and Stakeholder Grants as Cornerstones of a More Egalitarian Capitalism*. New York: Verso, 2006.
Alesina, Alberto and George-Marios Angeletos. "Fairness and Redistribution: US versus Europe." *National Bureau of Economic Research*. (2003) Working paper 9502. Available online at: www.nber.org/paperts/w9502
Alesina, Alberto and Eliana La Ferrara. "Who Trusts Others?" *Journal of Public Economics* 85 (2002) 2: 207–234.
Alesina, Alberto, Edward Glaeser and Bruce Sacerdote. "Why Doesn't the US Have a European-Type Welfare State?" *Brookings Papers on Economic Activity* 2 (2001): 187–277.
Anderson, Benedict. *Imagined Communities: Reflections on the Origin and Spread of Nationalism*, revised edition. London: Verso, 2006.
Arrow, Kenneth J. *Social Choice and Individual Values*. New Haven: Yale University Press, 1951.
Basalla, George. *The Evolution of Technology*. Cambridge: Cambridge University Press, 1988.
Berg, Andrew G. and Jonathan D. Ostry. "Equality and Efficiency." *International Monetary Fund, Finance & Development* 48 (2011) 3: 12–15.
Blasi, Joseph R., Richard B. Freeman and Douglas L. Kruse. *The Citizen's Share. Putting Ownership Back Into Democracy*. New Haven: Yale University Press, 2013.
Brandolini, Andrea and Timothy M. Smeeding. "Inequality Patterns in Western-Type Democracies: Cross-Country Differences and Time Changes." *Luxembourg Income Study*, Working Paper Series No. 458 (2007).
Breyer, Stephen. "The Uneasy Case for Copyright: A Study of Copyrights for Books, Photocopies, and Computer Programs." *Harvard Law Review* 84 (1970) 2: 281–355.
Büntgen, Ulf, Willy Tegel, Kurt Nicolussi, Michael McCormick, David Frank, Valerie Trouet, Jed O. Kaplan, Franz Herzig, Karl-Uwe Heussner, Heinz Wanner, Jürg Luterbacher and Jan Esper. "2500 Years of European Climate Variability and Human Susceptibility." *Science* 331 (2011) 6017: 578–582.
Cohen, Gerald A. *Self-ownership, Freedom and Equality*. Cambridge: Cambridge University Press, 1995.
Cohn, Norman. *The Pursuit of the Millennium*. New York: Oxford University Press, 1970.
Conyon, Martin J., Simon I. Peck, and Graham V. Sadler. "Compensation Consultants and Executive Pay: Evidence from the United States and the United Kingdom." *Academy of Management Perspectives* 23 (2009) 1: 43–55.
Costa, Dora and Matthew Kahn. "Understanding the American Decline in Social Capital, 1952–1998." *Kyklos* 56 (2003) 1: 17–46.
Cowen, Tyler. *The Great Stagnation*. New York: Dutton, 2011.
Daly, Herman E. *Beyond Growth: The Economics of Sustainable Development*. Boston: Beacon Press, 1994.
Daly, Herman E. *Steady-state Economics: The Economics of Biophysical Equilibrium and Moral Growth*. San Francisco: W. H. Freeman, 1991 [1977].
Deckopp, John R., Robert Mangel and Carol C. Circa. "Getting More Than You Pay For; Organizational Citizenship Behaviour and Pay For Performance Plans." *Academy of Management Journal* 42 (1999) 4: 420–428.

Drahos, Peter and John Braithwaite. *Information Feudalism*. New York: New Press, 2002.
Dworkin, Ronald. "What is Equality." *Philosophy and Public Affairs* 10 (1981) 3, 4: 185–246 and 283–245.
Dworkin, Ronald. *Sovereign Virtue. The Theory and Practice of Equality*. Cambridge: Harvard University Press, 2000.
Falk, Armin and Michael Kosfeld. "Distrust – The Hidden Cost of Control." *American Economic Review* 96 (2006) 5: 1611–1630.
Flannery, Kent and Joyce Marcus. *The Creation of Inequality*. Cambridge: Harvard University Press, 2012.
Frank, Thomas. *What's the Matter with Kansas?* New York: Holt, 2004.
Fraser, Nancy. "Rethinking the Public Sphere: A Contribution to the Critique of Actually Existing Democracy." *Social Text* 25/26 (1990): 56–80.
Fried, Morton. "On the Evolution of Social Stratification and the State." In Stanley Diamond (ed.) *Culture in History*, 713–731. New York: Columbia University Press, 1960.
Fuentes-Nieves, Ricardo and Nick Galasso. "Working for the Few. Political Capture and Economic Inequality." Oxfam International. Available online at: www.oxfam.org.uk
Furedi, Frank. *The Politics of Fear*. London: Continuum Books, 2005.
Granovetter, Mark. "Economic Action and Social Structure: the Problem of Embeddedness." *American Journal of Sociology* 91 (1985) 3: 481–510.
Grund, Christian and Christine Harbring. "Trust and Control at the Workplace: Evidence from Representatives Samples in Europe." Discussion Paper 4297 (2009). *Institute for the Study of Labor*. Bonn (Germany). Available online at: http://ftp.iza.org/dp4297.pdf
Habermas, Jürgen. *Legitimationsprobleme im Spätkapitalismus*. Frankfurt: Suhrkamp, 1973.
Habermas, Jürgen. *Theorie kommunikativen Handelns*. Vols. I, II. Frankfurt: Suhrkamp, 1981.
Habermas, Jürgen. *Vorstudien und Ergänzungen zur Theorie des kommunikativen Handelns*. Frankfurt: Suhrkamp, 1984.
Habermas, Jürgen. *Die nachholende Revolution*. Frankfurt: Suhrkamp, 1990.
Habermas, Jürgen and Niklas Luhmann. *Theorie der Gesellschaft oder Sozialtechnologie – Was leistet die Systemforschung?* Frankfurt: Suhrkamp, 1971.
Hacker, Jacob S. and Paul Pierson. "Winner-Take-All Politics: Public Policy, Political Organization, and the Precipitous Rise of Top Incomes in the United States." *Politics & Society* 38 (2010 a) 2: 152–204.
Hayek, Friedrich. *Verfassung der Freiheit*. In *Friedrich A. von Hayek. Gesammelte Schriften in Deutscher Sprache*, edited by Alfred Bosch. Section B, volume 3. Tübingen: Mohr Siebeck, 2001–2003 [1971].
Hayek, Friedrich. *Recht, Gesetzgebung und Freiheit. Volume 2: Die Illusion der sozialen Gerechtigkeit*. Tübingen: Mohr, 1981.
Helliwell, John F. "Well-being, Social Capital and Public Policy: What's New?" *The Economic Journal* 116 (2006) 510: C34–C45.
Helliwell, John F. and Haifang Huang. "How's your Government? International Evidence Linking Good Government and Well-being." *British Journal of Political Science* 38 (2008) 4: 595–619.
Hill, Christopher. *The World Turned Upside Down: Radical Ideas during the English Revolution*. London: Penguin, 1978.
Höffner, Eckhard. *Geschichte und Wesen des Urheberrechts*. München: Verlag Europäische Wirtschaft, 2010.

Jaffe, Adam and Josh Lerner. *Innovation and its Discontents. How Our Broken Patent System is Endangering Innovation and Progress, and What to Do About it*. Princeton: Princeton University Press, 2004.
Joas, Hans. *The Genesis of Values*. Chicago: University of Chicago Press, 2000.
Johnson, Simon and James Kwak. *13 Bankers: The Wall Street Takeover and the Next Financial Meltdown*. New York: Pantheon, 2010.
Kendrick, Christopher. *Utopia, Carnival, and Commonwealth in Renaissance England*. Toronto: University of Toronto Press, 2004.
Kersting, Wolfgang. *Theorien der sozialen Gerechtigkeit*. Stuttgart: J.B. Metzler, 2000.
Knack, Stephen and Philip Keefer. "Does Social Capital have an Economic Payoff? A Cross-Country Investigation." *Quarterly Journal of Economics* 112 (1997) 3: 1251–1288.
Koller, Frank. *Spark*. New York: Public Affairs, 2010.
Krippner, Greta. *Capitalizing on Crisis: The Political Origins of the Rise of Finance*. Cambridge: Harvard University Press, 2011.
Lampert, Heinz. *Lehrbuch der Sozialpolitik*. Berlin: Springer Verlag, 2007.
Lane, Christopher. *Shyness: How Normal Behaviour Became a Sickness*. New Haven: Yale University Press, 2007.
Law, Michael R., Jillian Kratzer and Irfan A. Dhalla. "The Increasing Inefficiency of Private Health Care in Canada." *Canadian Medical Association Journal* 186 (2014) 12: E470.
Layard, Richard. *Happiness: Lessons From a New Science*. London: Allen Lane, 2005.
Lerner, Josh. "150 Years of Patent Protection." *American Economic Review* 92 (2002) 2: 221–225.
Lessig, Lawrence. *Free Culture: How Big Media uses Technology and the Law to Lock Down Culture and Control Creativity*. New York: Penguin, 2004.
Light, Donald and Joel Lexchin. "Pharmaceutical Research and Development: What Do We Get For All that Money?" *British Journal of Medicine* 345 (2012) e4348. DOI: 10.1136/bmj.e4348
Locke, John. *Second Treatise on Government*. Raleigh N.C., Alex Catalogue: 1947 [1688]. Available online at: www.infomotions.com/alex
Logue, John and Jacquelyn Yates. *The Real World of Employee Ownership*. Ithaca: Cornell University Press, 2001.
Macfarlan, Shane J., Robert Quinlan and Mark Remiker. "Cooperative Behavior and Prosocial Reputation Dynamics in a Dominican Village." *Proceedings of the Royal Society B* 280 (2013) 1761: 20130557.
MacIntyre, Alasdair. *After Virtue: A Study in Moral Theory*. London: Duckworth, 1984 [1981].
Marx, Karl. *Grundrisse der Kritik der Politischen Ökonomie*. Moscow: Verlag für fremdsprachige Literatur, 1939–1941 [1857/1858].
Mayr, Ernst. "Behaviour Programs and Evolutionary Strategies." In Ernst Mayr (ed.) *Evolution and the Diversity of Life*. Cambridge: Harvard University Press, 1976.
Mazzucato, Mariana. *The Entrepreneurial State*. London: Anthem Press, 2013.
McDermott, John F.M. *Restoring Democracy to America. How to Free Markets and Politics from the Corporate Culture of Business and Government*. University Park, PA: Pennsylvania State University Press, 2010.
Michaels, Walter Benn. *The Trouble with Diversity: How we Learned to Love Identity and Ignore Inequality*. New York: Metropolitan Books, 2006.
Nolte, Ellen and Martin McKee. "Measuring the Health of Nations: Updating an Earlier Analysis." *Health Affairs* 27 (2008) 1: 58–71.

Nozick, Robert. *Anarchy, State, and Utopia.* New York: Basic Books, 1974.
Nussbaum, Martha C. *Frontiers of Justice: Disability, Nationality, Species Membership.* Cambridge, MA: Belknap Press, 2006.
OECD. *Growing Unequal? Income Distribution and Poverty in OECD Countries.* Paris: OECD Publications, 2008. DOI: 10.1787/9789264044197-en
Okun, Arthur M. *Equality and Efficiency, the Big Tradeoff.* Washington: The Brookings Institution, 1975.
Olsen, Gregg M. *The Politics of the Welfare State. Canada, Sweden and the United States.* Don Mills: Oxford University Press, 2002.
Olsen, Gregg M. *Power and Inequality.* Don Mills: Oxford University Press, 2011.
Paxton, Pamela. "Social Capital and Democracy: An Interdependent Relationship." *American Sociological Review* 67 (2002) 2: 254–277.
Pencavel, John. *Worker Participation: Lessons from the Worker Co-ops of the Pacific Northwest.* New York: Russell Sage Foundation, 2001.
Pigou, Cecil Arthur. *Wealth and Welfare.* London: MacMillan, 1912.
Piketty, Thomas. *Capital in the Twenty-First Century.* Cambridge, MA: Belknap Press, 2014.
Piketty, Thomas and Emmanuel Saez. "The Evolution of Top Incomes: A Historical and International Perspective." *The American Economic Review* 96 (2006) 2: 200–205.
Plesch, Dan and Stephanie Blankenburg. "Corporate Rights and Responsibilities: Restoring Legal Accountability." London: *Royal Society for the Encouragement of Arts, Manufacture & Commerce* (RSA) (2007): 2–35.
Pluchino, Allessandro, Andrea Rapisarda and Cesare Garofalo. "The Peter Principle Revisited: A Computational Study." *Physica* A, 389 (2010) 3: 467–472.
Putnam, Robert D. *Bowling Alone: The Collapse and Revival of American Community.* New York: Simon and Schuster, 2000.
Putnam, Robert D. *Democracies in Flux: The Evolution of Social Capital in Contemporary Society.* Oxford: Oxford University Press, 2002.
Putnam, Robert D. *Better Together: Restoring the American Community.* New York: Simon and Schuster, 2003.
Putnam, Robert. "E Pluribus Unum: Diversity and Community in the Twenty-first Century." *Scandinavian Political Studies* 30 (2007) 2: 137–174.
Rawls, John. "Kantian Constructivism in Moral Theory: The Dewey Lectures." *Journal of Philosophy* 77 (1980) 9: 515–572.
Rawls, John. "The Basic Liberties and Their Priority." In Sterling M. MacMurrin (ed.) *The Tanner Lectures on Human Values,* 1–89. Cambridge: Cambridge University Press, 1982.
Rawls, John. *A Theory of Justice.* Oxford: Clarendon Press, 1971.
Ray, Rebecca and John Schmitt. "No-vacation Nation USA – A Comparison of Leave and Holidays in OECD Countries." *European Economic and Employment Policy Brief* 3. Brussels: European Trade Union Institute, 2007. Available online at: www.law.harvard.edu/programs/lwp/papers/No_Holidays.pdf
Rehg, William. *Insight and Solidarity. The Discourse Ethics of Jürgen Habermas.* Berkeley: University of California Press, 1994.
Reich, Robert. "Why Creative Capitalism Gets in the Way of Democracy." In Michael E. Kinsley (ed.) *Creative Capitalism,* 91–99. New York: Simon & Schuster, 2008.
Ridley, Matt. *The Origins of Virtue.* Harmondsworth: Penguin, 1996.
Roemer, John E. *Analytical Marxism.* New York: Cambridge University Press, 1986.
Roth, Randolph. *American Homicide.* Cambridge: Belknap Press, 2009.
Rousseau, Jean Jacques. "On Social Contract or Principles of Political Right." In Alan

Ritter and Julia Conaway Bondanella (eds) *Rousseau's Political Writings*, 84–173. New York: W.W. Norton, 1988 [1762].

Shapiro, Susan P. "The Social Control of Impersonal Trust." *American Journal of Sociology* 93 (1987) 3: 623–658.

Sidgwick, Henry. *The Elements of Politics*. 1891. Available online at: www.laits.utexas.edu/poltheory/sidgwick/elempol/elempol.html

Smith, Adam. *The Theory of Moral Sentiments*. 4th edition. London, Edinburgh, 1774 [1759].

Sorensen, Aage B. "Toward a Sounder Basis for Class Analysis." *American Journal of Sociology* 105 (2000) 6: 1523–1558.

Stiglitz, Joseph. *The Price of Inequality*. New York: W.W. Norton, 2012.

United Nations Environment Program. "Global Environment Outlook." *Annual Report* 2012. Available online at: www.unep.org

Walker, Edward T. "Privatizing Participation. Civic Change and the Organizational Dynamics of Grassroots Lobbying Firms." *American Sociological Review* 74 (2009) 1: 83–105.

Walzer, Michael. *Spheres of Justice*. New York: Basic Books, 1983.

Weber, Eugen. *Peasants into Frenchmen. The Modernization of Rural France 1870–1914*. Stanford: Stanford University Press, 1976.

White, Deena. "Social Policy and Solidarity, Orphans of the New Model of Social Cohesion." *Canadian Journal of Sociology* 28 (2003) 1: 51–76.

Wilkinson, Richard G. *The Impact of Inequality: How to Make Sick Societies Healthier*. London: Routledge, 2005.

Wilkinson, Richard and Kate Pickett. *The Spirit Level: Why More Equal Societies Almost Always Do Better*. London: Allen Lane, 2009.

Wilson, Edward O. *On Human Nature*. Cambridge: Harvard University Press, 1978.

Wright, Eric Olin. "Class, Exploitation, and Economic Rents: Reflections on Sorensen's 'Sounder Basis'." *American Journal of Sociology* 105 (2000) 6: 1559–1571.

Wright, Eric Olin. *Envisioning Real Utopias*. New York: Verso, 2010.

Zeitlin, Irving. *Rulers and Ruled*. Toronto: University of Toronto Press, 1997.

8 Epilogue

Evolution never starts from scratch. It always modifies what is already there. So it is with the evolution of theories. Classical sociological explanations did not uncover the inner secrets of inequality, but Michels, Marx and Veblen came close, and all of them contributed valuable ideas. Sumner's and Marx's comments on the historical role of chance, Weber's observation that ideas could act like switchmen sending history in different directions, Pareto's reminder that non-rational rather than rational behavior is a routine feature of social life, Michels' and Mosca's recognition of the self-reinforcing properties of hierarchy, or Durkheim's and Parson's emphasis on the social significance of solidarity and shared goals provided clues for understanding the growth of structures of social inequality. Of similar importance were the many efforts, from Spencer to modern Neo-Darwinism, to use evolutionary theory to study human culture and to achieve a greater unity of biological and social sciences (Wilson 1998; Blute 2010). All of them saw culture as a natural, evolutionary product. Some of them went further and argued that it was time to move away from the "paranoid" search for hidden adaptive rationales in all biological and cultural processes (Godfrey-Smith 2009) and, following Darwin's comments on use and habit, to recognize cognitive, internal selection as an integral part of evolution (Niedenzu 2012).

This book has included these insights in a new theory of cultural evolution which can explain its arguably most controversial historical product: social inequality. The guiding idea was to treat culture not as a derivative of genetic selection, but as an evolutionary process in its own right, connected to, but also distinct from, genetic change. To understand this process requires the systematic application of a blind variation, selective retention perspective to the short-term lived experience of evolution. Here, social environments are highly variable. Genetic variation is replaced by blind cognitive novelty. Evaluation and selection are based on internally generated conscious preferences which produce a vast array of cultural traits. Only a small fraction of these is shaped by inheritance or is likely to affect the future survival of the human species. Individuals use their creativity to transform contingent environments into opportunities and risks and choose from them the cultural patterns and social structures with which they conduct their daily affairs. Being able to imagine novel uses for contingent environments and to envision goals and outcomes before actions are taken greatly increases the probability of finding subjective utility and creates the extraordinary complexity of human culture. However, highly variable social worlds and flexible selection criteria also cause high rates of individual error and the social reinforcement of redundant or harmful cultural practices.

Nonetheless, genetic and internal selection follow the first principle of all evolution: that the production of blind variety, whether genetic or cognitive, is the best response to uncertain environments. Both face the same theoretical problem: to explain "why and how, given the potential for radical discontinuities in system behavior, do some systems seem to evolve away from the extremes of complete order, inertia, and stasis on one hand and complete randomness and chaos on the other?" (Mathews et al. 1999: 446).

Social inequality belongs mostly to the rough and tumble arena of lived evolution. Contingent constraints and opportunities, arising along structural and motivational fault lines of social life, create a continuous potential for changes in the allocation of the results of collaborative actions. Some of these are subsequently stabilized by self-reinforcing dynamics and social control, and they are the primary reason why inequality is such a recurrent feature of human history. Individuals and groups are not inevitably carried to wealth and power by rational choice, inherited ability or the providential laws of the market. In fifteenth century Florence, Cosimo and Lorenzo Medici owed their rise to dominance to a ratchet effect of circumstances: fortuitous local events, the elimination of potential opponents by rival elites, and their own indecisiveness which gave them an unintended aura of impartiality (Padgett and Ansell 1993). In much the same way, the rise of the financial industry and its resurgence after the collapse of 2008 was due to a series of fortuitous developments (Krippner 2011; Tomaskovic-Devey and Lin 2011). The evolution of inequality structures is a meandering process shaped by contingency and creativity, by opportunity and error, and by consolidation and change.

Contingency and creativity have contradictory consequences. Contingency imposes constraints on human agency. Like its genetic counterpart it is wasteful and inefficient. In natural selection, failures and extinctions far outnumber successful adaptations. In internal selection, complex environments and variable internal selection criteria produce much higher rates of error, redundancy and harm, although these may have occasional unexpected benefits. The history of inventions is full of discoveries resulting from failed experiments and false theories.

The constraining effects of contingency have broad empirical consequences which interact with social inequality. In genetic evolution, contingency causes a continuous flow of imperfection: changing environments make past adaptations obsolete, while mutations open options for novel uses. In the far more complex short-term lived evolution, imperfect choices make up the bulk of cultural selection. Modern cultures produce extraordinary scientific and technical achievements, but also ineffective medicines, planned obsolescence, mountains of waste, drugged athletes and insufferable celebrities, and environmental destruction. Even in scientific research committed to norms of accuracy and objectivity, contingent factors such as competition between researchers, focus on new variables and lack of replication, financial interest, prevailing intellectual bias, and vague definitions of variables, research designs and analytical methods introduce high rates of false results (Ioannidis 2005; Nosek et al. 2015).

Social inequality does not improve this trend. Past theories often saw it as a catalyst of economic growth and social progress. Historical evidence does not support this assumption. Inequality structures have coincided with periods of major social change as well as with centuries of stagnation and social decline. They may create temporary benefits, but they are also likely to preserve and strengthen suboptimal or harmful cultural choices where these are profitable to small but powerful segments of societies. There is no hidden hand which ensures that social inequality steers cultural selection towards rational, functional or adaptive ends.

Nor does inequality optimize the process of matching personal ability or skill with organizational requirements. Cultural choices are typically based on limited information and volatile selection criteria. High error rates in personnel assessment and shifting organizational goals mean that on every level of sufficiently large organized human activity, the distribution of ability or performance, however defined or measured, will approximate a normal curve. This trend will not be affected by refinements in assessment or recruitment procedures. Pockets of excellence and incompetence will be found on all organizational levels although they need not run contiguous to rank or authority. Inequality can reward good performance but is just as likely to impede initiative and protect ineptitude. Meanwhile the bulk of operations are carried out by a large body of average but adequate individuals. Just as feudalism failed to breed a superior race of hereditary aristocrats, modern recruitment, aptitude tests and selective admissions have not eliminated inferior performance: 60 to 75 percent of business failures in the United States are due to managerial incompetence (King et al. 2009: R915). Social inequality cannot be counted on to serve as "an unconsciously evolved device by which societies insure that the most important positions are conscientiously filled by the most qualified people" (Davis and Moore 1966: 48).

Finally, contingency also means that the many historical dreams of an ideal society of perfect harmony and equality must remain beyond reach. The continuous noise of opportunities seen or missed, and of risk avoided and advantage foregone, which are typical of the overall process of cultural evolution creates a permanent low level of inequality. There can therefore be no culture entirely without inequality, just as there are no inequality structures which are entirely immune to change. This constant flow of chance variations in individual lives can provide starting conditions for inequality, but the crucial dynamic that leads to its further evolution lies in its ability to become self-reinforcing and to close access to alternative ways of distributing collective achievements. Among cultural institutions, inequality is unique in that it provides the material means for its own entrenchment.

These limitations are a natural part of life in an uncertain world. They are counteracted by the human ability to envision new uses for what exists, and for distributing collective achievements in ways that differ from the past. In internal selection we are simultaneously observers and participants, and the scope of our imagination matches or exceeds the constraints of contingency. We make our world, restricted by inheritance and environments, but enabled by the creative discovery of opportunities they offer, and by our ability to share our experiences with others and with subsequent generations.

Inequality imposes characteristic biases on internal and cultural selection. The concentration of strategic resources in private hands encourages unjustified claims of credit for the contributions of contingency and the work of others. It biases creativity by subordinating the free growth of innovation to vested interests, and it strengthens short-term private goals which undermine the solidarity necessary to pursue public goods. Ownership of strategic resources provides the tools of social control which can institutionalize all these biases over long periods of time.

This book has shown that such consequences are neither inevitable nor irreversible. Wealth and poverty are historical results of political choices, of control over strategic resources, and of ideology and social conflict. They have no universal causes, and there is no inherent necessity for their existence. There is therefore also no reason why we cannot critically examine its past and present forms, and imagine and actively pursue alternative, more egalitarian ways of sharing what we have achieved together. We can untangle the complex causes of inequality, follow the path of its evolution, and identify nodal events and choices which strengthened or weakened it along the way (Flannery and Marcus 2012). We can construct counterfactual "unrealized histories" (Augier and March 2011: 279) of possible but missed opportunities, and compare the costs and benefits of what did and what could have happened. For current inequality structures we can reveal the role of chance, the self-reinforcing effects of inheritance, incumbency and market control, and study the role of contemporary forms of social control in the maintenance of inequality. We can expose unjustified claims, show gaps between ideological obfuscation and distributive reality, and compare distributive policies in different societies together with their respective cost and benefits.

As for the future, Chapter 7 showed that even present-day capitalist societies differ widely in the way they share the results of joint efforts, implicit proof that efficiency and subjective satisfaction do not only not suffer but improve under conditions of greater equality. Such comparisons merely suggest more far-reaching distributive options. An ongoing European survey-based study of possible alternatives for life in the year 2020 (Siemens AG 2007) projects two types of future societies. One is a "decelerated," socially responsible market economy where people value the enjoyment of life more than individual success, continuity more than change, and where differences in wealth and income are gradually diminishing. A strong state supports external security, education and health. Because of a larger number of older people, citizens are willing to support a solidarity-based health system, but in order to reduce health costs they must also forego expensive therapies or exploratory diagnostics, except in cases of serious complications. This model accepts a no-growth or slow-growth economy where many families need two or three jobs to earn a comfortable living, and where businesses focus on providing inexpensive services and long-lasting products.

Such a society is very innovative and open to new technologies, especially those directed toward environmental sustainability, but it also restricts outside scrutiny of private life for commercial purposes. Technology-free zones become fashionable.

In the second model, a performance-oriented "me" society, the state recedes in favor of individual responsibility and self-interest. This society divides people into "time-poor, money rich" and "time rich, money poor." It is dominated by an economic and cultural elite. Conspicuous consumption, trickling down from rich to poor, is common. Competitive innovation produces moderate economic growth and rising disposable incomes. E-commerce and internet penetrate private and work life. Regulation in areas such as biotechnology, medicine or environmental protection is resisted. Competition for energy, mining, water and food proceeds with minimal controls, often at the expense of shortages in the countries of origin. Many people live in poverty because they do not have sufficient education or have become redundant because of increased skill demands. Employment security is limited to core employees with high skill levels, while routine tasks are performed by freelancers. Societal goals are shaped by business and consumer preferences. Short-term planning predominates. Collective and long-term goals are rarely addressed. Social services such as health care or pensions are limited. Wealthy patients rely on private clinics or medical tourism for advanced therapies.

This study is just one of many possible explorations of how we could live in the future. Its importance lies as much in what it envisions as in overcoming the powerful tendency of inequality structures to claim that theirs is the only possible way of distributing collectively achieved wealth. There are compelling evolutionary reasons for more equality; lived evolution thrives where it is present. Public opinion is surprisingly consistent in wanting fair distributions of income and wealth, in rejecting corporate excess, in coming to the aid of people in national or international crises, and in taking practical and, if necessary, costly action to pursue common objectives. This becomes more important as human biological history turns full circle. Cultural evolution had given the human species a large measure of independence in how to employ its genetic inheritance. Now, the growth of the world's population, projected to rise from the current 7.3 billion to 11.2 billion by 2100, the large-scale extinction of species and irreversible ecological damage, and growing national and international inequities of wealth and political power and the inevitable increase of social conflict may at some future date threaten our survival as a species. An evolutionary theory tells us that inequality is not an immutable fate. To make it transparent, to examine its costs, and to work towards fairer alternatives is an integral part of an evolutionary study of inequality.

Bibliography

Augier, Mie and James G. March. *The Roots, Rituals and Rhetoric of Change. North American Business Schools after the Second World War*. Stanford: Stanford Business Books, 2011.

Blute, Marion. *Darwinian Sociocultural Evolution.* Cambridge: Cambridge University Press, 2010.
Davis, Kingsley and Wilbert Moore. "Some Principles of Stratification." In Reinhard Bendix and Seymour M. Lipset (eds) *Class, Status, and Power*, 47–53. New York: Free Press, 1966 [1945].
Flannery, Kent and Joyce Marcus. *The Creation of Inequality.* Cambridge: Harvard University Press, 2012.
Godfrey-Smith, P. *Darwinian Populations and Natural Selection.* Oxford: Oxford University Press, 2009.
Ioannidis, John P. "Why Most Published Research Findings are False." *Public Library of Science Medicine* 2 (2005) 8, 694–701. DOI: 10.1371/journal.pmed.0020124
King, Andrew J., Dominic D.P. Johnson and Mark Van Vugt. "The Origins and Evolution of Leadership." *Current Biology* 18 (2009): R911–R916.
Krippner, Greta. *Capitalizing on Crisis: The Political Origins of the Rise of Finance.* Cambridge: Harvard University Press, 2011.
Mathews, Michael, Michael White and Rebecca Long. "Why Study Complexity Sciences in the Social Sciences?" *Human Relations* 52 (1999) 4: 439–462.
Niedenzu, Heinz-Jürgen. "Sociality-Normativity-Morality: The Explanatory Strategy of Günther Dux's Historico-Genetic Theory." In Harry F. Dahms and Lawrence Hazelrigg (eds) *Theorizing Modern Societies as a Dynamic Process. Current Perspectives in Social Theory*, 179–205. Bingley: Emerald Group, 2012.
Nosek, Brian et al. "Estimating the Reproducibility of Psychological Science." *Science* 349 (2015) 6251: aac4716 1–8.
Padgett, John F. and Christopher K. Ansell. "Robust Action and the Rise of the Medici, 1400–1434." *American Journal of Sociology* 98 (1993) 6: 1259–1319.
Siemens AG, 2007. *Horizons 2020.* Available online at: www.siemens.com/innovation/en/publikationen/publications_pof/pof_fall_2004/horizons2020.htm
Tomaskovic-Devey, Donald and Ken-Hou Lin. "Income Dynamics, Economic Rents, and the Financialization of the U.S. Economy." *American Sociological Review* 76 (2011) 4: 538–559.
Wilson, Edward O. *Consilience. The Unity of Knowledge.* New York: Random House, 1998.

Index

Abrutyn, Seth 166
Acemoglu, Daron 222, 224
Ackerman, Bruce 205, 211, 228n4
Adams, Robert McC. 157
Adkins, Daniel 129
agency: ambiguity in social sciences
  towards 44, 45, 101, 102, 128;
  contingency and 98, 211, 235; and
  internal selection 111, 128, 215; in Neo-
  Darwinism 5; rediscovery in natural and
  social science 101–4; in sociological
  theory 4–5, 46, 89–91; and theories of
  social justice 208–9, 210
Alchian, Armen A. 120, 122
Alesina, Alberto 221, 222
Alford, John R. 127
Allen, Peter M. 101
altruism 53, 102, 130, 211; Neo-Darwinist
  views of 103, 132n1, 197, 210
Alverson, Mats 123
Ames, Kenneth M. 142, 147
Anderson, Benedict 214
Aplin, Lucy 108
Apter, David 70
Ariely, Daniel 124
Arnold, Jeanne E. 155
Arrow, Kenneth J. 204
Arthur, W. Brian 111, 114, 124
Atkinson, Anthony B. 2
Augier, Mie 237
Augustin, Patrick 121

Bailey, David H. 121
Bakan, Joel 180
Baldus, Bernd 3, 19, 21, 22, 33, 100, 106,
  121, 193n6, 174, 180, 181, 191, 192
Barber, Benjamin R. 72
Barkow, Jerome 58, 59, 105
Baron, Robert S. 124
Barrell, John 180, 181

Barthes, Roland 178
Bartlett, Robert C. 9, 10, 114, 125
Basalla, George 120, 124, 132n2, 211
Becker, Gary 125
Bender, Barbara 166
Bennett, H.S. 12
Benson, Peter 185, 191
Berg, Andrew G. 227
Bergreen, Laurence 1
Bétaille, André 15, 17
Bettinger, Robert L. 145, 148–9
Betzig, Laura L. 94, 146
Binford, Lewis 145
Blasi, Joseph R. 216, 217
Bliss, Michael 32, 179, 180, 184
Bloch, Marc 9, 14
Blute, Marion 105, 234
Boehm, Christopher 108, 145, 149, 156
Bonnie, Kristin E. 108
Bonnycastle, Richard H. 31
Boudon, Raymond 4
Boulding, Kenneth E. 121, 132n5
Bourdieu, Pierre 118
Bowles, Samuel 118
Boyer, Pascal 58
Brackert, Helmut 13
Brady, David 2
Brandolini, Andrea 225
Breyer, Stephen 220
Brezina, Timothy 121
Briggs, Asa 33
Brody, Hugh 167n1
Brosnan, Sarah F. 155
Brown, Roger 178
Brumfiel, Elizabeth 148
Buchan, Nancy R. 155
Buck, Trevor 123
Buckle, Henry Thomas 44, 45
Bugnyar, Thomas 108
Büntgen, Ulf 219

Bur, Michael 10
Burch, Ernest S. 142
Burris, Val 118, 178
Burt, Ronald 123

Campbell, Donald T. 108
capitalism 19, 35, 41, 60, 92, 156, 174, 216, 219; Habermas on 205, 206; Marx on 63, 64, 65, 227; Weber on 82, 83, 86, 90
Carmichael, Lorne 123
Carneiro, Robert L. 146, 152
Carruthers, Bruce G. 178
Carson, John 94, 122, 128
caste 8, 22, 69, 119, 162; *Dharma* and *Karma* 18; historical origins 15; in India 3, 8, 15–19, 118, 186; rules of exclusion 16–17
Catalano, Ralph 126
Cavalli-Sforza, Luigi L. 105
Cawelti, John G. 180, 181
central problem: of theories of cultural evolution 107; of theories of distributive justice 207; of theories of social inequality 3, 22
chance: causal role in social processes i, 3, 5, 6, 7, 47n2, 54, 114, 175, 180; Darwin on 49, 111; in evolution 106, 107, 126, 112, 113; implications for distributive ethics 207; and merit in human life 127–31; neglect in social research 3, 4, 44–6, 99; reasons for overlooking role of 120–4; rediscovery in natural and social science 99–101; role in ancient Rome and Athens 120, 121; role in early industrialization 31; role in the growth of inequality structures 236, 237; in work of Marx, Spencer, Sumner and Durkheim 4, 234
Chang, Kwang-chih 145, 155
chaos, chaotic processes 68, 102, 235; in nature 99; in social life 100, 146
Childe, V. Gordon 151
Chinoy, Ely 187
choice 3, 30, 44, 61, 68, 86, 132, 192, 206, 235; in classical sociological theory 91, 99, 101–2, 128, 130, 146, 197; consolidation of distributive 118–19, 119–24; Darwin on 103; and distributive justice 204, 209, 210–11, 214, 215; in economic theory 42; imperfect 235, 236; Luhmann on 100, 114, 214; non-rational 3, 4, 5, 74, 75, 90, 101, 102, 121, 124, 175, 234; and opportunity 7, 125, 129, 131, 149; Pareto on 74, 90; rational 3, 4,

8, 42, 44, 46, 74, 90, 91, 99, 102, 103, 121, 173, 199, 201, 235; role in evolution of inequality 6, 8, 124, 126, 227, 237; role in internal selection 104, 105, 106–11, 112, 130, 132, 235; under uncertainty 110, 112, 120, 123, 124, 125, 129, 210, 215
Coelho, Philip 3
Cohen, Abner 146
Cohen, Gerald A. 228n2
Cohn, Norman 183, 228n1
Cole, Stephen 187
Coles, John E. 147
"common assets": Rawls on 202, 215; in theories of distributive justice 211, 212, 215; types of 223–4
complexity in social systems 123, 178, 210; avoidance by theories of justice 228; and causation 86–8, 100; of early societies 147; limits of social control in reducing 188–9; Luhmann on 100, 101, 115, 212; Parsons on 70; as a problem for theories of cultural evolution 94, 210, 235; Weber on 86
compounding effects: in the evolution of inequality 113, 119, 122; in path-dependence 124–5; of shifts in strategic resources 7, 114, 177
Comte, Auguste 2, 42, 43, 44, 45, 47, 59, 66, 69, 175, 212
contingency 86, 98, 101, 123, 127, 128, 235, 236, 237; and continuity in human history 174–5; and creativity 219–21, 235; in environments 219; and equality 211–12, 215; and evolution 98, 210, 235, 236; and human choice 123, 210; implications for distributive justice 207, 208, 210–11; and individual effort 127–31, 207; and internal selection 215; and opportunity 32; and ordering forces in the growth of inequality 113–14; in the growth of inequality 4, 22, 111; Luhmann on 100–1; Marx on 62, 207; Newton's struggle with 98; Rawls on 208; recognition in labor relations 216–19; rediscovery in natural and social science 98–101; role in cultural evolution 111, 113, 210–11; Skinner on 46; Weber on 86; *see also* chance
Conyon, Martin J. 216
cooperation 11, 127, 128, 149, 151, 155, 156, 165, 167, 174, 192, 207, 209, 215, 218, 227; among hunter-gatherers 143–8; Darwin on 49, 103, 126; and evolution of inequality 6, 113, 116–18,

cooperation *continued*
130–1; in game theory 103–4; in Mesopotamia 157–8; Marx on 60, 65; multiplier effect of 211, 212; Parsons on 70, 71; Rawls on 202, 209, 228; rediscovery in the social sciences 101–4; rejection by Neo-Darwinist evolutionists 103; and solidarity 212–14; Sumner on 53, 91; use in social control 175, 177, 178–9, 192; Veblen on 83; weakness of 117, 166, 167, 209

Costa, Dora 221, 222
Courtiol, Alexandre 126
Cowen, Tyler 220
Cowgill, George L. 154
creativity 124, 183; channeling by modern advertising 183; and equality 212, 215, 219–21; historical fear of 45; and inequality 235, 237; neglect by Neo-Darwinist evolutionists 104–5; neglect in the social sciences 102; Neo-Darwinist views of 105–6; role in internal selection 109–13, 211, 215, 234–5
cultural evolution i, 4, 98, 214, 220, 234; among animals 107–8; and emergence of harmful traits 58, 107, 113; and human preferences 105; and information exchange 220; and internal selection 106–11, 238; and lived evolution 6; Neo-Darwinist views of 5; of social inequality 111–13, 236; *see also* internal selection
Currie, Thomas 166
Curry, Andrew 142

Dallos, Csilla 149, 155
Daly, Herman E. 215
Darnton, Robert 186, 188
Darwin, Charles 49, 50, 107, 111, 215; on chance and opportunity in evolution 111; on cognitive abilities of animals 106; on continuity of animal and human evolution 5, 106; on evolution of cooperation 103, 126, 197; on the evolution of cultural traits harmful to human welfare 197; on human evolution 43, 103, 197; influence on Marx 59; influence on Nietzsche 81; and Neo-Darwinism 4, 44, 56, 104–6, 109; and Social Darwinism 49–50, 56; on social inequality 49–50; on the role of "use" and "habit" in evolution 106, 107, 234; reception by nineteenth century social science 43, 44

Davis, Kingsley 7, 72, 111, 236
De Waal, Frans 108
Dean, Lewis G. 127
deception: conditions for 130, 149, 150; counteracted by institutional trust 212; in Nazi propaganda 151; in social relations of trust 6, 113, 114–16, 119, 127, 131, 156, 175, 213, 215, 222; underestimated by theories of justice 209–10; weakness and cost of 117–18, 192, 214
Deckopp, John R. 214
defection: conditions for 127, 149, 150; counteracted by institutional trust 212; in social relations of cooperation 6, 113, 116–18, 119, 127, 131, 156, 215, 222; underestimated in theories of justice 209–10; weakness and cost of 117–18, 192
Demarest, Arthur 147, 148, 153, 160, 161
determinism: in classical physics 99; Max Weber's critique of 99; and Neo-Darwinism 5, 103, 130; and probability in social processes 101; in sociological theories 4, 5, 46, 98; in the work of Marx 87
Diakonis, Persi 111, 122
Diakonoff, Igor M. 158, 159, 160, 167n2
Diamond, Jared 148
Diamond, Sigmund 193n7
distributive justice i, 228; an evolutionary argument for 211–15; free rider problem 209, 210; Habermas' discourse ethic 205–7; libertarian views of 200–1; modern conceptions of 197–200; Neo-Darwinist views of 197; possible evolution in early human societies 126; Rawls on 201–3; in uncertain environments 210; Utilitarians and Sidgwick on 203–5
division of labor 33, 88, 179; Adam Smith on 34–5, 40; Durkheim on 66–8, 69, 102; Marx on 49, 87; social construction of 33–6
Dixon, Thomas 103
Dollery, Brian 3
Douglas, Kate 130
Douglas, Mary 110
Drahos, Peter 220
Duby, Georges 13, 14, 22
Dumont, Louis 15
Dunnell, Robert C. 146
Durham, William H. 57, 58, 105
Durkheim, Emile 2, 4, 43, 44, 45, 59, 65, 66–9, 70, 72, 73, 81, 88, 89, 91, 93, 156;

Index   243

anomic divisions of labor 69; "collective conscience" 66, 67; genesis of values 102, 131; long-term deception unlikely 173; organismic view of society 44; rejection of psychological explanations 46; "social facts" 99, 102; on social inequality 66–8; social role of trust 115; on solidarity 44, 66–8, 212, 221, 234; *see also* division of labor
Dutt, Nripendra Kumar 16
Dworkin, Ronald 205, 211, 228n4

Earle, Timothy 147, 148, 149, 152, 153, 154, 166, 178
Easton, David 190
Edelman, Murray J. 151, 179
egalitarian social structures i, 1, 3, 5, 6, 42, 62, 131, 148, 173, 205, 217, 226, 237; advantages of 149, 166, 174; early visions of 198; egalitarian behavior in young children 126–7; "egalitarian revolution" in early human evolution 103; Engels on 61, 87; French and American Revolution demands for 33, 179; Marx on 62, 87; origins of inequality in 155–7; Parsons on 88; persistence in unequal societies 155; Rousseau on 38; social control in 150, 191
Ehrenreich, Barbara 186
Eibl-Eibesfeldt, Irenäus 167n1
Elson, Ruth Miller 184, 190
Engels, Friedrich 42, 59, 60, 81, 86, 174; on early human society 61, 87, 142; on "primitive communism" 62, 87; on unforeseen consequences of human actions 87
Entine, John 57
equality i, 7, 8, 9, 14, 16, 28, 76, 79, 82, 88, 93, 122, 128, 147, 154, 157, 187, 197, 215, 236; in ancient Athens 226; contingency and 132, 211–12, 219; cooperation and 130, 167; cyclical history of inequality and 166, 174; early demands for 42, 174, 181, 192, 198; in early societies 1, 157–66; environment and 219–21, 212; evolutionary argument for greater 199, 205, 210–15, 226, 228, 238; Habermas on 206; nineteenth century reinterpretation of 33, 179, 180; in industrial work 216–19; libertarian view of 201; Locke on 205; Marx on 33, 65, 142, 226–7; Rawls on 202, 209–10; role of states in ensuring 221, 222–5; Sidgwick on 204, 205; Social Darwinist view of 54; solidarity and 212–14, 221–4; in "state of nature" 37, 38, 142, 225; trade-off between efficiency and 227, 237
Erdal, David 58, 156
Erikson, Kai T. 188
eugenics 56, 57, 94n1
Evans, Richard J. 151

Falk, Armin 124, 176, 214
Farmer, J. Doyne 121
Fehr, Ernst 103, 127
Feinman, Gary M. 147
feudal societies 3, 8–15, 17, 19, 22, 26, 30, 83, 94, 122, 125, 126, 129, 132, 151, 154, 157, 166, 173, 178, 183, 205, 206, 236; Marx on 61, 63, 64, 65, 86–7; social control in 12–15, 22, 119, 151, 155, 178, 183, 188–92, 193
Fichtenau, Heinrich 10, 11
Finley, Moses 121
first principle of evolution 6, 107, 235
Flannery, Kent, and Joyce Marcus 5, 125, 147, 148, 151, 153, 154, 155, 157, 159, 188, 211, 237
Fligstein, Neil 125
Flynn, James 93
Frank, Thomas 189, 222
Fraser, Nancy 221
free rider problem 192, 202, 209, 210; *see also* deception; defection
Freedman, Paul 12, 155
Freeman, James M. 17, 18, 118, 186
French Revolution 8, 45, 46, 125, 132, 179; and first public parks 219; impact on nineteenth century politics 33, 173, 212; impact on portrayal of lower classes in art 180; Marx on 33; as source of social tensions 28, 29, 42, 183, 101
Fried, Morton 173, 146, 222
Fruzetti, Lina 18
Fuentes-Nieves, Ricardo 216, 227
Fukuyama, Francis 167n2
Furedi, Frank 222

Gambetta, Diego 115
Garud, Raghu 124
Gavrilets, Sergey 126
Geertz, Clifford 161
George, C.H. 188
Ghiselin, Michael 103
Giddens, Anthony 5, 99
Gilens, Martin 114, 118, 178
Gilman, Antonio 148, 152, 175
Ginsburgh, Victor A. 122

Index

Gintis, Herbert 105
Godfrey-Smith, P. 234
Goffman, Erving 151, 176
Goldthorpe, John H. 8
Goode, William J. 119
Gordon, Scott 31
Gould, Stephen J. 56, 128, 132n2
Granovetter, Mark 214
Grätz, Tilo 187
Gregor, Thomas 149
Griffin, Donald R. 106
group selection 103
Gruber, Thibaud 108
Grund, Christian 214
Gunawardana, R.A.L.H. 148

Habermas, Jürgen 6, 205–7, 209, 210
Hacker, Jacob S. 3, 177, 216
Hacking, Ian 45, 46
Hahanou, Eric Komlavi 22
Hallpike, Christopher R. 112
Hamann, Katharina 126
Hamermesh, Daniel 121
Hamlin, Kiley J. 127
Hammond, John L. 31, 47n1, 179, 186
harmful cultural traits: cultural selection of i, 22, 58, 91, 116, 127, 148; Darwin on 187; disguised by social control 75, 82; and internal selection 110, 112–13, 235, 236; treatment in Neo-Darwinism 58; treatment in sociological theory 3–6, 22, 98, 101, 112; treatment in theories of justice 200, 203, 204, 211; stabilization of 119–24, 191
Harris, Marvin 145, 146
Harvey, Campbell R. 121
Haviland, William A. 153, 160
Hawkins, Mike 57, 94n1
Hayden, Brian 145, 146, 153, 154, 167n2
Hayek, Friedrich 200, 201
Heer, Friedrich 11, 14, 178
Helliwell, John F. 217
Henrich, Joseph 127
Herrnstein, Richard G. 57
Hess, Robert D. 184, 190
Hibbing, John R. 127
Higham, Charles 147
Hill, Christopher 228n1
Hobbes, Thomas 27, 36, 37, 91, 116, 130, 142, 175
Hobsbawm, Eric J. 30, 173, 174
Hodgson, Geoffrey M. 58, 105
Hodgson, Robert T. 122
Höffner, Eckhard 220
Hopkins, Keith 185

Hunt, Terry L. 119
hunter-gatherer societies 61, 126, 142–5, 147–8, 167; advantage of egalitarian distributive structures 149; authority in 144; developmental views of the evolution of 145–6; forms of reciprocity in 143–4; as precursors of modern systems of redistribution and social support 156, 157; starting processes of inequality in 151–5; vulnerability to invasion by inequality 149–50

ideology 80, 103, 104, 111, 117, 128, 131, 155, 186, 191, 198, 206, 209, 212, 222, 237; among *Machube* 21; in ancient Mesopotamia 160–1; in ancient Rome 165; in Aztec society 162; Comte's "religion of humanity" 175; in early capitalism 30–2, 35–6, 43, 56, 178–85; in European feudalism 11, 22, 26, 29, 180, 189; Marx on 61, 64–5, 76; in Maya society 146; in nineteenth century schoolbooks 33, 174, 180, 181, 190, 192
"imperfections": in evolution 104, 235; in internal selection 210; Newton on 98; Parsons on 88; Spencer on 55; treatment in economic theory 42; treatment in sociological theory 8; *see also* harmful cultural traits
inequality i, 3; in an African slave-holding society 19–22; biological explanations of 56–9, 105, 126–7; in caste societies 15–19; central problems for the study of 22–3; in contemporary societies 2, 227; continuity and change in ancient Rome 164–6; continuity and change in Central and South America 160–3; continuity and change in Mesopotamia 157–60; defined 7–8; Durkheim on 66–9; early functional explanations of 65; in early industrial societies 29–31; early sociological theories of 2, 4–5, 42–7; economic theories of 39–42; in European feudal societies 8–15; historical instability of 166–7; intelligence measurements as predictors of 56, 57, 93–4, 128; lack of legitimacy of early industrial forms of 31–2; as lived evolution 6; Marx on 59–65; and organizational causes 73–80; Parsons on 69–73; path-dependent evolution of 124–6; priorities for an evolutionary study of 131–2; psychological theories of 81–5; and strategic resources 7; subjective perception of 8

intelligent design 106
internal selection: in animals 107–8; as basis for evolutionary principles of blind resources for 109; distributive justice 210–11, 215; evolutionary role of 110–11, 126; in the evolution of social inequality 111–13, 234–6; explained 106–11; and human agency 111–12, 210, 215; of socially redundant or harmful traits 112–13, 119–24
Ioannidis, John P. 236
Isaac, Larry W. 5

Jacobsen, Thorkild 158
Jaeger, Mads Meier 121
Jaffe, Adam 220
Jahoda, Marie 187
Jencks, Christopher 122, 129
Jensen, Arthur R. 57
Joas, Hans 102, 210
Johnson, Simon 216
Jordaan, Ken 143
Judge, Timothy A. 121

Kahlenberg, Sonya M. 108
Kalckhoff, Andreas 10, 14
Kanakogi, Yasukiro 107
Kaplow, Jeffrey 187
Katz, Friedrich 162, 163
Keating, P.J. 32, 181
Keeley, Lawrence H. 146
Kelly, Robert L. 142, 145, 147
Kendrick, Christopher 228n1
Kersting, Wolfgang 207, 208, 209, 228n2
Kinder, Donald R. 191
King, Andrew J. 58, 236
Klein, Martin 19, 155
Klofstadt, Casey A. 121
Knack, Stephen 214
Koller, Frank 217
Kraus, Michael W. 177
Krippner, Greta 216, 235
Kuczynski, Jürgen 173, 174, 184
Kunisch, Johannes 47n2

Lachmann, Richard 125
Lampert, Heinz 219
Lane, Christopher 220
Lane, Robert E. 186
"latent" functions 102; in Neo-Darwinism 58
Law, Michael R. 224
Lawler, Edward J. 103, 127
laws of motion: influence on social science 99, 105; Newton's 99; not applicable to evolving systems 100
Layard, Richard 223
Le Bon, Gustave 81, 82, 90
LeBlanc, Steven A. 167n1
Lee, Richard B. 144, 145
Lenormand, Thomas 105
Lenski, Gerhard E. 128, 145, 167n2
Lerner, Josh 220
Lessig, Lawrence 220
Lewis, Herbert S. 148
Light, Donald 220
Lipton, Charles 32
lived evolution 6, 119, 235; and equality 132, 215, 238; and human agency 128–9, 211; explained 109–11, 234; relationship to genetic evolution 126, 130, 235; role of creativity in 109–10, 212, 235; *see also* cultural evolution
Locke, John 36, 199, 200, 205, 207, 209; on property and inequality 37–8
Lockwood, David 73
Loewenthal, Leo 190
Logue, John 218
Lopreato, Joseph 58
Lucas, Rex 86, 193n7
Luhmann, Niklas 102, 114, 115, 132n2, 167n2, 209, 210, 212, 214; on contingency 100; on complexity reduction 101, 123; on "legitimation by procedure" 123; on trust 114–15
Luncz, Lydia V. 108
Lynd, Robert S. 183

McAnany, Patricia A. 155, 160, 161, 166
McCall, Leslie 178
McCloskey, Robert G. 179
McDermott, John F.M. 216
MacDonald, Kevin 57
Macfarlan, Shane J. 214
McGlew, James F. 153
McGowan, John 102
Machalek, Richard 150
MacIntyre, Alasdair 209, 213
Mackenzie, Alexander 156
McLean, Paul D. 103
Macpherson, Crawford B. 38
Mahoney, James 99, 124
Mair, Lucy 152
Malinowski, Bronislaw 156
Malthus, Robert 40, 49, 50, 126
Mandeville, Bernard de 26, 27
Mann, Michael 125, 166, 167
Marglin, Stephen A. 36
Markley, Robert 98

Martin, Isaac 189
Marx Engels Werke (MEW) 33, 35, 49, 59, 60, 61, 62, 63, 64, 87, 89, 90, 101
Marx, Karl 2, 4, 5, 33, 41, 42, 59, 60, 61, 64, 72, 73, 74, 75, 77, 79, 80, 81, 85, 87, 91, 93, 114, 117, 129, 131, 142, 200, 222, 234; *Communist Manifesto* 226, 227; on contingency and chance in human history 4, 62, 86, 87, 200, 207–8; on creativity 61, 62; and Darwin 44, 49, 59; on expropriation and inequality 62–4; on "false consciousness" 89; on ideology 64–5; influence of Adam Smith on 39, 59; on "primitive communism" 61, 86, 87; similarities with Durkheim's and Parsons' view of ideal society 72, 173; similarities with Pareto 73, 125; similarities with Spencer 73, 89; on surplus 61, 62
Mathews, Michael 235
Mattausch, John 99
Maxwell, James Clerk 99
Mayr, Ernst 106, 210
Mazur, Allan 58
Mazzucato, Mariana 221
Meillassoux, Claude 15
Merton, Robert K. 88
Mervis, Jeffrey 3
Mesoudi, Alex 105, 109, 132n2
Michaels, Walter Benn 213, 222
Michels, Robert 36, 73, 77–9, 90, 114, 167, 234; ambiguity of "iron law" 92–3
Milanovic, Branko 2
Mill, John Stuart 27, 41, 203, 204
Mokyr, Joel 132n2
Montesquieu, Charles-Louis 44
Moodie, Susanna 27, 28
Mookherjee, Dilip 125
Moore, Alexander 147
Moore, Wilbert E. 102
Moorjani, Priya 15
Mosca, Gaetano 36, 73, 75–7, 79, 90, 113, 131, 234; on incompetence among ruling class members 77; on role of chance in the rise of ruling classes 90
Mullainathan, Sendhil 177
Mullen, Ann L 118
Mundy, John H. 14
Murra, John 163
Murray, Charles A. 57
Myles, John 3

Nakashima, Tamiji 112
Nakassis, Dimitri 157, 166
Nash, June 187
Nature Neuroscience 123

Neckerman, Kathryn M. 178
Nelson, Linden L. 104
Neo-Darwinism 57, 103, 109, 126, 130; and evolutionary ethics 210; explanations of social inequality 57–9; problems in the study of human culture 6, 105, 106, 234; transformation of Darwin's theory 4, 46, 104; *see also* Darwin, Charles
Neo-Liberalism 6, 56, 77, 213, 216, 221, 222, 225
Newman, Katherine 187
Newton, Isaac 44, 46; "Newtonian paradigm" in the social sciences 99, 100, 105; struggle with chance 98
Niedenzu, Heinz-Jürgen 234
Nietzsche, Friedrich 81–2, 90, 94n3
Nolte, Ellen 224
North, Douglass C. 124
Nosek, Brian 236
Nozick, Robert 199, 200–1, 202, 207, 208, 209, 228n4
Nussbaum, Martha C. 228n2

Oates, Joan 157, 158, 159, 160
O'Hanlon, Rosalind 16
Okun, Arthur M. 227
Olsen, Gregg M. 217, 223
operationalism 46
Organisation for Economic Co-operation and Development (OECD) 2, 217, 225
Ormerod, Paul 121, 122, 125

Padgett, John F. 235
Pagels, Elaine H. 111
Palmieri, Rachel 121
Pareto, Vilfredo 73–5, 77, 79, 89, 90, 92, 102, 125, 131, 203, 234; causes of the circulation of elites 74, 75; non-rational behavior common in social life 74; residues and derivations 74
Parish, Steven M. 17, 18, 19, 186
Parsons, Talcott 3, 65, 69–73, 89, 92, 101, 102, 115, 131, 156, 212, 214, 221; on historical origins of stratification 70; on Marxism 92; on poverty 88; on stratification as exchange 72–3, 88
path dependence 124–5
Paxton, Pamela 221
Payer, Lynn 121
Peel, John D.Y. 56
Peel, Mark 190
Pencavel, John 218
Penner, Rudolph G. 121
Piddocke, Stuart 145

Index 247

Pierson, Paul 124
Piff, Paul K. 131, 177
Pigou, Cecil Arthur 205
Piketty, Thomas 2, 3, 216
Pinker, Steven 94n2, 106
Piven, Frances F. 190
Plesch, Dan 216
Pluchino, Allessandro 228n5
Pokorny, Jennifer J. 108
Polanyi, Karl 156
Pollett, Thomas V. 59
Postgate, J. Nicholas 158, 159, 160
Pragmatism 102
property 1, 27, 29, 30, 32, 49, 92, 94, 123, 142, 146, 149, 150, 155, 156, 179, 191, 204, 209, 218, 219, 220; in ancient Rome 165; in caste society 18; Durkheim on 66; early economic theories of 39–42; eighteenth and nineteenth century debates about 27–32; in feudal Japan 23; Hobbes on 36, 37; of land in feudal Europe 9–11; libertarian views of 200–1; Locke on 37–8, 200, 207; Marx on 33, 61, 62, 63, 87, 207; in Mesopotamia 158, 159; Parsons on origins of 72; Plato on 197–8; political philosophy of 36–8; Rawls on 202; Rousseau on 38, 142, 178, 213; slaves as 20; Social Darwinist explanations of 56; Spencer on 51; Sumner on 53; Veblen on 84; Weber on origins of 80, 152
Putnam, Robert D. 212, 221, 222, 224

Rajan, Raghuram G. 132
Rapport, Michael 60
rationalism in social and biological theories 5, 70, 94, 98, 99, 101, 112; *see also* determinism
Rawls John 6, 199, 201–3, 205, 208, 209, 211, 215, 228n3, 228n4
Ray, Rebecca 217
Reader, John 166
reciprocity: balanced 143; in cooperative social relations 102; as general principle of early and modern cooperative structures 127; generalized 143, 149, 150; negative 143; Rawls on 202; vulnerability to inequality 152, 155
Rediker, Marcus 187
redistribution of wealth: in ancient Mesopotamia 158, 159; in ancient Rome 165; in Aztec society 161, 162; early forms as prototypes for modern redistribution 156, 166; in early societies 144, 149, 156, 157; and economic efficiency 217; in neo-liberal economic theory 199; Kant on 199; Libertarian view of 200, 201; Mandeville on 27; Michels on 77, 91; Mill on 41; Paine on 42; Rawls on 203; Spencer on 51, 55; state-organized 224–5; vulnerability to inequality 154
Redman, Charles L. 167n2
regions of opportunity for the evolution of inequality 6, 111, 113, 114, 130, 150, 166; *see also* starting processes for the evolution of inequality
Rehg, William 210
Reich, Robert 222
Reid, Douglas A. 33
Rennenkampff, Anke 121
retrodictive fallacy in the study of social inequality 4
Rice, Michael 145
Richerson, Peter J. 105
Ridgeway, Cecilia L. 130
Ridley, Matt 103, 213
Rinehart, James 186
Roemer, John E. 228n4
Roos, Patrick 127
Roscigno, Vincent 4
Roth, Randolph 222
Rousseau, Jean Jacques 2, 33, 36, 75, 142, 178, 200, 205, 213; on inequality 38
Roy, Donald F. 186
Rushton, Philippe J. 57
Russon, Anne 108
Ryerson, Stanley B. 29

Sabel, Charles 35, 111
Sahagun, Bernardino de 162
Sahlins, Marshall D. 129, 142, 143, 153, 155
Sapolsky, Robert 102, 108
Sauter, Disa A. 107
Schele, Linda 130, 146, 154, 160, 161
Schmidt, Klaus 147
Schoeck, Helmut 94n4
Segerstrale, Ullica 132n1
self-reinforcing social processes: in the evolution of inequality 6, 104, 111, 113–14, 118, 125, 126, 131, 132, 154, 234, 236, 237; in social control 177–8, 187, 192, 235; *see also* compounding effects
Sennett, Richard 187
Service, Elman R. 167n2
Shapiro, Susan P. 192, 214
Sharma, Ursula 18, 19

Index

Sidgwick, Henry 199, 204–5, 208, 211
Siemens AG 237
Sierminska, Eva 121
Silverblatt, Irene 163, 186, 192
Skinner, Burrhus F. 46; on contingency and explanation 46
Skocpol, Theda 124
Smith, Adam 27, 34, 41, 45, 51, 59, 198; on deception of laborers by employers 40; on the division of labor 34–6; economic theory of 39–40; "hidden hand" 40, 46, 199; on inequality and political unrest 34
Smith, Craig E. 107
Smith, Mike 99
Smith, Thomas C. 186
Smucker, Joseph 179
Soares, Joseph A. 118
social control i, 152, 160, 209, 210, 212; in Borgu slave society 20–2; in caste societies 17–19; complementary opportunities and 185–7; and the consolidation of inequality 3, 6, 118–19, 128, 131, 174–5; and the consolidation of redundancy and harm 119–23; control strategies in the Spanish conquest of Mexico 185–6; defection and 117; and dynamics of self-reinforcement 177–8, 235; and fear of social disorder 34, 117, 173–4; in feudal societies 12–15; interventive forms of 179–85; long-term changes in 124–6, 188–91; strategies of 118–19, 175–7; strengths and weaknesses of 191–2
Social Darwinism 49, 50, 52, 54–7, 93; ideological legacy of 56; legitimating effect in early industrialization 56; and social policy 54–5
Sober, Elliott 103
sociobiology 5, 57
Sokal, Alan 178
solidarity 16, 29, 33, 44, 66–8, 69, 70, 78, 88, 91, 102, 103, 115, 146, 234, 237; in ancient Athens 226; and cooperation 192; emotional and institutional 221, 222; and equality 212; and kinship 156; modern views of 221; Rousseau on general will 213; in Sweden 223; and trust 213–15; *see also* Durkheim, Emile
Sommerfeld, Ralf D. 121
Sorensen, Aage B. 114, 211
Spencer, Herbert 2, 4, 27, 43, 44, 49, 50, 51, 52, 54, 56, 59, 66, 73, 81, 82, 85, 87, 89, 91, 93, 102, 132, 221, 234; belief in "science of man" 59; on equality 54;

influence of Lamarck on 50; inheritance of acquired characteristics 50; "law of progress" 50; "law of rhythms" 87; militant and industrial societies 51; on the rise of "regulating classes" 52; on social policy 54–6; on the survival of the fittest 50–2
Srinivas, M.N. 16, 18
Starr, Paul 193n2
starting processes for the evolution of inequality 150–5; *see also* regions of opportunity for the evolution of inequality
"state of nature" described: by Engels 142; by Hobbes 36, 142; by Locke 37, 207; by Rousseau 38, 142
Stein, Mark 124
Steinbeis, Nikolaus 127
Steward, Julian H. 146
Stiglitz, Joseph 3, 211
stochasticity in lived evolution 110, 124, 131
Stone, Elizabeth C. 160
Stone, Lawrence 94
Stouffer, Samuel A. 184
strategic resources: compounding effects of 119; defined 7; and inequality 8, 22, 80, 104, 114, 215, 237
Streek, Wolfgang 124, 125
Sumner, William Graham 2, 4, 27, 52–6, 81, 86, 89, 91, 93, 114, 179, 234; "antagonistic cooperation" 53; competition and inequality 53; on "plutocracy" 54, 55, 91; role of chance in human history 54, 86; on social policy 54–6
Suttles, Wayne 142
Sutton, Francis X. 190
Sutton, John R. 124
Svensson, Eric I. 103
Swami, Viren 121

Tacitus, Publius Cornelius 119, 144
Tainter, Joseph A. 126
Taylor, Alex H. 110
Tepperman, Lorne 187
Tervo, Dougal G.R. 110
Testart, Alain 154
Thelen, Kathleen 124
Thomas, Elizabeth Marshall 167n1
Thompson, Edward P. 34, 35, 36, 174, 186
Thornton, Alex 102
Thurow, Lester 120
Tjosvold, Dean 117, 123
Tocqueville, Alexis de 27

Todorov, Alexander 121
Tomaskovic-Devey, Donald 235
Trigger, Bruce 144, 145, 146, 147, 156
trust 6, 102, 114–15, 127, 129, 130, 133, 144, 206, 218, 222, 223, 224; and cooperation 116–18, 130, 131, 174, 192; Durkheim on 66, 67, 115; Hobbes on 37, 116, 130; in human societies 102, 131; impersonal 212–14; Luhmann on 114–15; and origins of social inequality 122, 114, 151–5, 166; and social control 175, 176; Parsons on 71, 72, 115; weakness of 116, 166
Turnbull, Colin M. 144, 149, 150

uncertainty 6, 99, 204, 217; in lived evolution 100, 112, 111, 113, 118, 119, 124, 210, 236; Luhmann on 115; in social processes 108–10, 120–2, 123, 148, 149, 210, 217, 228; *see also* contingency; chance
unforeseen consequences i, 87, 98, 190, 210, 219
United Nations Environment Program 228
United States Congressional Budget Office 2
uniqueness of human culture: belief in the 5, 61, 101, 106, 110
Ur, Jason A. 157
Uzzi, Brian 103, 116

Vaish, Amrisha 127
Van den Berghe, Pierre L. 146
Veblen, Thorstein 81, 84–5, 90, 93, 129, 191, 234
Vergne, Jean-Philippe 124

Wahrman, Dror 182
Walker, Edward T. 222

Walzer, Michael 228n2
Warneken, Felix 127
Watts, Joseph 150
Weber, Eugen 214
Weber, Max 73, 77, 79–80, 81, 82–4, 91, 92, 114, 115, 206, 214; on counterfactual analysis 125; critique of modern inequality structures 90; critique of "social laws" 86, 99; normative and instrumental rationality 92, 210; on the origin of property rights 152; on the role of contingency in social processes 86, 234; on social closure and inequality 80, 152
Webster, David 146
Weeden, Kim A. 118
Wenke, Robert J. 146, 156
White, Deena 222
White, Lynn Jr. 180
Wilkinson, Richard G. 222, 235
Willer, Robb 130
Williams, George C. 103
Wilson, David 132n1
Wilson, Edward O. 5, 57, 94n1, 103, 105, 197, 210, 234
Winterhalder, Bruce 145
Wise, Sydney F. 181, 183
Woodburn, James 145, 156
Wright, Eric Olin 211, 216
Wright, Robert 57
Wright, Ronald 119

Yamamoto, Shinya 108

Zeitlin, Irving 228n1
Zeitlin, Lawrence R. 186, 191
Zentner, Marcel R. 107
Zvelebil, Marek 148

Taylor & Francis eBooks

Helping you to choose the right eBooks for your Library

Add Routledge titles to your library's digital collection today. Taylor and Francis ebooks contains over 50,000 titles in the Humanities, Social Sciences, Behavioural Sciences, Built Environment and Law.

Choose from a range of subject packages or create your own!

Benefits for you
- Free MARC records
- COUNTER-compliant usage statistics
- Flexible purchase and pricing options
- All titles DRM-free.

REQUEST YOUR FREE INSTITUTIONAL TRIAL TODAY

Free Trials Available
We offer free trials to qualifying academic, corporate and government customers.

Benefits for your user
- Off-site, anytime access via Athens or referring URL
- Print or copy pages or chapters
- Full content search
- Bookmark, highlight and annotate text
- Access to thousands of pages of quality research at the click of a button.

eCollections – Choose from over 30 subject eCollections, including:

Archaeology	Language Learning
Architecture	Law
Asian Studies	Literature
Business & Management	Media & Communication
Classical Studies	Middle East Studies
Construction	Music
Creative & Media Arts	Philosophy
Criminology & Criminal Justice	Planning
Economics	Politics
Education	Psychology & Mental Health
Energy	Religion
Engineering	Security
English Language & Linguistics	Social Work
Environment & Sustainability	Sociology
Geography	Sport
Health Studies	Theatre & Performance
History	Tourism, Hospitality & Events

For more information, pricing enquiries or to order a free trial, please contact your local sales team:
www.tandfebooks.com/page/sales

The home of Routledge books

www.tandfebooks.com

Printed in the United States
By Bookmasters